# ASPEN PUBLISHERS

# Quick Reference to ERISA Compliance

## 2009 Edition

*by Marjorie R. Martin*

This one-volume desk reference details the various reporting and disclosure requirements under the Employee Retirement Income Security Act of 1974 (ERISA) and other benefits-related legislation. Explanations are illustrated with numerous flowcharts, decision tables, and forms to help plan sponsors and plan administrators comply with ERISA. In addition, the volume provides an overview of fiduciary responsibilities, trust and plan document requirements, and special rules for group health plans. A glossary and topical index are also provided.

## Highlights of the 2009 Edition

The 2009 Edition includes the following updates and additions:

- The 2006 disclosure requirements, as well as PBGC premium and reporting changes, contained in the Pension Protection Act reflect guidance from the agencies released through July 2008.

- A brief overview of plan termination notice requirements has been added.

- The 28 notice requirements in Chapter 9 have been reorganized for easier reference.

**10/08**

**For questions concerning this shipment, billing, or other customer service matters, call our Customer Service Department at 1-800-234-1660.**

**For toll-free ordering, please call 1-800-638-8437.**

Wolters Kluwer
Law & Business

# QUICK
# REFERENCE
# TO

# ERISA

**2009**

# COMPLIANCE

ASPEN PUBLISHERS

# *QUICK REFERENCE TO*

# 2009 ERISA

## COMPLIANCE

Marjorie R. Martin, EA, MAAA, MSPA

**Contributing Editor**
George A. Andrews, Esq.

**Aon Consulting**

## Wolters Kluwer

### Law & Business

AUSTIN    BOSTON    CHICAGO    NEW YORK    THE NETHERLANDS

© 2009 Aspen Publishers. All Rights Reserved.

No part of this publication may be reproduced or transmitted in any form or by any means, electronic or mechanical, including photocopy, recording, or any information storage and retrieval system, without permission in writing from the publisher. Requests for permission to reproduce content should be directed to the Aspen Publishers website at *www.aspenpublishers.com*, or a letter of intent should be faxed to the permissions department at 212-771-0803.

Printed in the United States of America

ISBN 978-0-7355-7395-6

1 2 3 4 5 6 7 8 9 0

# About Wolters Kluwer Law & Business

Wolters Kluwer Law & Business is a leading provider of research information and workflow solutions in key specialty areas. The strengths of the individual brands of Aspen Publishers, CCH, Kluwer Law International and Loislaw are aligned within Wolters Kluwer Law & Business to provide comprehensive, in-depth solutions and expert-authored content for the legal, professional and education markets.

**CCH** was founded in 1913 and has served more than four generations of business professionals and their clients. The CCH products in the Wolters Kluwer Law & Business group are highly regarded electronic and print resources for legal, securities, antitrust and trade regulation, government contracting, banking, pension, payroll, employment and labor, and healthcare reimbursement and compliance professionals.

**Aspen Publishers** is a leading information provider for attorneys, business professionals and law students. Written by preeminent authorities, Aspen products offer analytical and practical information in a range of specialty practice areas from securities law and intellectual property to mergers and acquisitions and pension/benefits. Aspen's trusted legal education resources provide professors and students with high-quality, up-to-date and effective resources for successful instruction and study in all areas of the law.

**Kluwer Law International** supplies the global business community with comprehensive English-language international legal information. Legal practitioners, corporate counsel and business executives around the world rely on the Kluwer Law International journals, loose-leafs, books and electronic products for authoritative information in many areas of international legal practice.

**Loislaw** is a premier provider of digitized legal content to small law firm practitioners of various specializations. Loislaw provides attorneys with the ability to quickly and efficiently find the necessary legal information they need, when and where they need it, by facilitating access to primary law as well as state-specific law, records, forms and treatises.

Wolters Kluwer Law & Business, a unit of Wolters Kluwer, is headquartered in New York and Riverwoods, Illinois. Wolters Kluwer is a leading multinational publisher and information services company.

# ASPEN PUBLISHERS SUBSCRIPTION NOTICE

This Aspen Publishers product is updated on a periodic basis with supplements to reflect important changes in the subject matter. If you purchased this product directly from Aspen Publishers, we have already recorded your subscription for the update service.

If, however, you purchased this product from a bookstore and wish to receive future updates and revised or related volumes billed separately with a 30-day examination review, please contact our Customer Service Department at 1-800-234-1660 or send your name, company name (if applicable), address, and the title of the product to:

**ASPEN PUBLISHERS**
**7201 McKinney Circle**
**Frederick, MD 21704**

**Important Aspen Publishers Contact Information**

- To order any Aspen Publishers title, go to *www.aspenpublishers.com* or call 1-800-638-8437.

- To reinstate your manual update service, call 1-800-638-8437.

- To contact Customer Care, e-mail *customer.care@aspenpublishers.com,* call 1-800-234-1660, fax 1-800-901-9075, or mail correspondence to Order Department, Aspen Publishers, PO Box 990, Frederick, MD 21705.

- To review your account history or pay an invoice online, visit *www.aspenpublishers.com/payinvoices.*

# About the Author

**Marjorie R. Martin, EA, MAAA, MSPA**, is a Vice President in Aon Consulting's *Tax & ERISA Practice* in Aon's Somerset, New Jersey office. Ms. Martin has provided actuarial and retirement plan consulting support to professionals at national consulting firms for over 30 years. She is a Senior Advisor to the American Society of Pension Professionals & Actuaries (ASPPA) Government Affairs Committee and a member of the Technical Review Board for ASPPA's publication, *The ASPPA Journal*. Ms. Martin is also an editorial board member for the *Journal of Pensions Management*. She has contributed articles to many publications, including Aspen Publishers' *Journal of Pension Benefits*, and is a member of the annual Enrolled Actuaries Meeting *Gray Book* (IRS), *Blue Book* (PBGC), *and Green Book* (DOL) Committee; she is also a contributor to *Aspen Publishers' 457 Answer Book*; *SIMPLE, SEP and SARSEP Answer Book*; and the *Roth IRA Answer Book*.

Ms. Martin obtained her B.A. in Mathematics from Montclair State University in New Jersey and may be reached at *marge_martin@aon.com*.

Aon Consulting is a fully integrated human resources consulting organization that specializes in linking human resources strategies with business initiatives for improved performance. Aon Consulting offers services in employee benefits, human resources, compensation, and change management. Specific services include organizational analysis and human resources strategic planning, job design, competency modeling, recruitment and selection, compensation and reward systems, benefits design and management, training and development, human resources compliance and risk management, and individual and organizational change management.

Aon's integrated consulting approach ensures that clients are effectively attracting, retaining, and utilizing their people "assets." Aon Consulting applies an objective, global perspective that provides customized solutions and consistent administration for client programs.

# Table of Contents

# Introduction

*Quick Reference to ERISA Compliance* is a reference manual for employee benefit professionals who are responsible for complying with the reporting and disclosure requirements of the Employee Retirement Income Security Act of 1974 (ERISA).

This 2009 edition of the book reflects changes enacted in the Pension Protection Act of 2006 as they apply to plan years beginning after December 31, 2008. For changes that affect post plan year end reporting requirements, the new requirements will first apply to reports due in 2009.

The book contains 11 chapters, a glossary, and an index. Chapter 1 provides an overview of ERISA's reporting and disclosure requirements for employee benefit plans. Chapter 2 discusses plans subject to ERISA. Chapter 3 is devoted to plans that are exempt from ERISA's reporting and disclosure requirements.

Chapters 4 through 8 describe in detail the requirements for annual reports, summary annual reports, reports for the Pension Benefit Guaranty Corporation (PBGC), summary plan descriptions (SPDs), and summaries of material modifications (SMMs). Chapter 9 outlines the special notice requirements for retirement plans. Chapter 10 examines special requirements for health plans. Chapter 11 provides a summary of other important ERISA requirements.

To guide the user (usually, the plan sponsor or plan administrator is the entity legally responsible for meeting ERISA requirements) through the more complex reporting and disclosure requirements, the author has included numerous flowcharts, forms, tables, and model documents.

Readers who require assistance in complying with ERISA requirements should contact their nearest Aon Consulting Office.

# Chapter 1

# Overview

**Introduction**  This chapter provides an overview of the comprehensive reporting and disclosure requirements for ongoing employee benefit plans under the Employee Retirement Income Security Act of 1974 (ERISA).[1] It also provides a listing of the reporting and disclosure requirements of the Department of Labor (DOL), the Internal Revenue Service (IRS), and the Pension Benefit Guaranty Corporation (PBGC) and the deadlines for compliance.

**Reporting**  *Reporting* refers to government filing requirements. ERISA reporting requirements include:

- filing annual reports with the IRS, PBGC and DOL (via DOL);
- filing annual premium forms and event-based reports with the PBGC; and
- making certain documents available for inspection by the DOL.

**Disclosure**  *Disclosure* refers to materials that plan administrators must distribute or make available to plan participants and beneficiaries. ERISA disclosure requirements include:

- supplying plan participants with summary plan descriptions (SPDs), summaries of material modifications (SMMs), summary annual reports (SARs), special notices for pension plans, and special notices for health plans; and
- making certain documents are available for inspection by participants and certain beneficiaries and providing copies of such documents on request.

**Plan administrator**  A *plan administrator* is an individual, a group of individuals, or an entity (e.g., a corporation).[2] The plan administrator, who is responsible for certain plan duties, is usually named in the plan document. If the plan administrator is not named in the plan document, the plan sponsor generally serves as the plan administrator.

---

[1]  Pub. L. No. 93-406, 88 Stat. 832 (1974) (codified as amended at 29 U.S.C. § 1001).
[2]  ERISA § 3(16)(A).

**Plan sponsor**     A *plan sponsor* may be one of the following:[3]

- the employer;
- the employee organization;
- a joint board of trustees; or
- an entity representing parties establishing or maintaining the plan.

**Other requirements**     In addition to reporting and disclosure requirements, ERISA and other federal laws require plans to address the following:[4]

- Plan documentation
- Claims processing
- Records retention
- Fiduciary responsibilities and prohibited transactions
- Bonding
- Trust requirements
- Group health plan portability, access, and renewability
- Standards for group health plans
- Health care coverage reporting
- Medical child support orders
- Continuation of group health plan coverage

---

[3] ERISA § 3(16)(B).
[4] See detailed discussion of other requirements in Chapters 9, 10, and 11.

## Compliance Overview

| Form/Notice | Description | Requirement | Deadline |
|---|---|---|---|
| Annual Report (Form 5500 Series) | Includes information about plan type, administration, participation, funding, and finances. | File annual reports with the DOL for pension and welfare plans subject to ERISA. | Last day of 7th month after close of plan year (extension available). |
| Summary Annual Report (SAR) | Provides abstract of financial information in annual report. | Distribute summary annual reports for ERISA-covered pension and welfare plans to participants and certain beneficiaries (unless Notice of Pension Plan Funding Status provided). | 2 months after Form 5500 deadline. |
| Summary Plan Description (SPD) | Contains summary of benefits provided by one or more plans, including eligibility requirements, funding arrangements, claims procedures, and ERISA rights. | Distribute SPDs for ERISA-covered pension and welfare plans to participants and certain beneficiaries.<br><br>Provide SPDs to the DOL upon request. | New participant: 90 days after individual becomes participant.<br><br>New plan: no later than 120 days after plan becomes subject to SPD requirements.<br><br>Updated SPD: no later than 5 years plus 210 days after end of plan year in which SPD was last updated (10 years plus 210 days if, during 5-year period, changes to plan did not affect information in SPD). |
| SPD/Notice for SIMPLEs | Contain summary of benefits, eligibility, contribution timing and methods, distribution methods, and description of rollovers from SIMPLE plans. | Trustee distributes to employer, who then furnishes SPD to eligible employees. | Annually. Distribute to eligible employees in advance of 60-day election period. |

**Compliance Overview (*cont'd*)**

| Form/Notice | Description | Requirement | Deadline |
|---|---|---|---|
| Summary of Material Modifications (SMM) | Provides summary of changes to SPD information. | Distribute SMMs for ERISA-covered pension and welfare plans to participants and certain beneficiaries. Provide SMMs to the DOL upon request. | 210 days after close of plan year during which change was adopted. A reduction in covered services or benefits under a group health plan: 60 days after modification adopted or 90 days if descriptions are provided at regular intervals. |
| PBGC Form1-ES | Used to estimate and pay initial annual insurance premium to the PBGC. (Must later reconcile estimated payment.) | Submit initial estimated annual payment to the PBGC for defined benefit plans that report 500 or more participants for flat rate count. | Last day of 2nd full month after close of prior plan year. |
| PBGC Comprehensive Premium Payment Filing | Used to calculate and pay actual insurance premium due to the PBGC. | Submit electronically and pay actual premium payment to the PBGC for covered defined benefit plans. | 15th day of 10th full month following end of prior year; last day of 16th month if fewer than 100 participants. |
| PBGC Form 10 and Form 10 Advance | Used to notify the PBGC of reportable events. | Notify PBGC of specified events, such as reduction in active participants and certain business transactions. | Varies based on event and funding status. Generally 30 days after event; 10 days in advance for nonpublic companies for narrowed list of events. |
| PBGC Form 200 | Used to notify the PBGC of a failure to make required contributions to a single-employer defined benefit plan. | Plan sponsor that fails to make required contribution to single employer defined benefit plan submits Form 200 to PBGC if the plan's funding target attainment percentage is less than 100% and total unpaid balance of required contributions exceeds $1 million. | 10 days after the date required contribution is due. |
| PBGC 4010 Report | Notifies PBGC of plans with "at risk" (below 80 percent) funding target attainment percentage. | Plan sponsor files documents and financial information with PBGC. | 105 days after the close of the sponsor's information year. |

| Notice | Description | Timing |
|---|---|---|
| PBGC Notice of Cessation of Operations/Withdrawal | Notifies PBGC of employer-sponsor change to single-employer plan. | Within 60 days of cessation of operations or withdrawal. |
| Notice of Plan Termination | Notifies PBGC, participants, beneficiaries and bargaining agents of plan's termination. | Between 60 and 90 days prior to proposed termination date. |
| Notice of Right to Defer | Explains material features of distribution, right to delay distribution, and consequences of failure to defer. | Provide before distribution unless exception applies. | No more than 180 and no less than 30 days before distribution unless participant elects earlier distribution. |
| Notice of Qualified Joint and Survivor Annuity (QJSA) | Explains terms, conditions, and rights of joint and survivor annuity benefit. | Distribute notice to participants in defined benefit plans and certain defined contribution plans, if QJSA can be waived in favor of an optional form of distribution. | No less than 30 and no more than 180 days before the annuity starting date. Participants may waive 30-day period if distribution begins more than 7 days after explanation is provided. |
| Notice of Withholding and Rollover Treatment | Explains direct rollover rules, income tax withholding on distributions not directly rolled over, and tax consequences of eligible rollover distributions. | Distribute notice to any person who receives a qualified plan distribution eligible for rollover. | No more than 180 and no less than 30 days before distribution unless participant elects earlier distribution. |
| Notice of Suspension of Benefits | Notifies participant that pension benefits are suspended, or that the plan does not provide actuarial adjustment for deferral period. | Distribute notice to any participant in defined benefit plan whose benefits are suspended due to rehire or increased work hours or due to continued employment beyond normal retirement age. | During 1st month or payroll period in which benefits are suspended. |
| Notice of Receipt of Domestic Relations Order | States that domestic relations order has been received and explains plan's procedure for determining if order is qualified. | Distribute notice to participant and each alternate payee. Alternate payee is a spouse, former spouse, child, or other dependent that order recognizes as having right to receive all or portion of benefits payable under plan to participant. | "Promptly" on receipt of order. |

**Compliance Overview (*cont'd*)**

| Form/Notice | Description | Requirement | Deadline |
|---|---|---|---|
| Notice of Status of Domestic Relations Order | Informs participant and alternate payee(s) of result of determination procedure and whether the domestic relations order is considered qualified. | Distribute notice to participant and each alternate payee. | Within "reasonable period" after receipt of order. |
| Notice of Qualified Preretirement Survivor Annuity (QPSA) | Explains terms and conditions of pre-retirement survivor annuity benefit. | Provide notice to participants in defined benefit plans and certain defined contribution plans, if pre-retirement death benefits are not fully subsidized, or if participant is permitted to designate a nonspouse beneficiary. | Generally, the later of last day of (1) period starting on 1st day of plan year in which participant attains age 32 and ending on close of plan year preceding plan year in which participant attains age 35 or (2) 1 year after employee becomes participant. |
| Statement of Accrued Benefits—Defined Benefit Plans | Provides summary of participant's accrued and vested pension benefits. | Must disclose total benefit accrued, vested status, date of full vesting and an explanation of applicable offsets. | Vested participants in defined benefit plans must be given benefit statements at least once every three years (initial statement for a calendar year plan due February 14, 2010), or a plan administrator may provide annual notice of the availability of a statement upon request (initial notice due December 31, 2007). |
| Statement of Accrued Benefits—Defined Contribution Plans | Provides summary of participant's investments and vested status. | Must disclose information on investment values in individual's account based on most recent valuation, and provide an explanation of the importance of portfolio diversification, including a discussion of the inherent risk of holding more than 20% of assets in a single security along with a notice that further information on investing and diversification is available on the DOL website. | Quarterly statements are required for defined contribution plan participants and beneficiaries who have the right to direct the investment of plan assets (45-day safe harbor deadline); annual statements are required for those without such rights (safe harbor is Form 5500 due date). |

| | | |
|---|---|---|
| Notice of Distribution of Excess Deferrals and Contributions | Informs participants receiving distributions of excess deferrals or contributions that the distributions are includable in income. | Distribute notice to all participants who receive distributions of excess deferrals, excess contributions, or excess aggregate contributions. | At time of distribution. |
| ERISA 404(c) Notice | Advises participants of fund choices, rights, and obligations for investment choices. | Distribute to each participant permitted to direct investment of own account. | Prior to exercise of control. Notice of Qualified Change in Investment Options due at least 30 days, but no more than 60 days in advance. |
| Notice of QDIA, QACA, EACA | Tells employees eligible to participate in defined contribution plan about default investment and automatic contribution arrangements. | Distribute notice of QDIA to each eligible employee and beneficiary with assets to be invested in a qualified default investment alternative, and QACA or EACA notices to employers who will be enrolled in this plan under an automatic contribution arrangement if they do not affirmatively opt-out. | Generally, need to provide between 30 and 90 days in advance of plan year to meet safe harbor; by date of eligibility for newly eligible employees. |
| 401(k) Safe Harbor Notice | Advises participants of their rights and obligations under the plan. | Distribute to each employee eligible to participate in 401(k) plan claiming safe harbor status. | A reasonable period before any plan year. Deemed reasonable if at least 30 days, but not more than 90 days. |
| Notice of Eligible Investment Advice Arrangement | Explains fees, investment performance and affiliations of fiduciary advisor. | Distribute to participants in eligible investment advice arrangement. | Provide before providing advice, plus annually, plus at time of material change. |
| Notice of Right to Divest Employer Securities | Explains right to invest participant accounts and, if 3 years of service, employer accounts in options other than employer securities. Also explains importance of diversification. | Individual account plans holding publicly traded employer securities (other than certain ESOPs) distribute notice to eligible participants and beneficiaries. | 30 days before individual is eligible to divest. |
| Blackout Notice | Notice of temporary period (more than 3 business days) investment changes cannot be made. | Distribute notice to affected participants and beneficiaries, and employer if securities in plan. | 30 days in advance. |

**Compliance Overview** (*cont'd*)

| Form/Notice | Description | Requirement | Deadline |
|---|---|---|---|
| Notice of Pension Plan Funding Status | Advises affected parties of plan's funding status, assets, liabilities, material plan amendments, and limits on PBGC guaranteed benefits. | Distribute to affected parties in PBGC-covered plans. Affected parties include PBGC, employee organizations, participants, beneficiaries, and each contributing sponsor in multiemployer plan. | 120 days after plan year end. Plans with 100 or fewer participants distribute when filing Annual Report (Form 5500). |
| Notice of Benefit Distribution Restrictions Due to Plan's Funding Status | Advises participants and beneficiaries of restrictions on the payment of shutdown, unpredictable contingent event benefits, lump sums, and certain other distributions. | Provide written notice to participants and beneficiaries. Electronic or other form permitted to the extent reasonably accessible. | Within 30 days after becoming subject to limit. |
| Notice of Failure to Make Timely Contributions | Advises participants and beneficiaries of employer's failure to make required quarterly contributions within 60 days of due date. | Employer failing to make required quarterly contributions to pension plan (except multiemployer plans) distributes notice to participants, certain beneficiaries, and alternate payees under qualified domestic relations orders. | Awaiting guidance. Disclosure with Notice of Pension Plan Funding Status may be acceptable. |
| Notice of Significant Reduction in Benefit Accruals | Advises participants of pension plan amendment that significantly reduces or freezes their benefit accruals, including any elimination or reduction of an early retirement benefit or retirement type subsidy. | Distribute notice to plan participants, alternate payees under qualified domestic relations orders, and designated person of employee organization and contributing employers. | 45 days before effective date of amendment; 15 days before for small plans, multiemployer plans, and business transactions. 30 days after for certain transfers that do not reduce benefit accruals. |
| Notice of Transfer to Retiree Health Account | Advises affected parties of the transfer of excess defined benefit plan assets to a Section 401(h) retiree health account. | Employer must distribute notice to plan administrator, employee organization(s), IRS and the DOL. Plan administrator must, in turn, notify participants and beneficiaries. | No later than 60 days before the date of the transfer. |

| | | |
|---|---|---|
| Notice of Funding Waiver Application | Advises affected parties of employer's intention to apply for funding waiver. | Employer requesting funding waiver must notify affected parties. Affected parties include the PBGC, employee organizations, participants, beneficiaries, and alternate payees under qualified domestic relations orders. | Within 14 days before date application for waiver is filed with the IRS. |
| Multiemployer Notice of Critical/Endangered Status | Warns participants of possible benefit limits due to plan funding shortfalls. | Describe "adjustable" benefits that may be reduced to participants, beneficiaries, bargaining parties, PBGC, and DOL. | Within 30 days of actuary's certification of critical or endangered status. |
| Multiemployer Notice of Adjustable Benefit Reduction | Announces reductions to "adjustable" benefits bargained to address funding levels. | Describe benefit reductions and rights/remedies to participants, beneficiaries, contributing employers and bargaining organization. | 30 days before reductions are implemented. |
| Multiemployer Notice of Application for Extension to Pay Unfunded Liabilities | Warns parties of request to IRS for funding extension. | Notify participants, beneficiaries, alternate payees, and bargaining organization. | 14 days before sending application to IRS. |
| Notice to Interested Parties | Advises interested parties that plan sponsor intends to file an application with IRS for determination of qualified status of pension plan. | Must post or distribute notice to all interested parties before submitting application for determination with the IRS. | Not less than 10 and no more than 24 days before submitting application. |
| General Preexisting-Condition/Special Enrollment Notice | Explains existence and terms of preexisting-condition exclusion period in group health plan. | Distribute notice to each participant. | Provide as part of written application material. |
| Individual Preexisting-Condition Notice | Explains length of preexisting-condition exclusion period after applying credit for previous health plan coverage. | Distribute notice to participants who have any preexisting-condition exclusion period remaining after applying credit for prior coverage. | After receiving a certificate of creditable prior coverage and before preexisting-condition exclusion may be imposed. |

**Compliance Overview (cont'd)**

| Form/Notice | Description | Requirement | Deadline |
|---|---|---|---|
| Notice of Alternative Method of Crediting Coverage Under Group Health Plan | Informs enrollees, participants, and beneficiaries that the group health plan only credits similar types of prior coverage toward satisfying its preexisting-condition limitation period. | Prominently state in any plan disclosure statement and must distribute to each enrollee. | When individual enrolls in group health plan. |
| Certification of Group Health Plan Coverage | Certifies individual's period of creditable coverage and the waiting period (if any) imposed. | Distribute certificate to each individual who loses coverage under the plan. | If "practicable" at time of COBRA notice. |
| Women's Health and Cancer Rights Notice | Explains availability of breast reconstruction in connection with mastectomy. | Distribute to participants in group health plans that cover mastectomy. | Upon plan enrollment and annually thereafter. |
| COBRA General Notice | Describes basic COBRA rights for continuation coverage under group health plan. | Distribute written notice to each covered employee and spouse upon enrollment. | Within 90 days of date individual enrolls in group health plan. |
| COBRA Second Notice and Election | Describes basic COBRA rights and election form. | Distribute written notice and election to each qualified beneficiary. | Within 14 days after plan administrator is notified of a qualifying event. |
| Notice of Receipt of Medical Child Support Order | Acknowledges receipt of order and explains procedure. | Provide to participant and each alternative recipient. | Within a reasonable time. |
| HIPAA Privacy Notice | Describes plan's use of protected health information. | Provide to participants. | At enrollment and at least once every three years. |
| Medicare Part D Creditable Coverage Notice | Tells Medicare beneficiaries whether employer's drug coverage is as good as Part D. | Distribute notice to covered employees, retirees, spouses in employer group health plan if covered by Medicare. | Annually; when coverage ends; and upon request. |

# Chapter 2

# Plans Subject to ERISA

---

**Introduction**    Identifying plans subject to ERISA is important because these plans must comply with certain requirements such as filing annual reports and distributing summary plan descriptions to participants. This chapter describes ERISA's general coverage provisions and exemptions and definitions of pension and welfare plans. It also describes the suspension of reporting requirements for plans subject to Internal Revenue Code (Code) Section 6039D.

**Contents**    This chapter has five sections:

# A. General Coverage Provisions

ERISA's general coverage provisions form the framework for determining whether a plan is subject to ERISA's rules and regulations.

Unless specifically exempted, a plan is subject to ERISA if it is an employee benefit plan established or maintained by an employer engaged in commerce or in an industry or activity affecting commerce, or an organization (or group of organizations) representing employees engaged in commerce or in any industry or activity affecting commerce.[1]

**Employee benefit plan**

In general, an *employee benefit plan* is either a pension plan or a welfare plan, or a plan that is both a pension plan and a welfare plan.[2] However, a pension plan or welfare plan is generally *not* an employee benefit plan if it has no employees as participants.[3]

**Employer**

An *employer* is any person or entity (including a group or association of employers) acting directly as an employer or indirectly in an employer's interest in relation to an employee benefit plan.[4]

**Employee organization**

An *employee organization* is either:

- a labor union or organization in which employees participate and that exists in whole or in part to deal with employers about employee benefit plans or other matters incidental to employment relationships, or
- an employee's beneficiary association organized in whole or in part to establish an employee benefit plan.[5]

**Employee**

An *employee* is any individual employed by an employer.[6] Sole owners of a trade or business (whether or not incorporated) and partners

---

[1]  ERISA § 4(a).
[2]  ERISA § 3(3).
[3]  DOL Reg. § 2510.3-3(b).
[4]  ERISA § 3(5).
[5]  ERISA § 3(4).
[6]  ERISA § 3(6).

in a partnership (and their spouses) are not considered employees for the purposes of ERISA.[7]

**Note.** For qualified plan purposes, the term *employee* can include individuals characterized by an employer as leased employees and independent contractors, as determined by the facts and circumstances. Leased employees who meet specific criteria can be treated as employees for certain purposes.[8]

**Participant**    A *participant* is any employee or former employee of an employer, or any member or former member of an employee organization, who is eligible or may become eligible for benefits from an employee benefit plan, or whose beneficiaries may become eligible for such benefits.[9]

---

7 DOL Reg. § 2510.3-3(c).
8 I.R.C. § 414(n).
9 ERISA § 3(7).

# B. Plans Exempt from ERISA

Some employee benefit plans are exempt from ERISA. Those plans do not have to comply with ERISA's requirements. Among the plans exempt from ERISA coverage are:

- Governmental plans
- Church plans
- Plans maintained solely to comply with workers' compensation, unemployment compensation, or disability insurance laws
- Plans maintained outside the United States primarily for nonresident aliens
- Unfunded excess benefit plans[10]

## Governmental Plans

In general, a *governmental plan* is a plan established or maintained by the federal government or state and local governments and their agencies or instrumentalities for their employees.

Governmental plans include plans financed by contributions required under the Railroad Retirement Acts of 1935 and 1937 and any plan sponsored by an international organization exempt from United States taxes by the International Organization Immunities Act.

In addition, governmental plans include plans established and maintained by an Indian Tribal Government, its subdivision, or agency or instrumentality, where all participants are employees who provide essential government functions, but not commercial activity services.[11]

## Church Plans

In general, a *church plan* is a plan that a church or a convention or association of churches establishes and maintains for its employees,[12] including a plan established for employees of a tax-exempt organization

---

10    ERISA § 4(b).
11    ERISA § 3(32).
12    ERISA § 3(33).

that administers the plans of the church or convention controlled by or associated with a church or a convention or association of churches.[13]

**Note.** Pension plans sponsored by a church or a convention or association of churches may irrevocably elect to be covered under ERISA. If so, the plans must comply with ERISA's participation, funding, and vesting requirements.[14]

## Excess Benefit Plans

An *excess benefit plan* is a plan maintained by an employer to provide benefits that exceed the limits imposed by Code Section 415 on contributions and benefits.[15]

---

[13] ERISA §3(33)(a).
[14] I.R.C. §410(d).
[15] ERISA §3(36).

# C. Covered Pension Plans

**Definition**
In general, a *pension plan* is any plan, fund, or program established or maintained by an employer, employee organization, or both, to provide retirement income to employees or to enable employees to defer income for periods of time extending to the termination of covered employment or beyond.[16]

**Types of pension plans**
Plans that generally meet the above definition of pension plan include the following:

- Defined benefit plans (e.g., fixed or unit benefit plans and cash balance plans)
- Defined contribution plans (e.g., profit-sharing plans, Section 401(k) plans, employee stock option plans, thrift plans, target benefit plans, and money purchase pension plans)
- Simplified employee pension plans (SEPs)
- Nonqualified deferred compensation plans
- Section 457 deferred compensation plans of tax-exempt organizations

In addition, the following types of plans are pension plans if they meet certain conditions:[17]

- Severance pay plans
- Individual retirement accounts (IRAs)
- Tax-sheltered annuities (TSAs) or Section 403(b) annuities
- Supplemental payment plans
- Gratuitous payments to employees who retired prior to the enactment of ERISA
- Bonus programs

The preceding list of plan types meeting the definition of a pension plan is not all-inclusive. Whether a plan is a pension plan depends on the plan's express terms and on the facts and circumstances of the plan.[18]

---

[16]  ERISA § 3(2)(A).
[17]  DOL Reg. § 2510.3-2.
[18]  ERISA § 3(2)(A); DOL Adv. Ops. 81-27A, 90-17A.

For example, a stock purchase plan could be a pension plan if any of the following conditions apply:[19]

- The plan is administered in a way that provides retirement income to employees.
- The plan results in the deferral of employees' income extending to or beyond the termination of covered employment.
- Communications to plan participants indicate that the purpose of the plan is to provide employees with retirement income or to defer income to termination of covered employment or beyond.

---

## Severance Pay Plans

---

**Definition**

A *severance pay plan* is an arrangement under which an employer makes compensation payments to involuntarily terminated employees. Such a plan is a pension plan unless:

- payments are not contingent directly or indirectly on the employee's retirement;
- the total amount of the payments does not exceed two times the employee's annual compensation during the year immediately preceding his or her termination of employment; and
- all payments to any employee are completed within the later of 24 months after termination of employment or 24 months after the employee attains normal retirement age for employees terminating under a limited program of terminations, or within 24 months after termination of employment for any other employee.[20]

A severance pay plan that is not a pension plan is subject to ERISA as a *welfare* plan.

**Annual compensation**

The term *annual compensation* refers to an employee's total compensation (including wages, salary, and other benefits of monetary value) paid in cash, or otherwise, as consideration for the employee's service during the year, or which would have been paid at the employee's usual rate of compensation if the employee had worked a full year.[21]

---

[19]  DOL Adv. Op. 90-17A.
[20]  DOL Reg. § 2510.3-2(b)(1).
[21]  DOL Reg. § 2510.3-2(b)(2)(i).

**Limited program of terminations**

A *limited program of terminations* is a program that

- is scheduled for completion on a specific date or upon the occurrence of one or more specified events;
- specifies in advance the number, percentage, or class(es) of employees whose employment will be terminated; and
- makes available to the DOL for inspection a written document describing the program of terminations and containing enough information to show that the program meets all of these conditions.[22]

## Individual Retirement Accounts

**Definition**

An *individual retirement account* (IRA) is a trust created to establish a personal retirement program meeting the requirements of Code Section 408.[23]

An IRA is not generally a pension plan. However, if an IRA program is established and maintained by an employer or employee organization, it may be an ERISA-covered pension plan.

**Conditions**

An IRA program established or maintained by an employer or employee organization is an ERISA-covered pension plan unless all the following conditions apply:[24]

- The employer or employee association does not contribute to the program.
- The participation of employees or members in the program is completely voluntary.
- The employer or employee association does not receive any consideration other than reasonable compensation for services it renders in connection with collecting and remitting payroll deductions and dues checkoffs.
- The employer or employee's association's sole functions are, without endorsing the plan, to (1) permit the sponsor to publicize the program to employees/members of the association and (2) collect contributions through payroll deductions or dues checkoffs and remit them.

---

[22] DOL Reg. § 2510.3-2(b)(2)(ii).
[23] I.R.C. § 408(a).
[24] DOL Reg. § 2510.3-2(d).

**Endorsement**   An employer or employee organization that collects payroll deductions from employees or members for an IRA program does not endorse the IRA program in any way if it meets all of the following conditions:[25]

- Materials about the IRA program must clearly and prominently state in words the average employee or member can understand that:
  — the program is completely voluntary;
  — the employer or employee organization does not endorse the IRA sponsor or the funding media;
  — employees or members may choose other funding media that are outside the payroll deduction program;
  — an IRA may not be appropriate for everyone; and
  — the tax consequences of contributing to an IRA through payroll deduction are the same as those when contributions to an IRA are made outside the payroll deduction program.
- The employer is not the IRA sponsor or an affiliate of the sponsor.
- The funding medium must not have significant investments in employer securities and does not state that one of its purposes is to invest in such securities.
- For an IRA program resulting from an agreement between an employer and an employee organization, the funding medium does not have significant investments in an investment vehicle that is designed to benefit the organization by providing its members with more jobs or loans, or similar direct benefits, nor does the funding medium state that one of its objectives is to invest in such a vehicle.

An employer may encourage its employees to save for retirement by providing general information on the IRA payroll deduction program and other educational materials that explain the advisability of retirement savings without converting the program into an ERISA covered plan. However, the employer must make clear that its involvement in the program is limited to collecting the deducted amounts and remitting them promptly to the IRA sponsor and that it does not provide any additional benefit or promise any particular investment return on the employee's savings.[26]

---

## Tax-Sheltered Annuities

---

**Definition**   A *tax-sheltered annuity* (TSA) *program* is a program under which employees of certain tax-exempt organizations and public schools may defer income taxes on contributions to certain annuity contracts or

---

[25]   DOL Adv. Op. 81-80A.
[26]   DOL Reg. § 2509.99-1 Interpretive Bulletin.

custodial accounts.[27] Because TSA programs must meet the requirements of Code Section 403(b), they are commonly known as 403(b) plans.

**Conditions**

A TSA program established by and maintained by an employer is a pension plan under Title I of ERISA unless all the following apply:[28]

- Employee participation in the program is completely voluntary.
- Only an employee (or the employee's beneficiary or authorized representative) can enforce any rights under the annuity contract or custodial account.
- The employer's sole functions under the program are to:
  — permit annuity contractors to publicize their products to employees;
  — request information about proposed funding media, products, and annuity contractors;
  — summarize or compile information on the proposed funding media, products, or the annuity contractors to facilitate review and analysis by the employees;
  — collect salary reduction contributions, remit them to the insurer or custodian, and maintain contribution records;
  — hold in its name any group annuity contracts covering its employees; and
  — limit the number of funding media, products, or annuity contractors to a selection that affords employees a reasonable choice in light of the relevant circumstances.
- The employer does not receive any consideration other than reasonable reimbursement of its expenses incurred in performing its duties under employees' contribution agreements.

---

## Supplemental Payment Plans

---

**Definition**

A *supplemental payment plan* is an arrangement under which an employer makes payments to supplement an employee's retirement income.[29]

---

[27] I.R.C. § 403(b).
[28] DOL Reg. § 2510.3-2(f).
[29] DOL Reg. § 2510.3-2(g)(1).

**Conditions**     In general, a supplemental payment plan is an ERISA-covered pension plan. However, a supplemental payment plan is treated as an ERISA-covered welfare plan, rather than a pension plan, if supplemental payments made on or after September 26, 1980, meet all the following conditions:[30]

- The employer makes supplemental payments to plan participants or their beneficiaries from its general assets or from a separate trust.
- The monthly supplemental payments to participants or their beneficiaries do not exceed a certain amount determined by a formula specified in DOL regulations.
- The employer does not make supplemental payments before the last day of the month for which payments are computed.

**Note.** Special rules apply to employees who retired prior to 1977.

## Gratuitous Payments to Pre-ERISA Retirees

A program of voluntary, gratuitous payments to employees who retired prior to the enactment of ERISA is not an ERISA-covered pension plan if the program meets all the following conditions:[31]

- The employer makes the payments from general assets.
- The retirees separated from service prior to September 2, 1974.
- The payments to the retirees began before September 2, 1974.
- The employer annually notifies the retirees in writing that the payments are gratuitous and do not constitute a pension plan.

## Bonus Program

**Definition**     A *bonus program* is not an ERISA-covered pension plan if payments are made to some or all employees for work performed, unless the program systematically defers bonus payments until the termination of covered employment or beyond or provides retirement income to employees.[32]

---

[30]   *Id.*
[31]   DOL Reg. § 2510.3-2(e).
[32]   DOL Reg. § 2510.3-2(c).

# D. Covered Welfare Plans

In general, a welfare plan is any plan, fund, or program an employer or employee organization, or both, establish and maintain to provide certain benefits to participants and their beneficiaries through the purchase of insurance or other means.[33] The benefits may include:

- Medical, surgical, and/or hospital care benefits
- Sickness, accident, and/or disability benefits
- Death benefits
- Unemployment benefits
- Vacation
- Severance benefits
- Apprenticeship or other training
- Scholarship funds
- Day care
- Prepaid legal services
- Certain supplemental payments to retirees based on cost-of-living increases[34]

For details concerning types of ERISA-covered welfare benefits, see Table 2-1 at the end of this section.

**Excluded programs and practices**

DOL regulations identify certain programs and practices that are *not* ERISA-covered welfare plans.[35] They include:

- Certain payroll practices such as the payment of overtime pay, shift differentials, sick pay, vacation and holiday pay
- Certain on-premise facilities (other than day care centers) such as recreation and dining facilities
- On-premise facilities for treating minor injuries and illnesses or for rendering first aid during work hours
- Holiday gifts such as turkeys or hams
- Employee discount programs
- Hiring hall facilities
- Remembrance funds
- Strike funds
- Industry advancement programs

---

[33] ERISA § 3(1).
[34] DOL Reg. § 2510.3-2(g)(1).
[35] DOL Reg. § 2510.3-1.

- Payroll deductions for deposit in savings accounts owned by employees
- Unfunded scholarship programs
- Certain group or group-type insurance programs that are not established and maintained by an employer or employee organization ("voluntary employee-pay-all-programs")

For details concerning types of plans that are not ERISA-covered welfare plans, see Table 2-1 at the end of this section.

**Voluntary employee-pay-all programs**

A group or group-type insurance program is not an ERISA-covered welfare plan if it meets the following conditions:[36]

- Employees' or members' participation in the program is completely voluntary.
- The employer or employee organization does not contribute to the program.
- The employer or employee organization does not negotiate premiums or benefits with an insurer or similar organization or assist employees with claims.
- The employer or employee organization does not receive a contract relating to the plan in its name or choose the coverage and insurance carrier or similar organization.
- The employer or employee organization does not receive any consideration from the plan other than reimbursement of administrative expenses.
- The sole functions of the employer or employee organization, without endorsing the plan, are to (1) permit an insurer or similar organization to publicize the program and (2) collect premiums through payroll deductions or dues checkoffs and remit them to the insurer.

**Endorsement**

An employer would not be considered to "endorse" a group or group-type insurance merely by limiting the providers that it allows to market products in the workplace or selecting a single provider to which it will forward contributions.[37] Refer to Section C on Individual Retirement Accounts for a further discussion of actions that may, or may not be viewed as "endorsing" a plan.

---

36  DOL Reg. § 2510.31-1(j); DOL Adv. Ops. 77-54, 75-06.
37  DOL Field Assistance Bulletin 2006-2, Q2; DOL Reg. § 2509.99-1 Interpretive Bulletin.

**Cafeteria
Plans**

The provision of tax favored treatment in and of itself is not a benefit that would be subject to ERISA. But while DOL does not view a cafeteria plan to be a *separate* ERISA employee welfare benefit plan, such a plan would be viewed as *part* of an ERISA welfare benefit plan because it provides a mechanism for funding the plan with employee contributions. This leads to the conclusion that pre-tax contributions to a cafeteria plan for ERISA benefits are "plan assets" of the plan "as of the earliest date on which such contributions can reasonably be segregated from the employer's general assets."[38]

---

[38] DOL Adv. Op. 96-12A.

**Table 2-1**
**Identifying ERISA-Covered Welfare Plans**

*Note:* This table assumes a plan is not a voluntary employee-pay-all group or group-type insurance program.

| If Plan Provides | And Plan Is | And | Then Plan Is |
|---|---|---|---|
| death benefits | • a group term life insurance plan[1]<br><br>• an accident, death, and dismemberment plan[2]<br><br>• a split-dollar life insurance plan[3]<br><br>• a group universal life or whole life insurance plan[4] | → | an ERISA-covered welfare plan |
| | • a travel accident insurance plan | Coverage via employer credit card or reimbursed[5] | NOT an ERISA-covered welfare plan |
| | | Coverage under employer's insurance contract[6] | an ERISA-covered welfare plan |
| | a remembrance fund[7] | benefit is incidental | NOT an ERISA-covered welfare plan |
| | | benefit is not incidental ($1,500 is not incidental) | an ERISA-covered welfare plan |
| dependent care benefits | an employer-provided day care center[8] | → | |
| | a dependent care reimbursement program[9] | → | NOT an ERISA-covered welfare plan |
| disability benefits | a group long-term disability plan[10] | → | an ERISA-covered welfare plan |
| | • a group short-term disability plan[11]<br><br>• a sick pay program[12]<br><br>• a salary-continuation program[13] | benefits are funded | |
| | | benefits are paid solely from employer's general assets | NOT an ERISA-covered welfare plan |

**Table 2-1 (*cont'd*)**
**Identifying ERISA-Covered Welfare Plans**

| If Plan Provides | And Plan Is | And | Then Plan Is |
|---|---|---|---|
| educational benefits | an apprenticeship program[14] | ⟶ | an ERISA-covered welfare plan |
| | • a scholarship program[15] | program is funded | |
| | • an educational assistance program (I.R.C. § 127)[16]<br>• an in-house training program[17]<br>• a tuition-refund program[18] | benefits are paid solely from employer's general assets | NOT an ERISA-covered welfare plan |
| employment termination compensation benefits | a severance pay program[19] | benefits do not exceed twice an employee's annual compensation and meet other DOL requirements (see Section C) | an ERISA-covered welfare plan |
| | | benefits exceed twice an employee's annual compensation or do not meet other DOL requirements (see Section C) | an ERISA-covered *pension* plan |
| | a supplemental unemployment benefit plan[20] | ⟶ | an ERISA-covered welfare plan |
| | a strike fund[21] | ⟶ | NOT an ERISA-covered welfare plan |
| fringe benefits | • an employer-operated eating facility[22]<br>• an employee discount program[23] | ⟶ | NOT an ERISA-covered welfare plan |

**Table 2-1 (*cont'd*)**
**Identifying ERISA-Covered Welfare Plans**

| If Plan Provides | And Plan Is | And | Then Plan Is |
|---|---|---|---|
| health benefits | • a group health plan (i.e., medical, dental, vision, prescription drug)[24]<br><br>• health care FSA or HRA<br><br>• a physical exam program[25]<br><br>• an executive medical reimbursement program[26] | ⟶ | an ERISA-covered welfare plan |
| | an employee assistance program[27] | program provides more than referral services | |
| | | program provides referral services only | NOT an ERISA-covered welfare plan |
| | • an on-premise first aid program[28]<br><br>• a health savings account[29] | ⟶ | |
| legal services | a prepaid group legal services program | ⟶ | an ERISA-covered welfare plan |
| retirement benefits | a supplemental payment plan[30] | plan meets DOL requirements (see Section C) | an ERISA-covered welfare plan |
| | | plan does *not* meet DOL requirements | an ERISA-covered *pension* plan |
| vacation and recreational benefits | a vacation pay plan[31] | benefits are funded | an ERISA-covered welfare plan |
| | | benefits are paid solely from employer's general assets | NOT an ERISA-covered welfare plan |
| | a recreational facility[32] | ⟶ | |

---

| | |
|---|---|
| 1 | ERISA § 3(1). |
| 2 | *Id.* |
| 3 | DOL Adv. Op. 77-23. |
| 4 | ERISA § 3(1). |
| 5 | ERISA § 3(1); *see also* DOL Adv. Op. 81-77A. |
| 6 | DOL Adv. Op. 79-69A. |
| 7 | DOL Reg. § 2510.3-1(g); DOL Adv. Ops. 80-69A, 81-19A. |

[8]  ERISA § 3(1).

[9]  DOL Adv. Op. 88-10A.

[10]  DOL Adv. Ops. 80-38A, 85-9A.

[11]  DOL Reg. § 2510.3-1(b)(2); DOL Adv. Ops. 80-44A, 85-23A.

[12]  DOL Reg. § 2510.3-1(b)(2); DOL Adv. Ops. 81-71A, 81-87A.

[13]  *Id.*

[14]  ERISA § 3(1).

[15]  DOL Reg. § 2510.3-1(k).

[16]  DOL Adv. Op. 85-34A.

[17]  DOL Adv. Op. 83-32A.

[18]  DOL Reg. § 2510.3-1(k).

[19]  ERISA § 3(1); DOL Reg. § 2510.3-2(b); DOL Adv. Op. 77-27A.

[20]  DOL Adv. Op. 82-43A.

[21]  DOL Reg. § 2510.3-1(h).

[22]  DOL Reg. § 2510.3-1(c)(1).

[23]  DOL Reg. § 2510.3-1(e).

[24]  ERISA § 3(1); DOL Reg. § 2510.3-1(a)(2).

[25]  *Id.*

[26]  *Id.*

[27]  DOL Adv. Ops. 83-35A, 88-4A, 91-26A.

[28]  DOL Reg. § 2510.3-1(c)(2).

[29]  DOL Field Assistance Bulletin 2004-1. HSAs are not subject to ERISA unless the employer (1) limits the ability of eligible individuals to move their funds to another HSA beyond the restrictions already imposed by the Code; (2) imposes conditions on the use of HSA funds other than those permitted by the Code; (3) makes or influences investment decisions regarding HSA funds; (4) represents that an HSA is a benefit plan established or maintained by the employer; or (5) receives any payment or compensation in connection with an HSA.

[30]  DOL Reg. § 2510.3-2(g).

[31]  DOL Reg. § 2510.3-1(b)(3)(i); DOL Adv. Op. 79-14A.

[32]  DOL Reg. § 2510.3-1(c)(1); DOL Adv. Op. 85-38A.

# E. Covered Section 6039D Plans

Section 6039D was added to the Internal Revenue Code in 1984 to impose independent annual reporting requirements on certain welfare plans. Annual reporting was accomplished through the filing of Form 5500 together with Schedule F.

**Affected plans**   Initially Code Section 6039D applied to cafeteria plans, educational assistance plans, and adoption assistance plans.[39] Congress subsequently expanded Code Section 6039D to include accident and health plans (e.g., medical, dental, vision, accidental death and dismemberment, and long-term disability), group term life insurance plans, and dependent care plans. The IRS, however, delayed the effective date of the reporting requirements until further notice.

**Reporting requirements suspended**   In April 2002, the IRS indefinitely suspended the requirement that cafeteria plans, educational assistance programs, and adoption assistance programs file Form 5500 and Schedule F. The suspension applies to any plan years for which a Form 5500 has not yet been filed, including prior plan years.[40] Thus, there is no current requirement to file Schedule F for any plan.

The suspension of Schedule F is particularly significant for small cafeteria plans and non-ERISA governmental and church plans, which will no longer need to file Form 5500.

**Note.** ERISA-covered cafeteria plans that have 100 or more participants and that contain a health care FSA are still required to file Form 5500 and any applicable schedules other than Schedule F.

---

[39]   IRS Notice 90-24, 1990-1 C.B. 335.
[40]   IRS Notice 2002-24, 2002-16 I.R.B. 785.

# Chapter 3

# Reporting and Disclosure Exemptions and Electronic Distribution

---

**Introduction**     Chapter 2 discussed the types of employee benefit plans covered by ERISA. Those plans must comply with the ERISA reporting and disclosure requirements unless they are specifically exempted.

This chapter describes briefly the ERISA reporting and disclosure requirements and explains the types of plan exemptions. It also describes the Department of Labor's (DOL's) electronic distribution safe harbor and the Internal Revenue Service's (IRS's) rules for electronic plan communications.

**Contents**     This chapter has four sections:

# A. General Information

Most pension and welfare plans subject to ERISA must comply with ERISA's reporting and disclosure requirements.[1]

**ERISA reporting requirements**

The term *ERISA reporting requirements*, for purposes of this chapter, means the following reports and other information that plan administrators must file with or make available to the DOL and the Internal Revenue Service (IRS) under ERISA:

- Annual reports (see Chapter 4)
- Summary plan descriptions (SPDs) (see Chapter 7)
- Summary of material modifications (SMMs) (see Chapter 8)
- Plan documents and other plan information (see Chapter 11)

These requirements are found in Title I of ERISA.

**ERISA disclosure requirements**

The term *ERISA disclosure requirements*, for purposes of this chapter, means the following information that plan administrators must distribute or make available to plan participants and beneficiaries under ERISA:

- Summary annual reports (SARs) (see Chapter 5)
- SPDs (see Chapter 7)
- SMMs (see Chapter 8)
- Plan documents and participant notices (see Chapters 9, 10, and 11)

These requirements are also found in Title I of ERISA.

**Exemptions**

Types of pension and welfare plans subject to ERISA but exempt from some or all of ERISA's reporting and disclosure requirements are:

- Small welfare plans[2]
- Welfare plans in certain group insurance arrangements[3]
- Unfunded welfare plans[4]

---

[1]   ERISA § 101.
[2]   DOL Reg. § 2520.104-20.
[3]   DOL Reg. §§ 2520.104-21, 2520.104-43.
[4]   DOL Reg. § 2520.104b-10(g)(1).

- Employer-provided day care centers[5]
- Apprenticeship training programs[6]
- Simplified employee pension plans (SEPs)[7]
- Pension or welfare plans maintained primarily for a select group of management or highly compensated employees (HCEs)[8]
- Savings Incentive Match Plans for Employees (SIMPLEs)[9]
- Dues-financed pension or welfare plans[10]

Table 3-1 lists the various plan types and the particular reporting and disclosure requirements from which they are fully exempt provided certain definitions and conditions are met. Exemptions from financial reporting requirements in annual reports are covered in Chapter 4. For definitions and details about the conditions that a plan must satisfy to be eligible for exemption, see Section B in this chapter.

**Note.** The DOL has not announced whether medical savings accounts (MSAs) are subject to ERISA's reporting and disclosure requirements. Trustees of MSAs are required to file Form 5498-MSA with the IRS.[11]

Also note that 403(b) arrangements previously exempt from filing certain financial information will be treated the same as other pension plans for plan years beginning after 2008.

---

5   DOL Reg. § 2520.104-25.
6   DOL Reg. § 2520.104-22.
7   DOL Reg. §§ 2520.104-48, 2520.104-49.
8   DOL Reg. §§ 2520.104-23, 2520.104-24.
9   ERISA § 101(h).
10   DOL Reg. §§ 2520.104-26, 2520.104-27.
11   I.R.C. § 220.

**Table 3-1**
**ERISA Reporting and Disclosure Exemptions**

| If ERISA-Covered Plan Is: | And Plan Meets Following Conditions: | Then Plan Is Exempt from Reporting to Government Agencies and Disclosure to Plan Participants as Checked Below: | | | | |
| --- | --- | --- | --- | --- | --- | --- |
| | | Reporting Requirements | | Disclosure Requirements | | |
| | | Annual Report | DOL request for documents | SAR | SPD | SMM |
| A small welfare plan | • Covers fewer than 100 participants at beginning of plan year | | | | | |
| | • Is unfunded and fully insured, or partly unfunded and partly insured | ✓ | | ✓ | | |
| | • If contributory and insured, meets certain other requirements | | | | | |
| A welfare plan in group insurance arrangement | • Is a fully insured arrangement providing benefits for employees of two or more unrelated employers | | | | | |
| | • A trust or other entity holds insurance contracts | | | | | |
| | • Each plan in arrangement has fewer than 100 participants at beginning of plan year (does not apply to annual report exemption) | ✓ | | * | | |
| | • A trust or other entity files annual report for plan in arrangement (applies to annual report exemption for plans in arrangement covering 100 or more participants) | | | | | |
| | • Arrangement meets certain other requirements | | | | | |
| An unfunded welfare plan | Benefits are paid solely from general assets of employer or employee organization maintaining the plan | | | ✓ | | |

| Plan/Program | Characteristics | Col1 | Col2 | Col3 | Col4 | Col5 |
|---|---|---|---|---|---|---|
| An employer-provided day care facility | Includes facilities maintained by employers to provide day care for employees' dependents (dependent care reimbursement programs are not subject to ERISA) | ✓ | | | ✓ | ✓ |
| An apprenticeship training program | • Provides apprenticeship training benefits exclusively | ✓ | ✓ | ✓ | ✓ | ✓ |
| | • Meets certain other conditions and alternative reporting and disclosure requirements | | | | | |
| A simplified employee pension (SEP) plan | • Employer makes direct contributions to IRA established by employee | ✓ | ✓ | ✓ | ✓ | ✓ |
| | • Plan meets certain other conditions and alternative reporting and disclosure requirements | | | | | |
| A SIMPLE plan | • Employer has fewer than 100 employees and does not maintain another qualified plan | ✓ | ✓ | ✓ | | |
| | • Employees may contribute up to $6,000 per year | | | | | |
| | • Employer must make either matching or nonelective contributions | | | | | |
| | • Contributions are 100 percent vested at all times | | | | | |
| An executive pension or welfare plan | • Provides benefits primarily for select group of management or HCEs | ✓ | | | ✓ | ✓ |
| | • Is unfunded and insured, or partly unfunded and partly insured | | | | | |
| | • If a pension plan, meets certain alternative reporting requirements | | | | | |
| A dues-financed pension or welfare plan | • Is maintained by employee organization for its members and their beneficiaries | ✓ | | | ✓ | ✓ |
| | • Benefits are paid solely from organization's assets, derived in whole or in part from membership dues | | | | | |
| | • Files Report Form LM-2 or LM-3 | | | | | |
| | • Provides by-laws and supplemental information | | | | | |

* Group insurer provides SAR for arrangement.

# B. Exemptions for Various Types of Plans

---

### Small Welfare Plans

---

**Definition**  A *small welfare plan* is an employer-sponsored welfare benefit plan that covers fewer than 100 participants at the beginning of the plan year.[12]

**Exemption**  A small welfare benefit plan is exempt from filing annual and terminal[13] reports and from distributing SARs to plan participants.

**Conditions for exemption**  The plan must meet one of the following requirements:[14]

- The plan is unfunded (i.e., the employer or employee organization pays benefits as needed solely from its general assets.
- The plan is fully insured, and premiums are paid partly by the employer or employee organization from its general assets, or partly from the general assets of the employer and employee organization and partly from employee contributions.
- The plan is partly unfunded and partly insured.

Therefore, a plan that is funded in whole or in part through a trust does *not* fall within the scope of the small welfare plan exemption.

**Additional conditions for contributory plans**  If a plan requires employee contributions, it must, in addition to meeting the conditions listed above, meet *all* the following requirements to qualify for the small employer plan exemption:[15]

- The employer or employee organization forwards employee contributions to the insurer within three months of receipt.
- Employee contributions apply *only* to the insured part of the plan (with the exception of cafeteria plan contributions).

---

[12] DOL Reg. § 2520.104-20(a).
[13] There are no DOL regulations requiring terminal reports aside from terminal reports for abandoned plans as described in DOL Reg. § 2520.103-13.
[14] DOL Reg. § 2520.104-20(b)(2).
[15] DOL Reg. § 2520.104(b)(3).

- The employer or employee organization returns refunds to employees within three months of receipt from the insurer.
- Contributing employees are informed when they enroll in the plan of the plan's terms for refunds.

Use the flowchart in Figure 3-1 to determine whether a plan is a small welfare benefit plan exempt from filing annual reports with the DOL and from distributing SARs to plan participants.

**Trust requirements**

As noted previously, a plan that is funded in whole or in part through a trust is not "unfunded" and, therefore, does not fall within the scope of the small welfare plan exemption.

In general, the assets of most ERISA-covered pension and welfare plans must be held in trust.[16] Plan assets include amounts that participants or beneficiaries contribute directly to the plan as well as amounts withheld by the employer from participants' wages for plan contributions.[17] However, the DOL currently does not require salary reduction contributions to cafeteria plans to be held in trust and does not view such a plan as "funded" for purposes of the small welfare plan exemption.[18]

Employee contributions to an insured welfare plan are not required to be held in trust if the plan satisfies the requirements for exemption described above or the requirements for exemption from including an accountant's opinion in an annual report (see Chapter 4).[19] For details concerning trust requirements, see Chapter 11.

## Welfare Plans in Group Insurance Arrangements

**Definition**

A *group insurance arrangement* is a fully insured arrangement providing benefits for employees of two or more unrelated employers.[20] Multiemployer plans maintained according to collective bargaining arrangements are not group insurance arrangements.

---

[16] ERISA § 403(a).
[17] ERISA Tech. Rel. 92-01; DOL News Release (Aug. 27, 1993).
[18] *Id*.
[19] *Id*.
[20] DOL Reg. § 2520.104-21(b)(1).

**Figure 3-1**

## Determining Whether a Small Welfare Plan Is Exempt from Filing Annual Reports and Distributing SARs to Participants

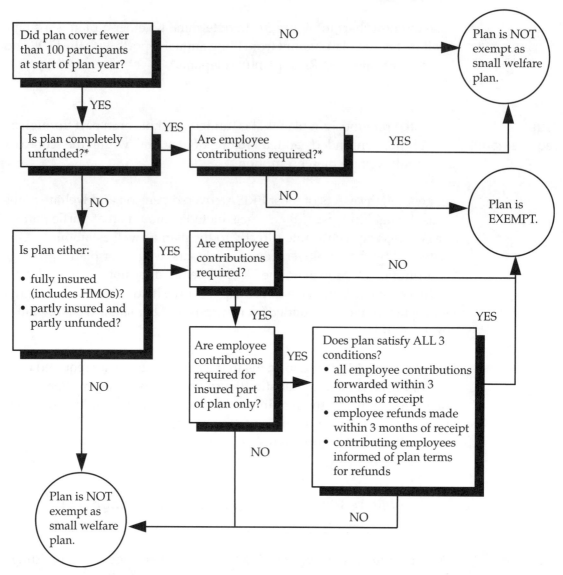

\* Employee contributions to cafeteria plans and certain other plans need not be held in trust; therefore, these contribution will not cause a plan to be "funded" for the purposes of this exemption.

**Exemption from filing annual reports**   A welfare benefit plan that is part of a group insurance arrangement is exempt from filing annual reports[21] with the DOL if the following conditions are met:[22]

- The group arrangement fully insures one or more welfare plans of each participating employer through insurance contracts.
- The contracts are purchased solely by the employers or else partly by employers and partly by participating employees.
- The insurance company makes all the benefit payments.
- A trust or other entity (such as a trade association) holds the insurance contracts and serves as a conduit for premium payments to the insurance carrier.
- The trust or other entity holding the group insurance contracts files annual reports on behalf of the plans participating in the arrangement.

Use the flowchart in Figure 3-2 to determine whether a welfare plan in a group insurance arrangement is exempt from filing annual reports.

---

## Unfunded Welfare Plans

---

**Definition**   An *unfunded welfare plan* is an employee welfare benefit plan that pays benefits solely from the general assets of the employer or employee organization maintaining the plan.[23]

**Exemption**   ERISA-covered unfunded welfare plans are exempt from distributing SARs to participants.[24]

*Note.* A medical reimbursement plan or health care flexible spending account (FSA) is an unfunded welfare plan if benefits are paid from the employer's general assets. A dependent care FSA is not a plan subject to ERISA.

**Trust requirements**   A plan funded in whole or in part through a trust is not "unfunded" and, therefore, does not fall within the scope of this exemption.

---

21   DOL Reg. § 2520.104-43.
22   DOL Reg. § 2520.104-43(b)(1).
23   DOL Reg. § 2520.104-44(b)(1)(i).
24   DOL Reg. § 2520.104b-10(g)(1).

**Figure 3-2**

## Determining Whether a Welfare Plan in a Group Insurance Arrangement Is Exempt from Filing Annual Reports

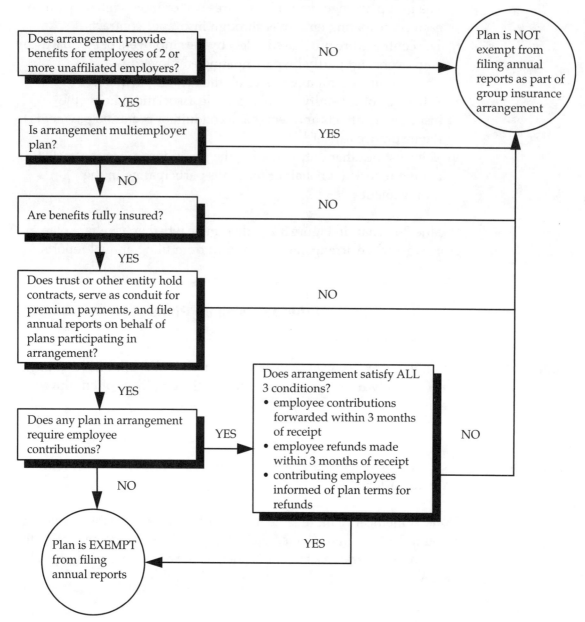

In general, the assets of most ERISA-covered pension and welfare plans must be held in trust.[25] Plan assets include amounts that participants or beneficiaries contribute directly to the plan as well as amounts withheld by the employer from participants' wages for plan contributions.[26] However, the DOL currently does not require salary reduction contributions to cafeteria plans to be held in trust.[27] Thus, cafeteria plan contributions will not cause a plan to be "funded" for purposes of this exemption.

For details concerning trust requirements, see Chapter 11.

## Employer-Provided Day Care Centers

**Definition**  ERISA regulations do not define the term *employer-provided day care center*.[28] However, the term encompasses a facility maintained by an employer to provide day care for dependents of its employees. The term does *not* include IRC § 129 employer reimbursement programs.[29]

**Exemption**  Employer-provided day care centers subject to ERISA are exempt from all ERISA reporting and disclosure requirements, except for providing plan documents and other plan information to the DOL upon request.[30]

## Apprenticeship Training Programs

**Definition**  An *apprenticeship training program* is an employee welfare benefit plan that exclusively provides apprenticeship training and other training benefits.[31]

---

25  ERISA § 403(a).
26  DOL Reg. § 2510.3-102.
27  DOL Tech. Rel. 92-01; DOL News Release 8/27/93.
28  DOL Reg. § 2520.104-25.
29  DOL Adv. Op. 88-10.
30  DOL Reg. § 2520.104-25.
31  DOL Reg. § 2520.104-22(a).

**Exemption**          An ERISA-covered apprentice training program is exempt from all
                       ERISA reporting and disclosure requirements if the program
                       administrator complies with *all* the following requirements:[32]

**Conditions for**     • The administrator files a notice with the DOL that contains the
**exemptions**           following information:[33]
                         — The plan name
                         — The plan sponsor's employer identification number (EIN)
                         — The plan administrator's name
                         — The name and location of an office (or person) from which (or
                           whom) interested persons may obtain (1) a description of any
                           existing or anticipated courses of study the plan sponsors or
                           establishes, including any prerequisites for enrolling in the
                           course; and (2) the procedure for enrolling in a such courses of
                           study
                       • The administrator takes steps to ensure the information in the notice
                         is given to the contributing employer's employees who may be
                         eligible to enroll in any course of study sponsored or established by
                         the plan.
                       • The administrator makes a copy of the notice available to employees
                         on request.

                       Use the flowchart in Figure 3-3 to determine whether an apprenticeship
                       training program is exempt from all ERISA reporting and disclosure
                       requirements.

## Simplified Employee Pension Plans

**Definition**         A Simplified employee pension plan (*SEP*) is an arrangement under
                       which an employer makes direct contributions to an individual
                       retirement account or annuity (IRA) established by an employee.[34]

**Exemption**          ERISA provides alternative methods of complying with the reporting
                       and disclosure requirements for SEPs meeting certain conditions.[35]

---

[32]  *Id.*
[33]  DOL Reg. § 2520.104-22(b).
[34]  I.R.C. § 408(k).
[35]  DOL Reg. §§ 2520.104-48, 2520.104-49.

**Figure 3-3**

## Determining Whether an Apprenticeship Training Program Is Exempt from ERISA Reporting and Filling Requirements

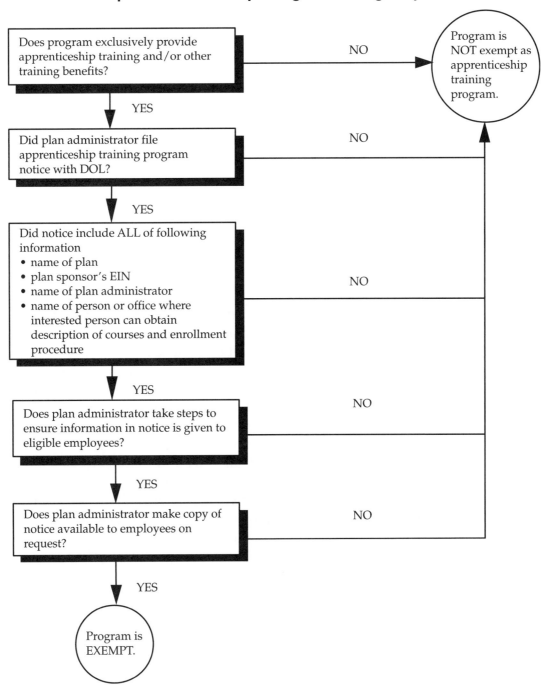

**Note.** No salary reduction SEPs (or SARSEPs) may be established after December 31, 1996. However, employers may continue to contribute to SARSEPs that were established before that date, and employees who were hired after December 31, 1996, may contribute to them.

Alternative methods are available for model SEPs created by completing Form 5305-SEP[36] and for other SEPs unless:

- the employer maintaining the SEPs selects, recommends or influences employees in the choice of IRAs to which the employer contributes; and
- employees' IRAs are subject to provisions that bar participants from withdrawing funds for any period of time.[37]

**Conditions for model SEPs**

A model SEP created by completing Form 5305-SEP is exempt from all ERISA reporting and disclosure requirements if the plan's administrator complies with *all* the following requirements:

- When an employee becomes eligible to participate in the SEP, the plan administrator gives the employee a copy of Form 5305-SEP, including the completed contribution agreement, general information and guidelines, and questions and answers.[38]
- After each calendar year-end, the plan administrator notifies each participant in writing of the employer's contribution (if any) made under the contribution agreement to the participant's IRA for that year.[39]
- If the employer selects, recommends, or in any other way influences employees to choose a particular IRA to which contribuions will be made and if that IRA restricts participants from withdrawing funds (other than restrictions the law imposes on all IRAs), the plan administrator gives each employee, at the time the employee becomes eligible to participate in the plan, a written explanation of the restrictions and a statement that other IRAs into which the participant may make contributions or rollovers may not be subject to the restrictions.[40]

---

[36] DOL Reg. § 2520.104-48.
[37] DOL Reg. § 2520.104-49.
[38] DOL Reg. § 2520.104-48(a).
[39] DOL Reg. § 2520.104-48(b).
[40] DOL Reg. § 2520.104-48(c).

**Conditions for other SEPs**

A SEP that is not barred from using the exemption as described above is exempt from all ERISA reporting and disclosure requirements if the plan administrator complies with all the following requirements:

- At the time an employee becomes eligible to participate in the SEP, the plan administrator gives the employee certain information in writing about the plan.[41] (See Table 3-2 for the list of required information.)
- The plan administrator notifies each participant in writing of the employer's contributions, if any, to the participant's IRA on or before the later of January 21 of the year following the year for which the employer made the contribution or 30 days after the employer made the contribution.[42]
- Within 30 days of the effective date of any amendment to the SEP, the plan administrator gives each participant a copy of the amendment and a written explanation of the amendment's effect.[43]

Use the flowcharts in Figures 3-4 and 3-5 to determine whether a model SEP and a non-model SEP is exempt from ERISA's reporting and disclosure requirements.

---

## Savings Incentive Match Plan for Employees

---

**Definition**

A *savings incentive match plan for employees* (SIMPLE) is an arrangement, sponsored by a small employer, that satisfies the following conditions:[44]

- The employer employs fewer than 100 employees who received at least $5,000 in compensation in the preceding year.
- The employer does not maintain another qualified plan.
- An employee may contribute up to $10,000 per year, adjusted for post-2004 inflation (See Appendix A).
- The employer must make either matching contributions or nonelective contributions.
- Contributions are fully vested at all times.

---

[41] DOL Reg. § 2520.104-49(a).
[42] DOL Reg. § 2520.104-49(c).
[43] DOL Reg. § 2520.104-49(d).
[44] I.R.C. § 408(p).

**Table 3-2**
**Notifying Employees Eligible for Non-Model SEP**

A non-model SEP meeting certain requirements is exempt from all ERISA reporting and disclosure requirements. One of the requirements is that the plan administrator must provide certain information to each employee at the time the employee becomes eligible to participate in the plan.

This table, based on DOL Regulations Section 2520.104-49(a), lists the required information organized into six categories:

1. Specific information about the SEP

2. General information about SEPs and IRAs

3. Statements about IRAs

4. A description of the IRS's disclosure requirement

5. A statement about additional information the plan administrator must give participants

6. Information about integration of plan benefits with Social Security benefits

If the SEP agreement is written in language that an average participant can understand, the plan administrator may give participants a copy of the agreement instead of the information in items 1, 2, 3, and 19 of this table. If disclosure materials furnished by the financial institution maintaining participants' IRAs contain the information required in item 4, the plan administrator can give participants the disclosure materials instead.

| Category | Item | Description |
|---|---|---|
| Specific information | 1 | Requirements for employee participation in SEP |
| | 2 | Formula used to allocate employer contributions made under SEP to participants' IRAs |
| | 3 | Name or title of person employer designated by the employer to provide additional information to participants about the SEP |
| | 4 | If the employer selects, recommends, or substantially influences employees to choose the IRAs to which it contributes, a clear explanation of the terms of<br><br>• The rate of return of those IRAs<br><br>• The restrictions on rollovers or withdrawals, including restrictions that allow rollovers or withdrawals but reduces earnings of the IRAs or impose other penalties |
| General information | 5 | What a SEP is and how it works |
| | 6 | Provisions of the law barring discrimination in favor of highly compensated employees |
| | 7 | Participants' right to receive contributions under a SEP and the allowable sources of contributions to participants' IRAs under the SEP |
| | 8 | The limits the law places on contributions to participants' SEP IRAs |

**Table 3-2 (*cont'd*)**
**Notifying Employees Eligible for Non-Model SEP**

| Category | Item | Description |
|---|---|---|
| General information (*cont'd*) | 9 | The consequences of excess contributions to participants' SEP IRAs and how to avoid excess contributions |
| | 10 | Participants' rights pertaining to contributions to their SEP IRAs |
| | 11 | How participants must treat contributions to their SEP IRAs for tax purposes |
| | 12 | The legal provisions on withdrawals from an IRA under the SEP and the consequences of early withdrawals |
| | 13 | The participant's ability to roll over or transfer funds from a SEP IRA to another IRA or to another IRA under a SEP, and how to roll over or transfer funds without causing adverse tax consequences |
| Statements about IRAs | 14 | A statement that other IRAs may have different rates of return and terms concerning, among other things, transfers and withdrawals from the IRAs |
| | 15 | A statement that if participants are entitled to make contributions or rollovers to IRAs, they can do so to an IRA other than the one to which the employer contributes under the SEP |
| | 16 | A statement that, depending on the terms of the IRA to which the employer contributes under the SEP, participants may be able to roll over or transfer funds from that IRA to another IRA |
| IRS required disclosure | 17 | A description of the disclosure the IRS requires the financial institution or other entity sponsoring the IRA into which the employer will contribute under the SEP to make to persons for whom an IRA has been established |
| Statement about participant information | 18 | A statement that in addition to the information employees receive at the time they become eligible to participate in the SEP, the plan administrator must furnish to each participant:<br><br>• A copy of any amendment to the SEP and an explanation of its effects within 30 days of its effective date<br><br>• Written notice of any employer contributions to the participant's IRAs on or before the *later* of:<br><br>—January 31 of the year following the year for which the employer made the contribution<br><br>—30 days after the employer made the contribution |

**Table 3-2 (cont'd)**
**Notifying Employees Eligible for Non-Model SEP**

| Category | Item | Description |
|---|---|---|
| Social Security integration<br><br>*Note:* Include items listed in this category only if the SEP is integrated with Social Security. | 19 | A statement that the Social Security taxes the employer pays for participants will be considered when determining the amount the employer will contribute to participants' IRAs under the SEP based on the allocation formula |
| | 20 | A description of how Social Security integration affects the employer's contributions |
| | 21 | The integration formula (which may be part of the allocation formula required in item 2 of this table) |

**Exemption**     Trustees of SIMPLEs are exempt from nearly all ERISA reporting and disclosure requirements,[45] except that they must provide abbreviated SPDs to employers annually.

**Notice requirements**     An employer that maintains a SIMPLE is required to distribute to each participating employee at least 61 days before the beginning of the plan year a notice that describes the terms of eligibility to make contributions and includes a copy of the SPD provided by the plan trustee.[46]

**Penalty for failure to provide SPD**     A trustee who fails to provide one or more SPDs may be assessed a penalty of $50 for each day the failure continues unless the trustee can show reasonable cause.[47]

An employer who fails to provide the SIMPLE notice to participating employees may be subject to a penalty of $50 per day until the notice is provided unless the employer can show reasonable cause.[48]

---

[45]  ERISA § 101(h).
[46]  ERISA § 101(h)(3).
[47]  I.R.C. §§ 6693(c)(2), (c)(3).
[48]  I.R.C. §§ 6693(c)(1), (c)(3).

## Figure 3-4

## Determining Whether a Model SEP Plan Is Exempt from ERISA Reporting and Disclosure Requirements

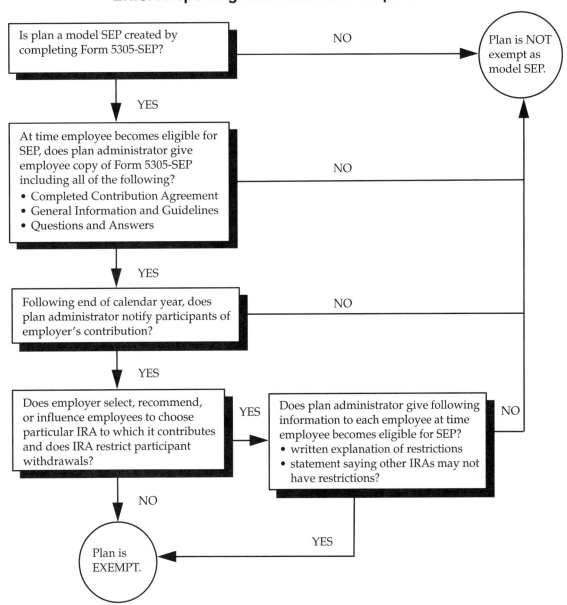

**Figure 3-5**

### Determining Whether a Non-Model SEP Plan Is Exempt from ERISA Reporting and Disclosure Requirements

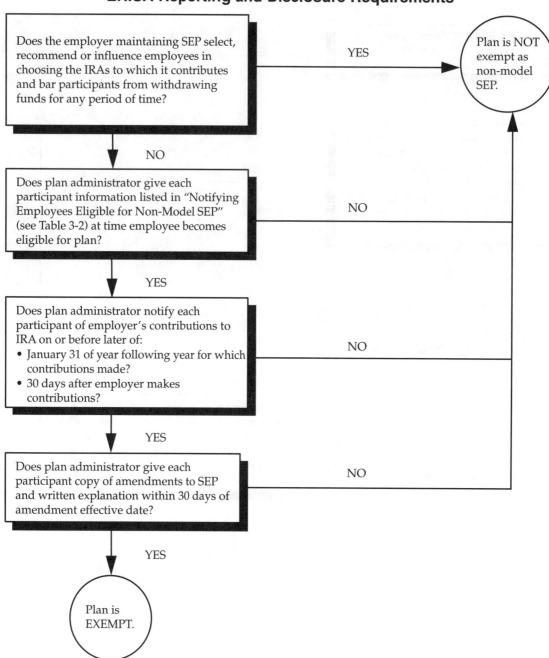

## Executive Pension and Welfare Plans

**Conditions for executive pension plans**

An executive pension plan is exempt from all ERISA reporting and disclosure requirements, except for providing plan documents to the DOL on request, provided the plan satisfies the following conditions:[49]

- The employer maintains the pension plan primarily to provide deferred compensation for a select group of management or highly compensated employees (HCEs).[50]
- The pension plan is unfunded or insured, or partly unfunded and partly insured (i.e., no part of the pension plan is funded through a trust or employee contributions).[51]
- The plan administrator satisfies alternative compliance requirements.[52]

**Alternative compliance requirements**

The alternative compliance requirements that the administrator of an executive pension plan must satisfy as a condition of the plan's exemption involves filing certain information with the DOL within 120 days after the plan first becomes subject to ERISA's reporting and disclosure requirements.[53] This required information includes:[54]

- The employer's name, address, and employer identification number (EIN)
- A statement saying the employer maintains the pension plan primarily to provide deferred compensation for a select group of management or HCES
- The number of plans and the number of participants in each

**Conditions for executive welfare plans**

Except for providing plan documents to the DOL on request, an *executive welfare plan* is exempt from all ERISA reporting and disclosure requirements if it meets both of the following conditions:[55]

- The employer maintains the welfare plan primarily to provide welfare benefits for a select group of management or HCEs.

---

[49]  DOL Reg. § 2520.104-23.
[50]  DOL Reg. § 2520.104-23(d)(1).
[51]  DOL Reg. § 2520.104-23(d)(2).
[52]  DOL Reg. § 2520.204-23(b).
[53]  DOL Reg. § 2520.104-23(b)(2).
[54]  DOL Reg. § 2520.104-23(b)(1).
[55]  DOL Reg. § 2520.104-24(c).

- The welfare plan is unfunded or insured, or partly unfunded and partly insured (i.e., no part of the welfare plan is funded through a trust or employee contributions).

The alternative compliance requirements for executive pension plans do *not* apply to executive welfare plans.

> **Example.** Eagleton Systems maintains a fully insured medical expense reimbursement plan for its key executives. The plan is noncontributory. The plan is exempt from all ERISA reporting and disclosure requirements except the requirement to provide plan documents to the DOL on request.

Use the decision table in Figure 3-6 to determine whether an ERISA-covered executive pension or welfare plan is exempt from all reporting and disclosure requirements, except for providing plan documents to the DOL upon request.

---

## Dues-Financed Pension and Welfare Plans

---

**Definition**

A *dues-financed pension plan or dues-financed welfare plan* is a plan that an employee organization maintains for its members and their beneficiaries.[56] Such a plan is unfunded. Benefits are paid solely from the organization's assets, which derive in whole or in part from membership dues.

**Alternative compliance requirements**

ERISA provides alternative methods for a dues-financed pension plan or welfare plan to comply with *some* reporting and disclosure requirements.[57] A dues-financed plan that files Report Form LM-2 or LM-3 in accordance with the Labor Management Reporting and Disclosure Act (LMRDA) and its regulations is exempt from filing annual reports with the DOL and from distributing SARs to plan participants.[58]

The organization maintaining the plan may supply a copy of the employee organization's constitution or its bylaws describing the plan and supplemental information to satisfy the SPD requirement.[59]

---

[56] DOL Reg. §§ 2520.104-26(b), 2520.104-27(b).
[57] DOL Reg. §§ 2520.104-26, 2520.104-27.
[58] DOL Reg. §§ 2520.104-26(a)(2), 2520.104-27(a)(2).
[59] DOL Reg. §§ 2520.104-26(a)(3), 2520.104-27(a)(3).

**Figure 3-6**

**Determining Whether an Executive Position or Welfare Plan Is
Exempt from All Reporting and Disclosure Requirements
Except for Providing Plan Documents to DOL on Request**

| If Plan Is: | And Employer: | And Plan Is: | And Plan Administrator: | Then Plan Is: |
|---|---|---|---|---|
| A pension plan | maintains plan primarily to provide deferred compensation to select management or HCEs | unfunded, insured, or partly unfunded and partly insured | meets alternative compliance requirements | **Exempt** |
| | | | does **not** meet alternative compliance requirements | **not** exempt as executive pension plan |
| | | **not** unfunded, insured, or partly unfunded and partly insured | | |
| | does **not** maintain plan primarily to provide deferred compensation to select management or HCEs | ⟶ | ⟶ | |
| A welfare plan | maintains plan primarily to provide welfare benefits to select management or HCEs | unfunded, insured, or partly unfunded and partly insured | ⟶ | **Exempt** |
| | | **not** unfunded, insured, or partly unfunded and partly insured | | **not** exempt as executive welfare plan |
| | does **not** maintain plan primarily to provide welfare benefits to select management or HCEs | ⟶ | ⟶ | |

**Additional requirement**

If any provision in the employee organization's constitution or bylaws states that a certain portion of members' dues or the organization's assets will be used solely for paying benefits, and those assets may legally be used for other purposes, then:

- the supplemental information provided to participants and beneficiaries must clearly state that membership dues or organization assets can be used for general purposes of the employee organization or may be subject to the claims of the organization's general creditors; and
- the organization's constitution or bylaws must accurately reflect the plan's status.[60]

Use the flowchart in Figure 3-7 to determine whether a dues-financed pension or welfare plan is exempt from ERISA's annual report and SAR requirements and the flowchart in Figure 3-8 to determine whether such a plan is exempt from the requirement to provide SPDs to participants and their beneficiaries.

---

[60]  DOL Reg. §§ 2520.104-26(a)(3)(ii), 2520.104-27(a)(3)(ii).

**Figure 3-7**

## Determining Whether a Dues-Financed Pension or Welfare Plan Is Exempt from Annual Report and SAR Requirements

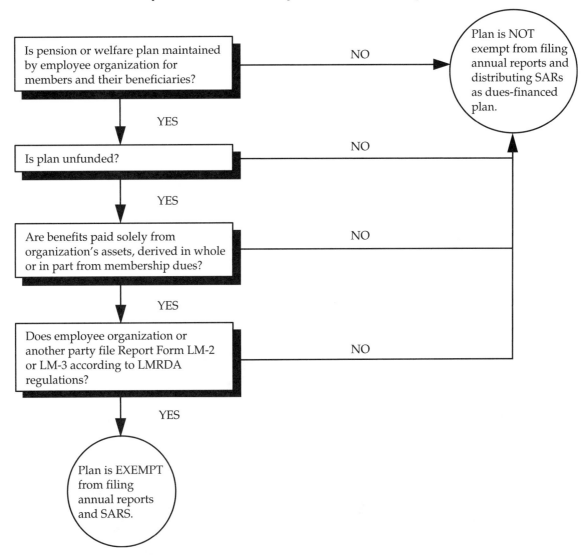

**Figure 3-8**

## Determining Whether a Dues-Financed Pension or Welfare Plan Is Exempt from SPD Disclosure Requirement

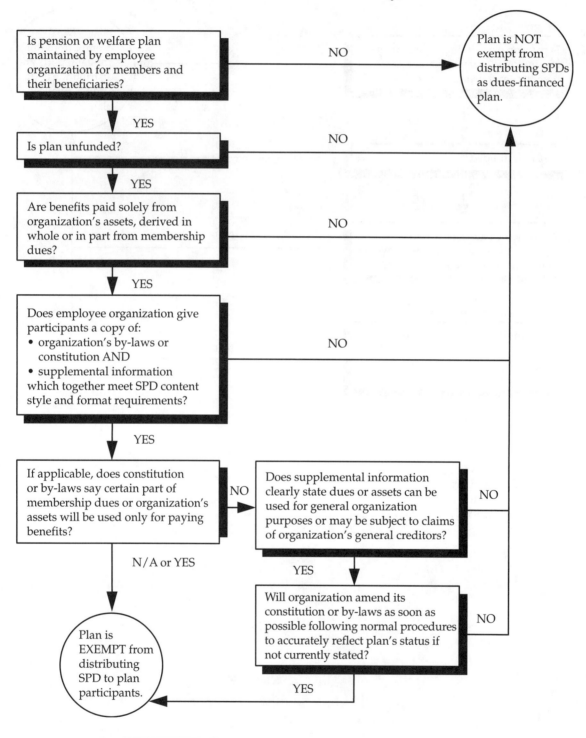

# C. DOL Electronic Distribution Safe Harbor

The DOL's safe harbor rules on the electronic delivery of disclosures required by ERISA apply to all employee benefit plans subject to ERISA's reporting and disclosure requirements.[61]

**Disclosures affected**

The rules apply to all disclosures required to be furnished by plans to plan participants or beneficiaries under Title I of ERISA, including:[62]

- SPDs, SMMs, SARs, and summaries of material reductions (SMRs);
- Individual benefit statements
- ERISA 404(c) investment-related information
- Notices under the Consolidated Omnibus Budget Reconciliation Act of 1985 (COBRA)
- Qualified domestic relations order (QDRO) notices
- Qualfied medical child support order (QMCSO) notices
- Participant loan information
- Creditable coverage and disclosures under the Health Insurance Portability and Accountability Act of 1996 (HIPAA)
- Suspension of benefits notices[63]

The rules do not apply, however, to certain disclosures under the IRS's jurisdiction (e.g., benefit distribution notices and spousal consent notices).[64]

**Who may receive electronic documents**

The safe harbor creates two categories of individuals who may receive disclosure material electronically:

- Participants who have the ability to effectively access documents furnished in electronic format at any location where they are reasonably expected to perform their duties as employees and with respect to whom access to the employer's or plan sponsor's electronic information system is an integral part of those duties (this would include employees who work at home or who may be traveling,

---

61   DOL Reg. § 2520.104b-1(c).
62   DOL Reg. § 2520.104b-1; Preamble at 67 Fed. Reg. 17,266 (2002).
63   IRS Reg. § 1.401(a)-21(a)(3)(i).
64   DOL Reg. § 2520.104b-1(e).

provided they have ready access to the employer's information system)[65]

- Participants, beneficiaries, and other persons entitled to receive documents in electronic or nonelectronic format under ERISA and who have consented (and have not withdrawn their consent) to receive documents through electronic media under certain conditions[66]

Before consenting, the individual must be provided a clear and conspicuous statement in electronic or nonelectronic form indicating:[67]

- The types of documents to which consent would apply
- The consent can be withdrawn any any time without charge
- The procedures for withdrawing consent and for updating recipients' addresses
- The right to request a paper version of an electronically furnished copy
- Any hardware and software requirements for assessing and retaining the documents

If there is a change in hardware or software requirements after the individual consents that may make it impossible to receive or retain the information, the individual may renew consent after being given a statement of the new requirements and the right to withdraw without consequences.[68]

**General safe harbor conditions**

Under the following conditions, a plan's use of electronic media would be deemed the equivalent of receiving the information in paper form:

- Each individual is notified, through electronic or other means at the time a document is furnished electronically, of the significance of the document when it is not otherwise reasonably evident as transmitted and that the individual has a right to request and receive a paper version of the document from the plan administrator.[69]
- The plan administrator takes appropriate and necessary measures reasonably calculated to ensure that the system for furnishing

---

[65]  DOL Reg. § 2520.104b-1(c)(2)(i).
[66]  DOL Reg. § 2520.104b-1(c)(2)(ii).
[67]  DOL Reg. § 2520.104b-1(c)(2)(ii)(C).
[68]  *Id.*
[69]  DOL Reg. §§ 2520.104b-1(c)(1)(iii), (iv).

documents results in actual receipt of transmitted information and protects the confidentiality of personal information relating to the individual's accounts and benefits.[70]

- The disclosures in electronic format are consistent with the applicable style, format, and content requirements applicable to the particular document (although the paper and electronic versions of the same required disclosure may differ).[71]

[70] DOL Reg. § 2520.104b-1(c)(i)(A) and (B).
[71] DOL Reg. § 2520.104b-1(c)(ii).

# D. IRS Rules for Electronic Plan Communications

**Overview**

IRS final regulations[72] coordinate the existing IRS electronic plan communication rules for certain employee benefit arrangements with the requirements of E-SIGN (Electronic Signatures in Global and National Commerce Act).[73] When providing notices, plan sponsors are allowed to choose between complying with either E-SIGN's consumer consent requirements or an exemption involving participants' "effective ability to access" electronic communications. A separate requirement applies to participant elections made in electronic form.

The regulations apply to any notice, election, or similar communication under IRS jurisdiction that is provided to or made by a participant under a retirement plan, health plan, cafeteria plan, educational assistance program, qualified transportation fringe program, Archer Medical Savings Account, or health savings account.[74] They do not apply to communications under the jurisdiction of the DOL or the PBGC such as suspension of benefits and COBRA notices.[75]

The electronic communication must be reasonably designed to provide notice to the recipient in a manner no less understandable than a written paper document. Also, at the time a notice is provided, the electronic transmission must alert the recipient to the significance of the transmittal (including the identification of the subject matter), and provide any instructions needed to access the notice in a manner that is readily understandable and accessible.[76]

**E-SIGN consumer consent requirements for notices**

To meet the E-SIGN option when providing notice, the recipient must be provided with a clear and conspicuous statement

---

[72]  IRS Reg. § 1.401(a)-21. Other IRS regulations amended to incorporate the new regulation include: regulations for loans [Section 1.72(p)-1], rollover explanations [Section 1.401(f)-1], distribution elections [Section 1.411(a)-11], survivor annuity explanations [Section 1.417(a)(3)-1], notice to interested parties [Section 1.7476-2], distribution withholding notices [Section 35.3405-1], and Section 204(h) notices [IRS Reg. § 54.4980F-1].

[73]  Public Law 106-229, 114 Stat. 463 (June 30, 2000). E-SIGN generally provides that electronic documents and signatures are given the same legal effect as their paper counterparts.

[74]  IRS Reg. § 1.401(a)-21(a)(2).

[75]  IRS Reg. § 1.401(a)-21(a)(3)(i).

[76]  IRS Reg. § 1.401(a)-21(a)(5).

containing the following disclosures before consenting to receive electronic notices:[77]

- The right, if any, to receive a paper document or other nonelectronic form, and how, after having provided consent, the recipient may obtain a paper copy and whether any fee will be charged
- The right to withdraw consent to receiving electronic notices on a prospective basis at any time, including the procedures and fees for withdrawing
- Whether the consent applies only to a particular transaction or to other identified transactions
- A description of procedures to update information needed to contact the recipient electronically
- The hardware or software needed to access and retain the notice

The recipient must affirmatively consent to the electronic delivery either electronically, in a manner that demonstrates that the recipient can access the communication in the applicable electronic media, or in writing.[78]

If a change in hardware or software creates a material risk that a recipient will not be able to access or retain a notice in electronic format, the recipient must receive a statement explaining the revised hardware or software requirements and the right to withdraw prior consent.[79] The recipient must then reaffirm consent to receive electronic delivery.[80]

For purposes of the consumer consent requirements, an oral communication or a recording of an oral communication is not an electronic record. Thus, oral communications may not be used or notices or consent.[81]

**Exemption from E-SIGN consumer consent requirements**

The alternative to the E-SIGN option is met[82]

- if the electronic medium used to provide a notice is a medium that the recipient has the effective ability to access; and
- if, at the time the notice is provided, the recipient is advised that he or she may request and receive the paper notice at no charge.

**Note.** Oral communications (e.g., telephonic voice response systems) are not barred.[83]

---

[77] IRS Reg. § 1.401(a)-21(b)(3).
[78] IRS Reg. § 1.401(a)-21(b)(2)(i).
[79] IRS Reg. § 1.401(a)-21(b)(4).
[80] IRS Reg. § 1.401(a)-21(b)(4)(ii).
[81] IRS Reg. § 1.401(a)-21(b)(1).
[82] IRS Reg. § 1.401(a)-21(c).
[83] IRS Reg. § 1.40(a)-21(f), examples 4 and 5.

**Rules for participant elections**

A participant election that is transmitted by electronic media is treated as being provided in writing or in written form if the following requirements are met:[84]

- The electronic medium used can be effectively accessed by the individual.
- The delivery system is reasonably designed to preclude any other individual from making the election (for example, by requiring that the individual making the election provide his or her account number and personal identification number).
- The electronic system provides the individual making the election with a reasonable opportunity to review, conform, modify, or rescind the terms of the election before the election becomes effective.
- The person making the election receives a confirmation of the effect of the election.
- In the case of an election that is required to be witnessed by a plan representative or a notary public (such as spousal consent to an alternative to the QJSA form of distribution), the signature, or electronic signature, is made in the physical presence of the plan representative or notary public (and E-SIGN standards and state laws applicable to notary publics are met).

**Record-keeping**

If an electronic record of an applicable notice is not maintained in a form that can be reproduced for later reference, then the legal effect, validity, or enforceability of the record may be denied.[85]

---

[84]  IRS Reg. § 1.401(a)-21(d).
[85]  IRS Reg. § 1.401(a)(21)-3(ii).

# Chapter 4

# Annual Reports

**Introduction**    Pension and welfare plans subject to annual report requirements must file Form 5500 with the Internal Revenue Service (IRS).

This chapter describes the types of plans that are required to file the Form 5500, explains which forms must be filed and when, details the requirements for obtaining an independent accountant's opinion, and discusses the penalties for noncompliance.

**Contents**    This chapter has eight sections:

# A. General Information

If a pension or welfare benefit plan is subject to annual reporting requirements, the plan administrator must file certain forms and schedules with the Department of Labor (DOL).

The reporting requirements under Internal Revenue Code (Code) Section 6039D have been suspended indefinitely (see Chapter 2, Section E).[1]

**Definitions**

The *annual report*, as its name indicates, is a report that is filed each year for a specific pension or welfare plan. The report includes information about the plan for a specified plan year: plan type, plan administration, participation, and funding and other financial information.

In general, information reported in an annual report relates to the plan year for which the report is filed.[2]

The *plan year* of a plan is the calendar, policy, or fiscal year on which the plan's records are kept.[3] The plan year should be stated in the plan document, and it need not coincide with any insurance policy years or other contract years that relate to the plan.

---

[1]  Notice 2002-24, 2002-16 I.R.B. 785.
[2]  Instructions for Form 5500, Section 5, available on the DOL's Web site, *www.dol.gov*.
[3]  ERISA § 3(39).

# B. Annual Report Form

The annual report consists of a single identifying Form 5500 and numerous schedules that must be completed, depending on plan type. The chart summarizing the schedules on the next two pages is reproduced from the 2007 Instructions. The 2007 chart reminds users of a new simplified reporting option for plans with fewer than 25 participants.

For 2008 plan years, further refinements will point out the new Schedule SB (for single-employer plans) and Schedule MB (for multiemployer plans) in lieu of Schedule B. For 2008, refinements to Schedule R will be added as well for multiemployer plans.[4]

**Formats**

Form 5500 is available in two different computer-scannable formats (1) hand print and (2) machine print.

Filers who choose the "hand print" format must enter data by hand or typewriter on specially designed paper. The "hand print" form and schedules can be filed only by mail sent to the address specified in the Instructions for Form 5500.

Filers who choose the "machine print" format may enter data using computer software and file the form and related schedules electronically. However, they still need to retain a paper copy with all required signatures as part of the plan's records. Alternatively, a filer who chooses the "machine print" format may print out the completed form and mail the paper copy with the required signatures to the address specified in the Form 5500 instructions.

DOL has issued final regulations under which all plans will be required to file their Form 5500 electronically beginning with filings for 2009 plan years (meaning the July 2010 filing for calendar year plans.)[5] Under this rule, the Internet will be the sole medium for transmitting ERISA filings.

**Simplified reporting option**

PPA requires the DOL to devise a simplified reporting form for plans with fewer than 25 participants. DOL has responded with a Short Form 5500 that will be available beginning with the filings for years after 2008 as part of the new electronic filing initiative. For 2007 and 2008 plan years, the Form 5500 instructions describe a simplified reporting option that uses current forms.

---

4   Instructions to Form 5500, Changes to Note.
5   DOL Reg. § 2520.104a-2; see also ERISA § 104(b)(5).

Caution: For 2008, file Schedule SB (single employer plans) or Schedule MB (multi employer plans) instead of Schedule B

## 2007 Quick Reference Chart for Form 5500, Schedules and Attachments[1]

| | Large Pension Plan | Small Pension Plan | Large Welfare Plan | Small Welfare Plan | DFE |
|---|---|---|---|---|---|
| **Form 5500** | Must complete. | Must complete. | Must complete. | Must complete.[2] | Must complete. |
| **Schedule A** (Insurance Information) | Must complete if plan has insurance contracts for benefits or investments. | Must complete if plan has insurance contracts for benefits or investments. | Must complete if plan has insurance contracts for benefits or investments. | Must complete if plan has insurance contracts for benefits or investments. | Must complete if MTIA, 103-12 IE, or GIA has insurance contracts for benefits or investments. |
| **Schedule B** (Actuarial Information) | Must complete if defined benefit plan and subject to minimum funding standards.[3] | Must complete if defined benefit plan and subject to minimum funding standards.[3] | Not required. | Not required. | Not required. |
| **Schedule C** (Service Provider Information) | Must complete if service provider was paid $5,000 or more and/or an accountant or actuary was terminated. | Not required. | Must complete if service provider was paid $5,000 or more and/or an accountant or actuary was terminated. | Not required. | MTIAs, GIAs, and 103-12 IEs must complete Part I if service provider paid $5,000 or more. GIAs and 103-12 IEs must complete Part II if accountant was terminated. |
| **Schedule D** (DFE/ Participating Plan Information) | Must complete Part I if plan participated in a CCT, PSA, MTIA, or 103-12 IE. | Must complete Part I if plan participated in a CCT, PSA, MTIA, or 103-12 IE. | Must complete Part I if plan participated in a CCT, PSA, MTIA, or 103-12 IE. | Must complete Part I if plan participated in a CCT, PSA, MTIA, or 103-12 IE. | All DFEs must complete Part II, and DFEs that invest in a CCT, PSA, or 103-12 IE must also complete Part I. |
| **Schedule E** (ESOP Annual Information) | Must complete if ESOP. | Must complete if ESOP. | Not required. | Not required. | Not required. |
| **Schedule G** (Financial Transaction Schedules) | Must complete if Schedule H, line 4b, 4c, or 4d is "Yes."[4] | Not required. | Must complete if Schedule H, line 4b, 4c, or 4d is "Yes."[2, 4] | Not required. | MTIAs, GIAs, and 103-12 IEs must complete if Schedule H, line 4b, 4c, or 4d is "Yes."[4] |
| **Schedule H** (Financial Information) | Must complete.[4] | Not required. | Must complete.[2, 4] | Not required. | All DFEs must complete Parts I, II, and III. MTIAs, 103-12 IEs, and GIAs must also complete Part IV.[4] |

**General Instructions to Form 5500**

4-4

| | Large Pension Plan | Small Pension Plan | Large Welfare Plan | Small Welfare Plan | DFE |
|---|---|---|---|---|---|
| **Schedule I** (Financial Information— Small Plan) | Not required. | Must complete. | Not required. | Must complete.[2] | Not required. |
| **Schedule R** (Retirement Plan Information) | Must complete.[5] | Must complete.[5] | Not required. | Not required. | Not required. |
| **Schedule SSA** (Annual Registration Statement Identifying Separated Participants With Deferred Vested Benefits) | Must complete if plan had separated participants with deferred vested benefits to report. | Must complete if plan had separated participants with deferred vested benefits to report. | Not required. | Not required. | Not required. |
| **Accountant's Report** | Must attach. | Not required unless Schedule I, line 4k, is checked "No." | Must attach.[2] | Not required. | Must attach for a GIA or 103-12 IE. |

[1] This chart provides only general guidance. Not all rules and requirements are reflected. Refer to specific Form 5500 instructions for complete information on filing requirements (e.g., **Who Must File** and **What To File**). For example, a pension plan is exempt from filing any schedules if the plan uses a Code section 403(b)(1) annuity, 403(b)(7) custodial account, or 408 individual retirement accounts or annuities as the sole funding vehicle for providing benefits. See **Limited Pension Plan Reporting**.

[2] Options if lower than 25 participants.

[3] Unfunded, fully insured and combination unfunded/insured welfare plans covering fewer than 100 participants at the beginning of the plan year that meet the requirements of 29 CFR 2520.104-20 are exempt from filing an annual report. (See **Who Must File** on page 2.) Such a plan with 100 or more participants must file an annual report, but is exempt under 29 CFR 2520.104-44 from the accountant's report requirement and completing Schedule H, but MUST complete Schedule G, Part III, to report any nonexempt transactions. See **What To File** on page 7.

[4] Certain money purchase defined contribution plans are required to complete Schedule B, lines 3, 9, and 10 in accordance with the instructions for Schedule R, line 5.

[5] Schedules of assets and reportable (5%) transactions also must be filed with the Form 5500 if Schedule H, line 4i or 4j is "Yes," but use of printed form not required.

[6] A pension plan is exempt from filing Schedule R if each of the following four conditions is met:

- The plan is not a defined benefit plan or otherwise subject to the minimum funding standards of Code section 412 or ERISA section 302.

- No in-kind distributions reportable on line 1 of Schedule R were distributed during the plan year.

- No benefits were distributed during the plan year which are reportable on Form 1099-R using an EIN other than that of the plan sponsor or plan administrator.

- In the case of a plan that is not a profit-sharing, ESOP or stock bonus plan, no plan benefits were distributed during the plan year in the form of a single sum distribution.

- For 2008, affected plans must file Schedule SB (single-employer plans) or MB (multiemployer plans) in lieu of Schedule B.

# C. Plans Required to File Annual Reports

**Affected plans**    An ERISA-covered pension or welfare benefit plan must file an annual report every year unless ERISA or DOL regulations specifically provide an exemption from annual reporting.

**Exempted plans**    Plans subject to ERISA but specifically exempt from annual reporting are:

- Small welfare plans[6]
- Welfare plans in certain group insurance arrangements[7]
- Employer-provided day care centers[8]
- Apprenticeship training programs[9]
- Simplified employee pension plans (SEPs)[10]
- Pension or welfare plans primarily for management or highly compensated employees (HCEs)[11]
- Dues-financed pension or welfare plans[12]
- Savings Incentive Match Plans for Employees (SIMPLEs)[13]

Most of these types of plans must meet certain conditions to be exempt from annual reporting. The conditions include, in some cases, meeting alternative compliance requirements. (For further discussion of the conditions of exemption, see Section B in Chapter 3.)

---

[6]  DOL Reg. § 2520.104-20.
[7]  DOL Reg. § 2520.104-43.
[8]  DOL Reg. § 2520.104-25.
[9]  DOL Reg. § 2520.104-22.
[10] DOL Reg. §§ 2520.104-48, 2520.104-49.
[11] DOL Reg. §§ 2520.104-23, 2520.104-24.
[12] DOL Reg. §§ 2520.104-26, 2520.104-27.
[13] ERISA § 101(h).

# D. Accountant's Opinion

Some plans are required to include an independent qualified public accountant's opinion when filing Form 5500.

---

**Pension Plans**

---

A pension plan must file an independent qualified public accountant's opinion with the Form 5500 unless it meets one of the following exemptions.

**General exemption**

A pension plan need not file an accountant's opinion if it meets either of the following conditions:

- Benefits are provided exclusively through fully guaranteed allocated insurance contracts and premiums are paid by the employer or employee organization from its general assets or partly from general assets and partly from employee contributions (and participant contributions are forwarded within three months of receipt and refunds are returned within three months).
- 403(b) tax deferred annuity contracts are the sole funding vehicle.[14]

**Note.** The 403(b) exemption has been eliminated for plan years beginning after 2008.[15]

**Restricted exemption for small pension plans**

A pension plan with fewer than 100 participants at the beginning of the plan year is exempt from the requirement to include the accountant's opinion if:

- at least 95 percent of the plan's assets are qualifying plan assets, or
- any person who handles plan assets that are not *qualifying plan assets* is bonded for at least the value of such funds.

---

14  DOL Reg. § 2520.104-44(b).
15  DOL Reg. § 2520.104-44(b), amended 72 Fed. Reg. 64728 (Nov. 16, 2007).

In addition, specific disclosures must be included in the Summary Annual Report (SAR) about plan asset vendors and the plan's surety bond.[16] For post-2007 plan years, DOL anticipates that these disclosures will be added to the PPA funding notice that replaces the SAR for defined benefit plans.[17]

*Qualifying plan assets* encompass qualifying employer securities; mutual fund shares; investment and annuity contracts issued by an insurance company; participant loans; and assets held by a bank or similar financial institution, insurance company, or registered broker-dealer; or an organization authorized to act as trustee for individual retirement accounts and annuities (IRAs).[18]

**SAR requirements for small pension exemption**

To qualify for the restricted exemption, a plan's SAR (Funding Notice, for post-2007 plan years as noted above) must include:

- The names of the financial institutions holding qualifying plan assets (other than employer securities, participant loans, and § 404(c) assets subject to participant direction)
- The name of the surety company issuing the bond if the plan has more than 5 percent of its assets in nonqualifying plan assets
- A notice indicating that participants and beneficiaries may, without charge, receive evidence of the required bond and statements from the financial institutions describing the qualifying plan assets
- A notice stating that participants should contact the DOL's regional offices if they are unable to examine or obtain copies of the above information[19]

DOL's model notice to address this requirement was added as an appendix to their regulation in 2007.[20]

## Welfare Plans

A welfare plan must file an independent qualified public accountant's opinion with the Form 5500 unless it had fewer than 100 participants at the beginning of the plan year[21] or it is (1) completely unfunded, (2) fully insured (includes health maintenance organizations), or (3) partly

---

[16]   DOL Reg. § 2520.104-46.
[17]   Footnote 8, 72 Fed. Reg. 64715 (Nov. 16, 2007).
[18]   DOL Reg. § 2520.104-46(b)(1)(ii).
[19]   DOL Reg. § 2520.104-46(b)(1)(i)(B).
[20]   DOL Reg. § 2520.104-46.
[21]   DOL Reg. § 2520.104-46(b)(2).

unfunded and partly insured. If the plan is fully insured or partly unfunded and partly insured, the insurer holds the plan assets in its general account, and premiums are paid by the employer or the employee organization from its general assets or partly from its general assets and partly from employee contributions (with participant contributions and refunds processed within three months).[22]

Use the flowchart in Figure 4-1 to determine whether a welfare plan must file an independent qualified public accountant's opinion with Form 5500.

**80-120 Rule**    If a pension or welfare plan had between 80 and 120 participants at the beginning of the plan year it may opt to file using the same approach as for the prior year. If this option is elected, an accountant's report is not required if the plan filed using one of the small plan exceptions. An accountant's opinion is filed if it had been applicable in the prior year.

## Cafeteria Plans

Employee contributions to cafeteria plans need not be held in trust. Therefore, a cafeteria plan that does not use a trust is not required to include an independent qualified public accountant's opinion in its annual report, provided it meets all the conditions for exemption.[23]

## Deferred Opinion

If a plan is required to file an independent qualified public accountant's opinion, it may be able to defer filing the opinion until the next plan year if the current year is the first of two consecutive plan years, one of which is a short plan year of seven months or less.[24]

**This year's annual report**    To defer filing the opinion, this plan year's annual report must include:

- Financial statements and schedules

---

[22]  DOL Reg. § 2520.104-44(b)(1).
[23]  ERISA Tech. Release 92-01; DOL News Release, 8/27/93.
[24]  DOL Reg. § 2520.104-50(b).

## Figure 4-1

## Determining Whether Accountant's Opinion Must Be Filed for Welfare Plan

*Note:* Under ERISA Technical Release 92-01 (as extended), employee contributions to cafeteria plans and certain other plans need not be held in trust. Therefore, these contributions will not cause a plan to be "funded" for purposes of determining if an accountant's opinion must be filed.

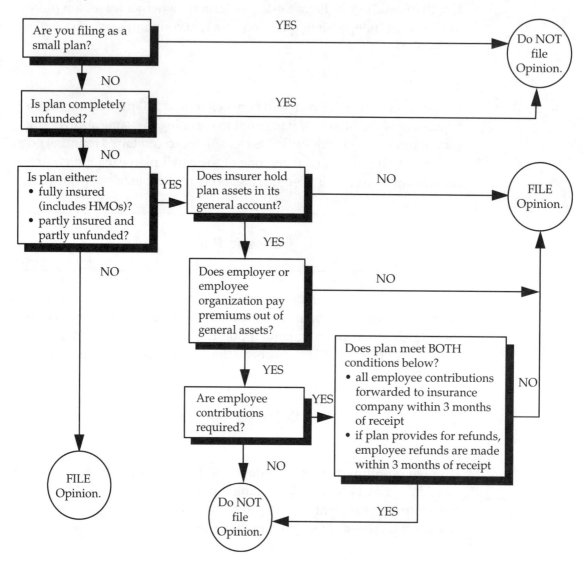

- An explanation of why the current plan year or the next plan year is a short year
- A statement that next year's annual report will include the independent qualified public accountant's opinion for both plan years[25]

**Next year's annual report**

To defer filing the opinion, the next year's annual report must include:

- Financial statements and schedules for both plan years
- The independent qualified public accountant's opinion for both plan years
- A description of any material difference between the unaudited financial information reported in this year's annual report and the audited information for this year reported in next year's annual report[26]

Use the flowchart in Figure 4-2 to determine whether the plan can defer filing the accountant's opinion until the following plan year.

---

[25]  DOL Reg. § 2520.104-50(b)(1).
[26]  DOL Reg. § 2520.104-50(b)(2).

## Figure 4-2

## Determining Whether Accountant's Opinion Can Be Deferred

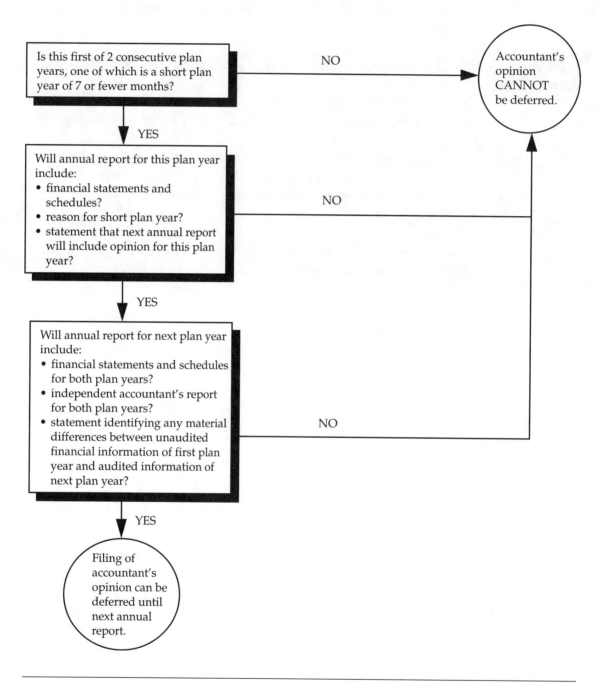

# E. Due Date

Once the plan determines which forms it must file, it needs to determine when to file them.

**General rule**

In general, the Form 5500 must be filed by the last day of the seventh month after the plan year ends.[27] This is true even if the plan year is a short plan year (i.e., less than 12 months).

If the deadline for filing falls on a Saturday, Sunday, or legal holiday, the annual report may be filed on the next succeeding day that is not a Saturday, Sunday, or legal holiday.[28]

*Caution.* While the weekend/holiday rule permits additional time for filing, it does not extend the time for making required minimum funding contributions.

> *Example 1.* A health plan has a plan year ending March 31. The date seven months after the plan year ending March 31, 2009, is October 31, 2009. Since October 31, 2009, falls on a Saturday, the plan's annual report must be filed by Monday, November 2, 2009.

> *Example 2.* A 401(k) plan has a plan year ending on December 31, 2008. The plan's annual report must be filed by July 31, 2009.

> *Example 3.* A pension plan has a plan year ending on November 20, 2008. Its annual report for the current plan year must be filed by June 30, 2009.

> *Example 4.* A long-term disability plan has a short plan year beginning January 1, 2008, and ending August 31, 2009. The plan's annual report must be filed by March 31, 2009.

**Request for extension**

If Form 5558, Application for Extension of Time To File Certain Employee Plan Returns, is filed with the IRS before the plan's annual report filing deadline, the plan is automatically granted a one-time extension of two and one-half months.[29]

---

27  Instructions for Form 5500, Section 2, When to File.
28  I.R.C. § 7503.
29  Instructions for Form 5500, Section 2, When to File.

Under this extension, the plan has a total of nine and one-half months from the end of the plan year, rather than seven months, to file its annual report. A copy of the completed extension request that was filed is attached to the Form 5500.

**Automatic extension**

A plan automatically receives an extension to the employer's federal income tax return due date for filing its annual report, provided all the following conditions are met:[30]

- The plan year and the tax year coincide.
- The IRS granted the employer an extension for filing its federal income tax return to a date later than the deadline for filing the annual report.
- A copy of the IRS's extension for filing the federal income tax return is attached to the annual report.

An extension granted under this provision may not be extended further by filing Form 5558.[31]

---

[30] *Id.*
[31] *Id.*

# F. Form EFast-1

For plan years beginning in 1999 or later, the Form 5500 may be filed electronically. Electronic filers must use Form EFAST-1 to apply for an electronic signature. Only individuals may apply for EFAST electronic signatures.

Copies of the Form EFAST-1 application and its instructions are available for viewing and may be downloaded at *www.efast.dol.gov*.

**Who must sign**  If an organization is filing Form 5500, an individual who is authorized to sign on behalf of the organization must sign the form. If an electronically filed Form 5500 requires more than one signature, each individual who signs must obtain his or her electronic signature by submitting a separate Form EFAST-1.

# G. Form M-1 for MEWAs and Others

Multiple-employer welfare arrangements (MEWAs) providing medical care benefits and certain collectively bargained plans with two or more employers are required to file Form M-1, Annual Report for Multiple Employer Welfare Arrangements (MEWAs) and Certain Entities Claiming Exceptions (ECEs).[32]

Collectively bargained plans providing medical benefits for the employees of more than one employer are required to file Form M-1 for the first three years the plan is in existence.

**Content**

Form M-1 asks whether the plan is in compliance with the Health Insurance Portability and Accountability Act of 1996 (HIPAA), the Mental Health Parity Act (MHPA), the Newborns' and Mothers' Health Protection Act (NMHPA), and the Women's Health and Cancer Rights Act of 1998 (WHCRA). The form also asks whether there has been any litigation or enforcement proceeding involving noncompliance.

**Due date**

Form M-1 is due by March 1; however, plan administrators can request a 60-day extension.

**MEWAs**

A *MEWA* is an arrangement that offers health or welfare coverage to the employees of two or more employers. The definition of MEWA excludes certain arrangements—those established or maintained under collective bargaining agreements, or by a rural electric cooperative, or by a rural telephone cooperative association.[33] (Form M-1 treats a collectively bargained arrangement in effect for less than three years as if it were a MEWA.)

The MEWA rules enable state insurance departments to regulate MEWAs, particularly MEWAs that are not fully insured. Some states regulate MEWAs as if they were insurers, others regulate them as special entities, and some prohibit them altogether.

---

[32] DOL Reg. § 2520.101-2.
[33] ERISA § 3(40).

Group health coverage offered by an employee leasing company (also known as a professional employer organization) to leased employees of two or more client employers is a MEWA that should file Form M-1 if the client employers, rather than the leasing company, control the leased employees' work or if the client employers and PEO claim co-employer status.[34]

**Exceptions**    Plans that do not have to file Form M-1 are the following:[35]

- A plan covering two or more businesses with a common control interest of at least 25 percent.
- An employer's health plan covering employees of a company that has spun off from the employer's controlled group. (Form M-1 is not required provided the arrangement does not extend beyond the end of the plan year following the year in which the change in control occurs.)
- A plan that covers nonemployees, such as independent contractors and outside corporate directors, if the total number of nonemployee participants does not exceed 1 percent of all participants.
- A plan that provides only exempted benefits, as defined under HIPAA, such as a limited scope dental plan.

---

[34]  Preamble to DOL Reg. § 2520.101-2; EBSA Information Letter, 05/08/06. DOL Adv. Op. 92-07A.
[35]  DOL Reg. § 2520.101-2(c)(2).

# H. Penalties for Noncompliance

Plan administrators are subject to both civil and criminal penalties for failure to provide copies of annual reports to participants or beneficiaries on request or failure or refusal to file annual reports.

## Civil Penalties

At its discretion, a court can impose civil penalties on a plan for failure to provide copies of annual reports to participants and certain beneficiaries on request.[36]

In addition, both the DOL and the IRS impose separate civil penalties for failure to file the following:

- Form 5500[37]
- Schedule B (Actuarial Information)[38]
- Schedule SSA (Annual Registration Statement Identifying Separated Participants With Deferred Vested Benefits)[39]

**Failure to disclose annual report**  A plan administrator who fails or refuses to provide a copy of an annual report within 30 days after receiving a request from a plan participant or beneficiary may be fined up to $110 a day. The penalty, imposed by a court, is payable to the participant or beneficiary filing the civil action.[40]

## DOL Penalties

**Failure to file annual report**  If a plan administrator fails or refuses to file an annual report required under ERISA, the DOL can assess a civil penalty of up to $1,100 a day from the date of failure or refusal.[41] Generally, plan administrators may

---

[36]  ERISA § 502(c)(1).
[37]  I.R.C. § 6652(e); ERISA § 502(c)(2).
[38]  I.R.C. § 6692.
[39]  I.R.C. § 6652(d)(1).
[40]  ERISA § 502(c)(1).
[41]  ERISA § 502(c)(2).

be assessed a penalty of $300 a day if the failure is discovered by the DOL.[42]

If the DOL rejects an annual report because it does not include certain required "material information," the report is treated as though it was never filed. However, the plan administrator has a 45-day grace period in which to submit an acceptable annual report.[43]

## Delinquent Filer Voluntary Compliance Program

The DOL generally assesses a penalty of $50 a day against plan administrators that voluntarily file late annual reports.[44] However, if a plan administrator files with the DOL under the Delinquent Filer Voluntary Compliance (DFVC) Program, this penalty is reduced to $10 per day.[45] Additionally, in the case of a single late annual report filing for a plan, the cumulative daily amount for a plan is capped at $750 for small plans and $2,000 for large plans.[46] When a plan has more than one delinquent annual report, the penalty is capped at $1,500 for small plans and $4,000 for large plans.[47]

The penalty for certain tax-exempt organizations is limited to $750 per submission. Apprenticeship programs and certain executive pension programs that have failed to file required registration statements can limit their non-filing penalty to $750 under this program.

**Note.** The IRS has also agreed to grant relief from its penalties for late filers who use the DFVC program.[48]

**Filing under the DFVC Program**

The DFVC Program is available only to a plan administrator that files before it is notified by the DOL in writing that an annual report is late.[49]

Filing is a two-part process.[50] First, the completed Form 5500(s) with applicable schedules must be sent to DOL at the appropriate ERISA Filing Acceptance System (EFAST) address or filed electronically in

---

42   DOL Notice, 92-158, 3/23/1992.
43   DOL Reg. § 2560.502c-2(b)(3).
44   DOL Notice, 92-158, 3/23/1992.
45   DOL Notice, § § 3.03(c)(1), 3.03(c)(2) at 67 Fed. Reg. 15,059 (2002).
46   Id.
47   Id.
48   DOL Notice § 5 at 67 Fed. Reg. 15,060 (2002); IRS Notice 2002-23.
49   DOL Notice, § 2.02 at 67 Fed. Reg. 15,058 (2002).
50   DOL Notice, § § 3.02(a)-(b), 3.03(a)-(b) at 67 Fed. Reg. 15,059 (2002).

accordance with EFAST electronic filing requirements. The plan administrator may use either (1) the Form 5500 issued for each plan year for which relief is sought or (2) the most current Form 5500 available.

Second, the plan administrator must send a signed and dated copy of the form, without any schedules or attachments, together with a check, payable to the U.S. Department of Labor, for the applicable penalty to:

By mail:

> DFVC Program DOL
> DOL
> P.O. Box 70933
> Charlotte, NC 28272-0933

By Private Delivery Service:

> DFVC Program DOL
> QLP Wholesale Lockbox-NC0810
> Lock Box 70933
> 1525 West WT Harris Blvd.
> Charlotte, NC 28262

---

## IRS Penalties

---

**Failure to file annual report**  The IRS may assess a penalty of $25 per day, up to a maximum of $15,000, for failure to file annual reports for certain retirement plans, including qualified plans.[51]

**Failure to file Schedule B**  If a plan administrator fails to file Schedule B, the IRS can assess a civil penalty of $1,000.[52]

**Failure to file Schedule SSA**  If a plan administrator fails to file Schedule SSA, the IRS can assess a civil penalty of $1 per day for each participant for whom the registration statement is not filed, up to a maximum of $5,000 for any plan year.[53]

---

[51] I.R.C. § 6652(e).
[52] I.R.C. § 6692.
[53] I.R.C. § 6652(d)(1).

## ERISA Criminal Penalties

For willfully failing to file annual reports, a plan administrator can be assessed a criminal penalty of up to $100,000 or imprisonment of up to ten years.

If an entity other than a natural person (e.g., a corporation) violates the annual reporting requirements, the DOL may assess a criminal penalty of $500,000.[54]

In addition, if a plan administrator knowingly makes a false statement or misrepresentation on the annual report, the DOL may assess a penalty of up to $10,000 or five years' imprisonment.[55]

---

[54] ERISA §501.
[55] 18 U.S.C. §1027.

# Chapter 5

# Summary Annual Reports

---

**Introduction**    Most ERISA-covered retirement and welfare plans must comply with ERISA's summary annual report (SAR) requirements. For post-2007 plan years, ERISA-covered defined benefit pension plans provide an annual funding notice. See Chapter 9.

This chapter begins by providing general information about SAR requirements and then describes affected plans, specific requirements due dates, and distribution methods.

**Contents**    This chapter has five sections:

| Section | Title | Page |
|---|---|---|
| A | General Information | 5-2 |
| B | Plans Subject to SAR Requirements | 5-3 |
| C | SAR Requirements | 5-4 |
| D | When and How to Distribute SAR Information | 5-14 |
| E | Multiemployer Plan Summary Report | 5-16 |

# A. General Information

Plan administrators of ERISA-covered pension (other than defined benefit plans described below) and welfare plans must generally distribute summary annual reports to participants and beneficiaries.

**PPA Revision**

For plan years beginning after December 31, 2007, plan administrators of defined benefit plans are no longer required to provide a summary annual report. Instead, these plans provide an annual funding notice.[1]

**Definition**

A *summary annual report* is an abstract of the information in a plan's Form 5500 annual report filed with the Department of Labor (DOL).

The primary purpose of a SAR is to inform participants and beneficiaries of the plan's financial condition.

**Disclosure requirement**

The SAR requirements are disclosure requirements. Thus, SARs must be distributed to participants and beneficiaries; they are *not* filed with the IRS or the DOL.

**Penalty for non-compliance**

If a plan administrator fails or refuses to provide a SAR within 30 days after receiving a request for one from a plan participant or eligible beneficiary, a court can impose a penalty of up to $110 per day.[2] This penalty is payable to the participant or beneficiary filing a civil action.

---

[1]   PPA § 503(f).
[2]   ERISA § 502(c)(1).

# B. Plans Subject to SAR Requirements

**Affected plans**   An ERISA-covered pension (other than defined benefit plans for post-2007 plan years) or welfare plan must comply with the SAR requirements, unless ERISA specifically exempts the plan from the requirements.

**Exemptions**   ERISA-covered plans exempt from the SAR requirements are

- Small welfare plans[3]
- Unfunded welfare plans[4]
- Employer-provided day care centers[5]
- Apprenticeship training programs[6]
- Simplified employee pension plans (SEPs)[7]
- Pension and welfare plans maintained primarily for management or highly compensated employees (HCEs)[8]
- Dues-financed pension and welfare plans[9]
- Savings Incentive Match Plans for Employees (SIMPLEs)[10]

Such plans are exempt *only* if they meet certain definitions and conditions. The conditions include, in some cases, meeting alternative compliance requirements. (For details concerning the conditions of exemption, see Chapter 3, Section B.)

**Note.** The DOL has not announced whether medical savings accounts (MSAs) are subject to ERISA's reporting and disclosure requirements. Savings Incentive Match Plans for Employees (SIMPLEs) are subject to special rules (see Chapter 3).

---

[3]   DOL Reg. §§ 2520.104-20, 2520.104b-10(g).
[4]   DOL Reg. §§ 2520.104-44(b)(1)(i), 2520.104b-10(g).
[5]   DOL Reg. §§ 2520.104-25, 2520.104b-10(g).
[6]   DOL Reg. §§ 2520.104-22, 2520.104b-10(g).
[7]   DOL Reg. §§ 2520.104-48, 2520.104-49.
[8]   DOL Reg. §§ 2520.104-23, 2520.104-24, 2520.104b-10(g).
[9]   DOL Reg. §§ 2520.104-26, 2520.104-27, 2520.104b-10(g).
[10]   ERISA § 101(h).

# C. SAR Requirements

If a plan is subject to the SAR requirements, it must distribute certain information to participants and certain beneficiaries. The particular information it must distribute depends on whether the plan is a pension plan (other than a defined benefit plan required to provide an annual funding notice for post-2007 plan years) or a welfare plan.[11]

The content of the SAR must follow one of the two prescribed SAR forms in ERISA regulations — one for pension plans, the other for welfare plans.

See Figure 5-2 for a SAR form for pension plans and Figure 5-3 for a SAR form for welfare plans.

**Completing SAR forms**

To complete the SAR, the plan administrator uses information from the plan's most recent Form 5500, Annual Return/Report of Employee Benefit Plan.[12]

The plan administrator may leave out any portion of the prescribed SAR form that does not apply to the plan or that requires information not included in the plan's annual report.[13]

The plan administrator may also add explanations if the administrator considers them necessary to summarize the annual report fairly.[14] However, the plan administrator must place such additional explanations at the end of the completed form under the heading "Additional Explanation."

**Note.** See Chapter 4, Section D, for information certain small plans must add for access to the accountant's opinion exception.

**Foreign language requirements**

Whether a plan is subject to the SAR foreign language requirements depends on the number of plan participants who are only literate in a particular foreign language.[15]

---

[11]   DOL Reg. § 2520.104b-10(d).
[12]   DOL Reg. § 2520.104b-10(d).
[13]   DOL Reg. § 2520.104b-10(d)(1).
[14]   DOL Reg. § 2520.104b-10(d)(2).
[15]   DOL Reg. § 2520.104b-10(e).

If the requirements apply, a statement must be prominently displayed in the English-language SAR, in the foreign language common to the participants, offering them assistance.

The actual assistance provided need not involve written materials. However, the assistance must be provided in the foreign language common to the participants. Furthermore, the statement must clearly state the procedures that participants are required follow to obtain assistance.

For plans covering fewer than 100 participants at the beginning of the plan year, the foreign language requirements apply if 25 percent or more of the participants are literate only in the same foreign language.[16]

For plans covering 100 or more participants at the beginning of the plan year, the foreign language requirements apply if (1) 500 or more participants are literate only in the same foreign language, or, if fewer (2) 10 percent or more of all plan participants are literate only in the same foreign language.[17]

Use the chart in Figure 5-1 to determine whether the SAR foreign language requirements apply to a plan.

**Furnishing additional documents**

If, after receiving a SAR, a participant or beneficiary requests additional annual report documents, the plan administrator must promptly comply with the request.[18]

**Charges for furnishing additional documents**

The plan administrator may charge a reasonable amount to cover the cost of furnishing copies of the full annual report or portions of the annual report. However, the charge may not include the cost of furnishing, either separately or as part of the full annual report, copies of the statement of assets and liabilities, the statement of income and expenses, and accompanying notes.

In general, a charge is reasonable if it is equal to the least expensive cost per page for copying.[19] However, a charge is not reasonable if it exceeds 25 cents per page. Any other charges for furnishing the information besides the copying charges (e.g., postage) are also not reasonable.

---

[16]   DOL Reg. § 2520.104b-10(e)(1).
[17]   DOL Reg. § 2520.104b-10(e)(2).
[18]   DOL Reg. § 2520.104b-10(f).
[19]   DOL Reg. § 2520.104b-30(b).

## Figure 5-1

## Determining Whether SAR Foreign Language Requirements Apply

| If, at Start of Plan Year, Plan Covered: | And Number of Participants Literate Only in Same Foreign Language Is: | Then Foreign Language Requirements: |
|---|---|---|
| Fewer than 100 participants | less than 25% of all participants | do NOT apply |
| | 25% or more of all participants | APPLY |
| 100 or more participants | • fewer than 500 participants, and<br>• less than 10% of all participants | do NOT apply |
| | • 500 or more participants or, if fewer,<br>• 10% or more of all participants | APPLY |

## Figure 5-2

## Summary Annual Report for Defined Contribution Pension Plans

**Instructions:** If the plan is a pension plan subject to the SAR requirements, it must distribute the following SAR form prescribed by DOL Regulations Section 2520.104b-10(d)(3) and ERISA Section 104(b)(3).

To complete the SAR for Pension Plans, use the cross-reference table at the end of the form.

---

### Summary Annual Report for (name of plan)

This is a summary of the annual report for (*name of plan and EIN*) for (*period covered by this report*). The annual report has been filed with the Pension and Welfare Benefit Administration, as required under the Employee Retirement Income Security Act of 1974 (ERISA).

#### Basic Financial Statement

Benefits under the plan are provided by __1__. Plan expenses were __2__. These expenses included __3__ in administrative expenses and __4__ in benefits paid to participants and beneficiaries, and __5__ in other expenses. A total of __6__ persons were participants in or beneficiaries of the plan at the end of the plan year, although not all of these persons had yet earned the right to receive benefits.

*Note: If your plan is funded solely by allocated insurance contracts, do not include the following paragraph in the SAR.*

The value of plan assets, after subtracting liabilities of the plan, was $__7a__ as of (*the end of the plan year*), compared to $__7b__ as of (*the beginning of the plan year*). During the plan year the plan experienced an (*increase*) (*decrease*) in its net assets of $__8__. This (*increase*) (*decrease*) includes unrealized appreciation or depreciation in the value of plan assets: that is, the difference between the value of the plan's assets at the end of the year and the value of the assets at the beginning of the year or the cost of assets acquired during the year. The plan had total income of $__9__, including employer contributions of $__9a__, employee contributions of $__9b__, (*gains*) (*losses*) of $__9c__ from the sale of assets, and earnings from investments of $__9d__.

*Note: If any funds are used to purchase allocated insurance contracts, include the following paragraph in the SAR.*

The plan has (a) contract(s) with (*name of insurance carrier*) which allocate(s) funds toward (*state whether individual policies, group deferred annuities or other*). The total premiums paid for the plan year ending (date) were $__10__.

## Figure 5-2 (*cont'd*)

### Summary Annual Report for Defined Contribution Pension Plans

**Minimum Funding Standards**

*Note: If the plan is a defined contribution plan (e.g., a money purchase or target benefit plan) covered by the minimum funding standards, include the following paragraph in the SAR.*

*[Enough money was contributed to the plan to keep it funded in accordance with the minimum funding standards of ERISA] [Not enough money was contributed to the plan to keep it funded in accordance with the minimum funding standards of ERISA. The amount of the deficit was $\_\_11\_\_ .]*

**Your Rights to Additional Information**

You have the right to receive a copy of the full annual report, or any part thereof, on request. The items listed below are included in that report: **[Note: list only those items that are actually included in the latest annual report.]**

1. an accountant's report;

2. financial information and information on payments to service providers;

3. assets held for investment;

4. fiduciary information, including non-exempt transactions between the plan and the parties- in-interest (that is, persons who have certain relationships with the plan);

5. loans or other obligations in default or classified as uncollectible;

6. leases in default or classified as uncollectible;

7. transactions in excess of 5 percent of the plan assets;

8. insurance information including sales commissions paid by insurance carriers;

9. information regarding any common or collective trusts, pooled separate accounts, master trusts or 103-12 investment entities in which the plan participates; and

To obtain a copy of the full annual report, or any part thereof, write or call the office of (*name*), who is (*state title: e.g., the plan administrator*), (*business address and telephone number*). The charge to cover copying costs will be ($\_\_\_) for the full annual report, or ($\_\_\_) per page for any part thereof.

You also have the right to receive from the plan administrator, on request and at no charge, a statement of the assets and liabilities of the plan and accompanying notes, or a statement of income and expenses of the plan and accompanying notes, or both. If you request a copy of the full annual report from the plan administrator, these two statements and accompanying notes will be included as part of that report. The charge to cover copying costs given above does not include a charge for the copying of these portions of the report because these portions are furnished without charge.

**Figure 5-2 (*cont'd*)**

**Summary Annual Report for Defined Contribution Pension Plans**

You also have the legally protected right to examine the annual report at the main office of the plan (*address*), (*at any other location where the report is available for examination*), and at the U.S. Department of Labor in Washington, D.C., or to obtain a copy from the U.S. Department of Labor upon payment of copying costs. Requests to the Department should be addressed to: Public Disclosure Room, Suite N-1513, Employee Benefits Security Administration, U.S. Department of Labor, 200 Constitution Avenue, N.W., Washington, D.C. 20210.

*Note: This address was correct at the time the guide went to press. However, government addresses occasionally change. Please confirm the address before distributing the SAR.*

*Note:* If the plan is taking advantage of the restricted exemption from the accountant's opinion requirement (see Chapter 4), this model language from Appendix A to DOL Reg. § 2520.104-46 may be used:

The U.S. Department of Labor's regulations require that an independent qualified public accountant audit the plan's financial statements unless certain conditions are met for the audit requirement to be waived. This plan met the audit waiver conditions for the plan year beginning (insert year) and therefore has not had an audit performed. Instead, the following information is provided to assist you in verifying that the assets reported on the (Form 5500 or Form 5500-SF—select as applicable) were actually held by the plan.

At the end of the (insert year) plan year, the plan had (include separate entries for each regulated financial institution holding or issuing qualifying plan assets):

[Set forth amounts and names of institutions as applicable where indicated], [(insert $ amount) in assets held by (insert name of bank)], [(insert $ amount) in securities held by (insert name of registered broker-dealer)], [(insert $ amount) in shares issued by (insert name of registered investment company)], [(insert $ amount) in investment or annuity contract issued by (insert name of insurance company)].

The plan receives year-end statements from these regulated financial institutions that confirm the above information. [Insert as applicable—The remainder of the plan's assets were (1) qualifying employer securities, (2) loans to participants, (3) held in individual participant accounts with investments directed by participants and beneficiaries and with account statements from regulated financial institutions furnished to the participant or beneficiary at least annually, or (4) other assets covered by a fidelity bond at least equal to the value of the assets and issued by an approved surety company.]

Plan participants and beneficiaries have a right, on request and free of charge, to get copies of the financial institution year-end statements and evidence of the fidelity bond. If you want to examine or get copies of the financial institution year-end statements or evidence of the fidelity bond, please contact [insert mailing address and any other available way to request copies such as e-mail and phone number].

If you are unable to obtain or examine copies of the regulated financial institution statements or evidence of the fidelity bond, you may contact the regional office of the U.S. Department of Labor's Employee Benefits Security Administration (EBSA) for assistance by calling toll-free 1-866-444-EBSA (3272). A listing of EBSA regional offices can be found at http://www.dol.gov/ebsa.

General information regarding the audit waiver conditions applicable to the plan can be found on the U.S. Department of Labor Web site at http://www.dol.gov/ebsa under the heading "Frequently Asked Questions."

## Figure 5-2 (*cont'd*)

## Summary Annual Report for Defined Contribution Pension Plans

| SAR Item | Form 5500 Large Plan Filer Line Items | Form 5500 Small Plan Filer Line Items |
|---|---|---|
| 1. Funding arrangement | Form 5500—9a | Same |
| 2. Total plan expenses | Sch. H—2j | Sch. I—2i |
| 3. Administrative expenses | Sch. H—2i(5) | Not applicable |
| 4. Benefits paid | Sch. H—2e(4) | Sch. I—2e |
| 5. Other expenses | Sch. H—Subtract the sum of 2e(4) & 2i(5) from 2j | Sch. I—2h |
| 6. Total participants | Form 5500—7f | Same |
| 7. Value of plan assets (net): | | |
|    a. End of plan year | Sch. H—1L [Col. (b)] | Sch. I—1c [Col. (b)] |
|    b. Beginning of plan year | Sch. H—1L [Col. (a)] | Sch. I—1c [Col. (a)] |
| 8. Change in net assets | Sch. H—Subtract 1L [Col. (a)] from 1L [Col. (b)] | Sch. I—Subtract 1c [Col. (a)] from 1c [Col. (b)] |
| 9. Total income | Sch. H—2d | Sch. I—2d |
|    a. Employer contributions | Sch. H—2a(1)(A) & 2a(2) if applicable | Sch. I—2a(1) & 2b if applicable |
|    b. Employee contributions | Sch. H—2a(1)(B) & 2a(2) if applicable | Sch. I—2a(2) & 2b if applicable |
|    c. Gains (losses) from sale of assets | Sch. H—2b(4)(C) | Not applicable |
|    d. Earnings from investments | Sch. H—Subtract the sum of 2a(3), 2b(4)(C) and 2c from 2d | Sch. I—2c |
| 10. Total insurance premiums | Total of all Schs. A—5b | Total of all Schs. A—5b |
| 11. Funding deficiency: | | |
|    Defined contribution plans | Sch. R—6c, if more than zero | Same |

## Figure 5-3

## Summary Annual Report for Welfare Plans

**Instructions:** If the plan is a welfare plan, it must distribute the following SAR form prescribed by DOL Regulations Section 2520.104b-10(d)(4).

To complete the SAR for Welfare Plans, use the cross-reference table at the end of this form.

---

### Summary Annual Report for (*name of plan*)

This is a summary annual report of the (*name of plan and EIN*) and (*type of welfare plan*) for (*period covered by this report*). The annual report has been filed with the Pension and Welfare Benefit Administration, as required under the Employee Retirement Income Security Act of 1974 (ERISA).

*Note: If any benefits under the plan are provided on an uninsured basis, include the following paragraph in the SAR.*

(Plan Sponsor) has committed itself to pay (*all, certain*) (*state type of*) claims incurred under the terms of the plan.

*Note: If any funds are used to purchase insurance contracts, include the following paragraph in the SAR.*

### Insurance Information

The plan has (a) contract(s) with __1__ to pay (*all, certain*) (*state type of*) claims incurred under the terms of the plan. The total premiums paid for the plan year ending (*date*) were $__2__.

*Note: If any portion of any insurance contract relating to the plan is experience-rated, include the following paragraph in the SAR.*

Because (*it is a*) (*they are*) so-called experience-rated contract(s), the premium costs are affected by, among other things, the number and size of claims. Of the total insurance premiums paid for the plan year ending (*date*), the premiums paid under such "experience-rated" contract(s) were $__3__ and the total of all benefit claims paid under the(se) experience-rated contract(s) during the plan year was $__4__.

*Note: If any funds of the plan are held in trust or in a separately maintained fund, include the following two paragraphs in the SAR.*

### Basic Financial Statement

The value of plan assets, after subtracting liabilities of the plan, was $__5a__ as of (*the end of the plan year*), compared to $__5b__ as of (*the beginning of the plan year*). During the plan year the plan experienced an (*increase*) (*decrease*) in its net assets of $__6__. This (*increase*) (*decrease*) includes unrealized appreciation or depreciation in the value of plan assets, that is, the difference be tween the value of plan assets at the end of the year and the value of the assets at the beginning of the year or the cost of assets acquired during the year. During the plan year, the plan had total income of $__7__, including employer contributions of $__7a__, employee contributions of $__7b__, realized (*gains*) (*losses*) of $__7c__ from the sale of assets, and earnings from investments of $__7d__.

Plan expenses were $__8__. These expenses included $__9__ in administrative expenses, $__10__ in benefits paid to participants and beneficiaries, and $__11__ in other expenses.

**Figure 5-3 (*cont'd*)**

**Summary Annual Report for Welfare Plans**

### Your Rights to Additional Information

You have the right to receive a copy of the full annual report, or any part thereof, on request. The items listed below are included in that report: [**Note: list only those items that are actually included in the latest annual report.**]

1.  an accountant's report;

2.  financial information and information on payments to service providers;

3.  assets held for investment;

4.  fiduciary information, including non-exempt transactions between the plan and parties-in-interest (that is, persons who have certain relationships with the plan);

5.  loans or other obligations in default or classified as uncollectible;

6.  leases in default or classified as uncollectible;

7.  transactions in excess of 5 percent of the plan assets;

8.  insurance information including sales commissions paid by insurance carriers; and

9.  information regarding any common or collective trusts, pooled separate accounts, master trusts, or 103-12 investment entities in which the plan participates.

To obtain a copy of the full annual report, or any part thereof, write or call the office of (*name*), who is (*state title: e.g., the plan administrator*), (*business address and telephone number*). The charge to cover copying costs will be ($__) for the full annual report, or ($__) per page for any part thereof.

You also have the right to receive from the plan administrator, on request and at no charge, a statement of the assets and liabilities of the plan and accompanying notes or a statement of income and expenses of the plan and accompanying notes, or both. If you request a copy of the full annual report from the plan administrator, these two statements and accompanying notes will be included as part of that report. The charge to cover copying costs given above does not include a charge for the copying of these portions of the report because these portions are furnished without charge.

You also have the legally protected right to examine the annual report at the main office of the plan (*address*), (*at any other locations where the report is available for examination*), and at the U.S. Department of Labor in Washington, D.C., or to obtain a copy from the U.S. Department of Labor upon payment of copying costs. Requests to the Department should be addressed to Public Disclosure Room, Suite N-1513, Employee Benefits Security Administration, U.S. Department of Labor, 200 Constitution Avenue, N.W., Washington, D.C. 20210.

*Note: This address was correct at the time the guide went to press. However, government addresses change frequently. Please confirm address before distributing the SAR.*

## Figure 5-3 (*cont'd*)

## Summary Annual Report for Welfare Plans

| SAR Item | *Form 5500 Large Plan Filer Line Items* | *Form 5500 Small Plan Filer Line Items* |
|---|---|---|
| 1. Name of insurance carrier | All Schs. A—1(a) | Same |
| 2. Total (experience rated and non-experienced rated) insurance premiums | All Schs. A—Sum of 8a(4) and 9(a) | Same |
| 3. Experience rated premiums | All Schs. A—8a(4) | Same |
| 4. Experience rated claims | All Schs. A—8b(4) | Same |
| 5. Value of plan assets(net): | | |
| a. End of plan year | Sch. H—1L [Col. (b)] | Sch. I—1c [Col. (b)] |
| b. Beginning of plan year | Sch. H—1L [Col. (a)] | Sch. I—1c [Col. (a)] |
| 6. Change in net assets | Sch. H—Subtract 1L [Col. (a)] from 1L [Col. (b)] | Sch. I—Subtract 1c [Col. (a)] from 1c [Col. (b)] |
| 7. Total income | Sch. H—2d | Sch. I—2d |
| a. Employer contributions | Sch. H—2a(1)(A) & 2a(2) if applicable | Sch. I—2a(1) & 2b if applicable |
| b. Employee contributions | Sch. H—2a(1)(B) & 2a(2) if applicable | Sch. I—2a(2) & 2b if applicable |
| c. Gains (losses) from sale of assets | Sch. H—2b(4)(C) | Not applicable |
| d. Earnings from investments | Sch. H—Subtract the sum of 2a(3), 2b(4)(C) and 2c from 2d | Sch. I—2c |
| 8. Total plan expenses | Sch. H—2j | Sch. I—2i |
| 9. Administrative expenses | Sch. H—2i(5) | Not applicable |
| 10. Benefits paid | Sch. H—2e(4) | Sch. I—2e |
| 11. Other expenses | Sch. H—Subtract the sum of 2e(4) & 2i(5) from 2j | Sch. I—2h |

# D. When and How to Distribute SAR Information

**Due date**   In general, a plan must distribute its SAR information within nine months after the close of the plan year.[20]

If the plan is a welfare plan in a group insurance arrangement, it generally must distribute the SAR information within nine months after the close of the fiscal year of the trust or other entity that files the annual report.[21]

If the IRS granted an extension for filing the plan's annual report, the plan can distribute the SAR information to participants and beneficiaries as late as two months after the extended filing date.[22]

> **Example 1.** Plan A has a calendar year plan year. The IRS did not grant the plan an extension for filing its annual report. Therefore, the plan administrator must distribute SAR information no later than September 30.

> **Example 2.** Plan B has a calendar year plan year. The IRS extended the plan's annual report filing deadline to October 15. Therefore, the plan administrator has until December 15 to distribute SAR information.

**Who must receive SAR information**   Plan administrators must distribute SAR information to plan participants and, in the case of *pension plans*, to beneficiaries receiving benefits.[23]

**Distribution methods**   When distributing SAR information to participants and beneficiaries, the plan must take measures to ensure these parties actually receive the information.[24]

---

20   DOL Reg. § 2520.104b-10(c).
21   DOL Reg. § 2520.104b-10(c)(1).
22   DOL Reg. § 2520.104b-10(c)(2).
23   DOL Reg. § 2520.104b-10(a).
24   DOL Reg. § § 2520.104b-1, 2520.104b-10(a).

The plan must use a distribution method or methods likely to result in full distribution.[25] Acceptable distribution methods include:

- In-hand delivery to employees at their worksites
- Special insert in an employee periodical if the distribution list is comprehensive, up-to-date, and accurate; and the periodical's front page prominently states the SAR is inserted
- First-class mail
- Second- or third-class mail if return and forwarding postage are guaranteed and address correction is requested
- Electronic distribution that satisfies the DOL's safe harbor requirements (see Chapter 3, Section C)

**Note.** Leaving a stack of SARs at a common worksite is not an acceptable distribution method.

**Insert in employee periodical**

If the plan wants to furnish SAR information by inserting it in an employee periodical, but some of the participants and beneficiaries are not on the mailing list, the plan may combine the periodical insert method with another distribution method. The plan can combine the two distribution methods if, together, the methods ensure that plan participants and beneficiaries actually receive the information.[26]

**Second- or third-class mail**

If the plan distributes SAR information by second- or third-class mail and later receives returned SAR information with a corrected mailing address, it must distribute the SAR information again by first-class mail or personal delivery to the participant at his or her worksite.[27]

---

[25] DOL Reg. § 2520.104b-1(b)(1).
[26] Id.
[27] Id.

# E. Multiemployer Plan Summary Report

For post-2007 plan years, administrators of multiemployer plans subject to the annual report requirement must provide summary reports to each employee organization, contributing employers, and the PBGC.[28]

**Contents**     The summary report to employers, unions, and PBGC must contain[29]:

- a description of the plan's contribution schedules and benefit formulas along with any modification made during the plan year
- the number of employers contributing to the plan
- a list of the employers that contributed more than 5% of the total contributions during the plan year
- the number of plan participants for whom no employer contributions were made for the plan year and for each of the two preceding plan years;
- whether the plan was in critical or endangered status for the plan year, and if so:
  — a list of the actions taken to improve the plan's funding status; and
  — instructions for obtaining a copy of the plan's improvement or rehabilitation plan along with actuarial and financial data that demonstrates any action taken by the plan toward fiscal improvement
- information on employers withdrawing from the plan
- information about plan merger activity
- information about any amortization extension or use of the shortfall funding method

The summary report must inform recipients of their right to obtain the annual report, SPD and SMMs upon written request, once during any 12-month period. The report must alert recipients to possible copying costs.[30]

---

[28]   ERISA § 104(d).
[29]   ERISA § 104(d)(1)(A) through (H).
[30]   ERISA § 104(d)(1)(I).

**Copying costs**   The administrator may impose reasonable charges for copying, mailing, and other costs of furnishing copies of the information.

**Due date**   The summary report must be provided within 30 days after the due date for filing the annual report.[31]

---

[31]   ERISA § 104(d)(1).

# Chapter 6

# PBGC Reporting Requirements

---

**Introduction**    Plan administrators for plans covered by the Pension Benefit Guaranty Corporation (PBGC) must pay insurance premiums and file certain forms, notify the PBGC of reportable events, and notify the PBGC of the failure to make timely contributions.

For plan years beginning after 2007, premium financial and actuarial information reporting rules are revised by the PPA.

**Contents**    This chapter has ten sections:

# A. Plans Subject to Coverage by PBGC Insurance Program

The PBGC is a federal agency that insures certain defined benefit pension benefits. If a plan terminates and cannot pay all the required pension benefits, the PBGC will step in and pay guaranteed benefits up to a specified maximum.

Most defined benefit pension plans are subject to coverage by the PBGC's Insurance Program.

**Covered plans** Qualified defined benefit pension plans are generally subject to coverage by the PBGC Insurance Program.[1]

**Exemptions** Pension plans exempt from coverage in the PBGC Insurance Program are:[2]

- Individual account plans (e.g., money purchase, profit-sharing, and stock bonus plans)
- Governmental plans, including those to which the Railroad Retirement Act applies
- Plans established by an Indian tribal government, a subdivision, or agency or instrumentality of either, where all participants are employees who provide essential government functions, but not commercial services
- Church plans that have not elected coverage under Internal Revenue Code participation, vesting, and funding requirements and under PBGC guarantees
- Fraternal and employees' beneficiary association plans and certain pre-1960 pension trusts to which no employer contributes
- Plans with no employer contributions since September 2, 1974
- Unfunded plans providing benefits for a select group of management or highly compensated employees
- Plans maintained outside the United States for nonresident aliens
- Excess benefit plans
- The individual account portion of a combined defined benefit/defined contribution plan (a.k.a. 414(k) plan)

---

[1]  ERISA § 4021(a).
[2]  ERISA § 4021(b).

- Plans established to comply with workers' compensation, unemployment compensation, or disability insurance laws
- Plans maintained exclusively for substantial owners of the employer
- Plans of international organizations exempt from taxation under the International Organizations Immunities Act
- Plans established by professional services employers that have 25 or fewer employees at all times

**Individual account plan exemption**

An individual account plan is a defined contribution that provides individual accounts for participants, with benefits based on contributions, income, expenses, gains and losses, and forfeitures to the participants.[3]

An individual account plan that promises a fixed benefit is not exempt from coverage if the employer or the employer's representative participated in the determination of that benefit.[4]

**Professional services employer exemption**

A *professional services employer* is any entity (e.g., a proprietorship, a partnership, or a corporation) owned or controlled by professional individuals who engage in providing professional services.[5]

Examples of professional individuals include physicians, dentists, attorneys, public accountants, public engineers, architects, actuaries, scientists, and performing artists.

---

[3] ERISA § 3(34).
[4] ERISA § 4021(c)(1).
[5] ERISA § 4021(c)(2).

# B. General Filing Requirements for PBGC Forms

Except for premium declarations, PBGC filings may be submitted by hand, mail, or commercial delivery service.[6] Premium declarations must be filed electronically, generally beginning in July 2006.[7]

**Electronic filing system**

The PBGC's electronic filing and payment system for premium declaration filings is called "My Plan Administration Account" (My PAA). There are three methods for electronically filing under the My PAA system, as follows:

- *My PAA data entry*: Filers enter premium data directly into My PAA; other members of the e-filing "team" (e.g., enrolled actuary, plan administrator) use My PAA's routing, certification, and other capabilities to complete the package.
- *Import Method*: This method allows filers using compatible software to import premium data from that software to My PAA's data entry and editing screens. This method gives filers full advantage of My PAA's routing, certification, and other capabilities.
- *Upload Method*: A premium data file can be uploaded to the PBGC through My PAA if the filer has compatible software. Under this method, there is only limited ability to use My PAA's certification capabilities and no ability to use its routing and other capabilities.

All plans are required to file electronically.[8] Plans may apply for exemptions on a case-by-case basis. Premium payments may be made electronically via My PAA—through ACH, electronic check, or credit—or outside of My PAA by paper check or wire transfer.

More information on My PAA and how to file electronically is accessible on the agency's Web site (*www.pbgc.gov*).

To keep information on electronic filings—including permitted methods, fax numbers, and e-mail addresses—current, the PBGC will

---

6  PBGC Reg. § 4000.3(a).
7  PBGC Reg. § 4000.3(b).
8  PBGC Reg. § 4000.3(a).

update its rules on its Web site, in its various printed forms and instruction packages, and through its customer service center:[9]

> Customer Service Center
> 1200 K Street, N.W.
> Washington, D.C., 20005-4026
> Tel: 1-800-400-7242 (for participants)
>       1-800-736-2444 (for practitioners)

**Date of filing**  Most forms are treated as filed on the date the submission is sent, as long as certain requirements are met.[10] The requirements vary, depending on the method of filing used. The PBGC may ask for evidence of when a submission was sent. However, the PBGC treats the following submissions as being filed when received (not sent) regardless of the submission method used:[11]

- Applications for benefits and related submissions (unless instructions to forms provide an earlier date)
- Advance notices of reportable events
- Notices of missed contributions exceeding $1 million
- Requests for approval of a multiemployer plan amendment

If a submission is received after 5 p.m. on a business day or at any time on a weekend or federal holiday, it is treated as received on the next business day.[12]

For submissions treated as filed when sent:

- If a submission is mailed and has a legible postmark, the postmarked date is considered the filing date. However, an earlier date may be proven. The same rules apply if a submission has a legible postmark made by a private postage meter.[13]
- If a submission is sent by a commercial delivery service, the filing date is the date of deposit. However, if the deposit is later than the last scheduled collection for the day, or on a day when there is no scheduled collection, the filing date is the next scheduled collection date.[14]

---

[9]  PBGC Reg. § 4000.3.
[10] PBGC Reg. § 4000.23(a).
[11] PBGC Reg. § 4000.23(b).
[12] PBGC Reg. § 4000.23(b)(3).
[13] PBGC Reg. § 4000.24.
[14] PBGC Reg. § 4000.26.

For electronic deliveries, the filing date for a submission is the transmission date, provided (1) the submission is sent to the proper address; (2) the technical requirements for that type of submission are met; and (3) when the transmission is sent as an attachment to an e-mail, the e-mail contains the name and telephone number of the person the PBGC should contact if the attachment cannot be read.[15]

---

[15] PBGC Reg. § 4000.29.

# C. Premium Payments

Both single employer and multiemployer plans covered by the PBGC Insurance Program must pay annual premiums. Any plan that is not a multiemployer plan (e.g., most multiple employer plans) is treated as a single employer plan for PBGC reporting purposes.

**Note.** The following description reflects regulations proposed, as of the publication date, by the PBGC to address PPA changes.

**Single employer plan premiums**

Single employer plans must pay PBGC premiums in two parts: the flat rate premium and the variable rate premium.

**Flat rate premium**

The *flat rate premium*, for single employer plans, is determined by multiplying the flat rate premium charge, $30, by the number of participants.[16] The premium is adjusted to reflect cost-of-living changes. The premium for the 2008 plan year is $33.[17]

**Variable rate premium**

The *variable rate premium*, for single employer plans, is determined by dividing the variable rate charge, $9 for every $1,000 or fraction thereof of unfunded vested benefits, by the number of participants.[18]

**Multiemployer plan premiums**

Multiemployer plans pay a flat rate premium.

The premium for multiemployer plans is determined by multiplying the premium rate, $8, by the number of participants in the plan.[19] This premium is adjusted to reflect cost-of-living changes. The premium for 2008 increased to $9.[20]

---

16   ERISA § 4006(a)(3)(A)(i).
17   PBGC Notice of flat premium rates, 72 Fed. Reg. 67765 (Nov. 30, 2007).
18   ERISA § 4006(a)(3)(E).
19   ERISA § 4006(a)(3)(A)(iii).
20   PBGC Notice of flat premium rates, 72 Fed. Reg. 67765 (Nov. 30, 2007).

**Participant Count**

The number of participants[21] on which premiums are based should be determined on the participant count date. For ongoing plans, the participant count date is the last day of the preceding plan year.[22]

For new or newly covered plans, the participant count date is the first day of the plan year (that is, the plan's effective date).[23] The transferee plan in a merger or the transferor in a spin-off counts participants as of the first day of the plan year if:

- the merger or spin-off is effective on the first day of the plan year; and
- the merger or spin-off is not de minimis or satisfies the multi-employer plan transfer rules in ERISA Section 1321.[24]

**Prorated premiums for short plan years**

Plan sponsors are allowed to pay a prorated premium for short plan years due to certain events.[25] The rule covers a short year that is

- the first year of a new or newly covered plan;
- created by a change in plan year;
- created by distribution of plan assets (other than excess assets) pursuant to a plan termination; or
- created by the appointment of a trustee for a single-employer plan under ERISA Section 4042.

However, the rule does *not* cover short plan years caused by a plan merger, consolidation, or spin-off. Premium refunds are not available in those situations. The prorated premium is determined by multiplying the full year's premium by the ratio of the number of months in the plan year (counting partial months as full months) to 12.

For plans paying a prorated premium with the Form 1-ES in anticipation of a plan amendment creating a short plan year, the premium underpayment penalty is waived if the amendment is later rescinded (by plan merger, for example).[26]

---

[21] PBGC Reg. § 4006.2.
[22] PBGC Reg. § 4006.5(c).
[23] PBGC Reg. § 4006.5(d).
[24] PBGC Reg. § 4006.5(e).
[25] PBGC Reg. § 4006.5(f).
[26] PBGC Reg. § 4007.8(i); examples in preamble at 65 Fed. Reg. 75160 (Dec. 1, 2000).

**Variable rate premium cap for small plans**

The variable rate premium for each participant is capped at $5 times the square of the number of participants if the number of employees at the beginning of the premium payment year is 25 or less.[27] The premium calculation takes into account all plan participants (including retirees and vested terminees) as of the close of the preceding plan year, but access to the limit is based on the number of *employees* at the beginning of the premium payment year. "Employees" includes employees (including leased employees) of all controlled or affiliated service groups of employers contributing to a plan as defined in the Internal Revenue Code Section 410(b)(1) coverage rules. Exclusions are not permitted for collective bargaining employees, employees not meeting a plan's age and service requirements, and employees in separate lines of business. The determination of whether the cap is available for a multiple employer plan is on a plan-wide, rather than an employer-by-employer, basis.[28]

**Termination premium**

The Deficit Reduction Act of 2005 created a new plan termination premium (generally $1,250 per participant), payable for three years following certain distress and involuntary plan terminations. The premium is determined by the number of participants on the day prior to the plan termination date and applies to all involuntary terminations and to distress terminations where at least one contributing sponsor or controlled group member is not the subject of bankruptcy liquidation. Special rules apply to the plan of a commercial passenger airline or airline catering service.[29]

**Responsibility for payment**

In the case of a single employer plan, the party responsible for the payment of premiums is the contributing sponsor or the plan administrator. In addition, all controlled group members share joint and several liability for the premiums the sponsor is required to pay.

In the case of a multiemployer plan, the plan administrator is responsible for the payment of premiums.[30]

---

[27] ERISA 4006(a)(3)(H).
[28] PBGC Reg. § 4006.3(b)(2)-(4).
[29] ERISA 4006(a)(7); PBGC Reg. § 4006.7.
[30] ERISA § 4007(e).

**Address for payment**

Premiums can generally be paid online using electronic funds transfer options or credit card.[31] Checks can be mailed to:[32]

| If you send your filing via the U.S. Postal Service (regular or certified mail) | If you use a delivery service that does not deliver to a P.O. Box |
|---|---|
| Pension Benefit Guaranty Corporation Dept. 77430 P.O. Box 77000 Detroit, MI 48277-0430 | Pension Benefit Guaranty Corporation JPMorgan Chase Bank, N.A. 9000 Haggerty Road Dept. 77430 Mail Code MI1-8244 Belleville, MI 48111 |

---

[31] 2008 PBGC Comprehensive Premium Payment Instructions, Appendix 3.
[32] 2008 PBGC Comprehensive Premium Payment Instructions, Appendix 5.

# D. PBGC Premium Payment Forms

If a defined benefit pension plan is subject to PBGC coverage under the PBGC Insurance Program, it must make annual premium payments and file the appropriate PBGC form electronically (see Section B).

PBGC provides separate instruction packages for Estimated Premium Payments and Comprehensive Premium Payments.

The forms, due dates, and the penalties for failing to file or for filing late are explained below. The PBGC's filing rules are explained in Section B.

**General due dates**

Estimated, flat rate, and variable rate premium due dates for pre-existing plans with no change in plan year for small, mid-size, and large calendar year plans for the 2009 premium payment year based on the plan's flat-rate premium participant count for the preceding plan year are as follows:[33]

|  | Small plans (under 100 participants) | Mid-size plans (100–499 participants) | Large plans (500 or more participants) |
|---|---|---|---|
| Flat-rate premium due | April 30, 2010 | October 15, 2009 | March 2, 2009 |
| Flat-rate premium reconciliation due | N/A | N/A | October 15, 2009. |
| Variable-rate premium due | April 30, 2010 | October 15, 2009 Estimate may be filed and paid. Rules provided for correcting VRP without penalty. | October 15, 2009 Estimate may be filed and paid. Rules provided for correcting VRP without penalty. |
| Latest VRP penalty starting date. If certain conditions are met, penalty is waived until this date or, if earlier, the date the final VRP is filed. | N/A | April 30, 2010 | April 30, 2010 |

---

[33] PBGC Reg. § 4007.11(a).

For the balance of this section, the two-month deadline is referred to as the "first filing due date," the 15th of the 10th month is referred to as the "second filing due date" and the 16th month deadline is the "third filing due date."

**Modified due dates**

For off-calendar plan years, these dates are modified accordingly to the last day of the second month, 15th day of the 10th month, and last day of the 16th month following the end of the plan year before the premium payment year.

If a due date falls on a Saturday, Sunday or federal holiday, file by the next business day.[34] For new and newly covered plans, flat and variable rate premiums are due by the third filing due date, or 90 days after adoption of the plan.[35]

---

## PBGC Form 1-ES

---

The e-filing of PBGC Form 1-ES, *Estimated Premium Payment*, is used for the initial premium calculation, based on an estimated participant count. This form is used to estimate the flat rate premium for single employer plans and the total premium for multiemployer plans.

**Affected plans**

If a plan reported 500 or more participants for the prior plan year, it must submit estimated premium payments.[36] Plans that submit estimated premium payments must also later submit a comprehensive premium filing to reconcile final flat rate counts and provide information about any variable premium due.[37]

**Exception**

Newly established or newly covered plans are not required to submit estimated premium payments.[38]

**Due date**

Estimated filings must be submitted by the first filing due date. For ongoing plans, the first filing due date is the last day of the second full month after the end of the prior plan year.[39]

---

34    PBGC Reg. § 4000.22.
35    PBGC Reg. § 4007.11(c).
36    PBGC Reg. § 4007.11(a)(3)(i).
37    PBGC Reg. § 4007.11(a)(3)(iii).
38    PBGC Reg. § 4007.11(c).
39    PBGC Reg. § 4007.11(a)(3)(i).

> *Example.* An ongoing plan has a calendar year plan year. For the 2009 plan year, the first filing due date for the plan is February 28, 2009.

For plans that have changed plan years, the first filing due date is the later of (1) the last day of the second full month after the end of the short plan year or (2) 30 days after the plan amendment changing the plan year is adopted.[40]

---

## PBGC Comprehensive Filing

---

The Comprehensive Premium Filing is used to calculate and pay the actual amount of flat-rate premium due to PBGC. All plans covered by the PBGC Insurance Program must file.[41]

The flat rate premium for single employer plans and the total premium for multiemployer plans are initially reported, or reconciled from the Form 1-ES estimate filing based on the actual participant count.

The Comprehensive Premium Filing is also used by single employer plans to report unfunded vested benefits and to compute the variable rate premium.[42]

**Due date**    The plan administrator must file by the second or third filing due date depending on the size of the plan (see the chart at the beginning of this section).

**Final filing due date**    For ongoing plans, other than small plans, the final filing due date is the second filing due date (if that day is a Saturday or a holiday, the due date is the next business day).[43]

> *Example.* An ongoing plan has a calendar plan year. The plan's final filing due date for the 2009 plan year is October 15, 2009.

---

40  PBGC Reg. § 4007.11(b).
41  2008 PBGC Comprehensive Premium Payment Instructions, Who Must File.
42  2008 PBGC Comprehensive Premium Payment Instructions, Description of Data Elements.
43  PBGC Reg. §§ 4007.11(a)(2)(i) and (3)(ii).

For small plans (fewer than 100 participants for the plan year preceding the premium payment year), the due date is the third filing due date.[44]

For new or newly covered plans, the final filing due date is the latest of:

- the last day of the 16th full month that begins on or after the first day of the premium payment year (the effective date, in the case of a new plan); or
- 90 days after the plan's adoption.[45]

For plans changing plan years, the final filing due date is the second or third filing due date as above, or 30 days after the amendment changing the plan year is adopted if later.[46]

Latest penalty free due date. Mid-sized and large plans have until the third filing due date as a penalty free deadline for corrections of the variable premium amount if the premium funding target is not known at the final (second) filing due date.[47]

---

## Penalties for Noncompliance

---

The PBGC may assess penalties for failure to file PBGC forms and for filing late (see section C for information on the party responsible for payment).

**Failure to file**    For failure to file the required PBGC forms, the PBGC may assess a penalty of up to $1,100 per day.[48] Before assessing the penalty, however, the PBGC will generally issue a preliminary notice to allow the plan to provide information that the agency should consider in making a penalty determination.[49] Plans have 30 days after a penalty is assessed to request further review.[50]

---

[44]  PBGC Reg. 4007.11(a)(1).
[45]  PBGC Reg. § 4007.11(c).
[46]  PBGC Reg. § 4007.11(b).
[47]  PBGC Reg. 4007.11(a)(2)(ii) and (3)(iv).
[48]  ERISA § 4071; PBGC Reg. § 4071.3.
[49]  PBGC Prop. Reg. § 4071.4, Appendix § 12.
[50]  PBGC Prop. Reg. § 4071.4, Appendix § 14.

**Late filings**     The PBGC will assess interest and late payment charges based on the outstanding premium payment due.[51]

**Interest charges**     The interest charged for late premium payments accrues from the day payment was due until the time of payment. The rate is the interest rate used for the underpayment of taxes. PBGC will not waive interest charges.[52] Interest is not charged after the date of PBGC's bill, however, if paid within 30 days of the date of the bill.[53]

**Late payment penalty charges**     Unless the PBGC grants a waiver, the late payment charge is equal to the greater of 5 percent of the unpaid premium per month (or fraction of a month) or $25. This late payment charge will not exceed 100 percent of the unpaid premium.[54]

    The late payment charge for plan sponsors who self-correct late premiums is reduced to 1 percent for each month the premium is late. To self-correct, a plan sponsor must pay the late premium before the PBGC issues a written notice (e.g., statement of account or past-due filing notice).[55]

**Underestimation of participant count**     The late payment charges apply to plans underestimating the participant count on the e-filing of Form 1-ES, unless the amount paid is at least

- 90 percent of the flat rate premium due or, if less,
- the prior year's final participant count multiplied by the current year flat rate and the remainder of the flat rate is paid by the final filing due date.[56]

**Waiver before filing due date**     Before the filing due date, the responsible payor may ask the PBGC to waive the late payment charge. To obtain a waiver, the plan must show substantial hardship would result from timely payments or other good cause and that it can pay the premium within 60 days after the due date.[57]

---

[51]  PBGC Reg. §§ 4007.7, 4007.8.
[52]  PBGC Op. Ltrs. 76-6 (Dec. 12, 1976) and 76-48 (Apr. 12, 1978).
[53]  PBGC Reg. § 4007.7(b).
[54]  ERISA § 4007(b); PBGC Reg. § 4007.8(a).
[55]  PBGC Reg. § 4007.8(a)(1).
[56]  PBGC Reg. § 4007.8(g).
[57]  ERISA § 4007(b)(1); PBGC Reg. § 4007.8(b).

**Waiver after the filing due date**

After the filing due date, the PBGC may waive all or part of a penalty if:

- the responsible payor demonstrates reasonable cause;[58]
- the responsible payor relied on an erroneous but not frivolous, interpretation of the law;[59] or
- the error was caused by a change in the law enacted shortly before the due date.[60]

Action or inaction of outside parties, such as actuaries, attorneys, and accountants, is not reasonable cause for a failure. It is considered in applying PBGC's waiver authority as if the outside individual were part of the employer's organization.[61]

**Reasonable cause**

In general, there is reasonable cause for a failure to pay a premium on time to the extent that the failure arises from circumstances beyond the payor's control that could not be avoided by the exercise of ordinary business care and prudence.[62] This does not include overlooking legal requirements.[63] The size of the organization and the size of the underpayment are considered.[64]

Facts that the PBGC considers to determine reasonable cause include the following:

- What caused the underpayment and when it happened
- What prevented the payment from being made
- Whether the failure could have been anticipated
- What the response was, including what steps were taken and how quick the response[65]

Situations that might justify a waiver for reasonable cause include the following:

- The unexpected absence of an individual responsible for paying the premium or filing the information
- A fire or other disaster that destroys relevant plan records
- The plan's reliance on erroneous advice given by a PBGC employee

---

58  PBGC Reg. § 4007, Appendix § 21(b)(2).
59  PBGC Reg. § 4007, Appendix § 21(b)(3).
60  PBGC Reg. § 4007, Appendix § 21(b)(3)(iii).
61  PBGC Reg. § 4007, Appendix § 21(c).
62  PBGC Reg. § 4007, Appendix § 22(a).
63  PBGC Reg. § 4007, Appendix § 22(b).
64  PBGC Reg. § 4007, Appendix § 22(d) and (e).
65  PBGC Reg. § 4007, Appendix § 23.

- The plan's inability to obtain the information required for compliance[66]

**Address for waivers**

Requests for waivers should be sent to the following address:[67]

By e-mail:

Premiums@pbgc.gov

By mail:

Pension Benefit Guaranty Corporation
Department 77840
P.O. Box 77000
Detroit, MI 48277-0840

By delivery service:

Pension Benefit Guaranty Corporation
JP Morgan Chase Bank, N.A.
9000 Haggerty Road
Department 77840
Mail Code M11-8244
Belleville, MI 48111

**Caution.** The above addresses were correct at the time this edition went to press. Because government addresses occasionally change, the addresses should be confirmed before a waiver request is sent.

---

[66] PBGC Reg. § 4007, Appendix § 24.
[67] 2008 PBGC Comprehensive Premium Payment Instructions, Appendix 2.

# E. Notice of Reportable Event

Generally, all plans covered by the PBGC Insurance Program must notify the PBGC of certain "reportable events."[68] For some events, notice is required in advance of the event; for others, notice is required after the event occurs.

The purpose of this notification is to warn the PBGC of possible plan difficulties so it can monitor the plan or possibly terminate it.

**Exceptions**

Multiemployer plans and certain terminating plans that have either distributed all plan assets or had a trustee appointed under ERISA are excused from reporting.[69]

In addition, PBGC has waived the requirement to report certain events and provides waivers for others if certain conditions are met.

**Forms**

To notify the PBGC of certain "reportable events," a plan may use either PBGC Form 10 or PBGC Form 10-Advance. The PBGC's filing rules are explained in Section B of this chapter.

**Reportable events**

Reporting is required for the following events:

- *Active Participant Reduction.* The number of active participants in the plan is less than 80 percent of the number at the beginning of the year or 75 percent of the number at the beginning of the prior plan year, unless a regulatory waiver applies.[70] (See discussion of active participant reduction waiver below.)
- *Failure to Make Minimum Funding Payment.* A required quarterly payment or payment to avoid a deficiency in the plan's funding standard account is not made. Filing Form 200 satisfies the notice of reportable event requirement.[71] (See Section F of this chapter.)
- *Inability to Pay Benefits When Due.* The plan cannot currently (or may not in the future be able to) pay benefits due under the plan.

---

[68]  ERISA § 4043(a) and (b).
[69]  PBGC Reg. § 4043.4(b) and (c).
[70]  ERISA § 4043(c)(3); PBGC Reg. § 4043.23.
[71]  ERISA § 4043(c)(5); PBGC Reg. §§ 4043.25, 4043.81.

However, delays necessary for verifying a participant's eligibility, for locating a participant, or for any other administrative reason that lasts less than the shorter of two months or two full benefit payment periods are excepted from this requirement. Notice is waived unless the plan covered 100 or fewer lives on each day during the prior year.[72]

- *Distributions to Substantial Owner.* The plan distributed $10,000 or more during a 12-month period to a substantial owner (for any reason other than death) and, after the distribution, the plan had unfunded vested benefits, unless a regulatory waiver applies as described further below.[73]

- *Change in Contributing Sponsor or Controlled Group.* A controlled group member ceases to be a member of the plan's controlled group. This does not include reorganizations involving a mere change in identity, form, or place of organization.[74] Reporting waivers for is event are discussed below.

- *Liquidation.* The employer or member of the employer's controlled group liquidates (or liquidates into another controlled group member), institutes proceedings to dissolve, or liquidates under federal or state bankruptcy proceedings.[75] Reporting waivers for this event are discussed below.

- *Extraordinary Dividend on Stock Redemption.* The employer or any member of the employer's controlled group declares an extraordinary dividend or redeems, during any 12-month period, 10 percent or more of the total combined voting power or total value of shares of all classes of stock for the entire controlled group.[76] Reporting waivers for this event are discussed below.

- *Transfer of Benefit Liabilities.* During any 12-month period, 3 percent or more of the benefit liabilities are transferred to an employer outside of the controlled group or to a plan maintained by an employer outside the controlled group.[77] Reporting waivers for this event are discussed below.

- *Application for Minimum Funding Waiver.* A plan files an application for a minimum-funding waiver with the IRS.[78] There is no waiver for this event.

- *Loan Default.* The employer or any controlled group member defaults on a loan with an outstanding balance of $10 million or more because (1) the borrower fails to make a required payment, (2) the lender accelerates the loan, or (3) the lender sends a written notification that

---

72 ERISA § 4043(c)(6); PBGC Reg. § 4043.26.
73 ERISA § 4043(c)(7); PBGC Reg. § 4043.27.
74 ERISA § 4043(c)(9); PBGC Reg. § 4043.29.
75 ERISA § 4043(c)(10); PBGC Reg. § 4043.30.
76 ERISA § 4043(c)(11); PBGC Reg. § 4043.31.
77 ERISA § 4043(c)(12); PBGC Reg. § 4043.32.
78 ERISA § 4043(c)(13); PBGC Reg. § 4043.33.

the loan is in default because the borrower's cash reserves drop below a certain level, the borrower experiences an unusual or catastrophic event, or the borrower fails to meet agreed-upon financial performance levels.[79] Reporting waivers for this event are discussed below.

- *Bankruptcy or Similar Settlement.* The employer or any controlled group member becomes involved in a bankruptcy, insolvency, or similar proceeding; a proceeding that effects a composition, extension, or settlement with creditors; executes a general assignment for the benefit of creditors; or undertakes to effect any other nonjudicial composition, extension, or settlement with substantially all of its creditors.[80] The notice requirement is waived if each affected entity is a foreign entity other than a foreign parent.

**Waivers (post-event filings only)**

Specific waivers for events as noted above follow. Note that *funding based waivers* mentioned for these rules generally include having no variable rate premium obligation for the current year or meeting specific asset to liability goals. The plan's enrolled actuary can assess the availability of these waivers.

**Active participant reduction waiver**

If the total number of active participants in a plan decreases to less than 80 percent of the total at the beginning of the plan year, or less than 75 percent of the total at the beginning of the previous year, the PBGC must be notified unless one of the following applies:

- The plan had fewer than 100 participants at the beginning of the current or prior plan year.[81]
- The plan meets a funding based waiver.[82]
- The plan is at least 80 percent funded for vested benefits as of the last day of the prior year, and the active participant reduction would not be reportable if only those reductions resulting from operations ceasing at one or more facilities were taken into account.[83]

**Failure to make minimum funding**

The notice requirement is waived if the required payment is made by the 30th day after its due date.[84]

---

[79] ERISA § 4043(c)(13); PBGC Reg. § 4043.34.
[80] ERISA § 4043(c)(13); PBGC Reg. § 4043.35.
[81] PBGC Reg. § 4043.23(c)(1).
[82] PBGC Reg. § 4043.23(c)(2).
[83] PBGC Reg. § 4043.23(c)(3).
[84] PBGC Reg. § 4043.25(c).

**payments waiver**

In addition, small employers need not file a 2008 notice of reportable event for failing to make quarterly contributions. This reportable event waiver applies to:

- employers with fewer than 100 participants in all defined benefit plans for the 2007 plan year; and
- employers with fewer than 500 participants in all defined benefit plans for the 2007 plan year that were not required to provide a variable rate premium participant notice for the 2007 plan year because the notice was not returned under PBGC regulations in effect for 2006 (e.g., the plan was at least 90 percent funded).[85]

**Distribution to substantial owner waiver**

A plan must notify the PBGC of a distribution to a substantial owner of $10,000 or more within a one-year period unless one of the following applies:

- Distributions made within a 12-month period ending on the date of the distribution do not exceed the Code Section 415 defined benefit dollar limit as of the reportable event date.[86] See Appendix A for the dollar limit adjusted to reflect changes in cost of living.
- The plan meets a *funding based waiver.*[87]
- Distributions during the one-year period ending on the reportable event date do not exceed 1 percent of the plan assets reported on Form 5500 for either of the two preceding plan years.[88]

**Change in contributing sponsor or controlled group waiver**

The requirement to notify PBGC of a change in contributing sponsor or controlled group is waived if:

- the departing entity represents a de minimis 10 percent segment of the plan's old controlled group;[89]
- each departing entity is a foreign entity other than a foreign parent;[90]
- the plan meets a *funding based waiver;*[91] or
- the contributing sponsor is a public company and vested benefits are 80 percent funded based on the fair market value of the plan's assets as of the last day of the prior plan year.[92]

---

85   PBGC Tech. Update 08-2.
86   PBGC Reg. § 4043.27(c)(1).
87   PBGC Reg. § 4043.27(c)(2).
88   PBGC Reg. § 4043.27(c)(3).
89   PBGC Reg. § 4043.29(c)(1).
90   PBGC Reg. § 4043.29(c)(2).
91   PBGC Reg. § 4043.29(c)(3).
92   PBGC Reg. § 4043.29(c)(4).

**Liquidation waiver**

The requirement to notify PBGC of a liquidation of a controlled group member is waived if:

- the liquidating entity represents a de minimis 10 percent segment of the plan's old controlled group and plan sponsorship continues within the controlled group;[93]
- each liquidating entity is a foreign entity other than a foreign parent;[94]
- plan sponsorship continues within the controlled group and the plan meets a *funding based waiver*;[95] or
- plan sponsorship continues within the controlled group, the contributing sponsor is a public company, and vested benefits are 80 percent funded based on the fair market value of the plan's assets as of the last day of the prior plan year.[96]

**Extraordinary dividend or stock redemption**

The requirement to notify PBGC of an extraordinary dividend or stock redemption is waived if:

- the entity making a distribution represents a de minimis 5 percent segment of the plan's controlled group;[97]
- each entity making a distribution is a foreign entity other than a foreign parent;[98]
- the entity making the distribution is a foreign parent and the distribution is made solely to other members of the controlled group;[99] or
- the plan meets a *funding based waiver*.[100]

**Transfer of benefit liabilities**

The requirement to notify PBGC of the transfer of benefit liabilities outside the plan sponsor's current controlled group is waived if:

- the entire plan is transferred to one other plan;[101]
- the transfer complies with IRC § 414(l) transfer requirements using reasonable assumptions and, when aggregated with other transfers during the plan year, consumes less than 3 percent of assets;[102]
- the transfer complies with IRC § 414(l) transfer requirements using PBGC annuity assumptions;[103] or

---

[93]  PBGC Reg. § 4043.30(c)(1).
[94]  PBGC Reg. § 4043.30(c)(2).
[95]  PBGC Reg. § 4043.30(c)(3).
[96]  PBGC Reg. § 4043.30(c)(4).
[97]  PBGC Reg. § 4043.31(c)(2).
[98]  PBGC Reg. § 4043.31(c)(3).
[99]  PBGC Reg. § 4043.31(c)(4).
[100]  PBGC Reg. § 4043.31(c)(5).
[101]  PBGC Reg. § 4043.32(c)(1).
[102]  PBGC Reg. § 4043.32(c)(2).
[103]  PBGC Reg. § 4043.32(c)(3).

- the transfer complies with IRC § 414(l) transfer requirements using reasonable assumptions and after the transfer each transferee and transferor plan is fully funded using PBGC annuity rates.[104]

**Loan Default**   The requirement to notify PBGC of a significant loan default by a controlled group employer is waived if:

- the default is cured, or waived by the lender, within 30 days, or the deadline in the loan agreement, if later;[105]
- the debtor is a foreign entity other than a foreign parent;[106] or
- the plan meets a funding based waiver.[107]

**Content requirements**   The Notice of Reportable Event sent to the PBGC must include general information and, for certain events, specific information relating to the particular reportable event.[108] For a detailed list of the items to include in the notice, see Table 6-1 at the end of this section.

**Due date**   Generally, either the employer or plan administrator must file the Notice of Reportable Event with the PBGC no later than 30 days after it knows or has reason to know that a reportable event has occurred.[109] In some cases, additional time linked to various Form 5500 and PBGC filing deadlines is provided.[110]

**Advance Notice**   For certain events, the PBGC requires the contributing plan sponsor (not the plan administrator) to provide notice 30 days *in advance* of certain events if the following conditions apply:[111]

- The sponsor and any other member of a controlled group to which the reportable event relates is a privately held company (i.e., does not file under the Securities Exchange Act of 1934); and
- The sponsor is a member of a controlled group with plans that, in the aggregate, have unfunded vested benefits of more than $50 million and a funded vested benefit percentage of less than 90 percent.

---

[104]   PBGC Reg. § 4043.32(c)(4).
[105]   PBGC Reg. § 4043.34(c)(1).
[106]   PBGC Reg. § 4043.34(c)(2).
[107]   PBGC Reg. § 4043.34(c)(3).
[108]   PBGC Reg. § 4043.3(b).
[109]   PBGC Reg. §§ 4043.3(a)(1), 4043.20.
[110]   PBGC Reg. §§ 4043.23(d), 4043.27(d), 4043.29(d), 4043.30(d), and 4043.31(d).
[111]   ERISA § 4043(b)(3); PBGC Reg. § 4043.61(b).

For these advance notice events, different waivers apply than for the post-event rules as described above. The reportable events that require advance notice are the following:

- A change in contributing sponsor or controlled group[112]
  *Waiver*: 500 or fewer participants in a transferred plan, or departing entities represent a de minimis 5 percent segment of the old controlled group
- The liquidation of a member of the sponsor's controlled group[113]
  *Waiver*: Liquidating entities represent a de minimis 5 percent segment of the old controlled group, and plan sponsorship continues with controlled group
- An extraordinary dividend or stock redemption[114]
  *Waiver*: Entities making distribution represent a de minimis 5 percent segment of controlled group
- The transfer of benefit liabilities outside the controlled group[115]
  *Waiver*: Same as for post-event report, except that waiver based on PBGC annuity assumptions is limited to transfers involving 500 or fewer participants
- Application for minimum funding waiver[116]
  *Waiver*: Not waived, but deadline is extended to 10 days after the request for the waiver is submitted
- A loan default by the sponsor or a member of its controlled group[117]
  *Waiver*: Notice requirement is waived if the default is cured or waived within 10 days, or lender's period if later. Notice deadline is extended to 10 days after default or the day after receipt of written notice, acceleration of the loan, or expiration of the cure period in the loan agreement, if later
- The bankruptcy or similar settlement of the sponsor or a member of its controlled group[118]
  *Waiver*: Not waived, but deadline is extended to 10 days after the date of the reportable event

If an advance notice is filed, there is no need to file a post-event notice after the reportable event occurs.[119]

For a summary of the post-event and advance reportable event notice requirements, see Table 6-2 at the end of this section.

---

[112]   ERISA § 4043(c)(9); PBGC Reg. § 4043.62.
[113]   ERISA § 4043(c)(10); PBGC Reg. § 4043.63.
[114]   ERISA § 4043(c)(11); PBGC Reg. § 4043.64.
[115]   ERISA § 4043(c)(12); PBGC Reg. § 4043.65.
[116]   ERISA § 4043(c)(13); PBGC Reg. § 4043.66.
[117]   ERISA § 4043(c)(13); PBGC Reg. § 4043.67.
[118]   ERISA § 4043(c)(13); PBGC Reg. § 4043.68.
[119]   ERISA § 4043(a).

**Mailing addresses**

PBGC Form 10, Post-Event Notice of Reportable Event and Form 10-Advance, Advance Notice of Reportable Event, along with required information must be sent to the PBGC by mail, commercial delivery service, or hand delivery to the following address:[120]

> Pension Benefit Guaranty Corporation
> Department of Insurance Supervision and Compliance
> 1200 K Street, N.W.
> Washington, D.C. 20005-4026

The Form 10 Post-Event Notice of Reportable Event may also be submitted by e-mail. The e-mail address is *post-event.report@pbgc.gov.*

The Form 10-Advance, Advance Notice of Reportable Event may also be submitted by e-mail. The e-mail address is *advance.report@pbgc.gov.*

The fax number for either form is: (202) 842-2643. To confirm receipt of a fax, the sender should call (202) 326-4070.

**Note.** These addresses should be checked against the current forms before notices are sent.

**Penalty for noncompliance**

The PBGC may assess a penalty of up to $1,100 per day for failure to provide a Notice of Reportable Event or an Advance Notice of Reportable Event.[121]

In deciding whether to assess a penalty, the PBGC may consider aggravating and mitigating factors.[122] However, the full $1,100 per day penalty is generally assessed for failure to file an Advance Notice of a Reportable Event.[123]

After a penalty has been assessed, a waiver may be obtained for reasonable cause.[124] (See prior discussion of the "reasonable cause" standard.)

---

[120]  PBGC Reg. § 4043.5; PBGC Form 10 Instructions and Form 10-Advance Instructions.
[121]  ERISA § 4071; PBGC Reg. §§ 4043.3(e), 4071.3.
[122]  Prop. Reg. § 4071.4, Appendix §§ 22–24.
[123]  Prop. Reg. § 4071.4, Appendix § 28(d).
[124]  Prop. Reg. § 4071.4, Appendix §§ 22(d), 31–35.

**Table 6-1**
**Notice of Reportable Event Content Requirements***

*The information listed in this table is from PBGC Regulations Section 4043.3, PBGC Form 10, and PBGC Form 10-Advance

| General Information | |
| --- | --- |
| 1 | Name of plan |
| 2 | Contributing sponsor's name, address, and telephone number and individual who should be contacted |
| 3 | Plan administrator's name, address, and telephone number and name of individual to contact. |
| 4 | Contributing sponsor's employer identification number (EIN) and plan number (PN) |
| 5 | Brief statement of the pertinent facts relating to the reportable event |
| 6 | Copy of the plan document currently in effect (i.e., a copy of the last plan restatement and all subsequent amendments) |
| 7 | Copy of the most recent actuarial statement and opinion (if any) relating to plan |
| 8 | Statement of any material change in the plan assets or liabilities occurring after the date of the most recent actuarial statement and opinion |

*Note.* If PBGC forms are used, many of these items are not required to be submitted as part of the initial filing. However, PBGC may request these or other items after reviewing the initial filing.

**Table 6-1 (*cont'd*)**
**Notice of Reportable Event Content Requirements**

| Item | Specific Information |
|---|---|
| Additional Information | If reportable event is *Active Participant Reduction*, include:<br><br>• A statement explaining the reason for the reduction (e.g., facility shutdown or sale)<br><br>• The number of active participants at the beginning of the preceding plan year, beginning of current plan year, and date of the event |
| | If reportable event is a *Failure to Make Minimum Funding Payment*, include:<br><br>• The due date and amount of the missed contribution and the due date and amount for the next payment<br><br>• The name of each controlled group plan member (if any) and its ownership relationship to other controlled group members<br><br>• The name, contributing sponsor, employer identification number (EIN), and plan number (PN) of each plan maintained by any controlled group member (if any)<br><br>• A copy of the most recent actuarial valuation |
| | If reportable event is *Inability to Pay Benefits When Due*, include:<br><br>• The date and amount of any missed benefit payments<br><br>• The next date on which the plan is expected to be unable to pay benefits, the amount of the projected shortfall, and the number of participants and beneficiaries affected by the projected shortfall<br><br>• The amount of the plan's liquid assets at the end of the quarter and the amount of disbursements for such quarter<br><br>• The name, address, and phone number of the plan trustee and custodian (if any)<br><br>• A copy of the most recent actuarial valuation |
| | If reportable event is *Distribution to a Substantial Owner*, include:<br><br>• The substantial owner's name, address, and telephone number<br><br>• The amount, form, and date of each distribution<br><br>• A copy of the most recent actuarial valuation for the plan |

**Table 6-1 (*cont'd*)**
**Notice of Reportable Event Content Requirements**

| Item | Specific Information |
|---|---|
| Additional Information (*cont'd*) | If reportable event is *Change in Contributing Sponsor or Controlled Group*, include:<br><br>• The expected effective date of event (for advance reporting only)<br><br>• The name of each member in the plan's old and new controlled groups, and the member's ownership relationship to the other members<br><br>• The name and plan number (PN) of each plan maintained by any member of the new or old controlled group, contributing sponsor, and the sponsor's name, and employer identification number (EIN)<br><br>• For advance reporting, a copy of the most recent audited (or, if not available, unaudited) financial statements, and the interim financial statements for the plan's contributing plan sponsor (both old and new, if change in plan sponsorship) and any persons who will cease to be in the controlled group |
| | If reportable event is *Liquidation*, include:<br><br>• The expected effective date of event (for advance reporting)<br><br>• The name of each controlled group member before and after the liquidation and its relationship to other members in the controlled group<br><br>• The name and plan number (PN) of each plan maintained by any member of the controlled group, contributing sponsor and the sponsor's name, and employer identification number (EIN)<br><br>• A copy of the most recent actuarial valuation for each plan in the controlled group (for advance reporting only) |
| | If reportable event is *Extraordinary Dividend or Stock Redemption*, include:<br><br>• The name and employer identification number (EIN) of person making the distribution<br><br>• The date and amount of any cash distributions during the fiscal year<br><br>• The date and amount of any non-cash distributions during the fiscal year, the fair market value of each asset distributed and the date(s) distributed<br><br>• A statement about whether the amounts were distributed to a controlled group member |
| | If reportable event is a *Transfer of Benefit Liabilities*, include:<br><br>• The name of the transferee plan and each contributing sponsor of each transferee plan, employer identification number (EIN), and plan number (PN)<br><br>• An explanation of the actuarial assumptions used to determine the value of benefit liabilities (and plan assets, if appropriate) for each transfer<br><br>• The estimate of the assets and liabilities transferred and the number of participants whose benefits are transferred<br><br>*Note: The PBGC will accept a copy of the Form 5310-A filed with the IRS to the extent it provides this information. See PBGC Form 10, Additional Information To Be Filed.* |

**Table 6-1 (*cont'd*)**
**Notice of Reportable Event Content Requirements**

| Item | Specific Information |
|---|---|
| Additional Information (*cont'd*) | If reportable event is an *Application for Minimum Funding Waiver*, include:<br><br>• A copy of the waiver application and all attachments |
| | If reportable event is a *Loan Default*, include:<br><br>• Copies of relevant loan documents (e.g., promissory note or security agreement)<br><br>• Due date(s) and amount(s) of any missed payment(s)<br><br>• A copy of any default notice from the lender<br><br>• A copy of any acceleration notice from the lender |
| | If reportable event is an *Application for Bankruptcy or Similar Settlement*, include:<br><br>• Copies of all papers filed in the relevant proceeding (including but not limited to petitions and supporting schedules) and docket sheet or other list of documents filed<br><br>• The last date for filing claims, if known<br><br>• The name, address, and phone number of any trustee or receiver (or similar person)<br><br>• The name of each controlled group plan member and its relationship to other members in the controlled group<br><br>• For each plan maintained by any controlled group member, the plan name, contributing sponsor's name, employer identification number (EIN), and plan number (PN)<br><br>• A copy of the most recent actuarial valuation for each plan in the controlled group |

**Table 6-2**
**PBGC Reportable Events Chart**

Plan administrators and contributing sponsors of single-employer defined benefit plans are required to notify the PBGC of a reportable event not later than 30 days after certain plan or corporate events have occurred. Contributing sponsors of a plan sponsored by any privately-owned entity with an aggregate unfunded vested benefit of more than $50 million and aggregated funded vested benefit percentage of less than 90 percent must give 30 days advance notice of certain reportable events. If applicable criteria are satisfied, the PBGC allows waivers of these requirements or extensions of the filing deadlines. This chart summarizes the events to watch for and available waivers.

| Reportable Event | Description | 30-Day Notice (Form 10) | Advance Notice (Form 10-Advance) |
|---|---|---|---|
| Minimum funding waiver | Application for minimum funding waiver. | Not waived. | Not waived, but deadline is extended to 10 days after the request for the waiver is submitted. |
| Failure to meet minimum funding standards | Failure to meet minimum funding standards or to pay amount required as a condition of a funding waiver. | Waived if: <br> 1. the required installment is paid by the 30th day after its due date; or <br> 2. in the case of quarterly contributions, <br> a) if the plan covered 100 or fewer lives on each day during the prior year; or <br> b) if the plan covered 500 or fewer lives and the variable rate premium Participant Notice was not needed for the current or prior year. <br> However, if any unpaid installment, when added to prior unpaid balances exceeds $1 million, Form 200 must be filed within 10 days of the payment's due date. | Not required. |
| Inability to pay benefits when due | Current inability to pay unless: <br> • need to verify eligibility <br> • can't locate <br> • administrative delay up to two months | Waived, unless plan covered 100 or fewer lives on each day during prior year. | Not required. |

| | | Waived if: | Waived if: |
|---|---|---|---|
| | Projected inability<br>• liquid assets less than 2 X disbursements for quarter | | |
| *Transfer of benefit liabilities* | Transfer of 3 percent or more of benefit *liabilities*, within any 12-month period to plan outside controlled group. | Waived if:<br>1. complete transfer of the entire plan to one other plan;<br>2. transfer complies with Code sec. 414(l) using reasonable assumptions and, when aggregated with other transfers during the plan year, consumes less than 3 percent of *assets*;<br>3. transfer complies with 414(l) using PBGC annuity assumptions; or<br>4. transfer complies with 414(l) using reasonable assumptions and after the transfer each transferee and transferor plan is fully funded using PBGC annuity rates. | Waived if:<br>1. complete transfer of the entire plan to one other plan;<br>2. transfer complies with Code sec. 414(l) using reasonable assumptions and, when aggregated with other transfers during the plan year, consumes less than 3 percent of *assets*;<br>3. transfer involves 500 or fewer participants and complies with 414(l) using PBGC annuity assumptions; or<br>4. transfer complies with 414(l) using reasonable assumptions and after the transfer each transferee and transferor plan is fully funded using PBGC annuity rates. |
| *Active participant reduction* | Number of active plan participants is reduced to less than 80 percent of the total number of active participants as of the beginning of the plan's current plan year, or to less than 75 percent of the total number of active participants as of the beginning of the plan's previous plan year. | Waived if:<br>1. plan has fewer than 100 participants as of the beginning of either the current or the previous plan year; or<br>2. plan meets select funding exceptions. | Not required. |

**Table 6-2 (cont'd)**
**PBGC Reportable Events Chart**

| Reportable Event | Description | 30-Day Notice (Form 10) | Advance Notice (Form 10-Advance) |
|---|---|---|---|
| Distribution to substantial owner | Non-death distributions to a substantial owner in excess of $10,000 leaving unfunded nonforfeitable benefits. | Waived, if:<br>1. total distribution does not exceed the defined benefit dollar limit for the year;<br>2. plan meets select funding exceptions; or<br>3. total distribution does not exceed 1 percent of assets at end of either of two preceding plan years. | Not required. |
| Change in contributing sponsor or controlled group | Transaction involving a change in sponsor or controlled group. | Waived if:<br>1. departing entity represents a de minimis 10 percent segment of the plan's old controlled group;<br>2. each departing entity is a foreign entity other than a foreign parent; or<br>3. plan meets select funding exceptions. | Waived if:<br>1. 500 or fewer participants in transferred plan; or<br>2. de minimis 5 percent segment |
| Liquidation | Liquidation of member of the contributing sponsor's controlled group. | Waived if:<br>1. liquidating entity represents a de minimis 10 percent segment of the plan's controlled group and plan sponsorship continues within controlled group;<br>2. each departing entity is a foreign entity other than a foreign parent; or<br>3. plan sponsorship continues within controlled group and the plan meets select funding exceptions. | Waived if:<br>1. de minimis 5 percent segment; and<br>2. plan sponsorship continues within controlled group |

| Event | Description | Waived | Notice deadline |
|---|---|---|---|
| *Extraordinary dividend on stock redemption* | Extraordinary dividend declared (more than current year and four year adjusted gross income) or more than 10 percent of the company's assets redeemed. | Waived if: 1. person making distribution is a de minimis 5 percent segment of the plan's controlled group; 2. person making distribution is a foreign entity other than a foreign parent; 3. foreign parent makes distribution solely to other members of the plan's controlled group; or 4. the plan meets select funding exceptions. | Waived if de minimis 5 percent segment. |
| *Loan default* | Member of plan's controlled group defaults on loan with outstanding balance of $10 million or more within 30 days without cure (10 days for plan's subject to advance notice rule). | Waived if: 1. default cured or waived within 30 days, or lender's period if later; 2. debtor is a foreign entity other than a foreign parent; or 3. the plan meets select funding exceptions. | Waived if default cured or waived within 10 days, or lender's period if later. Notice deadline extended to 10 days after default or day after receipt of written notice, acceleration of loan, or expiration of cure period in loan agreement, if later. |
| *Bankruptcy or similar settlement* | Bankruptcy, insolvency, or similar settlements of contributing sponsor. | Waived if entity is a foreign entity other than a foreign parent. | Not waived, but deadline extended to 10 days after date of reportable event. |

# F. Notice of Failure to Make Timely Contributions

A contributing sponsor (and the sponsor' parent corporation in the case of a "parent-subsidiary" controlled group) of a defined benefit plan that fails to make required quarterly contributions, or any other required contributions, resulting in an unpaid balance of more than $1 million, must provide the PBGC with Form 200, Notice of Failure to Make Required Contributions.[125] The PBGC's filing rules are explained in Section B.

**Form 200**

Form 200 provides information about the failure to make a required quarterly contribution or other required payment resulting in an accumulated unpaid balance of more than $1 million.[126] An enrolled actuary must certify certain plan funding information included in the filing.[127]

**Exceptions**

The notice requirement applies to all defined benefit plans (except multiemployer plans) covered by the PBGC Insurance Program for which the funding target attainment percentage is less than 100 percent.[128]

**PBGC lien**

If required contributions are not made, there is a lien in favor of the PBGC on all assets of the contributing sponsor, and if the contributing sponsor is part of a controlled group, on all assets of each member of the controlled group. The lien on the employer generally is in the amount of the entire missed contribution, including interest.[129]

**Note.** Filing Form 200 does not perfect the lien. Only the PBGC may perfect and enforce the lien.[130]

**Mailing address**

PBGC Form 200 and required information must be sent by mail, commercial delivery service, or hand delivery to the following address:[131]

---

[125] ERISA § 303(k)(4)(A); I.R.C. § 430(k)(4)(A); PBGC Reg. § 4043.81(a); PBGC Form 200. Notice of Failure to Make Timely Contributions, Who Must File?

[126] *Id.*

[127] PBGC Form 200 Instructions, Notice of Failure to Make Required Contributions, Specific Instructions, Pt. II. Plan Funding Information.

[128] ERISA § 303(k)(2); I.R.C. § 430(k)(2).

[129] ERISA § 303(k)(1), (3); I.R.C. § 430(k)(1), (3).

[130] ERISA § 303(k)(5); I.R.C. § 430(k)(5).

[131] PBGC Form 200 Instructions, Notice of Failure to Make Required Contributions, Where to File?

Pension Benefit Guaranty Corporation
Department of Insurance Supervision and Compliance
1200 K Street, N.W.
Washington, D.C. 20005-4026

Form 200 may also be submitted by e-mail and by fax. The e-mail address is *form200@pbgc.gov*. The fax number is: (202) 842-2643. To confirm receipt of a fax, the sender should call (202) 326-4070.

**Due date**

Form 200 must be filed with the PBGC within 10 days after the day the quarterly contribution or other payment was due.[132]

The filing date is the date on which Form 200 is received by the PBGC. If the last day of the period falls on a Saturday, Sunday, or federal holiday, the due date is the next business day. An electronic transmission will be deemed timely filed if the transmission is received by the PBGC on or before the filing deadline, the transmission contains at least items 1 through 8 on Form 200, and the PBGC receives the remaining required information, including the authorized signatures, no later than the first regular business day after the filing date.[133]

**Note.** The quarterly payment due dates for a calendar year plan are April 15, July 15, October 15, and January 15 of the following year.[134] Deadlines for off-calendar and short plan years are adjusted for corresponding periods.[135]

**Penalty for non-compliance**

The PBGC may assess a penalty of up to $1,100 a day for failure to file Form 200.[136] While the PBGC will consider aggravating and mitigating factors, it generally assesses the full penalty for failure to file Form 200.[137]

Once a penalty is assessed, however, a waiver may be obtained for reasonable cause.[138]

---

[132] ERISA § 303(k)(4)(A); I.R.C. § 430(k)(4)(A); PBGC Reg. § 4043.81(a)(1).
[133] PBGC Form 200 Instructions, Notice of Failure to Make Required Contributions, General Instructions, Filing Date.
[134] ERISA § 303(j)(3)(C); I.R.C. § 430(j)(3)(C)
[135] ERISA § 303(j)(3)(E); I.R.C. § 430(j)(3)(E).
[136] ERISA § 4071; PBGC Reg. § 4071.3.
[137] PBGC Prop. Reg. § 4071.4, Appendix §§ 22-24, 28(e).
[138] PBGC Prop. Reg. § 4071.4, Appendix §§ 22(d), 31-35.

# G. Annual Financial and Actuarial Information Reporting

For post-2007 fiscal years, sponsors of certain underfunded plans must report identifying, financial, and actuarial information annually to the PBGC.[139]

**Affected persons**

In general, a contributing sponsor of a plan and each member of the contributing sponsor's controlled group must file for an information year if:

- the funding target attainment percentage at the valuation date for the preceding plan year of any controlled plan ending in the information year is less than 80 percent;
- any member of a controlled group fails to make a required installment or other required payment to a plan, and, as a result, the conditions for imposition of a lien described in ERISA §§ 303(k)(1)(A) and (B) or Code §§ 430(k)(1)(A) and (B) have been met; or
- any plan maintained by a member of a controlled group has been granted one or more minimum funding waivers totaling in excess of $1 million and, as of the end of the plan year ending with the information year, any portion thereof is still outstanding.[140]

**Required information**

Each affected person (described above) must provide the PBGC annually with:

- such records, documents, or other information necessary to determine the liabilities and assets of plans;
- copies of such person's audited (or, if unavailable, unaudited) financial statements and such other financial information as the PBGC requires;[141]
- the amount of benefit liabilities under the plan determined using PBGC assumptions;
- the funding target of the plan determined as if the plan has been in at-risk status for at least 5 plan years; and
- the funding target attainment percentage of the plan.[142]

---

139  ERISA § 4010 and PBGC Reg. § 4010.1.
140  ERISA § 4010(b) and PBGC Reg. § 4010.4(a).
141  ERISA § 4010(a).
142  ERISA § 4010(d)(1).

The PBGC regulations issued prior to the enactment of the PPA described identifying, plan actuarial, and financial information required to meet the first two listed items. Rules for calculating values for the last three items, added by the PPA, have been proposed.[143]

**When filed**

The information must be filed no later than 105 days after the close of the filer's information year, with a possible extension for certain required actuarial information until 15 days after filing deadline for annual report.[144]

**Electronic filing**

Filing must be submitted electronically. Information on how to file electronically is available on the PBGC's website at http://www.pbgc.gov/practitioners/reporting-and-disclosure/content/page14529.html

**Waivers, extensions, exemptions**

PBGC may waive the filing requirement or may extend the applicable due date(s). The PBGC will exercise this discretion in appropriate cases where it finds convincing evidence supporting a waiver or extension. A request for a waiver or extension must be filed with the PBGC no later than 15 days before the due date and must state the facts and circumstances on which the request is based.[145] PBGC has proposed a waiver of the reporting requirement if the aggregate shortfall of all plans of a controlled group does not exceed $15 million. For this determination, plans with no shortfall are disregarded.[146]

In addition, actuarial information would not be submitted for plans with fewer than 500 participants and a funding shortfall below $15 million.[147] Actuarial information is not needed for overfunded plans, regardless of the number of participants.[148]

PBGC does not require financial or actuarial information from small noncontributing entities in the group (less than 5 percent of revenue and less than 5 percent (or $5 million) of operating income and net assets).[149]

---

[143] PBGC Reg. §§ 4010.6-9; Prop. Reg. § 4010.8.
[144] PBGC Reg. § 4010.10.
[145] PBGC Reg. § 4010.11.
[146] PBGC Prop. Reg. § 4010.11(a).
[147] PBGC Prop. Reg. § 4010.8(c).
[148] PBGC Reg. § 4010.8(c)(2).
[149] PBGC Reg. § 4010.4(d) [4(c) proposed].

**Penalty**    If all of the required information is not provided within the specified time limit, the PBGC may assess a separate penalty against the filer and each member of the filer's controlled group of up to $1,100 for each day that the failure continues.[150]

---

[150]    PBGC Reg. § 4010.13.

# H. Notice of Substantial Cessation of Operations or Withdrawal from Plan

If more than 20 percent of plan participants in a particular plan are separated from employment because an employer ceases operations at a facility in any location,[151] or if a substantial employer withdraws from a nonmultiemployer plan covering employees of unrelated employers,[152] then the plan administrator is required to notify the PBGC of the change. This is true even in the case where a multiple-employer plan is split into separate plans that continue to be maintained by the respective employers.[153]

In these situations, PBGC may seek a bond or escrow in the amount of the unfunded benefit liabilities.[154] In unusual circumstances, PBGC may pursue a partition of the plan[155] and treat a portion of the plan as a terminated plan and the remainder as a separate plan;[156] may accept an appropriate indemnity agreement among employers;[157] or may reach a negotiated arrangement with the employer.[158] In an appropriate case, PBGC may also consider initiating termination[159] and assessing liability.[160]

**Form of notice**  There is no prescribed format for the report. However, PBGC has said that a *Notice of a Substantial Cessation of Operations* may be filed with a *Reportable Event* notice of an active participant reduction if the filing identifies the "4062(e)" event and includes the applicable request for liability determination.[161]

---

[151]  ERISA § 4062(e).
[152]  ERISA § 4063(a).
[153]  2007 Blue Book Q&A 22. [Collection of agency questions from 2007 Enrolled Actuaries Meeting, available on PBGC's Website].
[154]  ERISA §§ 4063(b) and (c).
[155]  ERISA § 4063(d).
[156]  PBGC Opinion Letter 81-14.
[157]  ERISA § 4063(e).
[158]  ERISA § 4067.
[159]  ERISA § 4042(a).
[160]  ERISA §§ 4062 and 4064.
[161]  2007 Blue Book Q&A 20.

**Content**      The notification advises the PBGC of the cessation of operations or plan withdrawal and asks that the PBGC determine the liability of all parties.[162]

**Mailing address**      The report must be filed with the PBGC's Department of Insurance Supervision and Compliance. It may be faxed to DISC at 202-842-2643, e-mailed to *4063.report@pbgc.gov* or mailed to the following address:[163]

> Department of Insurance Supervision and Compliance
> 1200 K Street, NW
> Washington, DC 20005-4026

**Due date**      Notification must be made within 60 days after the cessation of operations or withdrawal.[164]

**Extension and waivers**      None. PBGC has indicated that a waiver is not available, for example, even for a small plan that is excused from reporting the active participant reduction *Reportable Event*.[165]

**Penalty for non-compliance**      The PBGC may assess a penalty of up to $1,100 a day for failure to provide notice.[166] Once a penalty is assessed, however, a waiver may be obtained for reasonable cause.[167]

**Related notification**      The plan administrator of a multiple employer plan should notify each substantial employer contributing to the plan of their status as a substantial employer within six months after the close of each plan year.[168]

---

[162]   ERISA § 4063(a).
[163]   2006 Blue Book Q&A 22.
[164]   ERISA § 4063(a)(1).
[165]   2007 Blue Book Q&A 21.
[166]   ERISA § 4071; PBGC Reg. § 4071.3.
[167]   PBGC Proposed Reg. § 4071.4, Appendix §§ 22(d), 31-35.
[168]   ERISA § 4066.

# I. Single Employer Plan Termination Notices

Plans covered by the PBGC Insurance Program can be terminated under ERISA rules for *Standard Terminations* or *Distress Terminations*. Plans that have sufficient funds to cover all benefits owed to participants and beneficiaries close out under the Standard Termination rules; plans that do not have sufficient funds close out under the Distress Termination rules if all controlled group entities related to the plan sponsor meet one of the distress termination criteria.

**Standard Termination Notices**

A **Notice of Intent to Terminate (NOIT)** is issued at least 60 days and not more than 90 days before the proposed termination date. The NOIT is provided to participants, beneficiaries of deceased participants, alternate payees under qualified domestic relations orders, and employee organizations representing participants.[169] A model NOIT is provided in Appendix B of the standard termination filing instructions (see figure 6-1).

A **Notice of Plan Benefits** is issued to participants, beneficiaries of deceased participants, and alternate payees no later than the date the plan administrator files the Standard Termination Notice (PBGC Form 500) with the PBGC.[170]

A **Standard Termination Notice** (PBGC Form 500, including the Schedule EA-S) is filed with the PBGC on or before the 180th day after the proposed termination date.[171] The PBGC has 60 days after receiving a complete Form 500 to review the termination for compliance with the law and regulations.[172]

A **Notice of Annuity Information** is provided to participants, beneficiaries of deceased participants, alternate payees under qualified domestic relations orders, and employee organizations representing participants no later than 45 days before the distribution date if benefits may be distributed in an annuity form.[173]

---

[169]   PBGC Reg. § 4041.23.
[170]   PBGC Reg. § 4041.24.
[171]   PBGC Reg. § 4041.25.
[172]   PBGC Reg. § 4041.26.
[173]   PBGC Reg. §§ 4041.23 (b)(5) and 4041.27.

A **Schedule MP** and the applicable attachment(s) are sent to the PBGC if the plan has Missing Participants.[174]

A **Notice of Annuity Contract** is provided to participants receiving their plan benefits in the form of an annuity no later than 30 days after the contract is available.[175]

A **Post-Distribution Certification** (PBGC Form 501) is filed with the PBGC no later than 30 days after all plan benefits are distributed. The PBGC will assess a penalty for late filings to the extent the certification is filed more than 90 days after the distribution deadline.[176]

**Distress Termination Notices**

A **Notice of Intent to Terminate (NOIT)** is issued at least 60 days and not more than 90 days before the proposed termination date. The NOIT is provided to participants, beneficiaries of deceased participants, alternate payees under qualified domestic relations orders, and employee organizations representing participants.[177] A model NOIT is provided in Appendix B of the distress termination filing instructions (see Figure 6-2).

A **NOIT** is filed with PBGC using Form 600 (with Schedule REP-D) on or after the date the NOIT is provided to affected parties listed above, but no later than 60 days before the proposed termination date.[178]

A **Distress Termination Notice** (PBGC Form 601, including the Schedule EA-D) is filed with the PBGC on or before the 120th day after the proposed termination date.[179]

A **Notice to Affected Parties** is provided if PBGC determines that the initial filing is noncompliant. The notice informs affected parties that the plan is not going to terminate or, if applicable, that the termination is invalid and that a new NOIT is being or will be issued.[180]

**Participant and benefit information** is filed with the PBGC by the later of (1) 120 days after the proposed termination date or (2) 30 days after receipt of the PBGC's determination that the requirements for a distress termination have been satisfied.[181]

---

[174]   PBGC Reg. § 4050.
[175]   PBGC Reg. § 4041.28 (d).
[176]   PBGC Reg. § 4041.29.
[177]   PBGC Reg. § 4041.43.
[178]   PBGC Reg. § 4041.43(a)(2), (4).
[179]   PBGC Reg. § 4041.45.
[180]   PBGC Reg. § 4041.46(e).
[181]   PBGC Reg. § 4041.45(b).

A **Post-Distribution Certification** (PBGC Form 602) is filed with the PBGC no later than 30 days after all plan benefits are distributed by plans that have sufficient assets to provide at least guaranteed benefits. The distribution and annuity contract notices described above for standard terminations would be used for this purpose.[182]

A **Schedule MP** and the applicable attachment(s) are sent to the PBGC if the plan has Missing Participants.[183]

Plan administrators must **disclose information submitted to PBGC** in connection with a distress termination filing (as well as in connection with PBGC-initiated terminations) upon request from a participant, beneficiary, or employee organization representing plan participants. Requested information must be provided by the plan administrator not later than 15 business days after receipt of the request for information. If the plan administrator has provided information in response to a request and later submits additional information to PBGC related to the proposed distress termination, the plan administrator would have to provide that additional information within 15 business days after the submission to any affected party that had made a previous request. Confidential information that may directly, or indirectly, identify an individual participant or beneficiary may not be disclosed unless authorized by court order.[184]

**Plan Termination Contact Information**

**Standard termination**[185] and coverage inquiries should be directed to (800) 736-2444. Written inquires, and PBGC Forms 500 and 501 may be delivered by hand, mail, or commercial delivery service to:

> Pension Benefit Guaranty Corporation
> Standard Termination Compliance Division, Suite 930
> 1200 K Street N.W.
> Washington, DC 20005-4026

**Distress termination**[186] and coverage inquiries should be directed to (800) 736-2444, ext 4100 or (202) 326-4242.

---

[182] PBGC Reg. § 4041.48, PBGC Distress Termination Filing Instructions.
[183] PBGC Reg. § 4050.
[184] PBGC Prop. Reg. § 4041.51.
[185] PBGC Standard Termination Filing Instructions.
[186] PBGC Form 600 Instructions.

Written inquires, and PBGC Form 600, Form 601, and Form 602 (if required) may be delivered by hand, mail, or commercial delivery service to:

Pension Benefit Guaranty Corporation
Distress Terminations
Department of Insurance Supervision and Compliance
Suite 270
1200 K Street, NW
Washington, DC 20005-4026

**Missing Participant**[187] forms (not payments) are sent to:

Processing and Technical Assistance Branch, Suite 930
1200 K Street NW
Washington, DC 20005-4026

If using the US postal service, the payment for designated benefits and/ or other amounts with a completed payment voucher must be sent to:

Pension Benefit Guaranty Corporation
P.O.Box 64523
Baltimore, MD 21264-4523

If using another delivery service or sending the payment via wire transfer, see the *Missing Participants Filing Instructions*.

Call (800) 736-2444 with inquires about the missing participant program.

---

[187] PBGC Missing Participant Filing Instructions.

## Figure 6-1

## Standard Termination
## MODEL NOTICE OF INTENT TO TERMINATE (NOIT)

*Source*: **PBGC Form 500, APPENDIX B**

---

Month/Day/Year

**NOTICE OF INTENT TO TERMINATE [PLAN NAME]**

The [plan administrator] intends to terminate the [plan name] in a standard termination. The law requires that we provide you with written notice of the proposed termination.

In order for this plan to terminate, plan assets must be sufficient to provide all plan benefits. If the proposed termination does not occur, the [plan administrator] will notify you in writing.

**NAME AND EIN OF EACH CONTRIBUTING SPONSOR:** [Name], EIN: [#########]

**PN:** [###]

**FOR CURRENT RETIREES:** [Include whichever statement applies]

- The proposed termination will not affect your [monthly] benefit amount.
- The proposed termination will affect your [monthly] benefit amount as follows: [explain]

**PROPOSED TERMINATION DATE:** MM/DD/YY

We will notify you in writing if the proposed termination date is changed to a later date.

**CONTACT PERSON:** If you have any questions concerning the plan's termination, contact:

[Name, Address, Phone Number]

**CESSATION OF ACCRUALS:** [Include <u>one</u> of the following statements, whichever applies.]

- Benefit accruals will cease as of the termination date, but will continue if the plan does not terminate;
- A plan amendment has been adopted under which benefit accruals will cease, in accordance with section 204(h) of ERISA, as of [insert either the proposed termination date or a specified date before the proposed termination date, whichever applies], whether or not the plan is terminated; or
- Benefit accruals ceased, in accordance with section 204(h) of ERISA, as of [insert specified date before the NOIT was issued].

**OBTAINING A SUMMARY PLAN DESCRIPTION:**

If you wish to obtain a copy of the summary plan description for your plan, you may [call or write . . . ] **[Include, if applicable:** A reasonable fee to cover the cost of furnishing the SPD may be charged. Please inquire at the time of your request.]

**NOTIFICATION OF PLAN BENEFITS:**

The [plan administrator] will provide you, at a later date, written notification regarding your benefits.

---

## Figure 6-1 (*cont'd*)

## Standard Termination
## MODEL NOTICE OF INTENT TO TERMINATE (NOIT)

**IDENTITY OF INSURER(S):** [For all participants and beneficiaries, except those who will receive benefits in the form of a nonconsensual lump sum, include whichever statement applies.]

- If you will receive a benefit in the form of an annuity, the [plan administrator] intends to purchase the annuity contract for your benefit from (one of) the following insurer(s) listed below. If we decide to select a different insurer, we will notify you in writing no later than 45 days before we purchase the annuity.
  [Insurer(s) Name and Address]
- If you will receive a benefit in the form of an annuity, the [plan administrator] intends to purchase an annuity contract for your benefit from an insurer to be selected at a later date. We will notify you in writing of the name and address of the insurer(s) from whom, or from among whom, we intend to purchase the annuity at least 45 days before we make the purchase.

**END OF PBGC GUARANTEE:**

- After plan assets have been distributed to provide all of your benefit, either through the purchase of an annuity contract or in another form permitted by the plan, PBGC's guarantee of your benefit ends.

**STATE GUARANTY ASSOCIATION COVERAGE:** [Required only first time insurer(s) is/ are identified]

- See enclosed notice.

**Figure 6-2**

**Distress Termination**
**MODEL NOTICE OF INTENT TO TERMINATE (NOIT)**

*Source*: PBGC Form 600, APPENDIX B

---

Month/Day/Year

**NOTICE OF INTENT TO TERMINATE [PLAN NAME]**

The [plan administrator] intends to terminate the [plan name] in a distress termination. The law requires that we provide you with written notice of the proposed termination. If the proposed termination does not occur, the [plan administrator] will notify you in writing.

**NAME AND EIN OF EACH CONTRIBUTING SPONSOR:** [Name] , EIN: [#########]

**PN:** [###]

**PROPOSED TERMINATION DATE:** [MM/DD/YY]

We will notify you if the proposed termination date is changed to a later date.

**CONTACT PERSON:** If you have any questions concerning the plan's termination, contact:

[Name, Address, Phone Number]

**CESSATION OF ACCRUALS:** [Include one of the following statements, whichever applies.]

- Benefit accruals will cease as of the termination date, but will continue if the plan does not terminate;
- A plan amendment has been adopted under which benefit accruals will cease, in accordance with section 204(h) of ERISA, as of [insert either the proposed termination date or a specified date before the proposed termination date, whichever applies], whether or not the plan is terminated; or
- Benefit accruals ceased, in accordance with section 204(h) of ERISA, as of [insert specified date before the NOIT was issued].

**OBTAINING A SUMMARY PLAN DESCRIPTION:**

If you wish to obtain a copy of the summary plan description for your plan, you may [call or write . . . ] **[Include, if applicable:** A reasonable fee to cover the cost of furnishing the SPD may be charged. Please inquire at the time of your request.]

**PLAN FUNDING LEVEL**

The plan does not have sufficient funds to pay all promised benefits. The Pension Benefit Guaranty Corporation (PBGC), a federal government agency, will assure that you receive pension benefits that are guaranteed by law.

**BENEFITS GUARANTEED BY PBGC:** PBGC pays most people all pension benefits, but some people may lose certain benefits that are not guaranteed.

**Figure 6-2 (*cont'd*)**

**Distress Termination**
**MODEL NOTICE OF INTENT TO TERMINATE (NOIT)**

---

**[Include all of the following that may apply to this plan's benefits.]**
The maximum guaranteed benefit that PBGC can pay is set by law each year. For pension plans ending in 2007, for example, the maximum guaranteed amount is $4,125.00 per month ($49,500 per year) for a worker who retires at age 65.

— The maximum benefit will be reduced for an individual who begins receiving payments before age 65.

— The maximum benefit also will be reduced if a pension includes benefits for a survivor or other beneficiary.

PBGC does not guarantee benefits that are not vested when the plan terminates, usually because the individual has not worked enough years for the company.

PBGC does not guarantee benefits for which an individual has not met all age, service, or other requirements at the time the plan terminates.

Benefit increases and new benefits that have been in place for less than a year are not guaranteed. Those that have been in place for less than 5 years are only partly guaranteed.

Early retirement payments that are greater than payments at normal retirement age may not be guaranteed. For example, a supplemental benefit that stops when an individual becomes eligible for Social Security may not be guaranteed.

Benefits other than pension benefits, such as health insurance, life insurance, death benefits, vacation pay, or severance pay are not guaranteed.

PBGC generally does not pay lump sums exceeding $5,000.

PBGC may recoup any pension payments that exceed PBGC's guarantee.

---

# J. Multiemployer Termination, Insolvency, Liability Notices

The plan sponsor of a multiemployer plan must notify the PBGC of a plan termination by amendment or by a mass withdrawal or total cessation of contributory obligations. Unlike single-employer plans, multiemployer plans continue to pay all vested benefits out of existing plan assets and withdrawal liability payments. PBGC's benefit guarantee is payable as financial assistance to the plan and only starts if and when the plan is unable to make payments at the statutorily guaranteed level. Multiemployer plans also notify participants and other interested parties of benefit reductions when insolvent and in reorganization.

Under PPA, participating employers may request information from the plan sponsor about their withdrawal liability even before the plan encounters difficulty. The ERISA § 101(l) notice informs participating employers of their potential withdrawal liability and the basis for the liability determination.

**Note:** See Chapter 9 for information on the participant notices that are required when a multiemployer plan is in critical or endangered status.

**Termination notice requirements**

A *notice of termination by plan amendment*, providing basic plan information,[188] is filed with the PBGC within 30 days after the amendment is adopted or effective, whichever is later.[189]

A *notice of termination due to mass withdrawal*, providing the basic information noted above, plus documents, valuation information and asset values,[190] is filed with the PBGC within 30 days after the last employer withdrew from the plan or 30 days after the first day of the first plan year for which no employer contributions were required under the plan, whichever is earlier.[191]

*Notices of benefit reductions* are provided by the plan sponsor of a plan that has been amended to reduce benefits under the mass withdrawal rules to participants and beneficiaries and the PBGC no later than 45 days after the amendment reducing benefits is adopted (or by the date the first

---

[188]   PBGC Reg. § 4041A.12(a).
[189]   PBGC Reg. § 4041A.11(c)(1).
[190]   PBGC Reg. § 4041A.12(b).
[191]   PBGC Reg. § 4041A.11(c)(2).

reduction occurs, if earlier).[192] Posting of notices is permitted for interested parties other than participants and beneficiaries with benefits in pay status, or expected to be in pay status by the end of the year after the year of adoption of the amendment.[193]

A *notice of benefit restoration* is provided to the PBGC if an amendment is adopted restoring benefits to previous levels.[194]

A *notice of insolvency* is filed with the PBGC, contributing employers, and bargaining parties no later than 30 days after the sponsor determines that the plan is or may become insolvent while under the mass withdrawal rules.[195] The notice is also provided to participants and beneficiaries in pay status and may be delivered with the first benefit payment made more than 30 days after the determination of insolvency.[196] Posting of notices is permitted for interested parties other than participants and beneficiaries with benefits in pay status.[197] In some cases, *annual updates* are required no later than 60 days before the beginning of the plan year for which the annual update is issued.[198]

*Notices of insolvency benefit level* are delivered to PBGC and interested parties (participants, beneficiaries, bargaining parties, contributing employers) within 60 days of the beginning of the insolvency year (or within 60 days after the insolvency determination under PBGC Reg. § 4041A.25(b), if later).[199]

**Reorganization notices**

For plans in reorganization, a *notice of insolvency* is filed with the PBGC, contributing employers, and bargaining parties no later than 30 days after the sponsor determines that the plan is or may become insolvent while under reorganization. The notice is also provided to participants and beneficiaries in pay status and may be delivered with the first benefit payment made more than 30 days after the determination of insolvency.[200] Posting of notices is permitted for interested parties other than participants and beneficiaries with benefits in pay status.[201]

*Notices of insolvency benefit level* for insolvent plans undergoing reorganization are delivered to PBGC and participants and beneficiaries in pay status or reasonably expected to enter pay status during the insolvency

---

[192]  PBGC Reg. § 4281.32.
[193]  PBGC Reg. § 4281.32(c).
[194]  PBGC Reg. § 4281.33.
[195]  PBGC Reg. § 4281.43.
[196]  PBGC Reg. § 4281.43(c).
[197]  PBGC Reg. § 4281.43(e).
[198]  PBGC Reg. § 4281.43(b).
[199]  PBGC Reg. § 4281.45(a) and (b).
[200]  PBGC Reg. § 4245.3.
[201]  PBGC Reg. § 4245.3(d).

year 60 days before the beginning of the insolvency year (or within 60 days after the insolvency determination if the determination is made fewer than 120 days before the beginning of the year).[202] Posting of notices is permitted for interested parties other than participants and beneficiaries with benefits in pay status, or reasonably expected to enter pay status, for the year covered by the notice.[203]

**IRS Notice**

Plan sponsors must notify IRS about certain insolvency determinations.[204] However, IRS and PBGC have indicated that notice to the PBGC will satisfy this requirement pending further regulations from the IRS.[205]

**Potential withdrawal liability notice**

In response to a written request from a contributing employer, the plan sponsor or administrator of a multiemployer plan must provide notice of:

- the contributing employer's estimated withdrawal liability on the last day of the preceding plan year; and
- how the estimated amount was determined.[206]

The explanation of the estimate must include:

- the actuarial assumptions and methods used to determine plan liabilities and assets;
- the data on employer contributions, unfunded vested benefits, annual changes in the plan's unfunded vested benefits; and
- any relevant limitations on the estimated withdrawal liability.[207]

The notice may be provided in written, electronic, or other appropriate form to the extent reasonably accessible to employers to whom the information is required to be provided.[208] The notice must be provided within 180 days of the request. DOL regulations may provide additional time for plans that determine withdrawal liability using the direct attribution method or alternative method.[209]

---

202  PBGC Reg. § 4245.5(a) and (c).
203  PBGC Reg. § 4245.5(e).
204  ERISA § 4245(e) and I.R.C. § 418E(e).
205  Preamble to PBGC Reg § 2674.1, 50 Fed. Reg. 12792 (April 1, 1985).
206  ERISA § 101(l)(1).
207  ERISA § 101(l)(1)(B).
208  ERISA § 101(l)(2)(B).
209  ERISA § 101(l)(2)(A).

# Chapter 7

# Summary Plan Descriptions

---

**Introduction**     Most ERISA pension and welfare plans must comply with the summary plan description (SPD) requirements. This chapter describes the style, format, and content requirements for SPDs, and the deadline for distributing SPDs.

This chapter also describes alternative compliance requirements with respect to SPDs for retirees, beneficiaries, and vested separated participants and for successor pension plans.

**Contents**     This chapter has seven sections:

# A. General Information

Plan administrators of most ERISA-covered pension and welfare plans must distribute summary plan descriptions to plan participants and certain beneficiaries and provide copies to the Department of Labor (DOL) upon request.

**Definition**

A *summary plan description* is a summary of the benefits provided by one or more plans. This summary must include all information required by ERISA, including a description of the benefits, eligibility requirements, funding arrangements, claims procedures, and participant rights under ERISA.

**Reporting requirement**

ERISA plans are not required to file SPDs with the DOL. Instead, plans must provide SPDs to the DOL upon request.[1]

**Disclosure requirement**

Unless an ERISA plan meets one of the exemptions, an SPD must be distributed to plan participants and certain beneficiaries.[2]

**Penalty for non-compliance**

If a plan administrator fails or refuses to provide an SPD within 30 days after receiving a request for one from a plan participant or eligible beneficiary, a court can impose a penalty of up to $110 per day.[3] This penalty is payable to the participant or beneficiary filing civil action.

If a plan administrator fails to provide the DOL with an SPD within 30 days after receiving the agency's request, the DOL may assess a penalty of up to $110 per day (maximum $1,100 per request). The DOL will not impose a penalty if the failure is beyond the plan administrator's reasonable control.[4]

---

[1] DOL Reg. § 2520.104a-8.
[2] ERISA § 104(b).
[3] ERISA § 502(c)(1).
[4] ERISA § 502(c)(6).

# B. Plans Required to Distribute SPDs

**Affected plans**  All pension and welfare plans subject to ERISA must comply with the SPD requirements unless ERISA specifically exempts them from the requirements.[5]

**Exemptions**  The following ERISA plans may be exempt from distributing SPDs to participants and beneficiaries:

- Pension and welfare plans maintained primarily for management or highly compensated employees (referred to as executive plans)[6]
- Dues-financed pension and welfare plans[7]
- Simplified employee pension plans (SEPs)[8]
- Employer-provided day care facilities[9]
- Apprenticeship training programs[10]

These plans are exempt only if they meet certain conditions. In some cases, the conditions include meeting alternative compliance requirements. (See Section B in Chapter 3 for discussion of conditions of exemption.)

---

[5]  ERISA §§ 102(a); 104(b)(1).
[6]  DOL Reg. §§ 2520.104-23, 2520.104-24.
[7]  DOL Reg. §§ 2520.104-26, 2520.104-27.
[8]  DOL Reg. §§ 2520.104-48, 2520.104-49.
[9]  DOL Reg. § 2520.104-25.
[10]  DOL Reg. § 2520.104-22.

# C. Style, Format, and Content Requirements

SPDs must comply with specific ERISA requirements that address, among other things, an SPD's style, format, and content.[11]

## Style and Format

The SPD style and format requirements cover writing style, general format, and foreign languages.[12]

**Writing style**    The SPD must be written in language that the average plan participant can understand, and it must be sufficiently comprehensive to inform participants and beneficiaries of their rights and obligations under the plan.[13]

To fulfill these requirements, factors such as the typical plan participant's level of comprehension and education and the complexity of the plan's terms must be considered. Technical jargon should be kept to a minimum or eliminated altogether. The SPD should contain examples and illustrations, cross-references, and a table of contents.

**General format**    Under the SPD format rules, the SPD:[14]

- Must not mislead, misinform, or fail to inform participants and beneficiaries about the plan
- Must not minimize any description of any exception, limit, reduction, or other restriction on benefits
- Must describe or summarize exceptions, limits, reductions, or other restrictions using style, captions, print type, and prominence that are no less prominent than those used to describe or summarize the plan's benefits
- Must present the plan's advantages and disadvantages without exaggerating the benefits or minmizing the limits

---

[11]    ERISA § 102(a).
[12]    DOL Reg. § 2520.102-2.
[13]    DOL Reg. § 2520.102-2(a).
[14]    DOL Reg. § 2520.102-2(b).

The plan does not have to describe the restrictions and limits in close proximity to the summary of the plan's benefits. If it does not describe them, however, it must include in the summary the page number(s) where participants can find the restrictions and limits.

**Foreign language requirements**

The foreign language requirements apply when a certain number of plan participants speak the same foreign language.[15]

If the requirements apply, the SPD must prominently display a notice in the foreign language common to the the participants, offering them assistance. The notice must clearly state the procedures the participants are to follow to obtain assistance. The following sample notice is from the DOL regulations.[16]

> This booklet contains a summary in English of your plan rights and benefits under Employer A Pension Plan. If you have difficulty understanding any part of this booklet, contact Mr. John Doe, the plan administrator, at his office in Room 123, 456 Main Street, Anywhere City, State 20001. Office hours are from 8:30 a.m. to 5:00 p.m. Monday through Friday. You may also call the plan administrator's office at 202-555-2345 for assistance.

The actual assistance provided does not have to involve written materials. However, the plan administrator must provide the assistance in the foreign language common to the participants and must give the participants a reasonable chance to become informed of their rights and obligations under the plan.

**Determining whether requirements apply**

For plans covering fewer than 100 participants at the beginning of the plan year, the foreign language requirements apply if 25 percent or more of the participants are literate only in the same foreign language.[17]

For plans covering 100 or more participants at the beginning of the plan year, the foreign language requirements apply if either:

- 500 or more participants are literate only in the same foreign language; or
- 10 percent or more of all plan participants are literate only in the same foreign language.[18]

---

[15] DOL Reg. § 2520.102-2(c).
[16] DOL Reg. § 2520.102-2(c)(2).
[17] DOL Reg. § 2520.102-2(c)(1).
[18] DOL Reg. § 2520.102-2(c)(2).

The following example is from the DOL regulations.[19]

> An employer maintains a pension plan that covers 1,000 participants. At the beginning of the plan year. 500 participants are literate only in Spanish and 101 are literate only in Vietnamese. Each of the 1,000 participants must receive an SPD that includes a notice written in Spanish and Vietnamese offering assistance.

Use Figure 7-1 to determine how to comply with the SPD style and format requirements and Figure 7-2 to determining whether foreign language requirements apply to a plan.

**Options for multiple SPDs**  If the plan provides different benefits for various classes of participants and beneficiaries, it can furnish separate SPDs to each class describing the benefits.[20] For example, if the plan provided salaried employees with benefits that are different from those for hourly employees, there can be two SPDs—one for each class.

**Rules for multiple SPDs**  If separate SPDs are created for different classes of participants and beneficiaries, each SPD must satisfy ERISA's style, format, and content requirements.[21] However, an SPD may omit information that does not apply to the class of participants who will receive it.

On the first page of each SPD, the class of participants to which the SPD applies and the plan's coverage of other classes must be clearly identified. If there are too many classes to list on page 1, the classes can be listed elsewhere, but page 1 must identify the location of this information.

---

[19]  *Id.*
[20]  DOL Reg. § 2520.102-4.
[21]  *Id.*

## Figure 7-1

## Complying with SPD Style, Format, and Foreign Language Requirements

| To Comply with: | Plan Must: |
|---|---|
| SPD writing style requirement | • Write the SPD so average plan participant can understand it.<br><br>• Ensure that SPD is comprehensive enough to inform participants/ beneficiaries of rights and obligations under plan. |
| SPD general format requirements | • Ensure that format does *not* mislead, misinform, or fail to inform participants/beneficiaries about plan.<br><br>• Avoid minimizing any description of any exception, limit, reduction, or other benefit restriction.<br><br>• Describe exceptions, limits, reductions, or other restrictions, using style, captions, print type, and prominence no less prominent than those used to describe plan benefits.<br><br>• Present plan's advantages and disadvantages without exaggerating benefits or minimizing limits. |
| SPD foreign language requirements | • Include a notice in SPD offering assistance in foreign language common to participants, if foreign language requirements apply (see Figure 7-2 on next page). |

## Figure 7-2

## Determining Whether Foreign Language Requirements Apply

| *If, at Start of Plan Year, Plan Covered:* | *And Number of Participants Literate Only in Same Foreign Language Is:* | *Then Foreign Language Requirements:* |
|---|---|---|
| fewer than 100 participants | less than 25% of *all* participants | do NOT apply |
| | 25% or more of *all* participants | APPLY |
| 100 or more participants | • fewer than 500 participants<br>and<br>• less than 10% of *all* participants | do NOT apply |
| | • 500 or more participants<br>or, if fewer,<br>• 10% or more of *all* participants | APPLY |

## SPD Content

ERISA requires a plan to include specific information in its SPD. The specific required information includes:[22]

- General information about the plan (e.g., name of plan, plan sponsor, and plan administrator)
- Eligibility requirements
- Summary of benefits
- Plan contributions and other funding information
- Claims procedures
- ERISA rights statement

The information provided must accurately reflect the plan contents as of a date no earlier than 120 days before the SPD is distributed.

See Figure 7-3 for the list of information that must be included in SPDs.

## ERISA Rights Statement

SPDs must explain participant (and beneficiary) rights under ERISA.[23] This explanation is called the ERISA rights statement.

In general, the ERISA rights statement must include all the information contained in the DOL's model ERISA rights statement.[24] See Figure 7-4.

The ERISA rights statement must appear in the SPD as a consolidated unit. Items that do not apply to the plan can be omitted, and statements that explain and describe the plan can be added. However, the additional statements cannot mislead, misinform, or fail to inform participants and beneficiaries about the plan. The statements also must be written in language that can be understood by the average participant.

In addition, the ERISA rights statement can mention rights that are described elsewhere in the SPD and state that the ERISA rights statement is required by federal law and regulation.

---

[22] DOL Reg. § 2520.102-3.
[23] ERISA § 104(c); DOL Reg. § 2520.102-3(t)(1).
[24] *Id.*

## Minimum Maternity Benefits Statement

Group health plans that provide maternity benefits must include a statement that describes the minimum maternity benefit standards established by the Newborns' and Mothers' Health Protection Act of 1996 (NMHPA) for plan years beginning on or after January 1, 1998.

The DOL has provided sample language that SPDs may use to satisfy the requirement of describing minimum maternity benefits.[25] See Figure 7-5.

## PBGC Insurance Protection Statement

Pension plans covered by the PBGC must contain a statement that benefits are insured and that additional information is available from the plan administrator or the PBGC (including the address).[26] See Figure 7-6 for the sample PBGC statement from DOL Regulations Section 2520.102-3(m)(3) as to which plans may be used to satisfy this requirement. Pension plans that are not covered by the PBGC must state that benefits are not insured and explain why.[27]

---

[25] DOL Reg. § 2520.102-3(u).
[26] DOL Reg. § 2520.102-3(m)(2).
[27] DOL Reg. § 2520.102-3(m)(1).

**Figure 7-3**

**SPD Content requirements**

*Note:* Information presented in this chart is from DOL Regulations Section 2520.102-3.

| Item | Description | Comment |
|------|-------------|---------|
| 1 | Name of plan and, if different, plan name commonly known to participants and beneficiaries. | |
| 2 | Name and address of:<br><br>• Employer, if plan is single employer plan<br><br>• Employee organization, if employee organization maintains plan<br><br>• Association, committee, joint board of trustees, parent, most significant employer in group of contributing employers, or similar representative, if the plan is a collectively bargained plan established or maintained by one or more employers<br><br>• Association, committee, joint board of trustees, parent, most significant employer in group of contributing employers, or similar representative, if two or more employers establish or maintain the plan | |
| 3 | Statement saying participants or beneficiaries can request, in writing:<br><br>• a complete list of sponsoring employers or employee organizations;<br><br>or<br><br>• information on whether a particular employer or employee organization is the plan sponsor and, if so, the sponsor's address. | Include this statement *only* if the plan is a collectively bargained plan or a plan maintained by two or more employers and the SPD does not include a complete list. |
| 4 | Plan sponsor's employer identification number (EIN) | |

## Figure 7-3 (*cont'd*)

## SPD Content Requirements

| Item | Description | Comment |
|---|---|---|
| 5 | Plan number | |
| 6 | Plan type | Examples of pension plan types include defined benefit plans, money purchase plans, and profit-sharing plans, 401(k), ERISA 404(c), etc.<br><br>Examples of welfare plan types include medical plans, dental plans, and disability plans. |
| 7 | Type of plan administration | Examples include administration by insurer, by third-party administrator, or by employer. |
| 8 | Whether a "health insurance issuer" is responsible for plan financing or administration (including payment of claims) and, if so, the name and address of the insurer or HMO. | Applies only to group health plans. |
| 9 | Plan administrator's name, business address, and business telephone number. | |
| 10 | Name of agent for service of legal process and address at which a person can serve legal process (e.g., subpoena). | |
| 11 | Statement saying a person may serve legal process to plan administrator or plan trustee. | |
| 12 | Name, title, and principal business address of each plan trustee. | |
| 13 | For a collectively bargained plan, a statement saying:<br><br>• plan is collectively bargained;<br><br>• participants or beneficiaries may request, in writing, copies of collective bargaining agreements related to plan; and<br><br>• collective bargaining agreements related to plan are available for inspection, as required by regulation. | A plan is collectively bargained if any collective bargaining agreement controls any plan duties, rights, or benefits. This is true even if the agreement is superseded in part for other purposes. |

**Figure 7-3 (*cont'd*)**

**SPD Content Requirements**

| Item | Description | Comment |
|------|-------------|---------|
| 14 | Description of participation eligibility requirements. | Examples include age and years of service. |
| 15 | For a pension plan, a statement describing<br><br>• plan's normal retirement age; and<br><br>• any other conditions participants must meet to become eligible to receive benefits. | This statement must include an explanation of qualified domestic relations order (QDRO) procedures or a statement that these procedures are available without charge.<br><br>For cash balance plans, a description of how a prior conversion may have affected benefits that classes of participants may have reasonably expected the plan to provide. |
| 16 | For a welfare plan, a statement describing conditions participants must meet to become eligible to receive benefits. | For health plans, this statement must include an explanation of qualified medical child support order (QMCSO) procedures or a statement that these procedures are available without charge. |
| 17 | Description or summary of benefits<br><br>For health plans: cost-sharing provisions that require participants or beneficiaries to pay premiums, copays, etc.; annual and lifetime caps and other plan limits; covered preventive services; coverage for existing or new drugs; coverage for medical tests, devices, and procedures; how to access in-network and out-of-network providers; restrictions on selecting primary or specialty care providers; restrictions on emergency care and preauthorization or utilization review procedures.<br><br>For plans with provider networks, a provider list may be furnished as a separate document that accompanies the plan's SPD. The SPD must still describe the network and state that the provider list is furnished automatically, without charge, as a separate document. | For welfare plans with extensive benefit schedules (e.g., medical plans), include only a general description if referring to detailed benefit schedules and if stating the schedules are available at no cost. |
| 18 | Group health plans providing maternity benefits must include a minimum maternity benefits standard statement. | The DOL's model statement may be used (see Figure 7-5). |
| 19 | For a pension plan, a statement describing any joint and survivor benefits and preretirement survivor benefits. | Include in the statement a description of any election or waiver requirements. |

## Figure 7-3 (*cont'd*)

## SPD Content Requirements

| Item | Description | Comment |
|---|---|---|
| 20 | Statement clearly identifying circumstances that could result in disqualification, ineligibility, claims denial, loss, forfeiture, or suspension of any benefits participants or beneficiaries might otherwise reasonably expect, including any provisions that may result in the imposition of a fee or charge on participants, beneficiaries, or their individual accounts. | Include in the statement information on the plan sponsor's or other's right to terminate the plan, the circumstances under which the plan may be terminated, the rights and obligations of plan participants upon termination, a summary of any plan provisions governing allocation and disposition of plan assets upon termination. |
| 21 | For a group health plan, a description of rights to continued coverage under COBRA. | Must include description of second election period for employees who become eligible for assistance under the Trade Act of 2002. |
| 22 | For a pension plan, a statement saying whether the PBGC insures the benefits. | |
| 23 | For a pension plan that the PBGC does *not* in sure, a statement explaining why plan is not insured. | |
| 24 | For a pension plan that the PBGC insures:<br><br>• a summary of PBGC benefit guarantee provisions;<br><br>• a statement saying further information about the PBGC's insurance program can be obtained from the plan administrator or the PBGC; and<br><br>• the PBGC's address. | To satisfy this requirement, the SPD may include the PBGC Insurance Protection Statement (see Figure 7-6). |
| 25 | For a pension plan, a description of plan provisions used to determine years of service for<br><br>• Eligibility to participate<br><br>• Vesting<br><br>• Breaks in service<br><br>• Benefit accrual | Describe the service required to accrue full benefits and how accruals are prorated for employees failing to complete a full year of service. |

## Figure 7-3 (*cont'd*)

## SPD Content Requirements

| Item | Description | Comment |
|------|-------------|---------|
| 26 | Sources of plan contributions. | Examples include employers, employee organizations, and employees. |
| 27 | Method for calculating contribution amounts. | In the case of a defined benefit plan, state without further explanation that the contribution is actuarially determined. |
| 28 | Funding arrangements (i.e., entity used for accumulation of assets or through which benefits are provided). | Examples include insurance companies and trust funds.<br><br>The SPD must identify any insurance company, trust fund, or any other institution, organization, or entity that maintains a fund for the plan or through which the plan is funded or benefits are provided. |
| 29 | Plan year end date. | |
| 30 | Procedures for filing claims for benefits, time limits for processing claims, and remedies available for redress of claims denied in whole or in part. If plan is a group health benefit plan, description must include DOL office where participants and beneficiaries may seek assistance regarding their rights under ERISA and under the Health Insurance Portability and Accountability Act of 1996. | Alternatively, the SPD may simply state that the claims procedure information will be furnished automatically, without charge, in a separate document.<br><br>(See Chapter 11 for claims procedure requirements.) |
| 31 | Statement explaining participants' ERISA rights. | See Model ERISA Rights Statement (Figure 7-4). |

## Figure 7-4

## Model ERISA Rights Statement

As a participant in [*name of plan*] you are entitled to certain rights and protections under the Employee Retirement Income Security Act of 1974 (ERISA). ERISA provides that all plan participants shall be entitled to:

### Receive Information About Your Plan and Benefits

Examine, without charge, at the plan administrator's office and at other specified locations such as worksites and union halls, all documents governing the plan, including insurance contracts and collective bargaining agreements, and a copy of the latest annual report (Form 5500 Series) filed by the plan with the U.S. Department of Labor and available at the Public Disclosure Room of the Employee Benefits Security Administration.

Obtain, upon written request to the plan administrator, copies of documents governing the operation of the plan, including insurance contracts and collective bargaining agreements, and copies of the latest annual report (Form 5500 Series) and updated summary plan description. The administrator may make a reasonable charge for the copies.

Receive a summary of the plan's annual financial report. The plan administrator is required by law to furnish each participant with a copy of this summary annual report.

Obtain a statement telling you whether you have a right to receive a pension at normal retirement age (age * * *) and if so, what your benefits would be at normal retirement age if you stop working under the plan now. If you do not have a right to a pension, the statement will tell you how many more years you have to work to get a right to a pension. This statement must be requested in writing and is not required to be given more than once every twelve (12) months. The plan must provide the statement free of charge.

### Continue Group Health Plan Coverage [*Include only if SPD covers health plans*]

Continue health care coverage for yourself, spouse or dependents if there is a loss of coverage under the plan as a result of a qualifying event. You or your dependents may have to pay for such coverage. Review this summary plan description and the documents governing the plan on the rules governing your COBRA continuation coverage rights.

Reduction or elimination of exclusionary periods of coverage for preexisting conditions under your group health plan, if you have creditable coverage from another plan. You should be provided a certificate of creditable coverage, free of charge, from your group health plan or health insurance issuer when you lose coverage under the plan, when you become entitled to elect COBRA continuation coverage, when your COBRA continuation coverage ceases, if you request it before losing coverage, or if you request it up to 24 months after losing coverage. Without evidence of creditable coverage, you may be subject to a preexisting condition exclusion for 12 months (18 months for late enrollees) after your enrollment date in your coverage.

**Figure 7-4 (*cont'd*)**

## Model ERISA Rights Statement

**Prudent Actions by Plan Fiduciaries**

In addition to creating rights for plan participants ERISA imposes duties upon the people who are responsible for the operation of the employee benefit plan. The people who operate your plan, called "fiduciaries" of the plan, have a duty to do so prudently and in the interest of you and other plan participants and beneficiaries. No one, including your employer, your union, or any other person, may fire you or otherwise discriminate against you in any way to prevent you from obtaining a [*pension, welfare*] benefit or exercising your rights under ERISA.

**Enforce Your Rights**

If your claim for a [*pension, welfare*] benefit is denied or ignored, in whole or in part, you have a right to know why this was done, to obtain copies of documents relating to the decision without charge, and to appeal any denial, all within certain time schedules.

Under ERISA, there are steps you can take to enforce the above rights. For instance, if you request a copy of plan documents or the latest annual report from the plan and do not receive them within 30 days, you may file suit in a Federal court. In such a case, the court may require the plan administrator to provide the materials and pay you up to $110 a day until you receive the materials, unless the materials were not sent because of reasons beyond the control of the administrator. If you have a claim for benefits that is denied or ignored, in whole or in part, you may file suit in a state or Federal court. In addition, if you disagree with the plan's decision or lack thereof concerning the qualified status of a domestic relations order or a medical child support order, you may file suit in Federal court. If it should happen that plan fiduciaries misuse the plan's money, or if you are discriminated against for asserting your rights, you may seek assistance from the U.S. Department of Labor, or you may file suit in a Federal court. The court will decide who should pay court costs and legal fees. If you are successful the court may order the person you have sued to pay these costs and fees. If you lose, the court may order you to pay these costs and fees if, for example, it finds your claim is frivolous.

**Assistance with Your Questions**

If you have any questions about your plan, you should contact the plan administrator. If you have any questions about this statement or about your rights under ERISA, or if you need assistance in obtaining documents from the plan administrator, you should contact the nearest office of the Employee Benefits Security Administration, U.S. Department of Labor, listed in your telephone directory or the Division of Technical Assistance and Inquiries, Employee Benefits Security Administration, U.S. Department of Labor, 200 Constitution Avenue N.W., Washington, D.C. 20210. You may also obtain certain publications about your rights and responsibilities under ERISA by calling the publications hotline of the Employee Benefits Security Administration.

## Figure 7-5

## Minimum Maternity Benefits Statement

*Note:* The DOL views this statement as sample language that plan sponsors may use in SPDs to satisfy the requirement to describe a plan's minimum maternity benefit standards. This model statement is from DOL Regulations Section 2520.102-3(u).

Group health plans and health insurance issuers generally may not, under Federal law, restrict benefits for any hospital length of stay in connection with childbirth for the mother or newborn child to less than 48 hours following a vaginal delivery, or less than 96 hours following a cesarean section. However, Federal law generally does not prohibit the mother's or newborn's attending provider, after consulting with the mother, from discharging the mother or her newborn earlier than 48 hours (or 96 hours as applicable). In any case, plans and issuers may not, under Federal law, require that a provider obtain authorization from the plan or the issuer for prescribing a length of stay not in excess of 48 hours (or 96 hours).

## Figure 7-6

## PBGC Insurance Protection Statement

> *Note:* This PBGC Insurance Protection Statement is from DOL Regulations Section 2520.102-3(m)(3).
>
> The address and telephone number included in the statement were accurate at the time this edition went to press. However, government addresses and telephone numbers occasionally change. To ensure accuracy, please confirm the address.

---

### PBGC Insurance Protection Statement (for Single Employer DB Plans)

Your pension benefits under this plan are insured by the Pension Benefit Guaranty Corporation (PBGC), a federal insurance agency. If the plan terminates (ends) without enough money to pay all benefits, the PBGC will step in to pay pension benefits. Most people receive all of the pension benefits they would have received under their plan, but some people may lose certain benefits.

The PBGC guarantee generally covers: (1) normal and early retirement benefits; (2) disability benefits if you become disabled before the plan terminates; and (3) certain benefits for your survivors.

The PBGC guarantee generally does not cover: (1) benefits greater than the maximum guaranteed amount set by law for the year in which the plan terminates; (2) some or all of benefit in creases and new benefits based on plan provisions that have been in place for fewer than 5 years at the time the plan terminates; (3) benefits that are not vested because you have not worked long enough for the company; (4) benefits for which you have not met all of the requirements at the time the plan terminates; (5) certain early retirement payments (such as supplemental benefits that stop when you become eligible for Social Security) that result in an early retirement monthly benefit greater than your monthly benefit at the plan's normal retirement age; and (6) non-pension benefits, such as health insurance, life insurance, certain death benefits, vacation pay, and severance pay.

Even if certain of your benefits are not guaranteed, you still may receive some of those benefits from the PBGC depending on how much money your plan has and on how much the PBGC collects from employers.

For more information about the PBGC and the benefits it guarantees, ask your plan administrator or contact the PBGC's Technical Assistance Division, 1200 K Street N.W., Suite 930, Washington, D.C. 20005-4026 or call 1-800-736-2444 or 202-326-4000 (not a toll-free number). TTY/TDD users may call the federal relay service toll-free at 1-800-877-8339 and ask to be connected to 202-326-4000. Additional information about the PBGC's pension insurance program is available through the PBGC's website on the Internet at http://www.pbgc.gov.

## Figure 7-6 (*cont'd*)

## PBGC Insurance Protection Statement

---

### PBGC Insurance Protection Statement (for Multiemployer DB Plans)

Your pension benefits under this multiemployer plan are insured by the Pension Benefit Guaranty Corporation (PBGC), a federal insurance agency. A multiemployer plan is a collectively bargained pension arrangement involving two or more unrelated employers, usually in a common industry.

Under the multiemployer plan program, the PBGC provides financial assistance through loans to plans that are insolvent. A multiemployer plan is considered insolvent if the plan is unable to pay benefits (at least equal to the PBGC's guaranteed benefit limit) when due.

The maximum benefit that the PBGC guarantees is set by law. Under the multiemployer program, the PBGC guarantee equals a participant's years of service multiplied by (1) 100% of the first $11 of the monthly benefit accrual and (2) 75% of the next $33. The PBGC's maximum guarantee limit is $35.75 per month times a participant's years of service. For example, the maximum annual guarantee for a retiree with 30 years of service would be $12,870.

The PBGC guarantee generally covers (1) normal and early retirement benefits; (2) disability benefits if you become disabled before the plan becomes insolvent; and (3) certain benefits for your survivors.

The PBGC guarantee generally does not cover (1) Benefits greater than the maximum guaranteed amount set by law; (2) benefit increases and new benefits based on plan provisions that have been in place for fewer than 5 years at the earlier of (i) the date the plan terminates or (ii) the time the plan becomes insolvent; (3) benefits that are not vested because you have not worked long enough; (4) benefits for which you have not met all of the requirements at the time the plan becomes insolvent; and (5) non-pension benefits, such as health insurance, life insurance, certain death benefits, vacation pay, and severance pay.

For more information about the PBGC and the benefits it guarantees, ask your plan administrator or contact the PBGC's Technical Assistance Division, 1200 K Street, N.W., Suite 930, Washington, D.C. 20005-4026 or call 1-800-736-2444 or 202-326-4000 (not a toll-free number). TTY/TDD users may call the federal relay service toll-free at 1-800-877-8339 and ask to be connected to 202-326-4000. Additional information about the PBGC's pension insurance program is available through the PBGC's website on the Internet at http://www.pbgc.gov.

---

# D. When and How to Distribute SPDs

---

### SPD Due Dates

---

ERISA has specific rules governing the time SPDs must be delivered to plan participants and the distribution method.

There are three different due dates for SPDs:

1.  The date the SPD must be distributed to new plan participants and beneficiaries[28]
2.  The date the initial SPD must be distributed[29]
3.  The date an updated SPD must be distributed[30]

Use the decision table in Figure 7-7 to determine when to distribute SPDs.

**New participants and beneficiaries**

The plan must distribute the SPD to a new participant (and any summary of material modifications not yet incorporated in the SPD) either:

*   90 days after the person becomes a plan participant (or, for a beneficiary, within 90 days after benefits begin); or (if later)
*   120 days after the plan becomes subject to the SPD requirements.

Group health plans that have had a material reduction in covered services must provide an SMM or updated SPD 60 days after the adoption of the modification. Alternatively, the employer may provide descriptions of material reductions at regular intervals of not more than 90 days.[31]

**Note.** The summary of material modifications (SMM) is a written summary describing a material modification to a plan. (For a discussion of SMM requirements, see Chapter 8.)

---

28   ERISA § 104(b)(1)(A).
29   ERISA § 104(b)(1)(B).
30   ERISA § 104(b)(1).
31   *Id.*

**Figure 7-7**

**Determining When to Distribute SPDs**

| If Situation Is This: | And There Were: | Then Plan Must: |
|---|---|---|
| person became new plan participant or beneficiary | ⟶ | give this person an SPD within:<br>• 90 days after person became participant (for beneficiary, 90 days after benefits begin)<br>or; if later<br>• 120 days after plan became subject to SPD requirements |
| plan is newly subject to SPD requirements | ⟶ | distribute SPD *no later* than 120 days after plan first subject to SPD requirements |
| plan already has SPD | changes to plan on or before 5-year period ended affecting information required in SPD | distribute updated SPD *no later* than 5 years + 210 days after end of plan year SPD last updated |
| | *no* changes to plan affecting information required in SPD | distribute updated SPD *no later* than 10 years + 210 days after end of plan year SPD last updated |
| plan is a group health plan | material reduction in covered services | distribute SMM or updated SPD *no later* than 60 days after modification adopted or 90 days if plan sponsor distributes updates at regular intervals |
| plan is a SIMPLE plan | ⟶ | annually |

**Initial SPDs**   A plan that is newly subject to the SPD requirements must distribute the initial SPD to plan participants no later than 120 days after it becomes subject to the requirements.[32]

**Updated SPDs**   Plans that already have an SPD must distribute the SPD to plan participants no later than five years plus 210 days after the end of the plan year during which the SPD was last updated.[33] However, if during the five-year period there were no changes to the plan information required in an SPD, the plan can distribute an updated version as late as ten years plus 210 days after the last update.[34] The five-year period ends five years from the last day of the plan year during which the SPD was last updated.

**Material reduction under group health plan**   A group health plan must provide either an updated SPD or an SMM describing a material reduction in covered services or benefits to participants and beneficiaries either:

- 60 days after the plan sponsor adopts the modification or change; or
- 90 days, if the plan sponsor distributes SPDs at regular intervals.[35]

(For further discussion of SMMs, see Chapter 8.)

> *Example 1.* A calendar-year plan's SPD was last updated on June 1, 2003. In March 2004, the employer made a change in the plan that affected the information required in the SPD. The five-year period ended on December 31, 2008. Since there was a change in the SPD required information during the five-year period, the plan administrator would have had to distribute an updated SPD to participants no later than July 29, 2009 (i.e., December 31, 2003 + five years + 210 days).

> *Example 2.* A calendar-year plan's SPD was last updated on May 1, 2003. On September 1, 2009, the employer made a change in the plan that affected the information in the SPD. The five-year period ended

---

[32]   DOL Reg. § 2520.104b-2(a)(2).
[33]   DOL Reg. § 2520.104b-2(b)(1).
[34]   DOL Reg. § 2520.104b-2(b)(2).
[35]   ERISA § 104(b)(1).

December 31, 2008. Since there were no changes in the SPD required information during the five-year period, the plan administrator can distribute updated SPDs as late as July 29, 2014 (i.e., December 31, 2003 + 10 years + 210 days).

## SPD Distribution Requirements

**Who must receive SPDs**

Plan administrators must distribute copies of SPDs to plan participants and, in the case of pension plans, to beneficiaries receiving benefits.[36]

**Distribution methods**

When distributing SPDs to plan participants and beneficiaries, the plan must take measures to ensure that the SPDs are actually received.[37]

The distribution method or methods used must be likely to result in full distribution. Two distribution methods can be combined if, together, they ensure that participants and beneficiaries actually receive the SPD.[38] Leaving a stack of SPDs in a common worksite is not an acceptable distribution method.

Acceptable distribution methods include:

- In-hand delivery to employees at their worksites
- Special insert in an employee periodical if:
  — the distribution list is comprehensive, up to date, and accurate; and
  — the front page prominently states the SPD is inserted.
  (*Note:* If some participants and beneficiaries are not on the mailing list, this method may be combined with another distribution method.)
- Electronic distribution if the distribution method or methods satisfy DOL safe harbor requirements (see Section C in Chapter 3)
- First-class mail
- Second-or third-class mail if return and forwarding postage are guaranteed and address corrections are requested

---

[36] DOL Reg. § 2520.104b-2(a).
[37] DOL Reg. § 2520.104b-1(b)(1).
[38] *Id.*

(*Note:* If SPDs are distributed by second-or third-class mail and an SPD is later returned with a corrected address, the plan administrator must distribute the SPD again by first-class mail or personal delivery to the participant at his or her worksite.[39])

---

[39]  *Id.*

# E. Retirees, Beneficiaries, and Vested Separated Participants

Pension plan sponsors can provide the same materials as provided to active plan participants, assuming that material describes the items applicable to retirees, beneficiaries, and vested separated participants or use one of three alternative methods for furnishing SPDs to retired participants, beneficiaries receiving benefits, and separated participants with vested interests.[40]

Two of the alternative methods apply to the initial SPD disclosure requirement. The third applies to updated SPDs.

## Initial SPDs

The alternative methods for meeting the initial SPD disclosure requirements cannot be used any *earlier* than the date of retirement (for a retiree), the date benefits begin (for a beneficiary), or the date of separation (for a vested separated participant).[41]

**Alternative method 1**

Under the first alternative method for meeting the initial SPD disclosure requirement for a retiree, beneficiary, or vested separated participant, the person is given a document that meets certain requirements instead of the initial SPD.[42]

The requirements a document must satisfy depend on whether the document is for retirees and beneficiaries or vested separated participants.

*For retirees and beneficiaries.* Under the first alternative method, the document given to retirees and beneficiaries must:

- Meet the SPD style and format requirements

---

[40]  DOL Reg. § 2520.104b-4.
[41]  DOL Reg. § 2520.104b-4(a)(4).
[42]  DOL Reg. §§ 2520.104b-4(a)(1), (2).

- Contain all the SPD required information,[43] except:
  — The name and address of the employee organization association, committee, joint board of trustees, parent, most significant contributing employer, or similar party maintaining the plan and accompanying statements (this requirement applies to collectively bargained plans or plans maintained by two or more employers)
  — Eligibility requirements for participation and benefits
  — Joint and survivor benefits and election and waiver requirements
  — Circumstances resulting in loss of benefits
  — How years of service are calculated when determining eligibility to participate, vesting, breaks in service, and years of participation for benefit accrual
  — Sources of plan contributions
- State retirees and beneficiaries will continue to receive the same benefit payments they receive at present and for the period agreed on at retirement, except as described in the document
- Describe any plan provision under which retirees' or beneficiaries' present benefit payments may be reduced, changed, terminated, forfeited, or suspended

*For vested separated beneficiaries.* The first alternative method document for vested separated participants must:

- Meet the SPD style and format requirements
- Contain all the SPD required information,[44] except:
  — The name and address of the employee organization association, committee, joint board of trustees, parent, most significant contributing employer, or similar party maintaining the plan and accompany statements (this requirement pertains to collectively bargained plans or plans maintained by two or more employers)
  — Eligibility requirements for participation and benefits
  — Circumstances resulting in loss of benefits
  — How years of service are calculated when determining eligibility To participate, vesting, breaks in service, and years of participation for benefit accrual
  — Sources of plan contributions
  — Plan year end date
- For participants who, at or after separation, were informed of their vested benefit amount or method used to compute their benefits, state that the participants were previously informed of this information and can request copies of this previously furnished information

---

[43]  DOL Reg. § 2520.104b-4(a)(1).
[44]  DOL Reg. § 2520.104b-4(a)(2).

- For participants who, at or after separation, were not informed of their vested benefit amount or method used to compute their benefits, state this information
- Describe the form in which the plan will pay benefits and for how long or describes the optional forms available
- Describe any plan provision under which benefits of vested and separated participants may be reduced, changed, terminated, forfeited, or suspended

**Alternative method 2**

Under the second alternative method for meeting the initial SPD disclosure requirements for retirees, beneficiaries, and vested separated participants, the plan must give these persons a document that satisfies the SPD style and format requirements and describes these persons' rights and obligations under the plan.[45]

**Alternative method 3**

For the updated SPD disclosure requirement, the plan does not have to give retirees, beneficiaries, and vested separated participants copies of updated SPDs if, instead, they are given[46] copies of the most recent SPD (and SMMs if they had not yet been incorporated in the SPD) on or after the date of retirement (for retirees), date benefit payments began (for beneficiaries), date of separation (for vested separated participants).

When updated SPDs are distributed to other participants, these participants must be given a notice stating that (1) their benefit rights are outlined in the earlier SPD and SMMs and (2) they can obtain a copy of the earlier SPD, any SMMs, and any updated SPD, without charge, on request.

---

[45] DOL Reg. § 2520.104b-4(a)(3)(i).
[46] DOL Reg. § 2520.104b-4(b).

# F. Successor Pension Plans

DOL provides an alternative method of complying with the SPD disclosure requirements for certain successor pension plans.[47]

**Definition**

A *successor pension plan* is the result of a pension plan merged into another pension plan.[48]

**When alternative method applies**

The alternative method for complying with the SPD disclosure requirements applies to successor pension plans in which some participants and beneficiaries not only have rights under the successor plan, but also retain rights under the merged (i.e., original) plan.[49]

The alternative method applies only to plan mergers that occur after the successor pension plan issues an initial SPD.

If the plan satisfies the requirements to use the alternative method, it need not describe the relevant terms of the merged plan in the successor plan's SPD that is furnished after the merger to participants and beneficiaries who retained rights under the merged plan.[50]

To satisfy the alternative method requirements, the plan must provide the following information, within 90 days after the merger takes effect, to affected participants and beneficiaries who are receiving benefits under the merged plan:[51]

- The most recent SPD for the successor plan
- Any SMMs to the successor plan not yet incorporated into the most recent SPD
- A separate statement containing:
  — a brief description of the merger;
  — a description of the merged and successor plan benefits applicable to the participants and beneficiaries; and
  — a notice saying the merged and successor plan documents and the plan merger documents (including any part of any corporate

---

47  DOL Reg. § 2520.104-4.
48  DOL Reg. § 2520.104-4(a).
49  *Id.*
50  *Id.*
51  DOL Reg. § 2520.104-4(b)(1).

merger documents describing or controlling the plan merger) are available for inspection and can be obtained, upon written request, for a duplication charge.

**Additional requirements**

In addition to the alternative compliance requirements described above, after the merger all subsequent SPDs for the successor plan must (1) clearly identify the class of participants and beneficiaries who retained rights under the predecessor plan and (2) state that the information listed above (alternative method requirements) is available for inspection and can be obtained, upon written request, for a duplication charge.[52]

---

52    DOL Reg.§ 2520.104-4(b)(2).

# G. Special Rules for SIMPLEs

Trustees of savings incentive match plans for employees (SIMPLEs) must provide plan sponsors with SPDs that meet specific content requirements every year. Plan sponsors must distribute these SPDs to eligible employees.

**Content requirements**

An SPD for a SIMPLE must contain the following information:[53]

- Employer's name and address
- Trustee's name and address
- Eligibility requirements
- Benefits provided under the plan
- The time and method for making salary reduction elections
- Procedures and effects of withdrawals and rollovers

**Distribution requirements**

Employers must provide a copy of the SPD and a required annual notice to each employee eligible to participate at least 61 days before the plan year begins.[54] (For details on the required notice, see Chapter 9).

**DOL penalty for failure to provide SPD**

A trustee who fails to provide the SPD may be assessed a penalty of $50 for each day the failure continues unless the trustee can provide reasonable cause.[55]

An employer who fails to provide the annual notice, which includes the SPD, may be assessed a penalty of $50 for each day the failure continues, absent a showing of reasonable cause.[56]

---

[53] ERISA § 101(h)(2); I.R.C. § 408(1)(2)(B).
[54] ERISA § 101(h)(3); I.R.C. § 408(p)(5)(C).
[55] I.R.C. §§ 6693(c)(2) and (3).
[56] I.R.C. §§ 6693(c)(1) and (3).

# Chapter 8

# Summary of Material Modifications

---

**Introduction**    A change in an ERISA-covered pension or welfare plan may require the distribution of a summary of material modifications (SMM) to participants and beneficiaries. SMMs are not filed with the Department of Labor (DOL), but must be provided to the DOL at the agency's request.

This chapter describes the requirements for SMMs, including the types of plans that must comply, the exceptions, and the distribution rules.

**Contents**    This chapter has four sections:

| Section | Title | Page |
|---------|-------|------|
| A | General Information | 8-2 |
| B | Plans Required to Distribute SMMs | 8-3 |
| C | Exceptions to SMM Requirements | 8-4 |
| D | Distribution of SMMs | 8-5 |

# A. General Information

**Definitions**
A *material modification* is a change in the information required to to be in a summary plan description (SPD).[1] (See Chapter 7 for details about required information in an SPD.) The SMM is a written summary describing a material modification to a plan that is provided to plan participants and beneficiaries.

**Style and format**
An SMM must be written in a way that the average plan participant can understand.[2]

The SMM must include enough detail to inform participants of their rights and obligations in connection with the material modifications. In addition, the SMM must not mislead, misinform, or fail to inform participants about material modifications to the plan.

**Penalty for noncompliance**
If a plan administrator fails or refuses to provide an SMM within 30 days after receiving a request for one from a plan participant or eligible beneficiary, a court can impose a penalty of up to $110 per day,[3] which is payable to the participant or beneficiary filing a civil action.

If a plan administrator fails to provide an SMM to the DOL within 30 days after receiving the agency's request, the DOL may assess a penalty of up to $110 per day (maximum $1,100 per request). The DOL will not impose a penalty if the failure is beyond the plan administrator's reasonable control.[4]

---

[1]   DOL Reg. §§ 2520.102-3, 2520.104b-3.
[2]   DOL Reg. § 2520.104b-3(a).
[3]   ERISA § 502(c)(1).
[4]   ERISA § 502(c)(6).

# B. Plans Required to Distribute SMMs

**Affected plans**   Pension and welfare plans subject to ERISA must comply with the SMM disclosure requirement unless they are specifically exempted from doing so.[5]

**Exempted plans**   The following ERISA-covered pension and welfare plans may be exempt from distributing SMMs to participants and beneficiaries:

- Pension and welfare plans maintained primarily for management or highly compensated employees (HCEs), also known as "executive plans"[6]
- Simplified employee pension (SEP) plans[7]
- Employer provided day care centers[8]
- Apprenticeship training programs[9]

The above plans are exempt only if they meet certain definitions and conditions. In some cases, the conditions include meeting alternative compliance requirements (see Section B in Chapter 3 for further discussion about conditions for exemption.).

---

[5]   ERISA §§ 102(a), 104(b)(1).
[6]   DOL Reg. §§ 2520.104-23, 2520.104-24.
[7]   DOL Reg. §§ 2520.104-48, 2520.104-49.
[8]   DOL Reg. § 2520.104-25.
[9]   DOL Reg. § 2520.104-22.

# C. Exceptions to SMM Requirements

**General rule**   An SMM is distributed to plan participants and beneficiaries only if the plan change is a material modification or changes information required to be included in an SPD.[10]

**Exceptions**   Even if a plan change is a material modification, an SMM need not be distributed to plan participants and beneficiaries if either of the following applies:

- The plan administrator describes the material modification in an updated SPD and files and distributes the SPD *before* distributing an SMM.[11]
- The adopted material modification is rescinded before it takes effect.[12]

---

[10]   DOL Reg. § 2520.104b-3(a).
[11]   DOL Reg. § 2520.104b-3(b).
[12]   DOL Reg. § 2520.104b-3(a).

# D. Distribution of SMMs

**Due date**

The deadline for distributing an SMM to plan participants and beneficiaries is 210 days after the close of the plan year during which the material modification was adopted.[13]

SMMs must be filed with the DOL within 30 days of the DOL's request to avoid the imposition of penalties.[14]

**Special rule for group health plans**

If a change to a group health plan results in a material reduction of covered services or benefits, then participants and beneficiaries must be notified (1) within 60 days after the modification is adopted, or (2) with communications provided at regular intervals if the plan sponsor provides communications at regular intervals of not more than 90 days.[15]

**Who must receive SMMs**

SMMs must be distributed to plan participants and, in the case of pension plans, to beneficiaries receiving benefits.[16]

**Retirees, vested separated participants, and beneficiaries**

If a material modification does not affect the rights of an individual retiree, vested separated participant, or beneficiary under a pension plan, an SMM does not need to be furnished to that individual unless the individual asks for a copy.[17]

*Example 1.* Employer G modifies the benefits under its defined benefit plan. Retirees, vested separated participants, and beneficiaries covered by Employer G's plan are not entitled to receive the new benefits. Thus, the change does not affect their rights under the plan and, therefore, they are not entitled to receive an SMM describing the change unless they ask for it.

*Example 2.* Plan P has a change in trustees. Because the retirees, vested separated participants, and beneficiaries covered by Plan P need to know who the plan trustees are to contact them with

---

13   DOL Reg. § 2520.104b-3(a).
14   ERISA § 502(c)(6).
15   ERISA § 104(b)(1).
16   DOL Reg. §§ 2520.104b-1(b), 2520.104b-3(a).
17   DOL Reg. § 2520.104b-4(c).

questions about the plan, the administrator of Plan P must distribute an SMM to these individuals describing the change.

**Distribution methods**

When an SMM is distributed to plan participants and beneficiaries, the plan must take measures to ensure that the SMM is actually received.[18] The method of distribution used must be likely to result in full distribution. Leaving a stack of SMMs at a common worksite is not an acceptable method of distribution.

Acceptable methods of distribution include the following:

- In-hand delivery to employees at their worksites
- Special insert in an employee periodical if:
  — the distribution list is comprehensive, up to date, and accurate; and
  — the front page of the periodical prominently states that an SMM is inserted.
- Electronic distribution if the distribution satisfies the DOL's safe harbor requirements for SPDs (See Section C in Chapter 3)
- First-class mail
- Second- or third-class mail if return and forwarding postage are guaranteed and address corrections are requested

If an SMM is to be distributed as an insert in an employee periodical, but some plan participants and beneficiaries are not on the mailing list, the plan may combine the periodical insert method with another distribution method to ensure that participants and beneficiaries actually receive the SMM.[19]

If SMMs are distributed by second- or third-class mail, and an SMM distributed by this method is returned with an address correction, the plan must distribute that SMM again by first-class mail or personal delivery to the participant at his or her worksite.[20]

---

[18]  DOL Reg. § 2520.104b-1(b)(1).
[19]  *Id.*
[20]  *Id.*

# Chapter 9

# Additional Notice Requirements for Retirement Plans

**Introduction**     Besides meeting the ERISA disclosure requirements discussed in previous sections of this guide, pension plan administrators must provide broadcast-type notices about specific events and rights that affect all plan participants and beneficiaries (such as a notice of a plan blackout period) and notices to address individual circumstances (such as procedures for processing benefit distributions and domestic relations orders).

This chapter provides an overview of these participant notice requirements.

**Contents**     This chapter has 28 sections:

| Section | Title | Page |
|---------|-------|------|
| N | Notice of Right to Divest Employer Stock in Defined Contribution Plan | 9-74 |
| O | Notice of Individual Account Plan Blackout Period | 9-78 |
| P | Notice of Qualified Change in Investment Options | 9-82 |
| Q | Notice for SIMPLE IRAs | 9-84 |
| R | Notice of Defined Benefit Pension Plan Funding | 9-86 |
| S | Notice of Funding Based Limitation on Distributions | 9-89 |
| T | Notice of Failure to Make Timely Contributions | 9-91 |
| U | Notice of Significant Reduction in Benefit Accruals | 9-93 |
| V | Notice of Transfer to Retiree Health Account | 9-98 |
| W | Notice of Multiemployer Plan's Critical or Endangered Status | 9-100 |
| X | Notice of Reduction to Adjustable Benefits | 9-105 |
| Y | Multiemployer Plan Funding Information Made Available on Request | 9-107 |
| Z | Notice of Funding Waiver Application | 9-109 |
| AA | Notice of Multiemployer Plan Application for Extension of Unfunded Liability Amortization | 9-112 |
| BB | Notice to Interested Parties | 9-116 |

# A. Consent to Distribution

**General rule**
In general, a qualified plan may not distribute benefits unless the plan administrator notifies the participant of his or her rights under the plan and the participant consents to the distribution.[1]

(See Section C in this chapter for discussion of a participant's waiver of the Qualified Joint and Survivor form of payment from certain pension plans.)

**PPA note**
The PPA expanded the 90-day maximum notice period to 180 days and added a requirement to explain the consequences of a failure to defer distribution.

**Exceptions**
A plan may make a distribution without notice and consent in the following circumstances:[2]

- The value of the participant's nonforfeitable total accrued benefit does not exceed $5,000.
- The participant has attained the later of:
  — *normal retirement age*, which is the earlier of (1) normal retirement age under plan provisions, or (2) age 65; or, if later, the fifth anniversary of the participant's entry date, or
  — age 62.
- The participant has died and benefits are payable to a non-spouse beneficiary.
- The distribution is pursuant to a qualified domestic relations order.
- The distribution is a minimum distribution required under Code Section 401(a)(9).

**Contents of notice**
The notice to the participant must include:

- a general description of the material features and relative values of optional forms of distribution (e.g., lump sums and single life annuities); and

---

[1]  I.R.C. § 411(a)(11).
[2]  IRS Reg. § 1.411(a)-11(c).

- the participant's right, if any, to defer receipt of the distribution[3] and the consequences of failing to defer receipt.

The requirement to mention the consequences of a failing to defer receipt of a distribution was added by Section 1102(b) of PPA for years beginning after December 31, 2006.

The IRS gives these three rules as a safe harbor for complying with this new disclosure rule:[4]

- In the case of a defined benefit plan, provide a description of how much larger benefits will be if the commencement of distributions is deferred. For this purposes, a plan administrator can use a generally applicable description as described in IRS' "relative value" regulation that includes the financial effect of deferring distributions based solely on the normal form of benefit.
- In the case of a defined contribution plan, provide a description indicating the investment options available under the plan (including fees) that will be available if distributions are deferred.
- For all plans, provide the portion of the summary plan description that contains any special rules that might materially affect a participant's decision to defer.

**Electronic distribution**

The notice and consent traditionally have been provided in writing. However, the IRS has issued regulations providing standards for electronic transmission of the notice.[5] See Section D in Chapter 3 for IRS rules for electronic plan communication.[6]

**Timing of notice**

In general, the notice must be given to the participant no more than 180[7] days and no fewer than 30 days before the annuity starting date. Alternatively, the plan administrator may base this 180/30-day time period on the date the distribution will actually begin.[8]

However, a plan may permit the participant to elect to begin receiving distributions before 30 days have elapsed if the participant was informed that he or she could have had at least 30 days to elect a distribution and the distribution begins more than seven days after the notice is provided.[9]

---

3  IRS Reg. § 1.411(a)-11(c)(2).
4  IRS Notice 2007-7, Q-33.
5  IRS Reg. §§ 1.401-21, 1.411(a)-11(f).
6  IRS Reg. § 1.411(a)-11(f).
7  PPA § 1102(a).
8  IRS Reg. §§ 1.411(a)-11(c)(2)(iii), 1.417(e)-1(b)(3).
9  IRS Reg. §§ 1.411(a)-11(c)(2)(iii), 1.417(e)-1(b)(3)(ii).

**Alternative timing rule**

The IRS has an alternative timing rule that allows a plan administrator to give full notice more than 180 days before a distribution if the plan administrator also provides a summary of the notice during the 180/30-day time period. Full notice may be given in either paper or electronic form, as long as the electronic notice offers the option to request a full written paper notice.[10]

**Summary notice under alternative timing rule**

The summary of the notice must:[11]

- refer the participant to the most recently provided full notice;
- advise the participant of the right to request and receive full notice without charge no fewer than 30 days (unless the participant waives this 30-day requirement) before the distribution date;
- advise the participant of any right to defer receipt of a distribution; and
- include a summary of the plan distribution options.

**Prohibitions**

No consent to a distribution is valid if a significant detriment is imposed by the plan for a failure to consent to a distribution.[12] However, charging a reasonable fee for account maintenance is not considered a "significant detriment."[13]

A defined contribution plan limiting investments to a money market fund for a participant who has terminated employment rather than offering the broad range of investment alternatives with materially different risk and return characteristics that are available to active participants imposes an impermissible significant detriment on a participant who does not consent to a distribution.[14]

---

[10]   IRS Reg. § 1.411(a)-11(f).
[11]   IRS Reg. § 1.411(a)-11(c)(2)(iii)(B)(3).
[12]   IRS Reg. § 1.411(a)-11(c)(2).
[13]   Rev. Rul. 2004-10.
[14]   Rev. Rul. 96-47.

# B. Notice of Qualified Joint and Survivor Annuity

**PPA note**    The PPA expanded the 90-day maximum notice period to 180 days. PPA also added the requirement to offer a qualified optional survivor annuity

**Definitions**    The *Notice of Qualified Joint and Survivor Annuity* (QJSA Notice) is a written explanation of the terms and conditions of a joint and survivor annuity benefit, the participant's right to waive the option, the rights of the participant's spouse, and the effect of revoking a waiver.[15]

A *qualified joint and survivor annuity* is an annuity that is payable for the life of the participant, with a benefit equal to at least 50 percent (but not more than 100 percent) of that amount payable to the spouse upon the participant's death.[16]

**Note.** A plan generally may not make a distribution of a participant's accrued benefits in a form other than a QJSA unless the present value of the nonforfeitable benefit is not greater than $5,000, or the participant has waived the QJSA and the participant's spouse has consented to the waiver.[17] However, if a plan provides two or more actuarially equivalent joint and survivor annuities, a participant may choose any of these options without spousal consent.[18]

**Affected plans**    Pension plans subject to the minimum funding standards (e.g., defined benefit plans, money purchase plans) must provide that benefits are available in the form of a QJSA. These rules also apply to plans that are not subject to the minimum funding requirements (e.g., stock bonus plans, profit-sharing plans) unless:[19]

- the plan's vested benefits are payable in full upon the participant's death to the participant's surviving spouse (or designated beneficiary if the spouse consents to a different beneficiary); and
- the participant elects payment in a form other than a life annuity.

---

[15]   I.R.C. §417(a)(3)(A).
[16]   I.R.C. §417(b).
[17]   IRS Reg. §1.417(e)-1(b)(1), (2).
[18]   IRS Reg. §1.401(a)-20, Q&A-16.
[19]   I.R.C. §401(a)(11)(B); IRS Reg. §1.401(a)-20, Q&A-3(a).

Thus, plans not subject to the minimum funding rules may be subject to the QJSA notice requirements for some participants but not others.[20]

**Exception**

In general, if the plan fully subsidizes the QJSA benefit and if a participant may not waive the benefit (or choose a beneficiary other than the spouse), the plan does *not* have to provide the Notice of Qualified Joint and Survivor Annuity.[21]

**Fully subsidized benefit**

A plan fully subsidizes the benefit if it does not charge the participant for the benefit by increasing employee contributions or decreasing other benefits.[22]

**Content requirements**

The notice must contain information about available distribution options, waiver, and consent rights.

*Optional forms:* For each of the optional forms of benefit presently available to the participant, a QJSA explanation must provide the following information:[23]

- a description of the optional form of benefit;
- a description of the eligibility conditions for the optional form of benefit;
- a description of the financial effect of electing the optional form of benefit (i.e., the amounts and timing of payments to the participant under the form of benefit during the participant's lifetime, and the amounts and timing of payments after the death of the participant);
- in the case of a defined benefit plan, a description of the relative value of the optional form of benefit compared to the value of the QJSA; and
- a description of any other material features of the optional form of benefit.

The QJSA explanation can provide specific information about the benefits available under the plan to the particular participant or generally applicable information with an offer to provide additional information about the participant's benefits under the plan upon

---

20  IRS Reg. § 1.401(a)-20, Q&A-4.
21  I.R.C. § 417(a)(5)(A).
22  I.R.C. § 417(a)(5)(B); IRS Reg. § 1.401(a)-20, Q&A 37.
23  IRS Reg. § 1.417(a)(3)-1(b) and (c).

request. IRS regulations provide detailed requirements for calculating and displaying the relative value of optional forms of payment.

*Waiver and consent rights*: The QJSA notice must inform the plan participant of the:[24]

- terms and conditions of the QJSA and the "qualified optional survivor annuity";
- participant's right to waive the QJSA;
- effect of the waiver;
- participant's right to change elections;
- effect of changing elections; and
- spouse's rights to consent to the election.

**Qualified optional survivor annuity**

The Qualified Optional Survivor Annuity (QOSA) must be offered in plan years beginning after 2007. The QOSA is an alternate joint and survivor form of benefit with a survivor percentage that varies based on the automatic percentage used for the QJSA. If the survivor percentage for the QJSA is less than 75 percent, the QOSA percent is 75 percent; if the survivor percentage for the QJSA is 75 percent or more, then the QJSA percentage is 50 percent. For example, for a plan that provides a 50 percent joint and survivor form for the QJSA, the QOSA is a 75 percent joint and survivor option.[25]

The QOSA must be at least actuarially equivalent to the plan's single life annuity payable at the same time as the QOSA. It need not be equivalent to the QJSA.[26]

**Due date**

In general, the notice must be provided to participants no fewer than 30 days and no more than 180 days before the annuity starting date.[27]

**Annuity starting date**

The *annuity starting date* is the first day of the first period for which an amount is payable as an annuity; in the case of benefits not payable in the form of an annuity, it is the date on which all events have occurred that entitle the participant to the benefit.[28] A payment is not considered to occur after the annuity starting date merely because payment is reasonably delayed for calculating the amount.[29]

---

[24] I.R.C. § 417(a)(3).
[25] I.R.C. § 417(g).
[26] IRS Notice 2008-30.
[27] I.R.C. § 417(a)(6)(A) as modified by PPA § 1102(a); IRS Reg. § 1.417(e)-1(b)(3).
[28] I.R.C. § 417(f)(2); IRS Reg. § 1.401(a)-20, Q&A-10(b)(1).
[29] IRS Reg. 1.401(a)-20, Q&A 10(b)(3).

**Early commencement of distributions**

A plan may start a participant's benefit less than 30 days after providing notice if the participant affirmatively elects a form of distribution and the following conditions are met:[30]

- The distribution must not begin until at least seven days after notice is provided.
- The participant must be informed that he or she has at least 30 days to consider whether to waive the QJSA and choose an alternative form of payment.
- The participant must be able to revoke a waiver at any time prior to the annuity starting date, or the end of the seven-day period if later.
- The notice must be provided before the annuity starting date.

**Retroactive annuity starting date**

A defined benefit plan may base benefits on a retroactive annuity starting date (RASD) if the plan provides for it, *and* the participant elects to use it.[31] A RASD is an annuity starting date that is before the date the QJSA notice is provided.[32] A plan may impose conditions on the use of RASD, such as limiting its use to annuity payment forms and not lump sum distributions.[33]

If a RASD is used, the notice must be provided no fewer than 30 days and no more than 180 days before the first benefit payment date. A participant's benefit election must be made after the written explanation is provided and on or before the date of the first payment. The plan may waive the 30-day notice requirement if the requirements for early commencement, described above, are satisfied.[34]

**Distribution methods**

Sending the QJSA notice to the participant's last known address by first-class mail and hand delivery are acceptable distribution methods. Posting the notice is not acceptable.[35] Electronic media can be used to provide the QJSA notice (see Section D in Chapter 3 for IRS rules for electronic plan communications).

---

[30] I.R.C. § 417(a)(7); IRS Reg. § 1.417(e)-1(b)(3).
[31] IRS Reg. § 1.417(e)-1(b)(3)(iv).
[32] IRS Reg. § 1.417(e)-1(b)(3)(iv)(B).
[33] IRS Reg. § 1.417(e)-1(b)(3)(iv)(A).
[34] IRS Reg. § 1.417(e)-1(b)(3)(vi).
[35] IRS Reg. § 1.417(a)(3)-1(a)(3).

# C. Notice of Withholding and Rollover Treatment

A plan administrator must provide a Notice of Withholding and Rollover Treatment to any participant or surviving spouse who receives a plan distribution from a qualified retirement plan that is eligible for rollover.[36]

**PPA note**

The PPA expanded the 90-day maximum notice period to 180 days.[37] PPA also added the option of a direct IRA rollover for nonspouse beneficiaries.

**Definition**

A *Notice of Withholding and Rollover Treatment* explains the direct rollover rules, income tax withholding on distributions not directly rolled over, and tax consequences of eligible rollover distributions.[38]

**Eligible rollover distribution**

In general, an *eligible rollover distribution* is any distribution to a participant or a surviving spouse of all or part of the balance to the credit of the participant in a qualified plan.[39]

Eligible rollover distributions do not include:[40]

- a series of substantially equal periodic payments (not less frequently than annually) made over the life of the participant or the joint lives of the participant and his or her beneficiary or over the life expectancy of a participant or the joint life expectancies of a participant and his or her designated beneficiary;
- payments made over a specified period of ten or more years;
- any hardship distributions; or
- any qualified disaster-relief distribution.

**Note.** Amounts paid to a participant from an annuity contract that has been distributed to him or her from a qualified plan may be an eligible rollover distribution.[41]

---

[36] I.R.C. § 402(f)(1); IRS Reg. § 1.402(f)-1, Q&A-1(a).
[37] PPA § 1102(a).
[38] I.R.C. § 402(f)(1); IRS Reg. § 1.402(f)-1, Q&A-1(a).
[39] I.R.C. §§ 402(c)(4) and (9).
[40] I.R.C. § 402(c)(4).
[41] IRS Reg. §§ 1.401(a)(31)-1, Q&A-17, 1.402(c)-2, Q&A-10.

A participant may roll over:

- an eligible rollover distribution from a qualified retirement plan, 403(b) tax-sheltered annuity plan, or a governmental Section 457 plan, to any other such "eligible retirement plan;"[42]
- a distribution from an IRA (other than a Roth IRA) to another IRA or an "eligible retirement plan;"[43]
- employee after-tax contributions distributed from a qualified plan to an IRA or another qualified retirement plan, as long as certain requirements are met.[44]

**Designated Roth accounts** Participants who have made designated Roth contributions under a plan may roll over their Roth accounts to a Roth IRA or, through a direct rollover, to another eligible employer plan that accepts Roth accounts.[45]

- *Rollovers to a Roth IRA.* A designated Roth account may be rolled over directly or indirectly to a Roth IRA. The five-year period during which earnings are taxable if distributed is based on the holding period in the Roth IRA and will not include the period in a plan.[46] Once a designated Roth account has been rolled over to a Roth IRA, the funds cannot later be rolled to an employer plan.[47]
- *Rollovers to an eligible employer plan.* Qualified plans, Section 403(b) tax sheltered annuities and governmental 457(b) plans that are eligible rollover plans and provide separate accounting for Roth rollover amounts and their earnings can accept rollovers. The plan administrator of the distributing plan provides the plan administrator of the recipient plan with either (1) a statement indicating the first year of the 5 taxable year period of the designated Roth account and the amount of the basis (the previously taxed Roth contributions), or (2) a statement that the distribution is a qualified distribution.[48] Unlike a Roth rollover to an IRA, a rollover of a designated Roth account to an employer plan that is qualified under section 401 or 403 allows the holding period from the original plan to be added to the period in the new plan.[49]

Beginning January 1, 2008, if limits based on income and filing status are met, participants may also directly roll non-Roth funds over to

---

42   I.R.C. §§ 402(c)(8)(B), 403(b)(8)(A)(ii), 457(e)(16).
43   I.R.C. § 408(d)(3).
44   I.R.C. §§ 401(a)(31)(B), 402(c)(2).
45   I.R.C. 402A(c)(3). A pending technical correction (Summer 2008) would clarify that such rollovers are not subject to the income limits on conversion rollovers.
46   Reg. § 1.408A-10, Q&A 4.
47   Reg. § 1.408A-10, Q&A 5.
48   Reg. § 1.402A-2, Q&A 2(a)(1).
49   Reg. § 1.402A-1, Q&A 4(b).

a Roth IRA with similar tax consequences to converting a traditional IRA to a Roth IRA.[50]

**Automatic rollovers of involuntary cashouts**

Qualified retirement plans that call for automatic cashout distributions must roll over to a designated IRA involuntary cashouts ($5,000 or less) that exceed $1,000 and are eligible for rollover, unless a plan participant affirmatively elects to receive the distribution or have the distribution transferred to a different IRA or a qualified plan.[51]

The DOL has issued regulations that provide a safe harbor for selecting the IRA provider used for the automatic rollover requirement.[52] IRS Guidance offers a model plan amendment and transition rules.[53]

**Nonspouse beneficiaries**

Plans may optionally offer to rollover distributions for nonspouse beneficiaries.[54]

**Content requirements**

The Notice of Withholding and Rollover Treatment must explain:[55]

- The rules under which a participant or spouse may directly roll over an eligible rollover distribution to an eligible retirement plan and that the automatic rollover rule (described above) applies to certain involuntary cashouts[56]
- The income tax withholding rules on distributions that are not directly rolled over to an eligible retirement plan[57]
- The rules under which an employee may defer income tax on a distribution rolled over to an eligible retirement plan within 60 days of the distribution
- If applicable, special rules regarding taxation of lump-sum distributions (e.g., five- or ten-year forward averaging)
- In the case of a rollover to an eligible retirement plan, any restrictions or tax consequences that may apply to the distribution of that rollover from such plan that are different from the rules that apply to an amount distributed from the distributing plan[58]

---

[50]  I.R.C. §§ 408A(c)(3)(B) and (d)(3); IRS Notice 2008-30.
[51]  I.R.C. § 401(a)(31)(B).
[52]  DOL Reg. § 2550.404a-2.
[53]  IRS Notice 2005-5.
[54]  IRS Notice 2007-7, Q&A 14. A pending technical correction (Summer 2008) would make this a mandatory requirement.
[55]  I.R.C. § 402(f)(1); IRS Reg. § 1.402(f)-1, Q&A-1.
[56]  I.R.C. § 402(f)(1)(A).
[57]  *See* I.R.C. § 3405.
[58]  I.R.C. § 402(f)(1)(E).

**Electronic distribution**

The notice and consent have traditionally been provided in writing. However, the IRS has issued regulations that provide standards for electronic transmission of the notice.

See Section D in Chapter 3 for IRS rules for electronic plan communications.

**Satisfying the notice requirement**

In general, to satisfy the notice requirement, a notice must be provided for every eligible rollover distribution. However, for a series of periodic payments that are eligible rollover distributions, the plan may satisfy the notice requirement by providing the notice before the first payment in the series and at least once annually for as long as the payments continue.[59]

See Figure 9-1A (on pages 9-16 through 9-24) for the IRS Model Notice "Special Tax Rules Regarding Plan Payments."

**Timing of notice**

The plan must provide the Notice of Withholding and Rollover Treatment no fewer than 30 days and no more than 180[60] days before the date of distribution or annuity starting date.

**Alternative timing rule**

Under an alternative timing rule, a plan may give full notice more than 180 days before the distribution if it also provides a summary of the notice during the 180/30-day time period.[61]

**Summary notice under alternative timing rule**

The summary of the notice must

- refer the participant to the most recently provided full notice; and
- advise the participant of the right to request and receive full notice without charge no fewer than 30 days (unless the participant waives the 30-day requirement) before the distribution date.

In contrast to the full notice, the summary can be provided orally through a well-designed telephone system in a manner no less understandable than a written paper summary.

**Note.** The 30-day requirement may be waived by the recipient if the plan administrator gives the recipient at least 30 days after receiving

---

[59]  IRS Reg. § 1.402(f)-1, Q&A-3.
[60]  PPA § 1102(a).
[61]  IRS Reg. § 1.402(f)-1, Q&A-2(b).

the notice to decide whether to make a direct rollover and brings the 30-day period to the recipient's attention by any reasonable method.[62]

**Penalty for non-compliance**

The IRS may assess a $100 penalty for each failure to provide the Notice of Withholding and Rollover Treatment, up to $50,000 in a calendar year.[63]

**Tax-sheltered annuities**

IRC Section 403(b) Tax-sheltered annuities (TSAs) are generally subject to the same rules as qualified plans, including the inability to roll over any hardship distributions of a participant's salary reduction contribution to a TSA. In most cases, amounts may be rolled over from a TSA to another TSA, qualified retirement plan, or individual retirement account.[64] In addition, for TSA distributions, the 402(f) notice must be provided within a "reasonable period of time." The administrator is deemed to have provided the notice within a reasonable period of time if it complies with the 180/30-day time period applicable to qualified plans.[65]

**Withholding rules for periodic payments and nonperiodic payments not eligible for rollover**

Specific income tax withholding requirements apply to qualified plan distributions that are not eligible to be rolled over:

- Periodic payments are subject to income tax withholding based on Circular E wage withholding tables.[66]
- Nonperiodic payments are subject to income tax withholding at a 10% rate.[67]

In both cases, the payee may elect not to have income tax withheld.

Payees must be notified of their withholding choices. The notices must include:[68]

- notice of the right to elect not to have withholding apply to any payment or distribution and instructions on how to make the election;

---

[62] IRS Reg. § 1.402(f)-1, Q&A-2(a).
[63] I.R.C. § 6652(i).
[64] I.R.C. § 403(b)(8) as amended by PPA '06.
[65] IRS Reg. § 1.403(b)-2, Q&A-3.
[66] I.R.C. 3405(a)(1)
[67] I.R.C. 3405(b)(1)
[68] Temp Reg. § 35.3405-1T. Question D-18.

- notice of the right to revoke the election at any time and a statement that the election remains effective until revoked;
- a warning that penalties may be incurred under the estimated tax payment rules if payments of estimated tax are not adequate and sufficient tax is not withheld from the or distribution; and
- information about imposing withholding on the full amount of the distribution where information about amounts excludable from gross income are not known.

When distributions are to be delivered outside the U.S. and its possessions, generally an election out of withholding is not allowed and a 30% income tax withholding rate applies.[69] However, payees who are nonresident aliens can avoid IRC 3405 withholding and apply the withholding rules under IRC 1441 or special treaty provisions by certifying on Form W-8 that they aren't a U.S. person and identifying the applicable treaty provision.

Sample notices of election and revocation rights are provided in Figures 9-X1 through 9X4.

**Withholding notice deadlines**

For periodic payments, the notice must be provided no earlier than six months before the date of the first distribution and at the time of the first distribution. In addition, a yearly notice of the right to make and revoke elections is required.[70]

For nonperiodic payments, the notice of the right to elect out of withholding must be provided no earlier than six months in advance and must be provided within sufficient time for the payee to make the election and send the reply to the payor before the distribution is made.[71]

**Penalty for non-compliance**

The IRS may assess a $10 penalty for each failure to provide these withholding notices, up to $5,000 in a calendar year.[72]

---

[69]   Reg. § 1.1441-1(b)(3)(iii)(C).
[70]   Temp Reg. § 35.3405-1T. Question D-4.
[71]   Temp Reg. § 35.3405-1T. Question D-9.
[72]   I.R.C. § 6652(h).

## Figure 9-1A

## Model Notice "Safe Harbor Explanation"
## of Pension-Rollover Rights (IRS Notice 2002-3)

### SPECIAL TAX NOTICE REGARDING PLAN PAYMENTS

*Caution.* **This notice has not been updated to reflect changes to Roth account options, nonspouse rollovers, etc. IRS and Treasury have a revised notice under development. Samples of a modified notice are available from the author upon request.**

This notice explains how you can continue to defer federal income tax on your retirement savings in the [INSERT NAME OF PLAN] (the "Plan") and contains important information you will need before you decide how to receive your Plan benefits.

This notice is provided to you by [INSERT NAME OF THE PLAN ADMINISTRATOR OR, IN THE CASE OF A § 403(b) TAX-SHELTERED ANNUITY, THE PAYOR] (your "Plan Administrator") because all or part of the payment that you will soon receive from the Plan may be eligible for rollover by you or your Plan Administrator to a traditional IRA or an eligible employer plan. A rollover is a payment by you or the Plan Administrator of all or part of your benefit to another plan or IRA that allows you to continue to postpone taxation of that benefit until it is paid to you. Your payment cannot be rolled over to a Roth IRA, a SIMPLE IRA, or a Coverdell Education Savings Account (formerly known as an education IRA). An "eligible employer plan" includes a plan qualified under section 401(a) of the Internal Revenue Code, including a 401(k) plan, profit-sharing plan, defined benefit plan, stock bonus plan, and money purchase plan; a section 403(a) annuity plan; a section 403(b) tax-sheltered annuity; and an eligible section 457(b) plan maintained by a governmental employer (governmental 457 plan).

An eligible employer plan is not legally required to accept a rollover. Before you decide to roll over your payment to another employer plan, you should find out whether the plan accepts roll-overs and, if so, the types of distributions it accepts as a rollover. You should also find out about any documents that are required to be completed before the receiving plan will accept a rollover. Even if a plan accepts rollovers, it might not accept rollovers of certain types of distributions, such as after-tax amounts. If this is the case, and your distribution includes after-tax amounts, you may wish instead to roll your distribution over to a traditional IRA or split your rollover amount between the employer plan in which you will participate and a traditional IRA. If an employer plan accepts your rollover, the plan may restrict subsequent distributions of the rollover amount or may require your spouse's consent for any subsequent distribution. A subsequent distribution from the plan that accepts your rollover may also be subject to different tax treatment than distributions from this Plan. Check with the administrator of the plan that is to receive your rollover prior to making the rollover.

If you have additional questions after reading this notice, you can contact your plan administrator at [INSERT PHONE NUMBER OR OTHER CONTACT INFORMATION].

### SUMMARY

There are two ways you may be able to receive a Plan payment that is eligible for rollover:

1. Certain payments can be made directly to a traditional IRA that you establish or to an eligible employer plan that will accept it and hold it for your benefit ("DIRECT ROLLOVER"); or

2. The payment can be PAID TO YOU.

**Figure 9-1A (*cont'd*)**

**Model Notice "Safe Harbor Explanation"**
**of Pension-Rollover Rights (IRS Notice 2002-3)**

---

If you choose a DIRECT ROLLOVER:

- Your payment will not be taxed in the current year and no income tax will be withheld.

- You choose whether your payment will be made directly to your traditional IRA or to an eligible employer plan that accepts your rollover. Your payment cannot be rolled over to a Roth IRA, a SIMPLE IRA, or a Coverdell Education Savings Account because these are not traditional IRAs.

- The taxable portion of your payment will be taxed later when you take it out of the traditional IRA or the eligible employer plan. Depending on the type of plan, the later distribution may be subject to different tax treatment than it would be if you received a taxable distribution from this Plan.

If you choose to have a Plan payment that is eligible for rollover PAID TO YOU:

- You will receive only 80% of the taxable amount of the payment, because the Plan Administrator is required to withhold 20% of that amount and send it to the IRS as income tax withholding to be credited against your taxes.

- The taxable amount of your payment will be taxed in the current year unless you roll it over. Under limited circumstances, you may be able to use special tax rules that could reduce the tax you owe. However, if you receive the payment before age 59$\frac{1}{2}$, you may have to pay an additional 10% tax.

- You can roll over all or part of the payment by paying it to your traditional IRA or to an eligible employer plan that accepts your rollover within 60 days after you receive the payment. The amount rolled over will not be taxed until you take it out of the traditional IRA or the eligible employer plan.

- If you want to roll over 100% of the payment to a traditional IRA or an eligible employer plan, you must find other money to replace the 20% of the taxable portion that was withheld. If you roll over only the 80% that you received, you will be taxed on the 20% that was withheld and that is not rolled over.

Your Right to Waive the 30-Day Notice Period. Generally, neither a direct rollover nor a payment can be made from the plan until at least 30 days after your receipt of this notice. Thus, after receiving this notice, you have at least 30 days to consider whether or not to have your withdrawal directly rolled over. If you do not wish to wait until this 30-day notice period ends before your election is processed, you may waive the notice period by making an affirmative election indicating whether or not you wish to make a direct rollover. Your withdrawal will then be processed in accordance with your election as soon as practical after it is received by the Plan Administrator.

---

## Figure 9-1A (*cont'd*)

## Model Notice "Safe Harbor Explanation" of Pension-Rollover Rights (IRS Notice 2002-3)

### MORE INFORMATION

I.   PAYMENTS THAT CAN AND CANNOT BE ROLLED OVER

II.   DIRECT ROLLOVER

III.   PAYMENT PAID TO YOU

IV.   SURVIVING SPOUSES, ALTERNATE PAYEES, AND OTHER BENEFICIARIES

### I. PAYMENTS THAT CAN AND CANNOT BE ROLLED OVER

Payments from the Plan may be "eligible rollover distributions." This means that they can be rolled over to a traditional IRA or to an eligible employer plan that accepts rollovers. Payments from a plan cannot be rolled over to a Roth IRA, a SIMPLE IRA, or a Coverdell Education Savings Account. Your Plan administrator should be able to tell you what portion of your payment is an eligible rollover distribution.

After-tax Contributions. If you made after-tax contributions to the Plan, these contributions may be rolled into either a traditional IRA or to certain employer plans that accept rollovers of the after-tax contributions. The following rules apply:

1.   Rollover into a Traditional IRA. You can roll over your after-tax contributions to a traditional IRA either directly or indirectly. Your plan administrator should be able to tell you how much of your payment is the taxable portion and how much is the after-tax portion.

     If you roll over after-tax contributions to a traditional IRA, it is your responsibility to keep track of, and report to the Service on the applicable forms, the amount of these after-tax contributions. This will enable the nontaxable amount of any future distributions from the traditional IRA to be determined.

     Once you roll over your after-tax contributions to a traditional IRA, those amounts CANNOT later be rolled over to an employer plan.

2.   Rollover into an Employer Plan. You can roll over after-tax contributions from an employer plan that is qualified under Code section 401(a) or a section 403(a) annuity plan to another such plan using a direct rollover if the other plan provides separate accounting for amounts rolled over, including separate accounting for the after-tax employee contributions and earnings on those contributions. You can also roll over after-tax contributions from a section 403(b) tax-sheltered annuity to another section 403(b) tax-sheltered annuity using a direct rollover if the other tax-sheltered annuity provides separate accounting for amounts rolled over, including separate accounting for the after-tax employee contributions and earnings on those contributions. You CANNOT roll over after-tax contributions to a governmental 457 plan. If you want to roll over your after-tax contributions to an employer plan that accepts these rollovers, you cannot have the after-tax contributions paid to you first. You must instruct the Plan Administrator of this Plan to make a direct rollover on your behalf. Also, you cannot first roll over after-tax contributions to a traditional IRA and then roll over that amount into an employer plan.

**Figure 9-1A (*cont'd*)**

**Model Notice "Safe Harbor Explanation"
of Pension-Rollover Rights (IRS Notice 2002-3)**

---

The following types of payments <u>cannot</u> be rolled over:

<u>Payments Spread over Long Periods.</u> You cannot roll over a payment if it is part of a series of equal (or almost equal) payments that are made at least once a year and that will last for:

- your lifetime (or a period measured by your life expectancy), or:

- your lifetime and your beneficiary's lifetime (or a period measured by your joint life expectancies), or

- a period of 10 years or more.

<u>Required Minimum Payments.</u> Beginning when you reach age 70½ or retire, whichever is later, a certain portion of your payment cannot be rolled over because it is a "required minimum payment" that must be paid to you. Special rules apply if you own more than 5% of your employer.

<u>Hardship Distributions.</u> A hardship distribution cannot be rolled over.

<u>ESOP Dividends.</u> Cash dividends paid to you on employer stock held in an employee stock ownership plan cannot be rolled over.

<u>Corrective Distributions.</u> A distribution that is made to correct a failed nondiscrimination test or because legal limits on certain contributions were exceeded cannot be rolled over.

<u>Loans Treated as Distributions.</u> The amount of a plan loan that becomes a taxable deemed distribution because of a default cannot be rolled over. However, a loan offset amount is eligible for rollover, as discussed in Part III below. Ask the Plan Administrator of this Plan if distribution of your loan qualifies for rollover treatment.

The Plan Administrator of this Plan should be able to tell you if your payment includes amounts which cannot be rolled over.

## II. <u>DIRECT ROLLOVER</u>

A DIRECT ROLLOVER is a direct payment of the amount of your Plan benefits to a traditional IRA or an eligible employer plan that will accept it. You can choose a DIRECT ROLLOVER of all or any portion of your payment that is an eligible rollover distribution, as described in Part I above. You are not taxed on any taxable portion of your payment for which you choose a DIRECT ROLLOVER until you later take it out of the traditional IRA or eligible employer plan. In addition, no income tax withholding is required for any taxable portion of your Plan benefits for which you choose a DIRECT ROLLOVER. This Plan might not let you choose a DIRECT ROLLOVER if your distributions for the year are less than $200.

<u>DIRECT ROLLOVER to a Traditional IRA.</u> You can open a traditional IRA to receive the direct rollover. If you choose to have your payment made directly to a traditional IRA, contact an IRA sponsor (usually a financial institution) to find out how to have your payment made in a direct rollover to a traditional IRA at that institution. If you are unsure of how to invest your money, you can temporarily establish a traditional IRA to receive the payment. However, in choosing a traditional IRA, you may wish to make sure that the traditional IRA you choose will allow you to move all or a part of your payment to another traditional IRA at a later date, without penalties or other limitations. See IRS Publication 590, Individual Retirement Arrangements, for more information on traditional IRAs (including limits on how often you can roll over between IRAs).

## Figure 9-1A (*cont'd*)

## Model Notice "Safe Harbor Explanation"
## of Pension-Rollover Rights (IRS Notice 2002-3)

DIRECT ROLLOVER to a Plan. If you are employed by a new employer that has an eligible employer plan, and you want a direct rollover to that plan, ask the plan administrator of that plan whether it will accept your rollover. An eligible employer plan is not legally required to accept a rollover. Even if your new employer's plan does not accept a rollover, you can choose a DIRECT ROLLOVER to a traditional IRA. If the employer plan accepts your rollover, the plan may provide restrictions on the circumstances under which you may later receive a distribution of the rollover amount or may require spousal consent to any subsequent distribution. Check with the plan administrator of that plan before making your decision.

DIRECT ROLLOVER of a Series of Payments. If you receive a payment that can be rolled over to a traditional IRA or an eligible employer plan that will accept it, and it is paid in a series of payments for less than 10 years, your choice to make or not make a DIRECT ROLLOVER for a payment will apply to all later payments in the series until you change your election. You are free to change your election for any later payment in the series.

Change in Tax Treatment Resulting from a DIRECT ROLLOVER. The tax treatment of any payment from the eligible employer plan or traditional IRA receiving your DIRECT ROLLOVER might be different than if you received your benefit in a taxable distribution directly from the Plan. For example, if you were born before January 1, 1936, you might be entitled to ten-year averaging or capital gain treatment, as explained below. However, if you have your benefit rolled over to a section 403(b) tax-sheltered annuity, a governmental 457 plan, or a traditional IRA in a DIRECT ROLLOVER, your benefit will no longer be eligible for that special treatment. See the sections below entitled "Additional 10% Tax if You Are under Age 59$^{1}/_{2}$" and "Special Tax Treatment if You Were Born before January 1, 1936."

## III. PAYMENT PAID TO YOU

If your payment can be rolled over (see Part I above) and the payment is made to you in cash, it is subject to 20% federal income tax withholding on the taxable portion (state tax withholding may also apply). The payment is taxed in the year you receive it unless, within 60 days, you roll it over to a traditional IRA or an eligible employer plan that accepts rollovers. If you do not roll it over, special tax rules may apply.

Income Tax Withholding:

Mandatory Withholding. If any portion of your payment can be rolled over under Part I above and you do not elect to make a DIRECT ROLLOVER, the Plan is required by law to withhold 20% of the taxable amount. This amount is sent to the IRS as federal income tax withholding. For example, if you can roll over a taxable payment of $10,000, only $8,000 will be paid to you because the Plan must withhold $2,000 as income tax. However, when you prepare your income tax return for the year, unless you make a rollover within 60 days (see "Sixty-Day Rollover Option" below), you must report the full $10,000 as a taxable payment from the Plan. You must report the $2,000 as tax withheld, and it will be credited against any income tax you owe for the year. There will be no income tax withholding if your payments for the year are less than $200.

Voluntary Withholding. If any portion of your payment is taxable but cannot be rolled over under Part I above, the mandatory withholding rules described above do not apply. In this case, you may elect not to have withholding apply to that portion. If you do nothing, an amount will be taken out of this portion of your payment for federal income tax withholding. To elect out of withholding, ask the Plan Administrator for the election form and related information.

**Figure 9-1A (*cont'd*)**

**Model Notice "Safe Harbor Explanation"
of Pension-Rollover Rights (IRS Notice 2002-3)**

Sixty-Day Rollover Option. If you receive a payment that can be rolled over under Part I above, you can still decide to roll over all or part of it to a traditional IRA or to an eligible employer plan that accepts rollovers. If you decide to roll over, you must contribute the amount of the payment you received to a traditional IRA or eligible employer plan within 60 days after you receive the payment. The portion of your payment that is rolled over will not be taxed until you take it out of the traditional IRA or the eligible employer plan.

You can roll over up to 100% of your payment that can be rolled over under Part I above, including an amount equal to the 20% of the taxable portion that was withheld. If you choose to roll over 100%, you must find other money within the 60-day period to contribute to the traditional IRA or the eligible employer plan, to replace the 20% that was withheld. On the other hand, if you roll over only the 80% of the taxable portion that you received, you will be taxed on the 20% that was withheld.

Example: The taxable portion of your payment that can be rolled over under Part I above is $10,000, and you choose to have it paid to you. You will receive $8,000, and $2,000 will be sent to the IRS as income tax withholding. Within 60 days after receiving the $8,000, you may roll over the entire $10,000 to a traditional IRA or an eligible employer plan. To do this, you roll over the $8,000 you received from the Plan, and you will have to find $2,000 from other sources (your savings, a loan, etc.). In this case, the entire $10,000 is not taxed until you take it out of the traditional IRA or an eligible employer plan. If you roll over the entire $10,000, when you file your income tax return you may get a refund of part or all of the $2,000 withheld.

If, on the other hand, you roll over only $8,000, the $2,000 you did not roll over is taxed in the year it was withheld. When you file your income tax return, you may get a refund of part of the $2,000 withheld. (However, any refund is likely to be larger if you roll over the entire $10,000.)

Additional 10% Tax If You Are under Age $59^1/_2$. If you receive a payment before you reach age $59^1/_2$ and you do not roll it over, then, in addition to the regular income tax, you may have to pay an extra tax equal to 10% of the taxable portion of the payment. The additional 10% tax generally does not apply to (1) payments that are paid after you separate from service with your employer during or after the year you reach age 55, (2) payments that are paid because you retire due to disability, (3) payments that are paid as equal (or almost equal) payments over your life or life expectancy (or your and your beneficiary's lives or life expectancies), (4) dividends paid with respect to stock by an employee stock ownership plan (ESOP) as described in Code section 404(k), (5) payments that are paid directly to the government to satisfy a federal tax levy, (6) payments that are paid to an alternate payee under a qualified domestic relations order, or (7) payments that do not exceed the amount of your deductible medical expenses. See IRS Form 5329 for more information on the additional 10% tax.

The additional 10% tax will not apply to distributions from a governmental 457 plan, except to the extent the distribution is attributable to an amount you rolled over to that plan (adjusted for investment returns) from another type of eligible employer plan or IRA. Any amount rolled over from a governmental 457 plan to another type of eligible employer plan or to a traditional IRA will become subject to the additional 10% tax if it is distributed to you before you reach age $59^1/_2$, unless one of the exceptions applies.

## Figure 9-1A (*cont'd*)

## Model Notice "Safe Harbor Explanation"
## of Pension-Rollover Rights (IRS Notice 2002-3)

Special Tax Treatment If You Were Born before January 1, 1936. If you receive a payment from a plan qualified under section 401(a) or a section 403(a) annuity plan that can be rolled over under Part I and you do not roll it over to a traditional IRA or an eligible employer plan, the payment will be taxed in the year you receive it. However, if the payment qualifies as a "lump sum distribution," it may be eligible for special tax treatment. (See also "Employer Stock or Securities", below.) A lump sum distribution is a payment, within one year, of your entire balance under the Plan (and certain other similar plans of the employer) that is payable to you after you have reached age 59$^1$/$_2$ or because you have separated from service with your employer (or, in the case of a self-employed individual, after you have reached age 59$^1$/$_2$ or have become disabled). For a payment to be treated as a lump sum distribution, you must have been a participant in the plan for at least five years before the year in which you received the distribution. The special tax treatment for lump sum distributions that may be available to you is described below.

Ten-Year Averaging. If you receive a lump sum distribution and you were born before January 1, 1936, you can make a one-time election to figure the tax on the payment by using "10-year averaging" (using 1986 tax rates). Ten-year averaging often reduces the tax you owe.

Capital Gain Treatment. If you receive a lump sum distribution and you were born before January 1, 1936, and you were a participant in the Plan before 1974, you may elect to have the part of your payment that is attributable to your pre-1974 participation in the Plan taxed as long-term capital gain at a rate of 20%.

There are other limits on the special tax treatment for lump sum distributions. For example, you can generally elect this special tax treatment only once in your lifetime, and the election applies to all lump sum distributions that you receive in that same year. You may not elect this special tax treatment if you rolled amounts into this Plan from a 403(b) tax-sheltered annuity contract, a governmental 457, or from an IRA not originally attributable to a qualified employer plan. If you have previously rolled over a distribution from this Plan (or certain other similar plans of the employer), you cannot use this special averaging treatment for later payments from the Plan. If you roll over your payment to a traditional IRA, governmental 457 plan, or 403(b) tax-sheltered annuity, you will not be able to use special tax treatment for later payments from that IRA, plan, or annuity. Also, if you roll over only a portion of your payment to a traditional IRA, governmental 457 plan, or 403(b) tax-sheltered annuity, this special tax treatment is not available for the rest of the payment. See IRS Form 4972 for additional information on lump sum distributions and how you elect the special tax treatment.

Employer Stock or Securities. There is a special rule for a payment from the Plan that includes employer stock (or other employer securities). To use this special rule, 1) the payment must qualify as a lump sum distribution, as described above, except that you do not need five years of plan participation, or 2) the employer stock included in the payment must be attributable to "after-tax" employee contributions, if any. Under this special rule, you may have the option of not paying tax on the "net unrealized appreciation" of the stock until you sell the stock. Net unrealized appreciation generally is the increase in the value of the employer stock while it was held by the Plan. For example, if employer stock was contributed to your Plan account when the stock was worth $1,000 but the stock was worth $1,200 when you received it, you would not have to pay tax on the $200 increase in value until you later sold the stock.

**Figure 9-1A (*cont'd*)**

**Model Notice "Safe Harbor Explanation"
of Pension-Rollover Rights (IRS Notice 2002-3)**

You may instead elect not to have the special rule apply to the net unrealized appreciation. In this case, your net unrealized appreciation will be taxed in the year you receive the stock, unless you roll over the stock. The stock can be rolled over to a traditional IRA or another eligible employer plan, either in a direct rollover or a rollover that you make yourself. Generally, you will no longer be able to use the special rule for net unrealized appreciation if you roll the stock over to a traditional IRA or another eligible employer plan.

If you receive only employer stock in a payment that can be rolled over, no amount will be withheld from the payment. If you receive cash or property other than employer stock, as well as employer stock, in a payment that can be rolled over, the 20% withholding amount will be based on the entire taxable amount paid to you (including the value of the employer stock determined by excluding the net unrealized appreciation). However, the amount withheld will be limited to the cash or property (excluding employer stock) paid to you.

If you receive employer stock in a payment that qualifies as a lump sum distribution, the special tax treatment for lump sum distributions described above (such as 10-year averaging) also may apply. See IRS Form 4972 for additional information on these rules.

Repayment of Plan Loans. If your employment ends and you have an outstanding loan from your Plan, your employer may reduce (or "offset") your balance in the Plan by the amount of the loan you have not repaid. The amount of your loan offset is treated as a distribution to you at the time of the offset and will be taxed unless you roll over an amount equal to the amount of your loan offset to another qualified employer plan or a traditional IRA within 60 days of the date of the offset. If the amount of your loan offset is the only amount you receive or are treated as having received, no amount will be withheld from it. If you receive other payments of cash or property from the Plan, the 20% withholding amount will be based on the entire amount paid to you, including the amount of the loan offset. The amount withheld will be limited to the amount of other cash or property paid to you (other than any employer securities). The amount of a defaulted plan loan that is a taxable deemed distribution cannot be rolled over.

## IV. SURVIVING SPOUSES, ALTERNATE PAYEES, AND OTHER BENEFICIARIES

In general, the rules summarized above that apply to payments to employees also apply to payments to surviving spouses of employees and to spouses or former spouses who are "alternate payees." You are an alternate payee if your interest in the Plan results from a "qualified domestic relations order," which is an order issued by a court, usually in connection with a divorce or legal separation.

If you are a surviving spouse or an alternate payee, you may choose to have a payment that can be rolled over, as described in Part I above, paid in a DIRECT ROLLOVER to a traditional IRA or to an eligible employer plan or paid to you. If you have the payment paid to you, you can keep it or roll it over yourself to a traditional IRA or to an eligible employer plan. Thus, you have the same choices as the employee.

If you are a beneficiary other than a surviving spouse or an alternate payee, you cannot choose a direct rollover, and you cannot roll over the payment yourself.

## Figure 9-1A (*cont'd*)

### Model Notice "Safe Harbor Explanation"
### of Pension-Rollover Rights (IRS Notice 2002-3)

If you are a surviving spouse, an alternate payee, or another beneficiary, your payment is generally not subject to the additional 10% tax described in Part III above, even if you are younger than age 59½.

If you are a surviving spouse, an alternate payee, or another beneficiary, you may be able to use the special tax treatment for lump sum distributions and the special rule for payments that include employer stock, as described in Part III above. If you receive a payment because of the employee's death, you may be able to treat the payment as a lump sum distribution if the employee met the appropriate age requirements, whether or not the employee had 5 years of participation in the Plan.

**HOW TO OBTAIN ADDITIONAL INFORMATION**

This notice summarizes only the federal (not state or local) tax rules that might apply to your payment. The rules described above are complex and contain many conditions and exceptions that are not included in this notice. Therefore, you may want to consult with the Plan Administrator or a professional tax advisor before you take a payment of your benefits from your Plan. Also, you can find more specific information on the tax treatment of payments from qualified employer plans in IRS Publication 575, Pension and Annuity Income, and IRS Publication 590, Individual Retirement Arrangements. These publications are available from your local IRS office, on the IRS's Internet Web site at *www.irs.gov*, or by calling 1-800-TAX-FORMS.

**Figure 9-1B**

**Sample**

## NOTICE OF WITHHOLDING ON PERIODIC PAYMENTS

(from Temp Reg. § 35.3405-1T, Question D-21)

---

The [pension] OR [annuity] payments you receive from the [insert name of plan or company] will be subject to Federal income tax withholding unless you elect not to have withholding apply. Withholding will only apply to the portion of your [pension] OR [annuity] payment that is already included in your income subject to Federal income tax and will be like wage withholding. Thus, there will be no withholding on the return of your own nondeductible contributions to the [plan] OR [contract].

You may elect not to have withholding apply to your [pension] OR [annuity] payments by returning the signed and dated election [manner may be specified] to [insert name and address]. Your election will remain in effect until you revoke it. You may revoke your election at any time by returning the signed and dated revocation to [insert appropriate name or address]. Any election or revocation will be effective no later than the January 1, May 1, July 1, or October 1 after it is received, so long as it is received at least 30 days before that date. You may make and revoke elections not to have withholding apply as often as you wish. Additional elections may be obtained from [insert name and address].

If you do not return the election by [insert date], Federal income tax will be withheld from the taxable portion of your [pension] OR [annuity] payments as if you were a married individual claiming three withholding allowances. As a result, no Federal income tax will be withheld if the taxable portion of your annual [pension] OR [annuity] payments are less than $5,400.

If you elect not to have withholding apply to your [pension] OR [annuity] payments, or if you do not have enough Federal income tax withheld from your [pension] OR [annuity] payments, you may be responsible for payment of estimated tax. You may incur penalties under the estimated tax rules if your withholding and estimated tax payments are not sufficient.

---

## Figure 9-1C

## Sample

## WITHHOLDING ELECTION FORM FOR PERIODIC PAYMENTS

(from Temp Reg. §35.3405-1T, Question D-22)

**NOTICE OF WITHHOLDING ON DISTRIBUTIONS OR WITHDRAWALS FROM ANNUITIES, IRA'S, PENSION, PROFIT SHARING, STOCK BONUS, AND OTHER DEFERRED COMPENSATION PLANS**

*Instructions:* Check Box A if you do not want any Federal income tax withheld from your [pension] OR [annuity]. Check Box B to revoke an election not to have withholding apply. Return the signed and dated election to [insert name and address]. Even if you elect not to have Federal income tax withheld, you are liable for payment of Federal income tax on the taxable portion of your [pension] OR [annuity]. You also may be subject to tax penalties under the estimated tax payment rules if your payments of estimated tax and withholding, if any, are not adequate.

    ☐ **A.** I do not want to have Federal income tax withheld from my [pension] OR [annuity].

    ☐ **B.** I want to have Federal income tax withheld from my [pension] OR [annuity].

Signed:

| Name | Date |
|------|------|

Return your completed election to: [insert name and address]

**Figure 9-1D**

**Sample**

## NOTICE OF WITHHOLDING ON NONPERIODIC PAYMENTS

(from Temp Reg. § 35.3405-1T, Question D-25)

---

The [distributions] OR [withdrawals] you receive from the [insert name of plan or company] are subject to Federal income tax withholding unless you elect not to have withholding apply. Withholding will only apply to the portion of your [distribution] OR [withdrawal] that is included in your income subject to Federal income tax. Thus, for example, there will be no withholding on the return of your own nondeductible contributions to the [plan] OR [contract].

You may elect not to have withholding apply to your [distribution] OR [withdrawal] payments by signing and dating the attached election and returning it [manner may be specified] to [insert name and address].

If you do not return the election by [insert date] receipt of your payments may be delayed. If you do not respond by the date your [distribution] OR [withdrawal] is scheduled to begin, Federal income tax will be withheld from the taxable portion of your [distribution] OR [withdrawal]. [Insert information on rates if desired].

If you elect not to have withholding apply to your [distribution] OR [withdrawal] payments, or if you do not have enough Federal income tax withheld from your [distribution] OR [withdrawal], you may be responsible for payment of estimated tax. You may incur penalties under the estimated tax rules if your withholding and estimated tax payments are not sufficient.

---

## Figure 9-1E

## Sample

## NONPERIODIC WITHHOLDING ELECTION FORM

(from Temp Reg. § 35.3405-1T, Question D-26)

**ELECTION FOR PAYEES OF NONPERIODIC PAYMENTS**

*Instructions:* If you do not want any Federal income tax withheld from your [distribution] OR [withdrawal], sign and date this election and return it to [insert name and address]. Even if you elect not to have Federal income tax withheld, you are liable for payment of Federal income tax on the taxable portion of your [distribution] OR [withdrawal]. You also may be subject to tax penalties under the estimated tax payment rules if your payments of estimated tax and withholding, if any, are not adequate.

I do not want to have Federal income tax withheld from my [distribution] OR [withdrawal].

Signed:

_____     _____
Name                                            Date

Return your completed election to: [insert name and address]

# D. Notice of Suspension of Benefits

**Definition**   A *Notice of Suspension of Benefits* is a written notification explaining that a participant's monthly pension plan benefits are suspended (that is, permanently forfeited).[73]

A pension plan administrator must distribute this notice to employees whose benefit payments are suspended upon reemployment or to employees who continue to work beyond normal retirement age even if they are not currently receiving benefits.[74]

**Exception**   The Notice of Suspension of Benefits need not be given to employees who continue to work beyond normal retirement age if these employees' benefits will be actuarially increased to reflect postponement of benefits. The suspension of benefit rules merely apply when there is a decrease in actuarial value.[75]

**Content requirements**   The notice must contain the following information:[76]

- Specific reasons why the benefits are suspended
- A general description of the plan's suspension provisions
- A copy of the plan's suspension provisions
- A statement explaining that the participant can find the applicable DOL regulations in Section 2530.203-3 of the Code of Federal Regulations
- A description of the review procedures for suspension decisions
- A description of the procedure and forms, if any, for notifying the plan that benefits should resume
- An explanation of any offset against post-suspension benefits for benefits that should have been suspended but were not, including:
  — period of employment affected
  — amount subject to the offset
  — how the offset will be made

If the plan's summary plan description (SPD) contains substantially the same information, the suspension notice may refer to the relevant

---

73   DOL Reg. § 2530.203-3(b)(4).
74   *Id.*
75   IRS Notice 82-23, 1982-2 C.B. 752.
76   DOL Reg. § 2530.203-3(b)(4).

portions of the SPD. However, the suspension notice must explain how a participant may obtain a copy of the SPD, and explain that a request for an SPD must be honored within 30 days.[77]

**Due date**

The Notice of Suspension of Benefits must be provided to the participant during the first month or payroll period in which benefits are suspended.[78]

**Distribution methods**

The notice may be distributed by first-class mail or personal delivery service.[79] The notice also may be distributed electronically pursuant to the DOL's electronic distribution safe harbor rules. (See discussion at Section C in Chapter 3.)

---

[77]  Id.
[78]  Id.
[79]  Id.

# E. Domestic Relations Order Notices

**Definitions**

A *domestic relations order* is a judgment, decree, or order[80]:

- made under a state's domestic relations law; and
- related to child support, alimony payments, or marital property rights for a spouse, former spouse, child, or other dependent of a participant.

A *qualified domestic relations order* is a domestic relations order that[81]:

- creates or recognizes the existence of an alternate payee's right to receive all or a portion of a participant's benefit;
- includes certain required information; and
- does not alter the amount or form of plan benefits.

An *alternate payee* is a spouse, former spouse, child, or other dependent of a participant who is recognized by the domestic relations order as having the right to receive all, or a portion of, the benefits payable under the plan to the participant.[82]

**Affected plans**

In general, qualified retirement plans and Tax-Sheltered Annuities (TSAs) that are subject to ERISA are subject to the QDRO rules. Governmental plans and church plans may also use these rules.[83]

**Notice requirements**

When a plan is served with a domestic relations order, the plan administrator must determine whether the order is a QDRO and whether it meets certain notice requirements.[84]

The rules for QDROs impose two notice requirements on the plan: (1) a Notice of Receipt of Domestic Relations Order, and (2) a Notice of Status of Domestic Relations Order.[85]

---

[80]  ERISA §206(d)(3)(B)(ii); I.R.C. §414(p)(1)(B).
[81]  ERISA §206(d)(3)(B)(i); I.R.C. §414(p)(1)(A).
[82]  ERISA §206(d)(3)(K); I.R.C. §414(p)(8).
[83]  ERISA §206(d)(1); I.R.C. §414(p)(11).
[84]  ERISA §206(d)(3)(G); I.R.C. §414(p)(6)(B).
[85]  ERISA §206(d)(3)(G)(i); I.R.C. §414(p)(6)(A).

**Required information**

To be qualified, a domestic relations order must include the following information:[86]

- participant's name and address;
- alternate payee's name and address;
- amount or percentage of the participant's benefits to be paid to the alternate payee or how the amount or percentage is determined;
- number of payments or period to which the order applies; and
- plan(s) to which the order relates.

**Amount and form of benefits**

To be qualified, a domestic relations order *cannot* require the plan to provide the following:[87]

- Any benefit type, form, or option not otherwise provided under the plan
- Increased benefits, determined on the basis of actuarial value
- Benefit payments to an alternate payee that are already required to be paid to another alternate payee under a prior QDRO

A domestic relations order may be issued after, or revise, another domestic relations order, provided certain conditions are met.[88]

**Written procedures**

Each plan must have procedures to determine the qualified status of a domestic relations order and administer distributions under qualified orders. These procedures must meet the following conditions:[89]

- Be in writing
- Provide prompt notification of the procedures to each person named in the order as entitled to benefits under the plan
- Permit an alternate payee to designate a representative to receive copies of all notices

## Notice of Receipt of Domestic Relations Order

Upon receipt of a domestic relations order, the plan administrator must provide a Notice of Receipt of Domestic Relations Order to the participant and each alternate payee.[90]

---

[86]  ERISA § 206(d)(3)(C); I.R.C. § 414(p)(2).
[87]  ERISA § 206(d)(3)(D); I.R.C. § 414(p)(3).
[88]  DOL Interim Final Rule § 2530.206(b).
[89]  ERISA § 206(d)(3)(G)(ii).
[90]  ERISA § 206(d)(3)(G)(i)(I); I.R.C. § 414(p)(6)(A)(i).

**Definition**    A *Notice of Receipt of Domestic Relations Order* is a written notification that states the plan administrator has received the domestic relations order and explains the plan's procedures for determining the qualified status of the order.[91]

**Who receives notice**    The plan administrator must provide the notice to the participant with respect to whom the domestic relations order was issued and to each alternate payee.[92] The notice may be provided electronically pursuant to the DOL's electronic distribution safe harbor rules. (See Section C in Chapter 3.)

**Content requirements**    The notice must state that the plan administrator has received the domestic relations order and explain the procedures for determining whether the order is qualified.[93]

**Due date**    The plan administrator is to provide the notice "promptly" upon receipt of a domestic relations order.[94] Neither the IRS nor the DOL specifies a due date.

## Notice of Status of Domestic Relations Order

**Introduction**    Once the determination has been made as to whether the domestic relations order is qualified, the plan administrator must provide a Notice of Status of Domestic Relations Order to the participant and each alternate payee.[95]

**Definition**    A *Notice of Status of Domestic Relations Order* is written notification that informs the participant and alternate payee(s) of the plan administrator's determination of the status of the domestic relations order.[96]

---

91    *Id.*
92    *Id.*
93    *Id.*
94    *Id.*
95    ERISA § 206(d)(3)(G)(i)(II); I.R.C. § 414(p)(6)(A)(ii).
96    *Id.*

**Who must receive notice**   The notice must be provided to the participant to whom the domestic relations order was issued and to each alternate payee.[97]

The notice must be mailed to these individuals at the addresses specified in the domestic relations order. The notice may be provided electronically pursuant to the DOL's electronic distribution safe harbor rules. (See Section C in Chapter 3.)

**Content requirements**   The notice must inform the participant and each alternate payee of the result of the determination procedure and specifically state whether the domestic relations order is qualified or not.[98]

**Due date**   The Notice of Status of Domestic Relations Order must be provided within a "reasonable period" after receiving the domestic relations order.[99] Neither the IRS nor the DOL specifies a due date.

---

[97]   *Id.*
[98]   ERISA §206(d)(3)(G)(i)(II); I.R.C. §414(p)(6)(A)(ii).
[99]   *Id.*

# F.  Notice of Qualified Pre-Retirement Survivor Annuity

**Definitions**  The *Notice of Qualified Pre-Retirement Survivor Annuity* is a written notice to plan participants explaining the terms and conditions of a preretirement survivor annuity benefit.[100]

A *qualified pre-retirement survivor annuity* is an annuity benefit payable to a deceased participant's surviving spouse for the life of the surviving spouse. The annuity starts no later than the month in which the participant would have attained the earliest retirement age under the plan and may not be less than the survivor benefit the spouse would have received had the participant retired and started QJSA payments.[101] A plan is not required to offer participants a QPSA based on the QOSA.[102]

**Affected plans**  Pension plans subject to the minimum funding standards (e.g., defined benefit plans, money purchase plans) must provide that death benefits are payable in the form of a qualified pre-retirement survivor annuity. These rules also apply to plans that are not subject to the minimum funding requirements (e.g., stock bonus plans, profit-sharing plans) unless[103]

- the participant's vested benefits in such a plan are payable in full upon the participant's death to the participant's surviving spouse (or designated beneficiary if the spouse consents to a different beneficiary) and
- the participant elects payments in a form other than a life annuity.

Thus, plans not subject to the minimum funding rules may be subject to the qualified pre-retirement survivor annuity notice requirements with respect to some participants but not others.[104]

**Exception**  In general, if the plan fully subsidizes the pre-retirement survivor annuity benefit and a participant may not waive the benefit (or choose a beneficiary other than the spouse), the plan does *not* need not provide

---

[100]  I.R.C. § 417(a)(3)(B).
[101]  I.R.C. § 417(c).
[102]  IRS Notice 2008-30.
[103]  I.R.C. § 401(a)(11)(B); IRS Reg. § 1.401(a)-20, Q&A-3(a).
[104]  IRS Reg. § 1.401(a)-20, Q&A-4.

the participant with the Notice of Qualified Pre-Retirement Survivor Annuity.[105]

**Fully subsidized benefit**

A plan fully subsidizes the benefit if it does not charge the participant for the benefit by increasing employee contributions or decreasing the accrued benefits.[106]

> *Example:* The QJSA in a defined benefit plan is the 50 percent Joint and Spouse form of benefit. On death, the spouse is provided a survivor benefit of 50 percent of the QJSA that the participant would have been paid had he retired, started the benefit, and then died. The plan is not required to provide a notice about the QPSA. There is no choice to be made on the part of the participant.

> *Example:* A money purchase plan provides that the participant's account balance is paid to the participant's spouse in the form of a lifetime annuity upon the death of the participant, but the participant can name a different beneficiary if the spouse consents to the distribution. The waiver of the QPSA by naming a different beneficiary is subject to the QPSA notice requirement.

**Content requirements**

The notice must contain the following information about the preretirement survivor annuity:[107]

- A general description
- The circumstances under which the annuity, if not waived, will be paid
- A description of the financial effect of the election of the annuity on the participant's benefits
- The participant's right to waive the QPSA
- The effect of the waiver
- The participant's spouse's rights to consent to the election
- The participant's right to change elections
- The effect of changing elections
- The financial effect of waiving the QPSA

**Content for money purchase plan**

The QPSA for a money purchase plan is an annuity for the life of the surviving spouse that has the same value as 50 percent (or more) of the participant's vested (including vesting upon death) account balance as of the date of death.[108] The participant's waiver of this benefit, and the spouse's consent, need not specify the payment form

---

[105]  I.R.C. § 417(a)(5)(A).
[106]  I.R.C. § 417(a)(5)(B).
[107]  I.R.C. § 417(a)(3)(B)(i); IRS Reg. § 1.417(a)(3)-1(b)(1).
[108]  I.R.C. 417(c)(2).

for the benefit—just the beneficiary.[109] Alternatively, a plan may permit the spouse to consent using a general consent that does not specify the beneficiary or form payment.[110] After the participant's death, the plan may allow the beneficiary to choose the form of payment.

The net result is that the QPSA waiver in the case of a money purchase plan centers on the designation of a beneficiary and the spouse's consent to the designation if the plan allows the beneficiary to choose the form of payment when benefits are payable.

A sample beneficiary designation form for a money purchase plan providing a 50 percent QPSA, allowing pre-age 35 designations, but limiting designations to a specific beneficiary rather than a blanket consent is provided in Figure 9-2.

**Due date**

The Notice of Qualified Pre-Retirement Survivor Annuity must be provided to participants during the applicable period.[111]

A plan may provide for an earlier waiver, but it must be invalid as of the beginning of the plan year participant's 35th birthday.[112]

**Applicable period**

The *applicable period* is whichever of the following periods ends last:[113]

- The period beginning with the first day of the plan year in which the participant attains age 32 and ending with the close of the plan year preceding the plan year in which the participant attains age 35
- One year before[114] or after the individual becomes a participant
- One year before or after the survivor benefit is no longer subsidized
- One year before or after the survivor annuity rules apply to the participant
- One year after separation from service in the case of a participant who separates before attaining age 35

**Distribution methods**

Sending the notice to the participant's last known address by first-class mail and hand delivery are acceptable distribution methods. Posting the notice is not acceptable.[115] (See Section D in Chapter 3 for IRS rules for electronic plan communications.)

---

109 IRS Reg. § 1.401(a)-20, Q&A 31(b)(2).
110 IRS Reg. § 1.401(a)-20, Q&A 31(c).
111 I.R.C. § 417(a)(3)(B)(i); IRS Reg. § 1.401(a)-20, Q&A-35(a).
112 IRS Reg § 1.401(a)-20, Q&A 33(b).
113 I.R.C. § 417(a)(3)(B)(ii); IRS Reg. § 1.401(a)-20, Q&A-35.
114 IRS Reg. § 1.401(a)-20, Q&A 35(c).
115 IRS Reg. § 1.417(a)(3)-1(a)(3).

**Figure 9-2**

**Sample Money Purchase 50 Percent QPSA Pre-Retirement
Beneficiary Designation form. Pre-Age 35 Designation Permitted;
Specific Beneficiary, Not Blanket Consent**

---

**\*\*PLAN NAME\*\***

**BENEFICIARY DESIGNATION FORM**

(Please print or type)

Please return this form to: [mailing address for Plan Administrator]

**A. EMPLOYEE INFORMATION**

| Name_____ | |
| Last      First      Middle | Social Security No. |
| Marital Status*:  ☐ Married      ☐ Single | |
| Office Location:_____ | |

**B. NOTICE OF SPOUSE'S SURVIVOR BENEFIT**

Upon your death, half of your account balance is payable to your spouse* if you were married at the time of your death; the remainder is payable to any beneficiaries you designate (which may also include your spouse). The portion of your account that is payable to your spouse is distributed in the form of a survivor annuity. Information about the amount of the survivor annuity and other payment choices will be provided before those distributions start. Alternatively, with the consent of your spouse, you may designate a different beneficiary to receive more than half of your account. Your spouse's consent must be witnessed by a notary or Representative of the Plan. If it is established to the satisfaction of a plan representative that you are not married or that your spouse cannot be located, spousal consent is not required. If you waive the minimum death benefit for your spouse before the beginning of the plan year in which you attain age 35, your waiver becomes invalid at that time and a new waiver is required to redesignate beneficiaries with your spouse's consent. If you make your waiver after you terminate employment, a new waiver is not required if you subsequently attain age 35. There is no charge to your account for this death benefit protection.

**C. BENEFICIARY DESIGNATION GUIDELINES**

In Section D below, you may designate your primary beneficiary(ies) and contingent beneficiary(ies). If more than one primary beneficiary is named, those who survive you will share the proceeds upon your death in the percentages you designate. A contingent beneficiary will receive the proceeds only in the event that no primary beneficiary survives you. In the event there is more than one contingent beneficiary, the contingent beneficiaries will share the proceeds in the percentages you designate. You may change your beneficiaries at any time (with your spouse's consent if you are married). If your marital status changes, be sure to complete a new beneficiary designation form.

**Figure 9-2 (*cont'd*)**

**Sample Money Purchase 50 Percent QPSA Pre-Retirement
Beneficiary Designation form. Pre-Age 35 Designation Permitted;
Specific Beneficiary, Not Blanket Consent**

---

## D. NAMED BENEFICIARIES

*Primary Beneficiaries*

| Name | Relationship | Address | Percent |
|------|-------------|---------|---------|
| Name | Relationship | Address | Percent |

*Contingent Beneficiaries*
If the above beneficiaries are not living at the time of my death, then my benefits should be paid to:

| Name | Relationship Percent | Address | Percent |
|------|---------------------|---------|---------|
| Name | Relationship Percent | Address | Percent |

## E. SPOUSAL CONSENT AND WAIVER

I understand that I have the right to half of my spouse's vested account in the Plan if my spouse dies before me. I agree to give up this right in favor of the beneficiaries listed above. I understand that my spouse cannot change the name of any beneficiary in the future unless I become the beneficiary of at least half of the account balance, or I agree to the change. I am signing this agreement voluntarily. I understand that if I do not sign this agreement, I will receive at least half of my spouse's vested account under the plan if my spouse dies before me. I further understand that my consent is irrevocable unless my spouse revokes either the primary or the secondary beneficiary designation.

| Signature of Spouse (must be witnessed) | Date |
|----------------------------------------|------|

## F. WITNESS FOR SPOUSE'S SIGNATURE (check 1 or 2 and complete as indicated)

1. ☐ Notary Public

   STATE OF _____, COUNTY OF _____ I, _____, a Notary Public in and for said county and state, DO HEREBY CERTIFY THAT _____ personally known to me to be the person whose name is subscribed above, appeared before me this ____ date of _____, 20__,

**Figure 9-2 (*cont'd*)**

**Sample Money Purchase 50 Percent QPSA Pre-Retirement
Beneficiary Designation form. Pre-Age 35 Designation Permitted;
Specific Beneficiary, Not Blanket Consent**

executed this spousal Consent statement and acknowledged to me that he/she did so as a free and voluntary act.

[Seal]

My commission expires _____ By _____

Notary Public

2.  ☐   Plan Representative

On _____, 20_____, before me personally came _____ and told me that he or she is the spouse of the participant or former participant named on this form and signed the spouse's consent. The identity of this person was verified by:

☐   Personal knowledge   ☐   Other _____

By _____
     Plan Representative

## G.  EMPLOYEE SIGNATURE AND CONSENT

The elections above are to remain in effect until changed by my written election, in accordance with the terms of the plan. I have read and understand the **NOTICE OF SPOUSE'S SURVI-VOR BENEFIT** and **BENEFICIARY DESIGNATION GUIDELINES**. I understand that if I have named someone other than my spouse as a primary beneficiary to receive more than half of my account, such designation is not valid unless my spouse consents in writing to the designation. I certify that the person I present as my spouse in the spousal consent section above is my legal spouse at this time.

Please check if applicable:   ☐ My spouse cannot be located.      ☐ I am not married

| | |
|---|---|
| _____ <br> Employee Signature | _____ <br> Date |

*Under federal rules used for purposes of this form, "marriage" is limited to a legal union only between one man and one woman as husband and wife, and a "spouse" is only a person of the opposite sex who is a husband or wife.

# G. Periodic Statement of Accrued Benefits

**PPA note**     PPA expanded existing requirement to provide individual statements of accrued benefits to plan participants and beneficiaries to include a requirement of quarterly statements for defined contribution plans that allow participants to direct the investment of their accounts. Requirements for defined benefit plans were expanded as well.

**General rule**     Most pension plan participants and certain beneficiaries are entitled to receive a *Statement of Accrued Benefits* that summarizes an individual's accrued and vested retirement benefits.[116]

**Who must receive statement**     A plan administrator must distribute a *Statement of Accrued Benefits* to the following individuals:

- Participants and beneficiaries (at prescribed times)[117]
- Participants and beneficiaries who request the statement[118]
- Terminated participants[119]
- Participants who incur a one-year break in service.[120]

**Frequency of statements**     Benefit statements for participants and beneficiaries in individual account plans must be provided:

- At least once each calendar quarter to a participant or beneficiary who has the right to direct the investment of assets in his or her account
- At least once each calendar year to a participant or beneficiary who does not have the right to direct the investment of assets
- Upon written request to other plan beneficiaries

Benefit statements for participants and beneficiaries in defined benefit plans must be provided:

- To a participant or beneficiary of the plan upon written request
- At least once every 3 years to each participant with a vested accrued benefit and who is employed by the employer maintaining the plan at the time the statement is to be furnished

---

[116] ERISA §§ 105(a), (c); ERISA § 209(a); I.R.C. § 6057(e).
[117] ERISA § 105(a)(1).
[118] ERISA §§ 105(a)(1)(A)(iii) and (B)(ii); ERISA § 209(a)(1)(A).
[119] ERISA § 105(c); ERISA § 209(a)(1)(B); I.R.C. § 6057(e).
[120] ERISA § 209(a)(1)(C).

Information in the triennial statements may be based on reasonable estimates.[121]

Administrators need not provide triennial statements if an alternative notice is provided at least once a year reminding participants of the option to obtain a statement upon request.[122]

Years in which no employee or former employee benefits under the plan need not be taken into account in determining the 3-year cycle for providing statements.[123]

**Content requirements**

Statements must include the following information on the basis of the latest available information:

- The total benefits accrued
- The vested pension benefits, if any, which have accrued, or the earliest date on which benefits will become vested

Statements are also required to include an explanation of any permitted disparity under Code § 401(l) or any floor-offset arrangement that may be applied in determining any accrued benefits.[124]

Individual account plan statements must provide values for each investment in an individual's account as of the most recent valuation date under the plan. This should include the value of assets held in the form of employer securities.[125]

Statements for participants who are permitted to direct the investment of their individual accounts should include:[126]

- An explanation of any limitations or restrictions on any right of the participant or beneficiary under the plan to direct an investment. Statements need not include limitations and restrictions imposed by investment funds, other investment vehicles, or by state or federal securities laws.[127]
- An explanation, written in a manner calculated to be understood by the average plan participant, of the importance, for the long-term retirement security of participants and beneficiaries, of a well-balanced and diversified investment portfolio, including a statement of the risk

---

121  ERISA § 105(a)(1)(B).
122  ERISA § 105(a)(3)(A).
123  ERISA § 105(a)(3)(B).
124  ERISA § 105(a)(2)(A)(ii).
125  ERISA § 105(a)(2)(B)(i).
126  ERISA § 105(a)(2)(B)(ii).
127  DOL Field Assistance Bulletin 2006-3, § 5.

that holding more than 20 percent of a portfolio in the security of one entity (such as employer securities) may not be adequately diversified. DOL has provided a model notice that may be used for this purpose.[128] See Figure 9-3A.

- A notice directing the participant or beneficiary to the Internet website of the DOL for sources of information on individual investing and diversification. Plan administrators may use the following Internet address for pension benefit statements: *www.dol.gov/ebsa/investing.html*.[129]

Statements for terminated participants must include the information reported on the Schedule SSA (Form 5500) registration statement and a notice of any benefits that are forfeited if the participant dies before a certain date.[130]

**Due dates**

To establish good-faith compliance in the absence of final DOL regulations, individual account plans should provide a *Statement of Accrued Benefits* within 45 days after the end of the reporting period (quarterly or annual as applicable).[131] For trustee-directed individual account plans, additional time is allowed. Such plans should provide statements by the date of filing Form 5500 (including extensions).[132]

Defined benefit plans opting to automatically provide periodic statements once every three years should provide the first statement under the PPA requirement for the 2009 plan year. If a defined benefit plan opts to use the alternative notice requirement reminding participants of the availability of statements upon request, the first notice should be provided by December 31, 2007.[133]

**Distribution methods**

Statements of accrued benefits may be provided in written, electronic, or other appropriate form to the extent such form is reasonably accessible to the participant or beneficiary.[134] (For a description of the DOL's electronic safe harbor distribution rules, see Section C in Chapter 3.) DOL also recognizes the IRS electronic distribution rules (Section D in Chapter 3) as good faith compliance with the requirement to provide these statements.[135]

---

[128]  DOL Field Assistance Bulletin 2006-3, § 6.
[129]  DOL Field Assistance Bulletin 2006-3, § 8.
[130]  ERISA § 105(c).
[131]  DOL Field Assistance Bulletin 2006-3, § 3.
[132]  DOL Field Assistance Bulletin 2007-3.
[133]  *Id.*
[134]  ERISA § 105(a)(2)(A)(iv).
[135]  DOL Field Assistance Bulletin 2006-3, § 2.

For plans that provide participants continuous access to benefit statement information through one or more secure websites, the DOL will view the availability of pension benefit statement information through such media as good faith compliance with the requirement to furnish benefit statement information, provided that participants and beneficiaries have been notified that the information is available and how to access the information or obtain a free paper copy.[136]

**Penalty for non-compliance**

Both the IRS and the DOL assess fines on employers or plan administrators who fail to furnish *Statements of Accrued Benefits.*

The IRS may fine the employer or plan administrator $50 for each occurrence for either willfully furnishing a false or fraudulent statement or willfully failing to furnish a statement of the information reported on the Schedule SSA (Form 5500) registration statement.[137]

The DOL may fine the employer or plan administrator a civil penalty of $11 for each occurrence if the employer fails to give the plan administrator the necessary information to prepare a statement.[138]

In addition, failure to provide statements can attract a penalty of $100 per day, per participant or beneficiary.[139]

---

[136]   *Id.*
[137]   I.R.C. § 6690.
[138]   ERISA § 209(b); DOL Reg. § 2575.209b-1.
[139]   ERISA § 502(c)(1).

**Figure 9-3A**

**DOL Model Notice on Importance of Well-Balanced and Diversified Investment Portfolio**

*Source:* DOL Field Assistance Bulletin 2006-3, §6.

To help achieve long-term retirement security, you should give careful consideration to the benefits of a well-balanced and diversified investment portfolio. Spreading your assets among different types of investments can help you achieve a favorable rate of return, while minimizing your overall risk of losing money. This is because market or other economic conditions that cause one category of assets, or one particular security, to perform very well often cause another asset category, or another particular security, to perform poorly. If you invest more than 20 percent of your retirement savings in any one company or industry, your savings may not be properly diversified. Although diversification is not a guarantee against loss, it is an effective strategy to help you manage investment risk.

In deciding how to invest your retirement savings, you should take into account all of your assets, including any retirement savings outside of the Plan. No single approach is right for everyone because, among other factors, individuals have different financial goals, different time horizons for meeting their goals, and different tolerances for risk.

It is also important to periodically review your investment portfolio, your investment objectives, and the investment options under the Plan to help ensure that your retirement savings will meet your retirement goals.

# H. Notice of Distribution of Excess Deferrals and Contributions

**Definitions**

A *Notice of Distribution of Excess Deferrals and Contributions* is written notification to plan participants who receive distributions (including interest) of excess deferrals, excess contributions, or excess aggregate contributions advising them these amounts are includable in income.[140] A plan administrator must provide this notice to any participant who receives these excess amounts.

*Excess deferrals* are pretax amounts participants contribute that exceed the maximum limit for the taxable year.[141]

*Excess contributions* are participants' pretax contributions that do not satisfy the nondiscrimination test (actual deferral percentage test) under Code Section 401(k).[142]

*Excess aggregate contributions* are participants' after-tax contributions or employer matching contributions that do not satisfy the nondiscrimination test (actual contribution percentage test) under Code Section 401(m).[143]

**Affected plans**

The notice requirements apply to 401(k) plans, 403(a) annuity plans, 403(b) salary reduction agreements, and 408(k)(6) salary reduction simplified employee pensions (SARSEPs).[144]

**Content requirements**

The notice must advise participants of receipt of excess amounts includable in gross income for the prior or current year and, for amounts taxable in a prior year, that an amended tax return must be filed if a return has already been filed for that year.[145]

*Note.* For excess deferrals, if the excess incurred a loss, the employer must include a statement showing the amount of the loss and stating that the employee must show the excess amount, unadjusted for the loss,

---

140 IRS Notice 87-77, 1987-2 C.B. 385; IRS Notice 89-32, 1989-1 C.B. 671.
141 IRS Reg. § 1.402(g)-1(e)(3).
142 IRS Reg. § 1.401(k)-6.
143 IRS Reg. § 1.401(m)-5.
144 IRS Notice 87-77, 1987-2 C.B. 385; IRS Notice 89-32 1989-1 C.B. 671.
145 *Id.*

on line 7 of his or her Form 1040 for the year of the deferral and show the loss in brackets as Other Income on the form for the year of the distribution.[146]

**Due date**

The notice must be provided to participants at the time of the distribution.[147]

---

[146] IRS Notice 89-32, 1989-1 C.B. 671.
[147] IRS Notice 87-77, 1987-2 C.B. 385.

# I. "404(c)" Notice for Plans Permitting Investment Direction by Plan Participants

**General rule**   ERISA allows plan fiduciaries to escape liability for the investment decisions made by plan participants who take control of the investment management of their own accounts.[148] Fiduciaries shed their responsibilities by prudently selecting a fund lineup that meets specific requirements[149] and by notifying participants and beneficiaries about fund choices, rights, and obligations.[150]

**Content**   A 404(c) notice must include the following information to ensure a participant or beneficiary has sufficient information to make informed decisions about the plan's investment alternatives:[151]

- An explanation that the plan is intended to be a plan described in section 404(c) of ERISA, and that the fiduciaries of the plan may be relieved of liability for any losses which are the direct and necessary result of investment instructions given by the participant or beneficiary.
- A description of the investment alternatives available under the plan. This should include a general description of the investment objectives and risk and return characteristics for each investment alternative and information about the type and diversification of assets in the alternative's portfolio.
- The names of any designated investment managers.
- An explanation of how and when participants and beneficiaries may give investment instructions—and when they may not do so. Restrictions on transfers between funds, limits on trading frequency and any restrictions on the exercise of voting, tender and similar rights.
- A description of transaction fees and expenses such as commissions, sales loads, deferred sales charges, redemption or exchange fees.
- A description of information available upon request and the name, address, and phone number of the person who will provide the information.

---

[148]   ERISA § 404(c).
[149]   DOL Reg. § 2550.404c-1(b)(3).
[150]   DOL Reg. § 2550.404c-1(b)(2)(i)(B).
[151]   *Id.*

- If employer securities are offered, a description of the procedures to assure confidentiality for the purchase, holding and sale of employer securities, and the exercise of voting, tender and similar rights, by participants and beneficiaries. In addition, the name, address and phone number of the plan fiduciary responsible for monitoring compliance with the procedures should be provided.
- For investment alternatives subject to the Securities Act of 1933, a copy of the most recent prospectus provided to the plan should be provided if the participant or beneficiary has no assets invested. The prospectus may be provided immediately before or after the participant's or beneficiary's initial investment. (Mutual Fund Profiles issued to comply with SEC rules may be used to satisfy this requirement under certain conditions.[152])
- Materials provided to the plan about pass-through voting, tender or similar rights that are incidental to holding an ownership interest in an investment alternative should be provided to participants and beneficiaries after they invest in an investment alternative. Information about plan provisions on the exercise of voting, tender or similar rights should be described.

In addition, the following information must be provided upon request:

- A description of the annual operating expenses of each investment alternative that reduce the rate of return to participants and beneficiaries, and the aggregate amount of such expenses expressed as a percentage of average net assets of the designated investment alternative.
- Copies of any prospectuses, financial statements and reports, and other materials about the investment alternatives available under the plan, if provided to the plan.
- A list of the assets in the portfolio of each investment alternative, their value (or proportion of the investment alternative) and, for fixed rate investment contracts issued by a bank, savings and loan association or insurance company, the name of the issuer, the term of the contract and the rate of return.
- Information about the value of shares or units in available investment alternatives as well as the past and current investment performance of the alternatives net of expenses.
- Information on the value of shares or units in investment alternatives held in the account of the participant or beneficiary.

---

[152] DOL Adv. Op. 2003-11A.

**Distribution methods**

The notice may be provided in written, electronic, or other appropriate form to the extent reasonably accessible to the recipient (see Section C in Chapter 3 for DOL rules on electronic plan communications).

**Consequences of non-compliance**

A fiduciary that allows participants or beneficiaries to control the investment of their account without providing notice and otherwise meeting the requirements of the 404(c) rule may retain responsibility for the prudent investment of the participant's account. If the participant or beneficiary exercises control within the confines of the DOL's regulation, then no fiduciary of the plan is liable for any loss that is the direct and necessary result of the participant's or beneficiary's exercise of control.[153]

**Proposed Changes**

Additional disclosure rules proposed by DOL in 2008[*] would expand the amount of information provided to participants in individually—directed account plans without regard to intended 404(c) status. Table 9-3B provides an overview of the proposed disclosures.

---

[153] DOL Reg. § 2550.404c-1(d)(2). However, at least one court of appeals has ruled that fiduciaries may be shielded from liability when permitting individual investment direction even if the DOL's safe harbor is not met. Jenkins v. Yager, 444 F.3d 916 (7th Cir. 2006).

[*] DOL Prop. Reg. § 2550. 404a-5.

## Table 9-3B

### Overview of Proposed Regulation § 2550.404a-5—Fiduciary requirements for disclosure in participant-directed individual account plans.
### July 23, 2008

| Category | Details Required | Deadline | Suggested Format |
|---|---|---|---|
| General Plan Information Description | • Circumstances under which participants and beneficiaries may give investment instructions<br>• Specific limitations on such instructions under the terms of the plan, including any restrictions on transfer to or from a designated investment alternative<br>• Plan provisions (or reference to plan provisions) about the exercise of voting, tender and similar rights and any restrictions on those rights associated with an investment in a designated investment alternative<br>• Specific designated investment alternatives offered under the plan<br>• The designated investment managers that serve the plan | On or before the date of plan eligibility and at least annually thereafter<br><br>Provide description of any material change not later than 30 days after the date of adoption | Summary Plan Description, or with Quarterly Benefit Statement |
| Administrative Expenses Description | • Any fees and expenses[1] for plan administrative services (e.g., legal, accounting, recordkeeping) that, to the extent not otherwise included in investment-related fees and expenses, may be charged to the plan<br>• The basis on which such charges will be allocated (e.g., pro rata, per capita) to, or affect the balance of, each individual account | On or before the date of plan eligibility and at least annually thereafter | Summary Plan Description, or with Quarterly Benefit Statement |
| Specific Administrative Expenses | • The dollar amount actually charged during the preceding quarter to the participant's or beneficiary's account for administrative services<br>• A description of the services provided to the participant or beneficiary for such amount (e.g., recordkeeping) | At least quarterly | Quarterly Benefit Statement |
| Individual Expenses Description | • Fees and expenses[1] that may be charged against the individual account of a participant or beneficiary for services provided on an individual, rather than plan, basis, such as for:<br>• Processing plan loans<br>• QDROs<br>• Investment advice or similar services charged on an individual basis | On or before the date of plan eligibility and at least annually thereafter | Summary Plan Description, or with Quarterly Benefit Statement |

| Category | Details Required | Deadline | Suggested Format |
|---|---|---|---|
| Specific Individual Expenses | • The dollar amount actually charged during the preceding quarter to the participant's or beneficiary's account for individual services<br>• A description of the services provided to the participant or beneficiary for such amount (e.g., processing plan loans) | At least quarterly | Quarterly Benefit Statement |
| Identifying Information for Each Designated Investment Alternative | • Name of the investment alternative<br>• An Internet Web site address that is sufficiently specific to lead participants and beneficiaries to supplemental information on the alternative, including:<br>  • name of the investment's issuer or provider<br>  • investment's principal strategies and attendant risks<br>  • assets in the investment's portfolio<br>  • investment's portfolio turnover<br>  • investment's performance<br>  • related fees and expenses[1]<br>• Type or category (e.g., money market fund, balanced fund, indexed fund, large-cap fund)<br>• Type of management (e.g., actively managed, passively managed) | On or before the date of plan eligibility and at least annually thereafter | Chart or similar format that is designed to facilitate a comparison of alternatives such as Appendix A model |
| Performance Data and Benchmarks for Each Designated Investment Alternative (other than Fixed Income) | • Average annual total return (percentage) of the investment for the following periods, if available:<br>  • 1-year, 5-year, and 10-year, measured as of the end of the applicable calendar year<br>• A statement that an investment's past performance is not necessarily an indication of how the investment will perform in the future.<br>• Name and returns of an appropriate broad-based securities market index over the 1-year, 5-year, and 10-year periods (must be independent unless the index is widely recognized and used) | On or before the date of plan eligibility and at least annually thereafter | Chart or similar format that is designed to facilitate a comparison of alternatives such as Appendix A model |
| Performance Data for Each Designated Fixed Income Investment Alternative | • Fixed rate of return<br>• Term of the investment | On or before the date of plan eligibility and at least annually thereafter | Chart or similar format that is designed to facilitate a comparison of alternatives such as Appendix A model |
| Fee & Expense Information for Each De- | • Amount and a description of each shareholder-type fee[1] (i.e., fees charged directly against a participant's or beneficiary's investment), such as:<br>  • Sales loads | On or before the date of plan eligibility and at least annually | Chart or similar format that is designed to facilitate |

| Category | Content | Timing | Format |
|---|---|---|---|
| signed Investment Alternative (other than Fixed Income) | • Sales charges<br>• Deferred sales charges<br>• Redemption fees<br>• Surrender charges<br>• Exchange fees<br>• Account fees<br>• Purchase fees<br>• Mortality and expense fees<br>• Total annual operating expenses of the investment expressed as a percentage (e.g., expense ratio)<br>• A statement indicating that fees and expenses are only one of several factors that participants and beneficiaries should consider when making investment decisions | thereafter | a comparison of alternatives such as Appendix A model |
| Fee & Expense Information for Each Designated Fixed Income Investment Alternative | • Amount and a description of any shareholder-type fees[1] that may apply to a purchase, transfer or withdrawal of the investment in whole or in part | On or before the date of plan eligibility and at least annually thereafter | Chart or similar format that is designed to facilitate a comparison of alternatives such as Appendix A model |
| Shareholder Rights Information | • Materials provided to the plan about the exercise of voting, tender and similar rights, to the extent that such rights are passed through to the participant or beneficiary under the terms of the plan | Subsequent to an investment | |
| Additional Financial Information | • Prospectuses (or any short-form or summary prospectus, the form of which has been approved by the SEC) or similar documents for designated investment alternatives that do not require prospectuses<br>• Copies of financial statements or reports, such as statements of additional information and shareholder reports, and of any other similar materials, to the extent such materials are provided to the plan<br>• A statement of the value of a share or unit of each designated investment alternative as well as the date of the valuation<br>• A list of the assets in the portfolio of each designated investment alternative which constitute plan assets within the meaning of 29 CFR 2510.3-101 and the value of each such asset (or the proportion of the investment which it comprises) | Upon request of a participant or beneficiary | |

[1] Expressed in monetary amount, formula, percentage of assets, or per capita charge

# J. Notice of 404(c) Plan's Default Investment Fund

Figure 9-4 at the end of Section L summarizes the QDIA, QACA, EACA, and 401(k) safe harbor notice requirements and provides a checklist. Figure 9-5 offers the sample provided by the IRS.

**PPA note**  This new PPA rule offers plan fiduciaries relief from responsibility for the investment choice made for a participant's account when the participant fails to respond to the offer to self-direct the investment of their account.

**General Rule**  In the absence of an affirmative election, a participant in an individual account plan that meets certain notice requirements is nonetheless treated as exercising control over the assets in his account if the plan invests the account in accordance with regulations prescribed by the DOL in a qualified default investment account (QDIA).[154]

**Content**  Each participant must receive a notice explaining the employee's right under the plan to designate how contributions and earnings will be invested and explaining how, in the absence of any investment election by the participant, such contributions and earnings will be invested in the plan's QDIA.[155] The notice must contain:[156]

- a description of the circumstances under which assets may be invested in the default, and an explanation of the plan's elective and automatic contribution arrangements;
- a description of the default, including a description of the investment objectives, risk and return characteristics (if applicable) and fees and expenses;
- a description of the right to direct investment of the assets to any other investment alternative under the plan including information on restrictions, fees and expenses; and
- an explanation of where to get information on the other investment alternatives under the plan.

---

[154]  ERISA § 404(c)(5).
[155]  ERISA § 404(c)(5)(B)(i)(I).
[156]  DOL Reg. § 2550.404c-5(d).

To further address the requirement to disclose fees and expenses, DOL has indicated that participants and beneficiaries generally should be provided: (1) information (amount and description) about shareholder-type fees such as sales loads, sales charges, deferred sales charges, redemption fees, surrender charges, exchange fees, account fees, purchase fees, and mortality and expense fees and (2) for investments with variable performance (such as mutual funds), the total annual operating expenses of the investment expressed as a percentage (e.g., expense ratio).[157] DOL's proposed regulations on fee and expense disclosures include these requirements. (See Figure 9-3B in Section I.)

**Due Date**

The notice must be provided within a reasonable period of time before each plan year.[158] The notice must be provided to plan participants at least 30 days prior to the first investment and 30 days before each subsequent plan year.[159] If participants are offered the opportunity to make permissible withdrawals under eligible automatic contribution arrangements (within 90 days of first default contribution), then the initial QDIA notice is due on or before the date of plan eligibility.[160]

**Distribution methods**

The notice should be written in a manner calculated to be understood by the average eligible employee and be sufficiently accurate and comprehensive to explain the employees' rights and obligations.[161] Electronic or other appropriate form should be acceptable to the extent reasonably accessible to the recipient (see Section C in Chapter 3 for DOL rules on electronic plan communications).

Fee and expense information may be provided in separate documents, though at the same time as the other information required by this disclosure rule. For example, a prospectus or profile prospectus of an investment alternative subject to the Securities Act of 1933 could be used.[162]

The QDIA Notice may be combined with 401(k) Safe Harbor Notices (see Section L) and the Notice of Automatic Contribution Arrangement (see Section K).[163]

---

157  DOL Field Assistance Bulletin 2008-03, Q 6.
158  ERISA § 404(c)(5)(B)(i)(I).
159  DOL Reg. § 2550.404c-5(c)(3).
160  DOL Reg. § 2550.404c-5(c)(3)(i)(B).
161  ERISA § 404(c)(5)(B)(ii).
162  DOL Field Assistance Bulletin 2008-03, Q 6.
163  DOL Field Assistance Bulletin 2008-03, Qs 8 and 10.

**Consequences of non-compliance**

Fiduciaries who automatically invest funds in a default investment without observing the requirements under the default investment rule retain responsibility for the investment choice.

# K. Notice of Automatic Contribution Arrangement

Figure 9-4 at the end of Section L summarizes the QDIA, QACA, EACA, and 401(k) safe harbor notice requirements and provides a checklist. Figure 9-5 offers the sample provided by the IRS.

**PPA note**

PPA allows plan sponsors to automatically enroll employees in their plans using an **automatic contributions arrangement** (ACA) without concern for violation of State law requirements constraining automatic deductions from employee paychecks. PPA also adds a second 401(k) safe harbor program that uses this new option (See QACA in Section L).

**General Rule**

ERISA overrides any state laws that directly or indirectly prohibit employers from using ACAs in their ERISA plans.[164] Employers who adopt ACAs that satisfy prescribed 401(k) rules (QACAs) need not perform annual nondiscrimination tests unless the plan permits after tax employee contributions.[165]

Employers who adopt **eligible** ACAs (EACAs),[166] but do not choose the QACA safe harbor option have extra time for penalty-free corrective distributions of excess contributions and excess aggregation contributions, if required by nondiscrimination tests applied to deferrals, after-tax employee contributions and employer matching contributions. An EACA affords the employer 6 months, rather than 2 1/2 months, for the task.[167]

An ACA is an arrangement to make automatic deferrals or contributions out of compensation until the participant specifically elects not to have such contributions made (or specifically elects to have such contributions made at a different percentage).[168] Contributions made under the arrangement are invested in the plan's default investment option (See Section J in this chapter).

---

[164] ERISA § 514(e)(1).
[165] I.R.C. § 401(k)(13).
[166] I.R.C. § 414(w)(3).
[167] I.R.C. § 4979(f)(1).
[168] ERISA § 514(e)(2).

An employer may allow employees to withdraw amounts contributed through an EACA within 90 days of the first elective contribution under the arrangement.[169]

**Content**

A *Notice of Automatic Contribution Arrangement* explains:[170]

- the participant's rights and obligations under the arrangement;
- the level of elective contributions that will be made on the participant's behalf if the participant does not make an affirmative election;
- the participant's right not to have elective contributions made on the participant's behalf (or to elect to have such contributions made at a different percentage);
- that the participant has a reasonable period of time, before the first elective contribution is made, to make such election;
- how contributions made under the arrangement will be invested in the absence of any investment election (if applicable) by the participant

In addition, a plan with an automatic contribution arrangement that intends to avail itself of the new safe harbor would need to observe the Notice requirements described in Section L *Notice of 401(k) Plan Safe Harbor*.[171] And a plan with an EACA that offers permissive withdrawals if elected within the initial 90-day initiation period must describe the employee's right to withdrawal and the procedure for making the withdrawal election.[172]

**Due date**

The notice should generally be provided within a reasonable period before the plan year.[173] For an employee who becomes eligible mid-year, the notice should be provided within a reasonable period of time before the employee becomes eligible.

The employee must be afforded sufficient advance notice to allow for an election to decline participation. Notice within 30 days (and no more than 90 days) in advance is deemed to satisfy the plan year notice requirement. Notice by the date of eligibility satisfies the rule for employees eligible after the 90-day cut-off.[174]

---

[169]  I.R.C. § 414(w)(2).
[170]  ERISA § 514(e)(3)(B), I.R.C. §§ 401(k)(13)(E)(ii) and 414(w)(4); and IRS Prop. Reg. § 414(w)-1(b)(3).
[171]  IRS Prop. Reg. § 1.414(w)-1(b)(3)(ii) and IRS Prop. Reg. § 1.401(k)-3(a)(2).
[172]  IRS Prop. Reg. § 1.414(w)-1(b)(3)(ii)(D).
[173]  ERISA § 514(e)(3)(A).
[174]  IRS Prop. Reg. § 1.414(w)-1(b)(3)(iii).

**Distribution methods**
The notice should be written in a manner calculated to be understood by the average eligible employee and be sufficiently accurate and comprehensive to explain the employees' rights and obligations.[175] Electronic or other appropriate form should be acceptable to the extent reasonably accessible to the recipient (see Section C in Chapter 3 for DOL rules on electronic plan communications).

The notice of Automatic Contribution Arrangement can be combined with the QDIA Notice (see Section J) and the 401(k) Safe Harbor Notice (see Section L).[176]

**Consequences of noncompliance**
Failure to satisfy the rules in ERISA §514(e)(3) can attract a penalty of $1,000 per day.[177] In the case of a plan using the QACA safe harbor, defaults in plan notices could lead to loss of safe harbor status. In addition, favorable taxation rules and the exception from in-service withdrawal restrictions (thus possible plan disqualification) for EACAs would be lost.

---

[175]  ERISA §514(e)(3)(A) and IRC §401(k)(13)(E)(i).
[176]  DOL Field Assistance Bulletin 2008-03, Qs 8 and 10.
[177]  ERISA §502(c)(4); DOL Prop. Reg. §2560.502c-4.

# L. Notice of 401(k) Plan Safe Harbor

*Figure 9-4, which begins on page 9-63, summarizes the QDIA, QACA, EACA, and 401(k) safe harbor notice requirements and provides a checklist. Figure 9-5, which follows on page 9-67 offers the sample provided by IRS.*

**PPA note**
The PPA adds an alternative safe harbor for plans with automatic contribution arrangements. See Section K of this Chapter.

**General rule**
If a 401(k) plan meets the nondiscrimination rules by using a safe harbor, a Notice of 401(k) Safe Harbor must be distributed to eligible employees.[178]

**Definition**
The *Notice of 401(k) Safe Harbor* is the written notice informing employees about their rights and obligations under the plan[179] under the traditional safe harbor or the Qualified Automatic Contribution Arrangement (QACA) safe harbor.

**Contents**
The notice must contain the following information:[180]

- the safe harbor matching or nonelective contribution formula used under the plan, including the levels of any safe harbor matching contributions available;
- any other plan contributions (or contributions to another plan on account of an employee's deferrals or after-tax contributions) and the conditions under which they are made;
- the plan to which safe harbor contributions will be made, if different from the 401(k) plan;
- the types and amounts of compensation that may be deferred under the plan;
- how to make elective contributions, including any administrative requirements;
- the time when elections may be made;
- withdrawal and vesting provisions under the plan; and

---

[178]  I.R.C. § 401(k)(12)(D); IRS Reg. § 1.401(k)-3(d).
[179]  *Id.*
[180]  IRS Reg. § 1.401(k)-3(d)(2)(ii).

- how to readily obtain more information about the plan (including an additional copy of the SPD), such as telephone numbers, addresses, and electronic addresses (if any) of the individuals from whom, or offices from which, employees can obtain such plan information.[181]

**Exception to content requirement**

The notice may cross-reference the relevant portions of an up-to-date SPD that has been provided (or concurrently is provided) to the employee. However, the notice must still accurately describe:

- the safe harbor matching or nonelective contribution formula used under the plan, including levels of any matching contributions available;
- how to make elective contributions, including any administrative requirements;
- the time when elections may be made;
- withdrawal and vesting provisions under the plan; and
- how to obtain additional information as described above.[182]

**Extra content for QACA**

The notice for the plan using the QACA safe harbor must describe:[183]

- the level of elective contribution that will be made for the employee if the employee does not make an affirmative election;
- the employee's right to opt out or choose a different level of participation; and
- how contributions will be invested, such as in the plan's QDIA.

**Due date**

The Notice of 401(k) Plan Safe Harbor must be provided within a reasonable period before the beginning of the plan year or before an employee first becomes eligible. This requirement is deemed met[184]

- for existing eligible employees, if provided at least 30 days and not more than 90 days before the beginning of each plan year; and
- for newly eligible employees, if provided not more than 90 days before an employee becomes eligible and not later than the date an employee becomes eligible.

A QACA notice must be provided sufficiently in advance to allow the employee to decline participation, and to make investment choices available other than QDIA.[185]

---

181  *Id.*
182  IRS Reg. § 1.401(k)-3(d)(2)(iii).
183  IRS Prop. Reg. § 1.401(k)-3(k)(4)(ii).
184  IRS Reg. § 1.401(k)-3(d)(3)(ii).
185  IRS Prop. Reg. § 1.401(k)-3(k)(4)(iii).

**Distribution methods**

The plan may provide written notice or an electronic notice that satisfies the IRS rules for electronic commumications.[186] (See Section D of Chapter 3.)

This Notice can be combined with the QDIA Notice (see Section J) and the 401(k) Safe Harbor Notice.[187]

**Exception for conditional safe harbor**

A plan sponsor is permitted to provide a contingent notice that meets the above requirements other than information about the specific safe harbor contributions to be made.[188] Such a notice explains that the plan may be amended during the plan year to include the safe harbor nonelective contribution and that, if the plan is amended, a follow-up notice will be provided. If the employer chooses to use the safe harbor option for the year, no later than 30 days before the last day of the plan year

- the plan must be amended to adopt the safe harbor, and
- a follow-up notice must be provided to eligible employees stating that the safe harbor nonelective contributions will be made for the plan year.

**Suspension of safe harbor matching contributions**

Plans using the safe harbor matching contribution option may be amended to suspend or reduce matching contributions on future employee before- and after-tax contributions by providing a supplemental notice 30 days in advance of the suspension and offering eligible employees a reasonable opportunity to change their elections prior to the reduction or suspension.[189] The notice explains:

- the consequences of the amendment that reduces or suspends matching contributions;
- the procedures for changing elections; and
- the effective date of the amendment.

---

[186] IRS Reg. § 1.401(k)-3(d)(1).
[187] DOL Field Assistance Bulletins 2008-03, Q8 and 10.
[188] IRS Reg. § 1.401(k)-3(f).
[189] IRS Reg. § 1.401(k)-3(g).

**Figure 9-4**

**Notice Requirements for 401(k) Plans***

| Notice | Non safe harbor plans | 401(k)(12) safe harbor plans ("old SH") | 401(k)(13) safe harbor plans (new QACA safe harbor) |
|---|---|---|---|
| **QDIA (advance and annual)** Provide this notice if the fiduciary wants insulation from responsibility for losses when investing in default alternative for participants who fail to make affirmative elections. *Use module A* | Optional | Optional | Optional |
| **EACA basic/ERISA 514(e)(3)** Provide this notice if using automatic enrollment to satisfy state law preemption notice requirement (for ERISA plans) and to obtain additional time for corrective refunds for failed ADP/ACP tests. Satisfaction of QDIA notice is deemed to satisfy this rule as well. *Use module B* | Required for ERISA plans (to meet ERISA 514(e)(3) notice mandate) Optional for non-ERISA plans | Required for ERISA plans (to meet ERISA 514(e)(3) notice mandate) Optional for non-ERISA plans | Required for ERISA plans (to meet ERISA 514(e)(3) notice mandate) Optional for non-ERISA plans |
| **QACA** Provide this notice if the plan sponsor adopts the 401(k)(13) nondiscrimination safe harbor. Include the notifications described below under "Safe Harbor status". *Use module B* | N/A | N/A | Required |
| **EACA with refunds** Provide this notice if the plan sponsor wants to allow participants to withdraw deferrals during initial 90-day window. This is in addition to the EACA basic notice. *Use module C* | Optional (Required for QDIA if less than 30-day notice of QDIA) | Optional (Required for QDIA if less than 30-day notice of QDIA) | Optional (Required for QDIA if less than 30-day notice of QDIA) |
| **Safe Harbor status** Provide this notice within reasonable period prior to the beginning of the plan year to inform participants of plan's safe harbor status/contribution rates/vesting. *Use module D* | N/A | Required | Required |

* QDIA and ERISA 514(e)(3) rules also apply for 403(b) plans, and EACA "basic" and "with refunds" rules can be used for 403(b) and 457 governmental plans as well.

| PPA 401(k) notice checklist | | |
|---|:---:|:---:|
| | *Yes* | *No* |
| ***All Notices*** | | |
| Is the notice sufficiently accurate and comprehensive to inform the employee of the employee's rights and obligations under the plan; and is the notice written in a manner calculated to be understood by the average employee eligible to participate in the plan? | ☐ | ☐ |
| ***Module A:* QDIA**<br>*Provide this notice if the fiduciary wants insulation from responsibility for losses when investing in default alternative for participants who fail to make affirmative elections.*<br>Ref: DOL Reg. § 2550.404c-5 | | |
| Does the notice describe the circumstances under which assets in the individual account of a participant or beneficiary may be invested on behalf of the participant or beneficiary in a QDIA? | ☐ | ☐ |
| If applicable, does the notice explain the circumstances under which elective contributions will be made for the participant, the percentage of such contributions, and the right of the participant to elect not to have such contributions made (or to elect a different percentage)? | ☐ | ☐ |
| Does the notice explain that participants and beneficiaries can direct the investment of their own account assets? | ☐ | ☐ |
| Does the notice describe the investment objectives, risk and return characteristics (if applicable), and fees and expenses under the QDIA? | ☐ | ☐ |
| Does the notice tell participants and beneficiaries that they can direct the investment of QDIA assets to any other investment alternative under the plan and describe any applicable restrictions, fees or expenses for making a transfer? | ☐ | ☐ |
| Does the notice explain where participants and beneficiaries can get investment information about the other investment alternatives available under the plan? | ☐ | ☐ |
| Does the plan give the participant a reasonable period of time, after receipt of the notice and before the first elective contribution is made, to make an election? (At least 30 days advance notice is required unless the plan allows permissible withdrawals under the EACA rule.) | ☐ | ☐ |
| ***Module B:* EACA basic and QACA**<br>*Provide this notice if using automatic enrollment to meet state law preemption notice requirement and to obtain additional time for corrective refunds for failed ADP/ACP tests. In addition, the safe harbor items in Module D must be included, if applicable.* **This module (other than the cross-reference requirement to Module D) is deemed satisfied if the notice satisfies Module A.**<br>Ref: Prop. Reg. §§ 1.401(k)-(3)(k)(4) and 1.414(w)-1(b)(3)(ii); ERISA § 514(e), QDIA final regulation preamble (72 FR 60457), and DOL Field Assistance Bulletin 2008-03, Q 8. | | |

|  | Yes | No |
|---|---|---|
| Does the notice explain the level of elective contributions that will be made on the employee's behalf and subtracted from compensation if the employee does not make an affirmative election? | ☐ | ☐ |
| Does the notice explain the participant's right not to have elective contributions taken from compensation (or to elect to have such contributions made at a different percentage)? | ☐ | ☐ |
| Does the plan give the participant a reasonable period of time, after receipt of the notice and before the first elective contribution is made, to make an election? (To satisfy the QDIA requirements, at least 30 days advance notice is required unless the plan allows permissible withdrawals under the EACA rule.) | ☐ | ☐ |
| Does the notice describe how contributions under the automatic contribution arrangement will be invested (including, in the case of an arrangement under which the employee may elect among 2 or more investment options, how contributions made under the automatic contribution arrangement will be invested in the absence of an investment election by the employee)? | ☐ | ☐ |
| *Module C:* **EACA with refunds** <br> *Provide this notice if the plan sponsor wants to allow participants to withdraw deferrals during initial 90-day window. (Required for EACA, and for QDIA if less than 30-day notice of QDIA)*Ref: Prop. Reg. §1.414(w)-1(b)(3)(ii)(D); |  |  |
| Does the notice describe the employee's right to withdraw deferrals made during the first 90 days and the procedures to elect the withdrawal? | ☐ | ☐ |
| *Module D:* **Safe Harbor status** <br> *Provide this notice within reasonable period prior to the beginning of the plan year to inform participants of plan's safe harbor status/contribution rates/vesting. Ref: Reg. §1.401(k)-3(d).* |  |  |
| Does the notice describe the safe harbor matching contribution or safe harbor nonelective contribution formula used under the plan (including a description of the levels of safe harbor matching contributions, if any, available under the plan)? | ☐ | ☐ |
| Does the notice describe any other contributions under the plan or matching contributions to another plan on account of elective contributions or employee contributions under the plan (including the potential for discretionary matching contributions) and the conditions under which such contributions are made? *[Okay to cross-reference SPD]* | ☐ | ☐ |
| Does the notice describe the plan to which safe harbor contributions will be made (if different than the plan containing the cash or deferred arrangement)? *[Okay to cross-reference SPD]* | ☐ | ☐ |
| Does the notice describe the type and amount of compensation that may be deferred under the plan? *[Okay to cross-reference SPD]* | ☐ | ☐ |
| Does the notice describe how to make cash or deferred elections, including any administrative requirements that apply to such elections? | ☐ | ☐ |

| | Yes | No |
|---|:---:|:---:|
| Does the notice describe the periods available under the plan for making cash or deferred elections? | ☐ | ☐ |
| Does the notice describe withdrawal and vesting provisions applicable to contributions under the plan? [IRS regulation does not permit the use of a cross-reference to the SPD to satisfy this requirement. But, note the limited cross-reference to the SPD included in IRS QACA/EACA sample] | ☐ | ☐ |
| Does the notice describe information that makes it easy to obtain additional information about the plan (including an additional copy of the summary plan description) such as telephone numbers, addresses and, if applicable, electronic addresses, of individuals or offices from whom employees can obtain such plan information? | ☐ | ☐ |

## Figure 9-5

## IRS Sample Automatic Enrollment and Default Investment Notice[1]

This IRS sample notice satisfies notice requirements under Code sections 401(k)(13) and 414(w) for a hypothetical QACA that permits EACA withdrawals and has certain other characteristics. Following coordination with the IRS, the DOL has indicated that use of this sample notice also satisfies the notice requirements under ERISA sections 404(c)(5) and 514(e)(3) and the DOL's default investment regulation for a hypothetical plan for which a fiduciary may wish to obtain relief under the regulation. A plan sponsor will need to add to, subtract from, or otherwise change the sample notice to the extent a plan's form and operations differ from the hypothetical QACA described in the sample notice, so that the actual notice accurately reflects the provisions of the plan. For example, a particular plan may satisfy the Code section 401(k)(13) employer contribution requirement through safe-harbor employer nonelective contributions to non-highly compensated employees, rather than through safe-harbor matching contributions to all eligible participants, or may provide employer nonelective contributions in addition to safe-harbor matching contributions. The plan sponsor will also need to provide details about a plan's QDIA, as directed in italicized notes to plan sponsors in the sample notice, and will need to fill in any blanks in the sample notice.

The hypothetical QACA described in the sample notice includes the following characteristics:

- The QACA is effective January 1, 2008. It is part of a calendar-year defined contribution plan that, before January 1, 2008, provided only for elective contributions under Code section 401(k) (but not for automatic elective contributions).

- The QACA provides for automatic elective contributions at the minimum level permitted under Code section 401(k)(13), and does not restrict employees' ability to elect other elective contribution levels, except to the extent required under other Code provisions (e.g., Code section 402(g)). The plan does not provide for designated Roth contributions described in Code section 402A.

- The QACA provides for matching contributions for all eligible participants at the minimum level permitted under Code section 401(k)(13), and does not provide for additional employer matching or nonelective contributions. The matching contributions are contributed to the plan on a payroll-by-payroll basis (based on the same definition of eligible compensation used to make elective contributions), and are subject to the minimum vesting schedule described in Code section 401(k)(13)(D)(iii)(I) (that is, full vesting upon completion of 2 years of service).

- Employees are eligible to participate in the plan on their date of hire.

- Participants make elective contribution and investment elections under the plan by returning specified election forms to the plan administrator, and may change their elections at any time without restriction.

- Affirmative contribution elections under the plan, whether made before or after the effective date of the QACA, continue in force until changed by the participant.

- The plan permits participants to withdraw automatic elective contributions during a 90- day window period described in Code section 414(w), and treats a withdrawal request as an election to not make further elective contributions to the plan (absent a contrary affirmative election).

---

[1] Special Edition IRS *employee plan news*, November 15, 2007.

## Figure 9-5 (*cont'd*)

## IRS Sample Automatic Enrollment and Default Investment Notice

- Plan participants may affirmatively choose among various available investment funds. Automatic elective contributions and related employer matching contributions are, absent contrary affirmative election, invested in a QDIA.

- The plan permits distributions and loans to the extent distributions and loans are permitted under Code sections 401(k)(2)(B) and 72(p)(2). Hardship distributions are permitted to the extent the deemed hardship requirements described in Treas. Reg. § 1.401(k)-1(d)(3)(iii)(B) and (iv)(E) are satisfied.

- The plan administrator has provided summary plan descriptions to participants that accurately describe eligible compensation, contribution limits, service crediting rules, investment election procedures, the investment funds available under the plan, and hardship withdrawal and loan rules.

Although the sample notice is designed for use in satisfying the QACA and EACA notice requirements, and the notice requirements under ERISA sections 404(c)(5) and 514(e)(3), plan sponsors may also find the sample notice to be helpful in drafting an employee explanation for an automatic contribution arrangement that is neither a QACA nor an EACA.

### [Plan Name] Plan (Plan) Automatic Enrollment Notice

Beginning in 2008, [ ] (Company) is making saving for retirement under our 401(k) Plan even easier. We are offering an automatic enrollment feature, and will make new Company matching contributions.

The new automatic enrollment feature won't change your contribution level if you already turned in a [ ] Form electing the level of your contributions to the Plan or electing not to contribute. Your earlier election will continue to be followed, and matching contributions will be made based on your contribution level. You can change your contribution level by turning in a new [ ] Form at any time. Matching contributions will then be based on your new contribution level.

If you have not turned in a contribution election form, you will be automatically enrolled in the Plan starting with your first paycheck in 2008. This means that amounts will be taken from your pay and contributed to the Plan. For pay during 2008, these automatic contributions will be 3% of your eligible pay each pay period. But, you can choose a different amount. You can choose to contribute more, less, or even nothing.

Keep in mind that the Company will match one dollar for each dollar you contribute, up to 1% of your eligible pay. The Company will also match 50 cents for each dollar you contribute that is between 1% and 6% of your eligible pay. So, to get the most from these matching contributions, you must contribute at least 6% of your eligible pay each pay period. This is more than the 3% automatic contribution rate. It may also be more than your current contribution rate.

This notice gives you important information about some Plan rules, including the Plan's automatic enrollment feature and Company matching contributions. The notice covers these points:

- Whether the Plan's automatic enrollment feature applies to you;

- What amounts will be automatically taken from your pay and contributed to the Plan;

- What other amounts the Company will contribute to your Plan account;

**Figure 9-5 (*cont'd*)**

## IRS Sample Automatic Enrollment and Default Investment Notice

- How your Plan account will be invested;

- When your Plan account will be vested (that is, not lost when you leave your job), and when you can get your Plan account; and

- How you can change your contributions.

You can find out more about the Plan in another document, the Plan's Summary Plan Description (SPD).

### 1. Does the Plan's automatic enrollment feature apply to me?

The Plan's automatic enrollment feature will not apply to you if you already elected (by turning in a [ ] Form to the Plan Administrator) to make contributions to the Plan or to not contribute. If you made an election, your contribution level will not automatically change. But, you can always change your contribution level by turning in a new contribution form.

If you have not elected a contribution level, you will be enrolled in the Plan starting with your first paycheck in 2008. This means money will be automatically taken from your pay and contributed to your Plan account. If you do not want to be enrolled, you need to turn in the enclosed contribution form to the Plan Administrator by [ ].

### 2. If I do nothing, how much will be taken from my pay and contributed to the Plan?

If you do not turn in a completed contribution form by [ ], 3% of your eligible pay for each pay period will be taken from your pay and contributed to the Plan. This will start with your first paycheck in 2008 and continue through the end of 2009. After 2009, your contribution level will increase by 1% each year (unless you choose a different level), until it reaches 6% of your eligible pay. To learn more about the Plan's definition of eligible pay, you can review the "[ ]" section of the Plan's SPD.

Your contributions to the Plan are taken out of your pay and are not subject to federal income tax at that time. Instead, they are contributed to your Plan account and can grow over time with earnings. Your account will be subject to federal income tax only when withdrawn. This helpful tax rule is a reason to save for retirement through Plan contributions.

Contributions will be taken out of your pay if you do nothing. But you are in charge of the amount that you contribute. You may decide to do nothing and become automatically enrolled, or you may choose to contribute an amount that better meets your needs. For example, you may want to get the full amount of the Company's matching contributions by contributing at least 6% of your eligible pay. You can change your contributions by turning in a new contribution form to the Plan Administrator at the address listed at the end of this notice.

If you want to contribute more to your account than would be provided automatically, there are limits on the maximum amount. These limits are described in the "[ ]" section of the Plan's SPD.

### 3. In addition to the contributions taken out of my pay, what amounts will the Company contribute to my Plan account?

Besides contributing the amounts taken from your pay, the Company will make other contributions to your Plan account. The Company will match, on a dollar-for-dollar basis, the first 1% of eligible pay you contribute each pay period. The Company will also match 50 cents for each dollar you contribute between 1% and 6% of your eligible pay each pay period.

## Figure 9-5 (*cont'd*)

## IRS Sample Automatic Enrollment and Default Investment Notice

These matching contributions will be made if you are automatically enrolled or if you choose your own contribution level.

The Company's matching contributions depend on the amount you contribute out of your pay each pay period.

For example:

If you earn $2,000 in eligible pay during a pay period and you elect to contribute 6% of your pay, the Company will deduct $120 from your pay for the pay period (that is, 6% x $2,000). The $120 will be put in your Plan account. The Company will also make matching contributions to your Plan account of $70 for the pay period. In other words, the Company will make a dollar-for-dollar matching contribution on your contributions up to 1% of eligible pay (100% of 1% x $2,000, or $20) plus a 50¢-per-dollar matching contribution on your contributions between 1% and 6% of eligible pay (50% of 5% x $2,000, or $50). Or, if you contribute 3% of your eligible pay for the pay period, the Company will take $60 out of your pay and put it in your Plan account, and will also make $40 in matching contributions for the pay period. Or, if you choose not to contribute to the Plan for a pay period, you will get no matching contributions for the pay period. Remember, you can always change the amount you contribute to the Plan by turning in a new contribution form.

### 4. How will my Plan account be invested?

The Plan lets you invest your account in a number of different investment funds. Unless you choose a different investment fund or funds, your Plan account will be invested in the [ ] Fund.

*[Note to plan sponsors: In order for the Plan's default investment to satisfy section 404(c)(5) of ERISA, the default investment fund must be a qualified default investment alternative ("QDIA") under DOL Reg. § 2550.404c-5. You must describe the Plan's QDIA, including its investment objectives, risk and return characteristics, and fees and expenses, and must describe other circumstances, if any, under which assets may be invested in the QDIA.]*

You can change how your Plan account is invested, among the Plan's offered investment funds, by turning in the enclosed [ ] Form to the Plan Administrator at the address listed at the end of this notice.

*[Note to plan sponsors: In order for the Plan's default investment to satisfy section 404(c)(5) of ERISA, you must describe any restrictions, fees, or expenses that apply when participants or beneficiaries transfer assets from the QDIA to other investment funds.]*

To learn more about the Plan's investment funds and procedures for changing how your Plan account is invested you can review the "[ ]" section of the Plan's SPD. Also, you can contact the Plan Administrator using the contact information at the end of this notice.

### 5. When will my Plan account be vested and available to me?

You will always be fully vested in your contributions to the Plan. You will also be fully vested in matching contributions when you complete two years of service. To be fully vested in Plan contributions means that the contributions (together with any investment gain or loss) will always belong to you, and you will not lose them when you leave your job. For more information about years of service, you can review the "[ ]" section of the Plan's SPD.

Even if you are vested in your Plan account, there are limits on when you may withdraw your funds. These limits may be important to you in deciding how much, if any, to contribute to the

**Figure 9-5 (*cont'd*)**

## IRS Sample Automatic Enrollment and Default Investment Notice

Plan. Generally you may only withdraw vested money after you leave your job, reach age 59-1/2, or become disabled. Also, there is generally an extra 10% tax on distributions before age 59-1/2. Your beneficiary can get any vested amount remaining in your account when you die.

You also can borrow certain amounts from your vested Plan account, and may be able to take out certain vested money if you have a hardship. Hardship distributions are limited to the dollar amount of your contributions. They may not be taken from earnings or matching contributions. Hardship distributions must be for a specified reason—for qualifying medical expenses, costs of purchasing your principal residence (or preventing eviction from or foreclosure on your principal residence, or repairing qualifying damages to your principal residence), qualifying post-secondary education expenses, or qualifying burial or funeral expenses. Before you can take a hardship distribution, you must have taken other permitted withdrawals and loans from qualifying Company plans. If you take a hardship distribution, you may not contribute to the Plan or other qualifying Company plans for 6 months.

You can learn more about the Plan's hardship withdrawal and loan rules in the "[ ]" and "[ ]" sections of the Plan's SPD. You can also learn more about the extra 10% tax in IRS Publication 575, Pension and Annuity Income.

### 6. Can I change the amount of my contributions?

You can always change the amount you contribute to the Plan. If you know now that you do not want to contribute to the Plan (and you haven't already elected not to contribute), you will want to turn in a contribution form electing zero contributions by [ ]. That way, you avoid any automatic contributions.

But, if you do not turn in the form in time to prevent automatic contributions, you can withdraw the automatic contributions for a short time, despite the general limits on Plan withdrawals. During the 90 days after automatic contributions are first taken from your pay, you can withdraw the prior automatic contributions by turning in a [ ] Form to the Plan Administrator. The amount you withdraw will be adjusted for any gain or loss. If you take out your automatic contributions, you lose Company contributions that matched the automatic contributions. Also, your withdrawal will be subject to federal income tax (but not the extra 10% tax that normally applies to early distributions). If you take out automatic contributions, the Company will treat you as having chosen to make no further contributions. However, you can always choose to continue or restart your contributions by turning in a contribution form.

If you have any questions about how the Plan works or your rights and obligations under the Plan, or if you would like a copy of the Plan's SPD or other Plan documents, please contact the Plan Administrator at:

[Plan administrator name]

[Address]

[Telephone number]

[E-mail address]

# M. Notice of Eligible Investment Advice Arrangement

**PPA note**    PPA allows defined contribution plan fiduciaries to provide investment advice to plan participants.

**General rule**    Fiduciary advisors can offer participants access to computer programs and personal investment advisors without violating the ERISA prohibited transaction restrictions if the advice is provided under an eligible investment advice arrangement.[190] Before providing advice, the fiduciary advisor provides a notice to participants about fees, investment performance and affiliations.

**Content**    A *Notice of Eligible Investment Advice Arrangement* should disclose:[191]

- The role of any party that has a material affiliation or contractual relationship with the financial adviser in developing the investment advice program and in the selection of available investment options.
- The past performance and historical rates of return of the available investment options.
- All fees or other compensation that the fiduciary adviser or any affiliate will receive (including compensation provided by any third party) for providing the advice or in connection with the sale, acquisition, or holding of the security or other property.
- Any material affiliation or material contractual relationship of the fiduciary adviser or affiliates in the security or other property.
- How, and under what circumstances, any participant or beneficiary information provided under the arrangement will be used or disclosed.
- The types of services provided by the fiduciary adviser in connection with providing investment advice.
- That the adviser is acting as a fiduciary of the plan in providing the advice.
- That a recipient of the advice may separately arrange for obtaining advice from another adviser who could have no material affiliation with and receive no fees or other compensation in connection with the security or other property.

---

[190]    ERISA §§ 408(b)(14), 408(g)(1); I.R.C. § 4975(f)(8)(A).
[191]    ERISA § 408(g)(6); I.R.C. § 4975(f)(8)(F).

In addition, the fiduciary adviser must provide any disclosure required by applicable securities laws.[192]

**Due date**

The notice must be provided before providing advice[193] and no less frequently than annually and contemporaneously with any material change.[194]

**Distribution methods**

The notice should be written in a manner calculated to be understood by the average plan participant and be sufficiently accurate and comprehensive to explain the required information.[195] Electronic or other appropriate form should be acceptable to the extent reasonably accessible to the recipient (see Section C in Chapter 3 for DOL rules on electronic plan communications).

**Consequences of non-compliance**

Providing advice without observing the requirements of the exemption would expose the fiduciary to prohibited transaction penalties.

---

192 ERISA § 408(g)(7)(A); I.R.C. § 4975(f)(8)(G)(i).
193 ERISA § 408(g)(6)(A); I.R.C. § 4975(f)(8)(F)(i).
194 ERISA § 408(g)(6)(B); I.R.C. § 4975(f)(8)(F)(ii).
195 ERISA § 408(g)(8); I.R.C. § 4975(f)(8)(H).

# N. Notice of Right to Divest Employer Stock in Defined Contribution Plan

**PPA note**    In response to concerns that participants are investing too heavily in the stock of their employer, this notice requirement was added to ERISA to assure that plan participants are informed about their rights (as expanded by PPA) to diversify assets held for retirement purposes by divesting holdings in employer stock. The diversification requirements generally apply to plan years beginning after 2006 with a delay for collectively-bargained plans to as late as after 2008.

**General rule**    For employer nonelective or matching contributions, defined contribution plans must allow participants to diversify out of employer stock after three years of vesting service. Participants must be allowed to diversify their employee elective deferral or after-tax contributions out of employer stock without a waiting period requirement.[196] The plan administrator provides a *Notice of Right to Divest* to inform participants of these rights.

A participant would be viewed as having completed the requisite three years on the last day of the plan's vesting computation period that constitutes the completion of the third year of service, or the third anniversary of hire for a plan that either uses the elapsed time method or that does not define the vesting computation period because the plan provides for full and immediate vesting.[197]

**Affected plans**    The diversification requirements apply to defined contribution plans with publicly-traded employer stock and do not apply to stand-alone ESOPs without elective, employee, or matching contributions. Investments through a diversified mutual fund or similar regulated pooled investment vehicle are generally exempt.

---

[196]    ERISA § 204(j), I.R.C. 401(a)(35), IRS Notice 2006-107 and IRS Prop. Reg. § 1.401(a)(35)-1.
[197]    IRS Prop. Reg. § 1.401(a)(35)-1(c)(3).

**Content**
The notice must describe the rules applicable to divesting plan assets invested in employer stock and describe the importance of diversifying the investment of retirement account assets.[198]

See Figure 9-6 for model language provided by IRS.[199]

**Due date**
The *Notice of Right to Divest* must be provided no later than 30 days before the first date on which an individual is eligible to redirect the investment of the proceeds from the divestment of employer securities.[200]

For individual account plans that provided participant and beneficiaries comparable diversification rights prior to January 1, 2007, DOL concluded that it would not be necessary to provide a stand-alone diversification notice. Instead, plans may comply with this requirement by providing the relevant diversification notice with periodic benefit statements under the *Periodic Statement of Accrued Benefits* requirement[201] (see Section G in this chapter).

**Distribution methods**
The notice may be provided in written, electronic, or other appropriate form to the extent reasonably accessible to the recipient (see Section D in Chapter 3 for IRS rules on electronic plan communications).

**Penalty for non-compliance**
Failure to provide the notice can attract a penalty of $100 per day, per participant or beneficiary.[202]

---

[198]  ERISA § 101(m).
[199]  IRS Notice 2006-107.
[200]  ERISA § 101(m).
[201]  DOL Field Assistance Bulletin 2006-3, § 7.
[202]  ERISA § 502(c)(7); DOL Reg. § 2560.502C-7.

## Figure 9-6

## Model *Notice of Right to Divest* Employer Stock

This model from IRS Notice 2006-107 may need to be adapted to reflect particular plan provisions. For example, changes would generally be necessary if:

- the plan has more than one class of employer securities,

- the plan provides diversification rights for participants with fewer than three years of service,

- some of the plan's investment options are closed,

- the plan receives participant elections electronically, or

- the transition rule at § 401(a)(35)(H) is being applied.

### Notice of Your Rights Concerning Employer Securities

This notice informs you of an important change in Federal law that provides specific rights concerning investments in employer securities (company stock). Because you may now or in the future have investments in company stock under the [*insert name of plan*], you should take the time to read this notice carefully.

### Your Rights Concerning Employer Securities

For plan years beginning after December 31, 2006, the Plan must allow you to elect to move any portion of your account that is invested in company stock from that investment into other investment alternatives under the Plan. This right extends to all of the company stock held under the Plan, except that it does not apply to your account balance attributable to [*identify any accounts to which the rights apply only after three years of service*] until you have three years of service. [*Insert description of any advance notice requirement before a diversification election becomes effective.*] You may contact the person identified below for specific information regarding this new right, including how to make this election. In deciding whether to exercise this right, you will want to give careful consideration to the information below that describes the importance of diversification. All of the investment options under the Plan are available to you if you decide to diversify out of company stock.

### The Importance of Diversifying Your Retirement Savings

To help achieve long-term retirement security, you should give careful consideration to the benefits of a well-balanced and diversified investment portfolio. Spreading your assets among different types of investments can help you achieve a favorable rate of return, while minimizing your overall risk of losing money. This is because market or other economic conditions that cause one category of assets, or one particular security, to perform very well often cause another asset category, or another particular security, to perform poorly. If you invest more than 20% of your retirement savings in any one company or industry, your savings may not be properly diversified. Although diversification is not a guarantee against loss, it is an effective strategy to help you manage investment risk.

In deciding how to invest your retirement savings, you should take into account all of your assets, including any retirement savings outside of the Plan. No single approach is right for everyone because, among other factors, individuals have different financial goals, different time horizons for meeting their goals, and different tolerances for risk. Therefore, you should carefully consider the rights described in this notice and how these rights affect the amount of money that you invest in company stock through the Plan.

**Figure 9-6 (*cont'd*)**

**Model *Notice of Right to Divest* Employer Stock**

It is also important to periodically review your investment portfolio, your investment objectives, and the investment options under the Plan to help ensure that your retirement savings will meet your retirement goals.

**For More Information**

If you have any questions about your rights under this new law, including how to make this election, contact [*enter name and contact information*].

# O. Notice of Individual Account Plan Blackout Period

**Definition**   A *blackout period* is defined as any period during which the ability of participants or beneficiaries under an individual account plan to direct or diversify assets credited to their accounts, or obtain loans or distributions from the plan, is temporarily suspended, limited, or restricted.[203]

**General rule**   Administrators of 401(k) plans and other defined contribution plans are required to provide plan participants with a written notice of a "blackout period" that lasts more than three consecutive business days. The notice must be sent at least 30 days, but not more than 60 days, before the blackout occurs.[204]

However, the 30-day advance notice requirement does not apply if a plan fiduciary reasonably determines in writing that:[205]

- delaying the blackout period to provide advance notice would conflict with ERISA's requirement to act prudently on behalf of plan participants; or
- failing to provide the notice is due to unforeseeable events or circumstances beyond the reasonable control of the plan administrator.

In these two situations, notice of the blackout period must be provided as soon as reasonably possible unless a notice before the end of the blackout period is impractical. Similarly, a notice can be provided as soon as reasonably possible, instead of 30 days in advance, to participants affected by a blackout period in connection with a corporate merger or acquisition.[206] If a blackout period changes after a notice is provided, another notice with the changes must be provided as soon as reasonably practicable.[207]

---

[203]   ERISA § 101(i)(7).
[204]   ERISA § 101(i)(2)(B); DOL Reg. § 2520.101-3(b)(2).
[205]   ERISA § 101(i)(2)(C).
[206]   ERISA § 101(i)(3); DOL Reg. § 2520.101-3(b)(2)(ii)(C).
[207]   DOL Reg. § 2520.101-3(b)(4).

**Exceptions**

The 30-day advance notice requirement does not apply to periods similar to blackouts that:[208]

- are regularly scheduled and described in the SPD (or SMM, or materials describing the plan's investment alternatives);
- apply to participants and alternate payees in connection with a QDRO; or
- are required by securities laws.

**Content and delivery**

The blackout notice must:[209]

- describe the reasons for the blackout, and the expected beginning and ending dates of the blackout period;
- identify the investments and other rights affected; and
- instruct participants to evaluate current investment decisions in light of the impending blackout period.

The blackout notice must be in writing but can be delivered electronically to recipients who have reasonable access to electronic delivery. The plan administrator must also provide timely notice to the sponsoring employer.[210]

See Figure 9-7 for the DOL's Model Notice of Pension Fund Blackout.

**Penalties for non-compliance**

The DOL can assess a civil penalty against the plan administrator of up to $100 a day for failing to provide the blackout notice.[211]

**SEC notice requirement**

The Sarbanes-Oxley Act imposes restrictions on insider trading during defined contribution plan blackout periods.[212] The Act bars directors and executive officers from selling or otherwise transferring their public company stock acquired through their service to the company if at least half of the participants or beneficiaries in the company's defined contribution plans cannot trade (i.e., sell or transfer) their company stock during a blackout period affecting the plans. The company must notify directors, officers, and SEC of the blackout period. The company, or shareholders on behalf of the company, can recover from the directors and executive officers their profits on the disposition of their company stock in violation of this insider trading rule.

---

208    ERISA § 101(i)(7); DOL Reg. § 2520.101-3(d)(1).
209    ERISA § 101(i)(2)(A).
210    ERISA §§ 101(i)(2)(D), (E).
211    ERISA § 502(c)(7).
212    Regulation BTR (Blackout Trading Restriction); SEC Release 34-47225; 68 Fed. Reg. 4388 (Jan. 28, 2003).

**SEC notice content**  The notice of blackout period to SEC and affected directors and executive officers must include:

- the reason or reasons for the blackout period;
- a description of the plan transactions to be suspended during, or otherwise affected by, the blackout period;
- the description of the class of equity securities subject to the blackout period;
- the length of the blackout period; and
- the name, address, and telephone number of the person who will respond to inquiries about the blackout period, or, in the absence of such a designation, the issuer's human resources director or person performing equivalent functions.

**Notice timing**  The notice to the directors and executive officers must be provided no later than:

- five business days after the company receives the blackout notice from the plan administrator; or
- fifteen calendar days before the actual or expected beginning date of the blackout period, if the company does not receive a blackout notice from the plan administrator.

Advance notice is not required when an unforeseeable event or circumstance beyond the company's reasonable control prevents it from providing advance notice.

The notice to SEC must be provided with a Form 8-K on the same day notice is provided to the directors and executive officers. A foreign private issuer subject to the blackout trading restriction must file as an exhibit to its annual report on Form 20-F or 40-F a copy of each notice provided to directors and executive officers during the most recently completed fiscal year, unless the notice previously was provided to SEC on Form 6-K.

**Figure 9-7**

**DOL Model Notice of Pension Fund Blackout**

*Source:* DOL Regulations Section 2520.101-3(e).

---

**Important Notice Concerning Your Rights Under the
[Enter Name of Individual Account Plan]**

[Enter date of notice]

1. This notice is to inform you that the [enter name of plan] will be [enter reasons for blackout period, as appropriate: changing investment options, changing recordkeepers, etc.].

2. As a result of these changes, you temporarily will be unable to [enter as appropriate: direct or diversify investments in your individual accounts (if only specific investments are subject to the blackout, those investments should be specifically identified), obtain a loan from the plan, or obtain a distribution from the plan]. This period, during which you will be unable to exercise these rights otherwise available under the plan, is called a "blackout period." Whether or not you are planning retirement in the near future, we encourage you to carefully consider how this blackout period may affect your retirement planning, as well as your overall financial plan.

3. The blackout period for the plan [enter the following as appropriate: is expected to begin on [enter date] and end [enter date]/is expected to begin during the week of [enter date] and end during the week of [enter date]. During these weeks, you can determine whether the blackout period has started or ended by [enter instructions for using toll-free number or accessing web site].

4. [In the case of investments affected by the blackout period, add the following: During blackout period you will be unable to direct or diversify the assets held in your plan account. For this reason, it is very important that you review and consider the appropriateness of your current investments in light of your inability to direct or diversify those investments during the blackout period. For your long-term retirement security, you should give careful consideration to the importance of a well-balanced and diversified investment portfolio, taking into account all your assets, income and investments.] [If the plan permits investments in individual securities, add the following: You should be aware that there is a risk to holding substantial portions of your assets in the securities of any one company, as individual securities tend to have wider price swings, up and down, in short periods of time, than investments in diversified funds. Stocks that have wide price swings might have a large loss during the blackout period, and you would not be able to direct the sale of such stocks from your account during the blackout period.]

5. [If timely notice cannot be provided (see paragraph (b)(1)(v) of this section) enter: (A) Federal law generally requires that you be furnished notice of a blackout period at least 30 days in advance of the last date on which you could exercise your affected rights immediately before the commencement of any blackout period in order to provide you with sufficient time to consider the effect of the blackout period on your retirement and financial plans. (B) [Enter explanation of reasons for inability to furnish 30 days advance notice.]]

6. If you have any questions concerning this notice, you should contact [enter name, address and telephone number of the plan administrator or other contact responsible for answering questions about the blackout period].

---

# P. Notice of Qualified Change in Investment Options

**PPA note**    This new PPA rule offers plan fiduciaries an official mechanism for dealing with modifications to the fund lineup offered under a defined contribution plan claiming the ERISA 404(c) safe harbor.

**General rule**    Fiduciaries who seek to retain insulation from fiduciary liability for participant direction of investments under the ERISA 404(c) safe harbor when changing the lineup of funds offered under a plan can do so with a "qualified change in investment options."[213] A qualified change in investment options allows for the reallocation of investments (a.k.a., "mapping") in a participant or beneficiary's account among replacement options that have reasonably similar risk and rate of return characteristics to the options previously selected by the participant or beneficiary. Participants and beneficiaries must be notified in advance of the change.

**Content**    The *Notice of Qualified Change in Investment Options* must provide information about the change including a comparison of the existing and new investment options and an explanation that, in the absence of affirmative investment instructions from the participant or beneficiary to the contrary, the account of the participant or beneficiary will be invested in the replacement options identified in the notice.[214]

**Due date**    The notice must be provided at least 30 days and no more than 60 days prior to the effective date of the change.[215]

**Distribution methods**    The notice may be provided in written form.[216] Electronic or other appropriate form should be acceptable to the extent reasonably accessible to the recipient (see Section C in Chapter 3 for DOL rules on electronic plan communications).

---

[213]  ERISA § 404(c)(4).
[214]  ERISA § 404(c)(4)(C)(i).
[215]  *Id.*
[216]  *Id.*

**Consequ-
ences of non-
compliance**

Fiduciaries who fail to observe the requirements for a qualified change in investment options lose the protection of the ERISA 404(c) safe harbor for the transactions that map existing investment choices to the new options. Subsequent investment choices made by participants and beneficiaries would fall under the safe harbor assuming the general rules for meeting the safe harbor are satisfied.

# Q. Notice for SIMPLE IRAs

Employers who maintain SIMPLE IRAs must provide a SIMPLE Notice to each employee at least 61 days before the beginning of the plan year.[217]

**Definition**

The *SIMPLE Notice* notifies employees of their opportunity to elect to make salary deferrals (or modify a prior election) and provides a summary description of the plan.[218] This notice may be used to provide information about a reduced matching contribution or nonelective contribution.[219]

**Content requirements**

The SIMPLE Notice must contain the following information:[220]

- A statement notifying employees of their opportunity to contribute to the plan
- A copy of the summary description, provided to the employer by the SIMPLE IRA trustee, which contains:
  — the employer's name and address
  — the trustee's name and address
  — a description of the plan's eligibility requirements
  — a description of the plan's benefits
  — the time and methods for electing to contribute
  — procedures for withdrawing from the plan, and the effects of any withdrawal (including rollovers)

See Figure 9-8 for the IRS Model Notice for SIMPLE Plans.

**Due date**

The *SIMPLE Notice* must be provided to employees immediately before the 60-day election period preceding each January 1, during which employees may elect to make salary deferrals.[221]

---

[217]   ERISA § 101(h)(3).
[218]   ERISA §§ 101(h)(2) and (3); IRS Notice 98-4, Q G-1, 1998-1 C.B. 269.
[219]   IRS Notice 98-4, Q G-2, 1998-1 C.B. 269.
[220]   ERISA §§ 101(h)(2), (3); IRS Notice 98-4, Qs G-1 and H-1, 1998-1 C.B. 269.
[221]   ERISA § 101(h)(3); IRS Notice 98-4, Q G-1, 1998-1 C.B. 269.

## Figure 9-8

## IRS Model Notice for SIMPLE Plans

*Note:* This model statement appears in IRS Form 5305-SIMPLE.

---

### Model Notification to Eligible Employees

1.  Opportunity to Participate in the SIMPLE Plan

    You are eligible to make salary reduction contributions to the _____ (*insert name of plan*) SIMPLE plan. This notice and the attached summary description provide you with information that you should consider before you decide whether to start, continue, or change your salary reduction agreement.

2.  Employer Contribution Election

    For the _____ (*insert year*) calendar year, the employer elects to contribute to your SIMPLE IRA [*employer must select either (1), (2), or (3)*]:

    ☐ (1) A matching contribution equal to your salary reduction contributions up to a limit of 3% of your compensation for the year;

    ☐ (2) A matching contribution equal to your salary reduction contributions up to a limit of __% (*employer must insert a number from 1 to 3 and is subject to certain restrictions*) of your compensation for the year; or

    ☐ (3) A nonelective contribution equal to 2% of your compensation for the year (limited to $225,000*) if you are an employee who makes at least $_____ (*employer must insert an amount that is $5,000 or less*) in compensation for the year.

3.  Administrative Procedures

    If you decide to start or change your salary reduction agreement, you must complete the salary reduction agreement and return it to _____ (*employer should designate a place or individual*) by _____ (*employer should insert a date that is not less than 60 days after notice is given*).

*This amount will be adjusted to reflect any annual cost-of-living increases to the IRC Section 401(a)(17) limit announced by the IRS.

---

# R. Notice of Defined Benefit Pension Plan Funding

**PPA change**

For plan years beginning after 2007, all ERISA covered defined benefit plans are subject to a funding notice requirement. The rules are modified from the existing rules for multiemployer plans to reflect the PPA changes to the minimum funding requirements and expand the level of disclosure.

**General rule**

The administrator of a defined benefit plan must send an annual notice to plan participants, beneficiaries, labor organizations, contributing employers to multiemployer plans, and the PBGC disclosing information on the plan's funding status.[222]

The administrator of a plan receiving financial assistance from the PBGC is not required to furnish the notice.[223]

**Content**

The notice must include:[224]

- the name of the plan;
- the address and phone number of the plan administrator and the plan's principal administrative officer (if different from the plan administrator);
- each plan sponsor's employer identification number;
- the plan number;
- a statement whether the plan is 100 percent funded for the current and two prior plan years, and if not, the actual percentages for each year (single employer plans report this funded status based on the plan's funding target attainment percentage; multiemployer plans disclose using actuarial liabilities determined on prescribed assumptions);
- for single employer plans, a statement of the plan's assets and liabilities as determined for minimum funding purposes for the current and prior two years, and as determined for PBGC premium purposes for the current year; for multiemployer plans, a statement of the value of the plan's assets and liabilities for the plan year as the last day of the reported plan year and the preceding two plan years;

---

[222] ERISA § 101(f).
[223] DOL Reg. § 2520.101-4(b).
[224] ERISA § 101(f)(2).

- information on the number of plan participants, including active participants as well as retired and separated participants either receiving benefits or eligible to receive benefits in the future;
- a description of the plan's funding policy and the asset allocation of investments under the plan (expressed as percentages of total assets) as of the end of the plan year;
- an explanation of any plan amendments, scheduled benefit increases or reductions, or other known event taking effect in the current plan year and having a material effect on plan liabilities or assets for the year, along with a projection to the end of the plan year of the effect of the change on plan liabilities;
- a summary of the rules governing the termination of a single employer plan or reorganization or insolvency of multiemployer plans, as applicable;
- a description of the benefits guaranteed and limitations on benefit payments under the PBGC's single or multiemployer program, as applicable;
- for a multiemployer plan, whether the plan was in critical or endangered status for such plan year and, if so, information about any funding improvement plan, rehabilitation plan, or modification of the plan and how to obtain a copy along with actuarial and financial data about the plan;
- a statement that a copy of the annual report of the plan can be obtained from the DOL or plan sponsor/administrator's website or Intranet (or from the multiemployer plan administrator on request from a contributing sponsor or labor organization representing plan participants); and
- if applicable, a statement that contributing sponsors and related controlled group entities were required to provide "4010" information for the plan year (due to a funding target attainment percentage below 80 percent, funding waivers in excess of $1,000,000, or funding shortfalls subjecting those entities to a PBGC lien).

The notice may also include any additional information that the plan administrator elects to include, provided that such information is:

- necessary or helpful to understanding the mandatory information on the notice;
- set forth following the above mandatory requirements and is under the heading "Additional Explanation."[225]

---

[225] DOL Reg. § 2520.101-4(b)(9).

**Distribution methods**   The notice may be distributed in the same manner as Summary Plan Descriptions (see Section D in Chapter 7). Electronic distribution is also permissible if DOL safe harbor requirements are satisfied (see Chapter 3, Section C).[226]

**Due date**   The notice must be furnished within 120 days after the close of the plan year. Small plans (100 or fewer participants) can provide notices at the same time as the plan's Form 5500 is filed.

---

[226]   DOL Reg. § 2520.101-4(e).

# S. Notice of Funding Based Limitation on Distributions

**PPA note**  PPA added this notice requirement for plan years beginning after 2007. Plans maintained under a collective bargaining agreement can wait to implement restrictions until their next negotiations, but no later than plan years starting on or after January 1, 2010.[227]

**Definition**  The Notice of Funding Based Limitation on Distributions is a written notice to participants and beneficiaries about limits on the amount that can be paid from the plan while the plan's adjusted funding target attainment percentage for the plan year is sub-par.[228]

**Affected plans**  Certain single employer defined benefit plans become subject to restrictions on the amount that can be currently distributed from the plan when plan assets drop below 80 percent of plan liabilities. At that point, plan distributions that are not in straight life annuity form are limited to 50 percent of the amount otherwise available. If funding drops below 60 percent, no nonannuity form (e.g., lump sums) can be paid and shutdown benefits, unpredictable contingent event benefits, and the accrual of additional benefits are constrained.[229]

**Due date**  The plan administrator of a single employer plan must provide a written notice to plan participants and beneficiaries within 30 days after:

- the plan becomes subject to a limit on the payment of nonannuity benefits (e.g., lump sums), shutdown benefits, or other unpredictable contingent event benefits;
- limits on benefit accruals because of severe funding shortfalls (funding target attainment percentage less than 60 percent) become applicable; or
- IRS regulations require.[230]

---

[227]  PPA § 113(b)(2), PL 109-280, 8/17/2006.
[228]  ERISA § 101(j).
[229]  ERISA §§ 206(g)(1), (3) and (4); I.R.C. § 436(b), (d) and (e).
[230]  ERISA § 101(j).

**Distribution methods**   The notice should be in writing, but may be in electronic or other form to the extent reasonably accessible to the recipient. (See Section D in Chapter 3 for IRS rules on electronic plan communications)[231]

**Penalty for non-compliance**   Failure to provide the notice can attract a penalty of $1,000 per day.[232]

---

[231]   ERISA § 101(j).
[232]   ERISA § 502(c)(4) and DOL Prop. Reg. § 2560.502c-4.

# T. Notice of Failure to Make Timely Contributions

**PPA note**    PPA did not change this notice requirement. However, it did eliminate the ERISA § 4011 Participant Notice for plan years beginning after 2006. The last § 4011 Participant Notice would have been due two months after the plan's Form 5500 due date for the 2005 plan year. Plan sponsors will need to provide notice separately rather than relying on disclosure through notices provided to comply with that rule. Starting with plan years beginning after 2007, a new ERISA § 101(f) funding notice is to be provided no later than 120 days after the end of the plan year (e.g., first one by the end of April 2009 for a calendar plan year). Small plans will have until the due date for their Form 5500. Presumably disclosure of missed contributions in that notice will satisfy the ERISA § 101(d) requirement as well.

**General rule**    An employer that fails to make a required quarterly contribution within 60 days after it is due must provide participants and beneficiaries with a *Notice of Failure to Make Timely Contributions.*[233]

This is a written notice advising participants and beneficiaries of the employer's failure to make a required quarterly contribution or other payment required to meet minimum funding standards.[234]

**Affected plans**    The Notice of Failure to Make Timely Contributions requirement applies to all employers maintaining any type of ERISA pension plan except multiemployer plans.[235]

**Exception**    An employer that has applied for a funding waiver does *not* have to distribute a Notice of Failure to Make Timely Contributions.[236] However, if the IRS denies the funding waiver request, the employer is required to distribute the notice.[237]

---

[233]  ERISA § 101(d).
[234]  ERISA § 101(d)(1).
[235]  *Id.*
[236]  ERISA § 101(d)(2).
[237]  *Id.*

**Who must receive notice**    The Notice of Failure to Make Timely Contributions must be distributed to plan participants, beneficiaries, and alternate payees under QDROs.[238]

**Due date**    The notice must be provided at the time and in the manner specified by the DOL. The DOL has not provided guidance on this topic, but indirectly DOL has said that disclosure in a plan's ERISA § 4011 Participant Notice will satisfy this requirement.[239] The § 4011 notice is due two months after the due date for the plan's Form 5500 for the previous plan year. (See introductory PPA note.) If an employer applied for a funding waiver, and the IRS denies the request, that employer must distribute the notice within 60 days of the IRS's denial.[240]

**Penalty for non-compliance**    An employer may be liable for a penalty of $110 per day to each participant for not providing the Notice of Failure to Make Timely Contributions.[241]

**Related requirements**    See Sections E and F in Chapter 6 for PBGC notice requirements. Failure to make timely contributions may also subject the employer to excise taxes.[242]

---

[238]    ERISA § 101(d)(1).
[239]    1995 Preamble to PBGC Reg. § 4011.1-11.
[240]    ERISA § 101(d)(2).
[241]    ERISA § 502(c)(3); DOL Reg. § 2575.502c-3.
[242]    I.R.C. §§ 4971(a) and (f).

# U. Notice of Significant Reduction in Benefit Accruals

**PPA note**     The PPA expanded this notice requirement to add employers who have an obligation to contribute to the plan to the list of notice recipients.

**General rule**     If a plan subject to the minimum funding standards is amended to reduce or freeze future accruals significantly, the plan administrator must provide a Notice of Significant Reduction in Benefit Accruals to plan participants.

**Definition**     The *Notice of Significant Reduction in Benefit Accruals*, also known as the "ERISA § 204(h)/IRC § 4980F Notice," advises participants of a plan amendment that significantly reduces or freezes their benefit accruals, including any elimination or reduction of an early retirement benefit or retirement-type subsidy.[243]

**Exceptions**     The notice requirements do not apply to plans that are amended solely to limit compensation under the maximum compensation rules of Code Section 401(a)(17).[244]

The notice requirements generally do not apply to reductions resulting from the transition to the revised equivalency factors prescribed by PPA for lump sums and other 417(e) forms of benefit to the extent the previous factors were I.R.C. 417(e) factors.[245]

The notice timing and content requirements are satisfied through these other notice requirements in the case of amendments effective on or after January 1, 2008:[246]

- ERISA § 101(j) notices that apply when I.R.C. § 436 restrictions on accruals, shutdown benefits, and accelerated benefit payments (e.g., lump sums) are adopted

---

[243]  ERISA § 204(h)(9); I.R.C. § 4980F(f)(3).
[244]  IRS Ann. 93-146, 1993-40 I.R.B. 16; Rev. Proc. 94-13, 1994-1 C.B, 566.
[245]  IRS Prop. Reg. § 4980F-1, Q&A 8(d).
[246]  IRS Prop. Reg. § 4980F-1, Q&A 9(g).

- Notices required for multiemployer plans in reorganization, [ERISA § 4244A(b)] insolvency, [ERISA § 4245(e)] or reducing plan benefits [ERISA § 4281(c)]
- Notices required by other guidance in connection with retroactive amendments under I.R.C. § 412(d)(2), [former § 412(c)(8)]

**Affected plans**  Tax qualified defined benefit plans (other than governmental and nonelecting church plans), and money purchase plans subject to the minimum funding requirements are required to provide this notice.[247] The ERISA § 204(h) requirement also applies to any other defined benefit plan that is subject to the Participation and Vesting rules in ERISA (§§ 201 to 211). Thus a defined benefit plan that does not meet the qualification rules is subject to the notice requirement unless it is exempt (such as an unfunded excess benefit plan or unfunded deferred compensation plan for a select group of management or highly compensated employees).

**Who must receive notice**  The notice must be distributed to plan participants, alternate payees under QDROs, and each employee organization representing plan participants whose future benefit accrual rate under the plan may reasonably be expected to be significantly reduced by the plan amendment.[248] In addition, the notice must be provided to each employer who has an obligation to contribute to the plan.[249]

**Content requirements**  The Notice of Significant Reduction in Benefit Accruals must be written in a manner calculated to be understood by the average plan participant and must provide sufficient information (as determined in IRS regulations) to make the effect of the plan amendment understandable to affected individuals.[250]

IRS regulations require the notice to include a description of the plan provisions before the amendment, plan provisions after the amendment, and the effective date of the amendment.[251]

The notice may be provided in narrative form, like an SPD.[252]

---

[247] ERISA § 204(h)(8)(B); I.R.C. § 4980F(f)(2).
[248] ERISA § 204(h)(8); I.R.C. § 4980F(f)(1).
[249] ERISA § 204(h)(1); I.R.C. § 4980F(e)(1).
[250] ERISA § 204(h)(2); I.R.C. § 4980F(e)(2).
[251] IRS Reg. § 54.4980F-1, Q&A-11(a)(3).
[252] 2002 Preamble to Prop. IRS Reg. § 54.4980F-1.

**Additional requirements**

If the magnitude of the amendment is not readily apparent from the above required information (e.g., in cases of a change from a traditional defined benefit formula to a cash balance formula), IRS regulations would require the plan to provide a further explanation, or examples.[253]

**Due date**

The notice must be provided within a reasonable period of time before the effective date of the plan amendment.[254] IRS regulations have a general timing rule and a special timing rule, depending on the nature of the amendment.

*Note.* Notice may be provided prior to the adoption of the plan amendment if no material modification occurs before adoption.

**General and special timing rule**

IRS regulations generally require the Notice of Significant Reduction in Benefit Accruals to be provided at least 45 days before the effective date of the amendment.[255] For retroactive amendments such as those allowed by PPA, this deadline would be based on the date the plan is operated in accordance with the change.[256]

The regulations accommodate special timing rules for the following circumstances:[257]

- *Business Acquisitions and Dispositions/Small and Multiemployer Plans certain Airline Plans.* The notice must be provided at least 15 days before the effective date of an amendment in connection with a business acquisition or disposition, or involving a small plan (i.e., fewer than 100 participants), a multiemployer plan, or certain commercial airlines or their catering services.
- *Merger or Plan-to-Plan Transfer.* The notice may be provided up to 30 days **after** the effective date of an amendment involving a plan-to-plan transfer or merger in connection with a business acquisition or disposition where the change only affects an early retirement benefit or retirement-type subsidy (but not the rate of future benefit accruals).

*Special PPA rule.* Cash balance plans that eliminate the minimum lump sum based on a projected normal retirement benefit (a.k.a. "whipsaw")

---

[253] IRS Reg. §54.4980F-1, Q&A-11(a)(4).
[254] ERISA §204(h)(3); I.R.C. §4980F(e)(3).
[255] IRS Reg. §54.4980F-1, Q&A 9(a).
[256] IRS Prop. Reg. §4980F-1, Q&A 9(g)(2).
[257] IRS Prop. Reg. §4980F-1, Q&A 9(f).

as permitted under the PPA are not required to grandfather the value that existed at the time of the amendment if the amendment is adopted on or before the last day of the first plan year starting after 2008. IRS, however, ruled that a Notice of Significant Reduction in Benefit Accruals must be provided at least 30 days before the date the amendment is first effective. If an amendment is adopted retroactively, then the notice must be provided at least 30 days before the earliest date the plan is *operated* using the new rule.[258] For years beginning after 2008, 45-day notice would be required.[259]

**Penalty for non-compliance**

For plans subject to IRC § 4980F, the IRS penalty for failure to provide the notice is $100 per day per applicable individual for the noncompliance period.[260] The **noncompliance period** begins on the date the failure first occurs and ends on the date the notice to which the failure relates is provided or the failure is otherwise corrected.

**Waiver of penalty**

No penalty is imposed on the employer for failure to provide the notice in the following circumstances:

- the failure was not known and reasonable diligence was exercised to meet the notice requirement;[261] or
- reasonable diligence was exercised to meet the notice requirement and notice was provided within 30 days from the date of knowledge of the failure (or date failure should have been known using reasonable diligence).[262]

IRS regulations clarify that the penalty would not apply only if the person responsible for the penalty exercised reasonable diligence in attempting to deliver the notice and believed the notice was timely delivered to the applicable individuals.[263]

In any event, if there was reasonable diligence to meet the notice requirement, the penalty will not exceed $500,000 for the taxable year.[264]

---

[258]   IRS Notice 2007-6.
[259]   IRS Prop. Reg. § 4980F-1, Q&A 18-(b)(3)(iii).
[260]   I.R.C. § 4980F(b).
[261]   I.R.C. § 4980F(c)(1).
[262]   I.R.C. § 4980F(c)(2).
[263]   IRS Reg. § 54.4980F-1, Q&A-15(b).
[264]   I.R.C. § 4980F(c)(3).

Finally, in the case of failure to notify due to reasonable cause, the IRS may waive the penalty to the extent payment would be excessive in relation to the failure involved.[265]

**Consequences of egregious failure to provide notice**

If there is an egregious failure by the plan sponsor to comply with the notice requirement, the plan provisions will apply as if the plan amendment entitled all affected individuals to the greater of:

- the benefits to which they would have been entitled without the amendment; or
- the benefits under the plan with such amendment.[266]

**Egregious failure**

There is an *egregious failure* to provide notice if the failure is within the control of the plan sponsor and is:

- an intentional failure;
- a failure to provide most of the applicable individuals with most of the information they are required to receive; or
- a failure that is determined to be egregious under IRS regulations.[267]

**Format and manner of delivery**

IRS regulations require the notice be provided in one of the following formats:

- Paper format, distributed first-class mail, hand delivery, or enclosed with another notice (e.g., the PBGC Notice of Intent to Terminate). Posting a paper copy is not acceptable.
- Electronic format that satisfies IRS' rules for electronic plan communications (see Section D of Chapter 3).[268]

---

[265] I.R.C. § 4980F(c)(4).
[266] ERISA § 204(h)(6)(A).
[267] ERISA § 204(h)(6)(B).
[268] IRS Reg. § 54.4980F-1, Q&A 13

# V. Notice of Transfer to Retiree Health Account

**Definition**

A *Notice of Transfer to Retiree Health Account* is a written notice advising participants and beneficiaries of the transfer of excess defined benefit plan assets to a Section 401(h) retiree health account.[269] A second transfer notice is required for notifying the DOL, IRS, plan administrator, and employee organizations representing participants in the plan.[270] The plan administrator of a defined benefit pension plan that makes a qualified transfer of excess assets to a Section 401(h) retiree health account provides the notice to participants.[271] The employer provides notice to the agencies, plan administrator, and bargaining organization.[272]

**Contents for participant notice**

The Notice of Transfer to Retiree Health Account must identify the plan and identify the amount of:[273]

- excess pension assets and portion to be transferred;
- health benefit liabilities expected to be provided with the transferred assets; and
- participant's vested pension benefits immediately after the transfer.

**Contents for agency notice**

The Notice of Transfer to Retiree Health Account provided by the employer to the agencies, plan administrator and bargaining representative identifies the plan (name, address and EIN of the employer and the name, EIN and plan number of the plan) along with:

- the amount of the transfer;
- a detailed accounting of assets projected to be held by the plan immediately before and after the transfer;
- the current liabilities under the plan at the time of transfer; and
- the filing date and the date on which the transfer is; intended to take place.[274]

*PPA Note.* Transfers can only be considered by well funded plans where assets exceed 125 percent of liabilities. Prior to PPA, the threshold was

---

[269]  ERISA § 101(e)(1).
[270]  ERISA § 101(e)(2).
[271]  ERISA § 101(e)(1).
[272]  ERISA § 101(e)(2).
[273]  ERISA § 101(e)(1); ERISA Tech. Release 91-1.
[274]  ERISA Tech. Release 91-1; Announcement 92-54, 1992-13 I.R.B 35.

based on "current liabilities"; for transfers after PPA, the threshold is based on the plan's "funding target" and "target normal cost."

**Filing agency notice**

The notice to the agencies is filed with the DOL. DOL provides access to the notice information to IRS.[275] The address for the filing is:

> Section 101(e)(2) Notice
> Room N5644
> Division of Reports, PWBA
> U.S. Department of Labor
> 200 Constitution Avenue, N.W.
> Washington, DC 20210

**Delivery to others**

The notice should be in writing, but can be delivered electronically to recipients if DOL safe harbor requirements are satisfied (see Chapter 3, Section C). A copy of the agency notice is required to be available for inspection in the principal office of the plan administrator.[276]

**Due date**

The notices are provided to participants, beneficiaries, DOL, plan administrators, and bargaining representatives no later than 60 days before the date of the qualified transfer.[277]

**Penalty for non-compliance**

A plan administrator employer or administrator who fails to provide the Notice of Transfer to Retiree Health Account may be liable for a $110 per day, per person penalty from the date of the failure.[278]

---

[275]  *Id.*
[276]  ERISA § 101(e)(2)(A).
[277]  ERISA Tech. Release 91-1; Announcement 92-54, 1992-13 I.R.B 35.
[278]  ERISA §§ 502(c)(1) and 502(c)(3); DOL Reg. §§ 2575.502c-1 and 2575.502c-3.

# W. Notice of Multiemployer Plan's Critical or Endangered Status

**PPA note**     This PPA notice requirement informs participants of the risk of benefit limitations when a multiemployer plan's funding status falls below established thresholds.

**General rule**     If a multiemployer plan's funding status is "endangered" (i.e., less than 80 percent funded or expected to have a funding deficiency in the next six years), the plan sponsor must develop a "funding improvement plan" to improve funding levels over a 10 to 15 year period. If a multiemployer plan's status is "critical" (i.e., less than 65 percent funded and face certain types of insufficiencies such as a projected inability to pay benefits) the sponsor must develop a rehabilitation plan that will correct funding over a ten-year period. The initial plan is to be based on a cutback of future accruals to a level that can be supported by current contribution levels. If that's not sufficient, a second plan would be based on an increase in contributions. Benefits other than basic core accrued normal retirement benefits may be reduced under certain circumstances. Payments in excess of the monthly amount paid under a single life annuity (plus social security supplements) cannot be paid if the plan is in critical status.[279]

Employer surcharges apply once a plan enters critical status; the surcharge is 5 percent the first year and 10 percent until certain criteria are met under the rehabilitation plan.

**Content**     The plan sponsor of a multiemployer plan that is or will be in endangered or critical status for a plan year must provide a *Notice of Multiemployer Plan's Critical or Endangered Status* to participants and beneficiaries, the bargaining parties, the PBGC, and the DOL.[280]

If there is a certification that the plan is or will be in critical status, the notice must explain the possibility that:

- "adjustable benefits" may be reduced;
- such reductions may apply to participants and beneficiaries whose benefit commencement date is on or after the date notice is provided for the first plan year in which the plan is in critical status; and

---

[279]   ERISA § 305(f)(2)(A)(i); I.R.C. § 432(f)(2)(A)(i).
[280]   ERISA § 305(b)(3)(D); I.R.C. § 432(b)(3)(D).

- if the plan provides benefits in a form that is restricted, an explanation that the plan cannot pay single sums and similar benefits that are greater than the monthly amount due under a single life annuity.[281]

The model notice for plans in critical status provided by the DOL satisfies this content requirement. See Figure 9-9.[282] The DOL believes this model may be useful in preparing notices required to be furnished by plans in endangered status.[283]

**Definition**     An "adjustable benefit" includes:[284]

- Benefits, rights, and features under the plan, including post-retirement death benefits, 60-month guarantees, disability benefits not yet in pay status, and similar benefits
- Early retirement benefits or retirement-type subsidies and any benefit payment option (other than the qualified joint-and survivor annuity)
- Benefit increases that would not be eligible for a PBGC guarantee as of the first day of the initial critical year because the increases were adopted (or, if later, took effect) less than 60 months before such first day

**Due date**     The notice must be provided not later than 30 days after the date of the actuary's certification of the plan's endangered or critical status.[285]

**Distribution methods**     Electronic or other appropriate form should be acceptable to the extent reasonably accessible to the recipient (see Section C in Chapter 3 for DOL rules on electronic plan communications).

For the notice to DOL, the following address may be used:

U.S. Department of Labor
Employee Benefits Security Administration
Public Disclosure Room, N-1513,
200 Constitution Ave., N.W.,
Washington, DC 20210.

Alternatively, notices may be e-mailed to *criticalstatusnotice@dol.gov*.[286]

---

[281]  IRS Prop. Reg. § 1.432(b)-1(e)(2).
[282]  *Id.*
[283]  Preamble to DOL Prop. Reg. § 2540.305-1, 73 Fed. Reg. 15,688 (Mar. 25, 2008).
[284]  ERISA § 305(e)(8)(A)(iv); I.R.C. § 432(2)(8)(A)(iv).
[285]  ERISA § 305(b)(3)(D)(i); I.R.C. § 432(b)(3)(D)(i).
[286]  Preamble to DOL Prop. Reg. § 2540.305-1, 73 Fed. Reg. 15688 (Mar. 25, 2008).

## Figure 9-9

## DOL Model Notice of Critical Status[287]

**Notice of Critical Status**
**For**

[Insert name of pension plan]

This is to inform you that on [enter date] the plan actuary certified to the U.S. Department of the Treasury, and also to the plan sponsor, that the plan [enter "is" or "will be"] in critical status for the plan year beginning [enter beginning date of plan year]. Federal law requires that you receive this notice.

### Critical Status

The plan is considered to be in critical status because it has funding or liquidity problems, or both. More specifically, the plan's actuary determined that [complete and insert appropriate explanation(s) from the options below].

*[Option one: "the plan's funded percentage for [enter plan year] is less than 65%, and the sum of the fair market value of its current assets plus the present value of expected employer contributions through [enter end of the 6th plan year following the current plan year] is less than the present value of all benefits projected to be payable (plus administrative expenses) through [enter end of the 6th plan year following the current plan year."]*

*[Option two: "the plan has an accumulated funding deficiency for the current plan year."]*

*[Option three: "over the next three plan years, the plan is projected to have an accumulated funding deficiency for the [enter appropriate plan year or years]."]*

*[Option four: "the funded percentage of the plan is 65% or less, and over the next four plan years, the plan is projected to have an accumulated funding deficiency for the [enter appropriate plan year or years]."]*

*[Option five: "the sum of the plan's normal cost and interest on the unfunded benefits for the current plan year exceeds the present value of all expected contributions for the year; the present value of vested benefits of inactive participants is greater than the present value of vested benefits of active participants; and the plan has an accumulated funding deficiency for the current plan year."]*

*[Option six: "the sum of the plan's normal cost and interest on the unfunded benefits for the current plan year exceeds the present value of all expected contributions for the year; the present value of vested benefits of inactive participants is greater than the present value of vested benefits of active participants; and over the next four plan years, the plan is projected to have an accumulated funding deficiency for the [enter appropriate plan year or years.]."]*

*[Option seven: "the sum of the fair market value of the plan's current assets plus the present value of expected employer contributions through [enter date that is the end of the plan year that is the 4th plan year following the current plan year] is less than the present value of all benefits payable through [enter date that is the end of the plan year that is the 4th plan year following the current plan year]."]*

*[Option eight: "the plan was in critical status last year and over the next 9 years, the plan is projected to have an accumulated funding deficiency for the [enter appropriate plan year or years]."]*

*[Instructions: Insert the following discussion entitled Rehabilitation Plan and Possibility of Reduction in Benefits only if the plan is in critical status and adjustable benefits have not yet been reduced (e.g., the*

---

[287]   DOL Prop. Reg. § 2540.305-1(b).

**Figure 9-9 (*cont'd*)**

**DOL Model Notice of Critical Status**

*initial critical status year). Where adjustable benefits have already been reduced, insert the discussion below entitled Rehabilitation Plan.]*

### Rehabilitation Plan and Possibility of Reduction in Benefits

Federal law requires pension plans in critical status to adopt a rehabilitation plan aimed at restoring the financial health of the plan. The law permits pension plans to reduce, or even eliminate, benefits called "adjustable benefits" as part of a rehabilitation plan. If the trustees of the plan determine that benefit reductions are necessary, you will receive a separate notice in the future identifying and explaining the effect of those reductions. Any reduction of adjustable benefits (other than a repeal of a recent benefit increase, as described below) will not reduce the level of a participant's basic benefit payable at normal retirement. In addition, the reductions may only apply to participants and beneficiaries whose benefit commencement date is on or after [enter the date notice is or was provided for the first plan year in which the plan is in critical status]. But you should know that whether or not the plan reduces adjustable benefits in the future, effective as of [enter date notice is or was provided for the first plan year in which the plan is in critical status or January 1, 2008, whichever is later], the plan is not permitted to pay lump sum benefits (or any other payment in excess of the monthly amount paid under a single life annuity) while it is in critical status.

### Rehabilitation Plan

Federal law requires pension plans in critical status to adopt a rehabilitation plan aimed at restoring the financial health of the plan. This is the [enter number] year the plan has been in critical status. The law permits pension plans to reduce, or even eliminate, benefits called "adjustable benefits" as part of a rehabilitation plan. On [enter date], you were notified that the plan reduced or eliminated adjustable benefits. On [enter date of initial critical status notice], you were notified that as of [enter date] the plan is not permitted to pay lump sum benefits (or any other payment in excess of the monthly amount paid under a single life annuity) while it is in critical status. If the trustees of the plan determine that further benefit reductions are necessary, you will receive a separate notice in the future identifying and explaining the effect of those reductions. Any reduction of adjustable benefits (other than a repeal of a recent benefit increase, as described below) will not reduce the level of a participant's basic benefit payable at normal retirement. In addition, the reductions may only apply to participants and beneficiaries whose benefit commencement date is on or after [enter the date notice is or was provided for the first plan year in which the plan is in critical status].

### Adjustable Benefits

The plan offers the following adjustable benefits which may be reduced or eliminated as part of any rehabilitation plan the pension plan may adopt [check appropriate box or boxes]:

☐ Post-retirement death benefits;

☐ Sixty-month payment guarantees;

☐ Disability benefits (if not yet in pay status);

☐ Early retirement benefit or retirement-type subsidy;

☐ Benefit payment options other than a qualified joint- and survivor annuity (QJSA);

## Figure 9-9 (*cont'd*)

## DOL Model Notice of Critical Status

☐ Recent benefit increases (i.e, occurring in past 5 years);

☐ Other similar benefits, rights, or features under the plan [provide identification]

_____

_____

_____

### Employer Surcharge

The law requires that all contributing employers pay to the plan a surcharge to help correct the plan's financial situation. The amount of the surcharge is equal to a percentage of the amount an employer is otherwise required to contribute to the plan under the applicable collective bargaining agreement. With some exceptions, a 5% surcharge is applicable in the initial critical year and a 10% surcharge is applicable for each succeeding plan year thereafter in which the plan is in critical status.

### Where to Get More Information

For more information about this Notice, you may contact [enter name of plan administrator] at [enter phone number and address (including e-mail address if appropriate)]. You have a right to receive a copy of the rehabilitation plan from the plan.

# X. Notice of Reduction to Adjustable Benefits

**PPA note**     PPA calls for benefit adjustments in connection with rehabilitation plans of multiemployer plans in critical status.

**General rule**     The plan sponsor of a multiemployer plan in critical status provides notice and implements reductions to adjustable benefits which the plan sponsor deems appropriate, based upon the outcome of collective bargaining over the schedule or schedules presented to the union for addressing the plan's critical status.[288]

**Definition**     An "adjustable benefit" includes:[289]

- benefits, rights, and features under the plan, including post-retirement death benefits, 60-month guarantees, disability benefits not yet in pay status, and similar benefits;
- early retirement benefits or retirement-type subsidies and any benefit payment option (other than the qualified joint-and-survivor annuity); and
- benefit increases that would not be eligible for a PBGC guarantee as of the first day of the initial critical year because the increases were adopted (or, if later, took effect) less than 60 months before such first day.

**Content**     A *Notice of Reduction to Adjustable Benefits* should include sufficient information to allow participants and beneficiaries to understand the effect of any reduction of their benefits.[290] The notice should include:

- an estimate (on an annual or monthly basis) of any affected adjustable benefit that a participant or beneficiary would otherwise have been eligible for as of the effective date of the reduction;
- information about the rights and remedies of plan participants and beneficiaries; and
- contact information and assistance where appropriate.

---

[288]   ERISA § 305(e)(8)(A)(i); I.R.C. § 432(c)(8)(A)(i).
[289]   ERISA § 305(e)(8)(A)(iv); I.R.C. § 432(e)(8)(A)(iv).
[290]   ERISA § 305(e)(8)(C)(ii); I.R.C. § 432(e)(8)(C)(ii).

**Due Date**   No reduction may be made to adjustable benefits unless notice of the reduction has been given at least 30 days before the general effective date of the reduction for all participants and beneficiaries to:

- plan participants and beneficiaries;
- each employer who has an obligation to contribute under the plan; and
- each employee organization representing plan participants.[291]

**Distribution methods**   The notice should be written in a manner calculated to be understood by the average plan participant and may be provided in written, electronic or other appropriate form to the extent reasonably accessible to the recipient[292] (see Section C in Chapter 3 for DOL rules on electronic plan communications). DOL is charged with providing a model notice.

---

[291]   ERISA § 305(e)(8)(C)(i); I.R.C. § 432(e)(8)(C)(i).
[292]   ERISA § 305(e)(8)(C)(iii); I.R.C. § 432(e)(8)(C)(iii).

# Y. Multiemployer Plan Funding Information Made Available on Request

**PPA note**      This requirement is part of the PPA package aimed at informing plan participants about the security of their benefits.

**General rule**      Multiemployer plan administrators are required to furnish copies of actuarial and financial reports, upon request, to any plan participant or beneficiary, employee representative, or any employer that has an obligation to contribute to the plan.[293]

The information available for production under this requirement includes:[294]

- the periodic actuarial report (including any sensitivity testing) for any plan year that has been in the plan's possession for at least 30 days;
- any quarterly, semi-annual, or annual financial report prepared for the plan that has been in the plan's possession for at least 30 days; and
- any application filed with IRS asking for an extension of the time permitted for amortizing plan liabilities and IRS' response to the application.

Plan administrators are not required to disclose:

- information or data that served as the basis behind or underlying a report or application; and
- information that the plan administrator reasonably determines to be either individually identifiable for any plan participant, beneficiary, employee, fiduciary, or contributing employer, or proprietary information about the plan, any contributing employer, or entity providing services to the plan (though disclosure that such information is being withheld is required if the information had been requested).[295]

**Due date**      The information must be provided within 30 days after the request.[296]

---

[293] ERISA § 101(k).
[294] ERISA § 101(k)(1).
[295] DOL Prop. Reg. § 2520.101-6(c)(2).
[296] ERISA § 101(k)(2)(A).

**Distribution methods**

The information may be provided in written, electronic, or other appropriate form to the extent reasonably accessible to the recipient (see Section D in Chapter 3 for IRS rules on electronic plan communications).[297] Any individually identifiable information or proprietary information about the plan, contributing employer or service provider should be redacted from the information.[298]

Plan administrators need not respond to more than one request per party, per 12-month period and may charge a reasonable fee for processing costs.

**Penalty for non-compliance**

Failure to provide the notice can attract a penalty of $1,000 per day.[299]

---

[297] ERISA § 101(k)(2)(B).
[298] ERISA § 101(k)(2)(C).
[299] ERISA § 502(c)(4) and DOL Prop. Reg. § 2560.502c-4.

# Z. Notice of Funding Waiver Application

**Definition**

A *Notice of Funding Waiver Application* is an advance notice advising affected parties of an employer's intention to apply for a funding waiver.[300]

**PPA note**

The basic rules for obtaining a funding waiver were not changed by PPA, merely reorganized.

**Affected parties**

Employers requesting funding waivers must notify affected parties and their delegates.[301] Affected parties include:[302]

- employee organizations representing employees covered by the plan;
- plan participants;
- beneficiaries of deceased participants;
- alternate payees under qualified domestic relations orders (QDROs); and
- PBGC.

**Content requirements**

A Notice of Funding Waiver Application must contain certain information and statements.[303]

See Figure 9-10 for the IRS Model Notice of Funding Waiver Application.

**Due date**

The Notice of Funding Waiver Application must be delivered to affected parties within 14 days before the date the employer files the application for waiver with the IRS.[304]

**Distribution methods**

The Notice of Funding Waiver Application must be delivered individually, by hand or mail, to each affected party's last-known address.[305]

Posting the notice on a bulletin board is not an acceptable distribution method.

---

[300]  I.R.C. § 412(c)(6).
[301]  *Id.*
[302]  Rev. Proc. 2004-15, 2004-7 I.R.B. 490.
[303]  *Id.*
[304]  Rev. Proc. 2004-15, 2004-7 I.R.B. 490, § 2.02.
[305]  *Id.*

## Figure 9-10

## Model Notice of Funding Waiver Application to Employee Organizations (Unions), Participants, Beneficiaries, and Alternate Payees

*Source*: Revenue Procedure 2004-15, modified to reflect the PPA 2006 changes to relevant Code and ERISA sections.

*Note*: The address listed in this sample notice was correct at the time this edition went to press. However, government addresses occasionally change. To ensure accuracy, users should confirm the address.

---

This notice is to inform you that an application for a waiver of the minimum funding standard under § 412(c) of the Internal Revenue Code (Code) and section 303 of the Employee Retirement Income Security Act of 1974 (ERISA) has been submitted by [INSERT PLAN SPONSOR'S NAME] to the Internal Revenue Service (Service) for the [INSERT PLAN NAME] for the plan year beginning [INSERT DATE].

Under § 412(c)(6)(B) of the Code and section 302(c)(6)(B) of ERISA, the Service will consider any relevant information submitted concerning this application for a waiver of the minimum funding standard. You may send this information to the following address:

> Director, Employee Plans
> Internal Revenue Service
> Attn: SE:T:EP:RA:T:A
> 1111 Constitution Avenue, N.W.
> Washington, D.C. 20224

Any such information should be submitted as soon as possible after you have received this notice. Due to the disclosure restrictions of § 6103 of the Code, the Service can not provide any information with respect to the waiver request itself.

In accordance with section 104 of ERISA and section 2520.104b-10 of the Department of Labor Regulations (29 C.F.R. Part 2520), annual financial reports for this plan, which include employer contributions made to the plan and the accumulated funding deficiency for the plan for any plan year, are available for inspection at the Department of Labor in Washington, D.C. Copies of such reports may be obtained upon request and upon payment of copying costs from the following address:

> Public Disclosure Room
> Room N-5507
> Employee Benefits Security Administration
> U.S. Department of Labor
> 200 Constitution Avenue, N.W.
> Washington, D.C. 20210

---

**Figure 9-10 (*cont'd*)**

## Model Notice of Funding Waiver Application to Employee Organizations (Unions), Participants, Beneficiaries, and Alternate Payees

As required by section 104(b)(2) of ERISA, copies of the latest annual plan report are available for inspection at the principal office of the plan administrator, who is located at [INSERT ADDRESS]. Copies of the annual report may be obtained upon request and upon payment of a copying charge of [INSERT CHARGE] by writing to the plan administrator at the above address.

The following information is provided pursuant to § 412(c)(6)(A) of the Code and section 302(c)(6)(A) of ERISA:

Present Value of Vested Benefits      $_____

Present Value of Benefits, calculated as though the plan terminated      $_____

Fair Market Value of Plan Assets      $_____

The above present values were calculated using an interest rate of [INSERT INTEREST RATE].


[SIGNATURE OF APPROPRIATE OFFICER OF THE PLAN SPONSOR]


[INSERT NAME]


[INSERT TITLE]


*Note:* You may have to provide additional information under a collective bargaining agreement.

# AA. Notice of Multiemployer Plan Application for Extension of Unfunded Liability Amortization

**PPA note**    For plan years beginning after 2007, this type of extension is only available to multiemployer plans.

**General rule**    A multiemployer defined benefit plan board of trustees may request approval from the IRS to extend, for up to 10 years, the period of time that the plan is required to amortize any of its unfunded liabilities.[306]

The request for an extension generally must be submitted to the IRS by the last day of the plan year for which the extension is intended to take effect, but the IRS will consider late requests if there is good cause.[307]

The applicant must provide written notice of the application to each participant, beneficiary, alternative payee, and employee organization representing employees covered under the plan.[308]

**Due date and distribution methods**    The notice of application for extension of unfunded liability amortization must be hand-delivered or mailed to the last known address of each participant, beneficiary, alternative payee, and employee organization (union) within 14 days prior to the date of the application. Posting of the notice on bulletin boards is not sufficient to satisfy this requirement.[309]

**Content**    The notice must include a description of the extent to which the plan is funded for benefits that are guaranteed by the PBGC and for benefit liabilities as of the application date.[310] Specifically, the notice must include (1) the present value of vested benefits, (2) the present value of benefits calculated as though the plan had terminated, (3) the fair market value of plan assets, and (4) the interest rate(s) used to determine the present value of such benefits.[311]

---

[306]  ERISA § 304(d); I.R.C. 431(d).
[307]  Rev. Proc. 2004-44, 2004-31 I.R.B. 134.
[308]  ERISA § 304(d)(3); I.R.C. § 431(d)(3).
[309]  Rev. Proc. 2004-44, 2004-31 I.R.B. 134.
[310]  ERISA § 304(d)(3); I.R.C. § 431(d)(3).
[311]  Rev. Proc. 2004-44, 2004-31 I.R.B. 134.

Compliance with the content requirements is satisfied by providing a notice substantially in the form set forth in the IRS Model Notice (see Figure 9-11).[312] No additional information is required by the IRS; however, additional information may be provided as required under a collective bargaining agreement.[313]

---

[312]  *Id.*
[313]  *Id.*

## Figure 9-11

### IRS Model Notice[314] of Application for an Extension of an Amortization Period to Employee Organizations (Unions), Participants, Beneficiaries, and Alternate Payees

This notice is to inform you that an application for an extension of an amortization period for unfunded liability under § 431(d) of the Internal Revenue Code (Code) and section 304(d) of the Employee Retirement Income Security Act of 1974 (ERISA) has been submitted by [INSERT APPLICANT'S NAME] to the Internal Revenue Service (Service) for the [INSERT PLAN NAME] for the plan year beginning [INSERT DATE].

Under § 431(d)(3)(B) of the Code and section 304(d)(3)(B) of ERISA, the Service will consider any relevant information submitted concerning this application for an extension of the amortization period for unfunded liability. You may send this information to the following address:

Director, Employee Plans
Internal Revenue Service
Attn: SE:T:EP:RA:T:A
1111 Constitution Avenue, N.W.
Washington, D.C. 20224

Any such information should be submitted as soon as possible after you have received this notice. Due to the disclosure restrictions of § 6103 of the Code, the Service cannot provide any information with respect to the extension request itself.

In accordance with section 104 of ERISA and section 2520.104b-10 of the Department of Labor Regulations (29 C.F.R. Part 2520), annual financial reports for this plan, which include employer contributions made to the plan for any plan year, are available for inspection at the Department of Labor in Washington, D.C. Copies of such reports may be obtained upon request and upon payment of copying costs from the following address:

Public Disclosure Room
Room N-5507
Employee Benefits Security Administration
U.S. Department of Labor
200 Constitution Avenue, N.W.
Washington, D.C. 20210

As required by section 104(b)(2) of ERISA, copies of the latest annual plan report are available for inspection at the principal office of the plan administrator, who is located at [INSERT ADDRESS]. Copies of the annual report may be obtained upon request and upon payment of a copying charge of [INSERT CHARGE] by writing to the plan administrator at the above address.

---

[314] Citations modified to reflect changes made by PPA '06.

**Figure 9-11 (*cont'd*)**

**IRS Model Notice of Application for an Extension of
an Amortization Period to Employee Organizations (Unions),
Participants, Beneficiaries, and Alternate Payees**

The following information is provided pursuant to § 431(d)(3)(A) of the Code and section 304(d)(3)(A) of ERISA:

Present Value of Vested Benefits      $_____

Present Value of Benefits, calculated as though the plan terminated      $_____

Fair Market Value of Plan Assets      $_____

The above present values were calculated using an interest rate or rates of [INSERT INTEREST RATE(S)].

[SIGNATURE OF APPROPRIATE OFFICER OF THE BOARD OF TRUSTEES]

[INSERT NAME]

[INSERT TITLE]

# BB.  Notice to Interested Parties

**General rule**  A plan administrator must distribute a Notice to Interested Parties before submitting an application to the IRS about a pension plan's qualified status.[315]

*Note.* Sponsors of plans that are not subject to IRC section 410, such as state or local governmental plans, are not required to distribute the Notice to Interested Parties.[316]

**Definitions**  The *Notice to Interested Parties* advises interested parties that the plan sponsor intends to file an application for an IRS determination on the plan's qualified status.[317] The notice also informs interested parties that they have the right to:[318]

- file comments with the IRS;
- ask the DOL to comment on their behalf; and
- request additional information.

Whether a person is an interested party depends on the type of plan or type of application the plan is filing with the IRS. In general, *interested parties* include all current employees who[319]

- participate in the plan;
- would be eligible to participate in the plan if they met the age and service requirements or elected to make mandatory contributions; and
- are employed at the same principal place of employment as any employee described above.

Special rules apply to collectively bargained plans, plan terminations, certain plan amendments, and controlled groups.

**Collectively bargained plans**  If the plan administrator is filing an application for determination for a collectively bargained plan for any reason except plan termination, the interested parties include all current employees covered by the

---

[315]  ERISA § 3001(a); IRS Reg. § 1.7476-1(a)(1); Rev. Proc. 2008-6, 2008-1 I.R.B. 192.
[316]  IRS Reg. § 1.7476-1(b)(7).
[317]  IRS Reg. § 1.7476-1(a)(1).
[318]  IRS Procedural Reg. § 601.201(o)(3)(xvi).
[319]  IRS Reg. § 1.7476-1(b).

collective bargaining agreement as well as the representative of the collective bargaining unit.[320]

**Plan terminations**

If the plan administrator is filing an application for determination for a terminating plan, interested parties include all current employees with accrued benefits, all former employees with vested deferred benefits, and all beneficiaries (of deceased employees) who are currently receiving benefits.[321]

**Certain plan amendments**

If a plan administrator is filing an application for determination for a plan amendment that does not alter plan participation provisions, and if the IRS previously approved the plan, interested parties include all current employees who participate in the plan or would be eligible to participate in the plan if they met the age and service requirements or elected to make mandatory employee contributions.[322]

**Content requirements**

The Notice to Interested Parties must be in writing and must contain certain identifying information, numbers, and statements.[323]

See Figure 9-12 for the specific information that must be included in the Notice to Interested Parties.

**Distribution methods**

For active employees, the plan may distribute the Notice to Interested Parties by any method that reasonably ensures all interested parties receive a timely and adequate notice.[324] The determination of whether the notification is timely and adequate is based on facts and circumstances.[325] Because acts and circumstances vary depending on the interested party, it is possible that more than one delivery method (e.g., both electronic and nonelectronic writing) may be required to ensure timely and adequate notice to all interested parties.[326]

**Due date**

Regardless of the method of distribution used, the Notice to Interested Parties must be delivered not less than 10 and no more than 24 days before the plan's application for determination is submitted to the IRS.[327]

---

[320] IRS Reg. §§ 1.7476-1(b)(4); 1.7476-2(c)(1).
[321] IRS Reg. § 1.7476-1(b)(5).
[322] IRS Reg. § 1.7476-1(b)(3).
[323] IRS Procedural Reg. § 601.201(o)(3)(xvi), Rev. Proc. 2008-6, 2008-1 I.R.B. 192.
[324] IRS Reg. § 1.7476-2.
[325] IRS Reg. § 1.7476-2(c)(1).
[326] Id.
[327] IRS Reg. § 601.201(o)(3)(xv).

## Figure 9-12

## Notice to Interested Parties

*Source:* Revenue Procedure 2008-6.

*Note:* Applications for an IRS determination letter sent by Express Mail or a private delivery service should be sent to: Internal Revenue Service, 201 West Rivercenter Blvd, Attn: Extracting Stop 312, Covington, KY 41011.

The above address and those in the sample notice were correct at the time this edition went to press. To ensure accuracy, users should confirm the addresses in the current year Revenue Procedure (i.e., Rev. Proc. in 200x-6). Before sending in an application.

---

### Notice to Interested Parties

1. Notice to: (class or classes of interested parties)

   An application is to be made to the Internal Revenue Service for an advance determination on the qualification of the following employee pension benefit plan:

2. (plan name)

3. (plan number)

4. (name and address of applicant)

5. (applicant's EIN)

6. (name and address of plan administrator)

7. The application will be filed on _____, for an advance determination as to whether the plan meets the qualification requirements of section 401 or section 403(a) of the Internal Revenue Code of 1986, with respect to the plan's _____ (initial qualification, amendment, termination or partial termination). The application will be filed with:

   EP Determinations
   Internal Revenue Service
   P.O. Box 192
   Covington, KY 41012-0192

8. The employees eligible to participate under the plan are: (describe by class).

9. The Internal Revenue Service (has, has not) previously issued a determination letter with respect to the qualification of this plan.

### Rights of Interested Parties

10. You have the right to submit to EP Determinations, at the above address, either individually or jointly with other interested parties, your comments as to whether this plan meets the qualification requirements of the Internal Revenue Code.

    You may instead, individually or jointly with other interested parties, request the Department of Labor to submit, on your behalf, comments to EP Determinations regarding qualification of the plan. If the Department declines to comment on all or some of the matters you raise, you may, individually, or jointly if your request was made to the Department jointly, submit your comments on these matters directly to EP Determinations.

---

## Figure 9-12 (*cont'd*)

## Notice to Interested Parties

---

**Requests for Comments by the Department of Labor**

11. The Department of Labor may not comment on behalf of interested parties unless requested to do so by the lesser of 10 employees or 10 percent of the employees who qualify as interested parties. The number of persons needed for the Department to comment with respect to this plan is _____. If you request the Department to comment, your request must be in writing and must specify the matters upon which comments are requested, and must also include:

   a. the information contained in items 2 through 5 of this Notice; and

   b. the number of persons needed for the Department to comment.

   A request to the Department to comment should be addressed as follows:

   Deputy Assistant Secretary
   Employee Benefits Security Administration
   ATTN: 3001 Comment Request
   U.S. Department of Labor
   200 Constitution Avenue, N.W.
   Washington, D.C. 20210

**Comments to the Internal Revenue Service**

12. Comments submitted by you to EP Determinations must be in writing and received by them by _____ (45 days from filing date). However, if there are matters that you request the Department of Labor to comment upon on your behalf, and the Department declines, you may submit comments on these matters to EP Determinations to be received by them within 15 days from the time the Department notifies you that it will not comment on a particular matter, or by (45 days from filing date) _____, whichever is later, but not after _____ (60 days from filing date). A request to the Department to comment on your behalf must be received by it by _____ (15 days from filing date) if you wish to preserve your right to comment on a matter upon which the Department declines to comment, or by (25 days from filing date) if you wish to waive that right.

**Additional Information**

13. Detailed instructions regarding the requirements for notification of interested parties may be found in sections 17 and 18 of Revenue Procedure 2008-6. Additional information concerning this application (including, where applicable, an updated copy of the plan and related trust; the application for determination; any additional documents dealing with the application that have been submitted to the Service; and copies of section 17 of Revenue Procedure 2008-6) are available at _____ during the hours of _____ for inspection and copying. (There is a nominal charge for copying and/or mailing.)

Date posted or mailed: _____.

---

# Chapter 10

# Special Requirements for Health Plans

**Introduction**   Health plans, unless they are specifically exempted, are required to satisfy certain requirements in addition to the reporting and disclosure requirements under the Employee Retirement Income Security Act of 1974 (ERISA). This chapter provides an overview of those additional requirements.

**Contents**   This chapter has 12 sections:

# A. Health Plan Access and Renewability Requirements

The Health Insurance Portability and Accountability Act of 1996 (HIPAA) amended ERISA provisions for group health plans to implement rules that govern preexisting condition limitations and to establish special enrollment periods.

**Exceptions**

This section does not apply to any group health plan that, on the first day of the current plan year, covered fewer than two current employees.[1]

It also does not apply to benefits provided under one or more of the following:[2]

- Accident or disability income insurance or any combination of the two
- Liability insurance, including general liability insurance, automobile liability insurance and coverage issued as a supplement to liability insurance
- Workers' compensation or similar insurance
- Automobile medical payment insurance
- Credit-only insurance
- Coverage for on-site medical clinics
- Coverage for other similar insurance benefits for medical care that is secondary or incidental to other insurance benefits, as specified in regulations

**Limited exceptions**

The requirements described in this section do not apply to the following:

- Separately offered coverage that provides
  - limited vision or or dental benefits
  - benefits for long-term care, nursing home care, home health care, community-based care, or any combination thereof
  - other limited benefits as stated in the regulations[3]
- Independent noncoordinated coverage that provides
  - coverage for a specific disease or illness
  - hospital indemnity or other fixed indemnity insurance[4]
- Coverage provided under a separate policy that supplements Medicare, Medicaid, or a group health plan.[5] The cost of this supplemental coverage may not be more than 15% of the plan's primary coverage.[6]

---

[1]  ERISA § 732(a).
[2]  ERISA § 733(c)(1).
[3]  ERISA § 733(c)(2).
[4]  ERISA § 733(c)(3).
[5]  ERISA § 733(c)(4).
[6]  DOL Field Assistance Bulletin No. 2007-04.

**Preexisting conditions**

Group health plans can impose preexisting-condition limitations on coverage for new enrollees (employees or dependents). Plans may refuse to cover or limit coverage of preexisting conditions of a new enrollee for up to 12 months (18 months for a late enrollee) for a health condition that was treated or diagnosed in the six months before enrollment.[7] *This maximum, however, is offset by prior creditable coverage.*[8]

Preexisting-condition exclusions cannot be applied to newborns and children adopted or placed for adoption who are under age 18 and who have creditable coverage within 30 days of birth or adoption. Preexisting-condition exclusions also cannot include pregnancy.[9]

A plan may not impose a preexisting-condition exclusion unless it has informed participants and their dependents in writing of the exclusion.[10] (See Figure 10-1.) The plan must also notify the individual of the length of the exclusion for that individual after applying any credit for prior coverage.[11] Figure 10-1 is a model notice provided by the DOL.[12]

**Special enrollment periods**

When employees marry, give birth to a child, or adopt a child, special enrollment rules apply. Plans must allow employees to enroll themselves, their spouses, and their dependents within 30 days of the date of the event, if the employees were otherwise eligible to enroll.[13] Plans cannot impose preexisting condition limitations on newborns or adopted children who enroll during these special enrollment periods.[14]

If an employee initially (or during a subsequent open enrollment period[15]) refused coverage on behalf of himself or herself, his or her spouse, or his or her dependents because of other coverage, and that other coverage is terminated as a result of loss of eligibility or cessation of employee contributions, those individuals have the right to enroll in the employer's plan within 30 days of the event.[16]

When an employee initially declines group health coverage, the employer's plan can require that the employee declare in writing that the reason is the existence of other group health coverage. At that time, the plan must notify the employee that failure to provide such a statement will mean the loss of the special enrollment right.[17]

---

7   ERISA § 701(a)(1), (2).
8   ERISA § 701(a)(3).
9   ERISA § 701(d).
10  DOL Reg. § 2590.701-3(c).
11  DOL Reg. § 2590.701-3(e).
12  DOL Reg. § 2590.701-3(c)(4).
13  ERISA § 701(f); DOL Reg. § 2590.701-6(b).
14  ERISA §§ 701(d), 701(f)(2)(C).
15  DOL Reg. §§ 2590.701-6(a)(2)(ii)(A)(2) and (iii) Example (2).
16  ERISA § 701(f)(1).
17  *Id.*

## Figure 10-1

## Preexisting-Condition Exclusions

*Note:* If a plan uses this model notice prepared by the DOL, it will be deemed in compliance with the general preexisting-condition exclusion notice requirement.

---

This plan imposes a preexisting-condition exclusion. This means that if you have a medical condition before coming to our plan, you might have to wait a certain period of time before the plan will provide coverage for that condition. This exclusion applies only to conditions for which medical advice, diagnosis, care, or treatment was recommended or received within a six-month period. Generally, this six-month period ends the day before your coverage becomes effective. However, if you were in a waiting period for coverage, the six-month period ends on the day before the waiting period begins. The preexisting-condition exclusion does not apply to pregnancy or to a child who is enrolled in the plan within 30 days after birth, adoption, or placement for adoption.

This exclusion may last up to 12 months (18 months if you are a late enrollee) from your first day of coverage, or, if you were in a waiting period, from the first day of your waiting period. However, you can reduce the length of this exclusion period by the number of days of your prior "creditable coverage." Most prior health coverage is creditable coverage and can be used to reduce the preexisting-condition exclusion if you have not experienced a break in coverage of at least 63 days. To reduce the 12-month (or 18-month) exclusion period by your creditable coverage, you should give us a copy of any certificates of creditable coverage you have. If you do not have a certificate, but you do have prior health coverage, we will help you obtain one from your prior plan or issuer. There are also ways that you can show you have creditable coverage. Please contact us if you need help demonstrating creditable coverage.

All questions about the preexisting-condition exclusion should be directed to Individual B at Address M or Telephone N.

---

**Notice of special enrollment rights**

When an employee first becomes eligible to enroll in the employer's health plan, the plan must give the employee a written notice describing his or her special enrollment rights.[18]

The DOL has prepared a safe harbor model Notice of Special Enrollment. (See Figure 10-2.)

**Waiting periods**

Any waiting periods imposed by a health plan on newly enrolled employees must run concurrently with any preexisting-condition limitation period.[19]

**Creditable coverage**

Group health plans are required to reduce any preexisting-condition limitation period by the amount of creditable time a new enrollee was covered under a health plan before enrollment.

*Creditable coverage* includes group health plan coverage, individual coverage, Medicare, Medicaid, and other governmental plans.[20] It does not include prior coverage, if there was a break in coverage of 63 days or longer before enrollment. Waiting periods are not counted for break-in-coverage determinations.[21] Under proposed rules, this 63-day period will be tolled for up to 44 days or until a certificate of creditable coverage is provided by the prior health plan.[22]

**Administering creditable coverage**

Health plans may administer creditable coverage in two ways—the standard method or the alternative method.[23] Under the standard method, new enrollees only need to provide certification that they had prior health plan coverage of any type.[24]

Under the alternative method, health plans and insurers can request more information on the types of prior coverage.[25] A health plan may request information on the employee's type of prior coverage only if the plan credits similar types of coverage. The plan credits coverage for each particular class of benefits if the prior plan provided any level of benefits for that class or category. The alternative method must be applied on a uniform basis for all participants and beneficiaries.[26]

---

[18]  DOL Reg. § 2590.701-6(c).
[19]  DOL Reg. § 2590.701-3(a)(3).
[20]  ERISA § 701(c)(1).
[21]  ERISA § 701(c)(2).
[22]  DOL Prop. Reg. § 2590.701-4(b).
[23]  ERISA § 701(c)(3).
[24]  ERISA § 701(c)(3)(A).
[25]  ERISA § 701(c)(3)(B).
[26]  *Id.*

**Figure 10-2**

**Notice of Special Enrollment**

*Note:* If a plan uses this model notice prepared by the DOL, it will be deemed to have complied with the content requirements for the notice as required under HIPAA.

---

If you are declining enrollment for yourself or your dependents (including your spouse) because of other health insurance or group health plan coverage, you may be able to enroll yourself and your dependents in this plan if you or your dependents lose eligibility for that other coverage (or if the employer stops contributing toward your or your dependents' other coverage). However, you must request enrollment within [*insert "30 days" or any longer period that applies under the plan*] after you or your dependents' other coverage ends (or after the employer stops contributing toward the other coverage).

In addition, if you have a new dependent as a result of marriage, birth, adoption, or placement for adoption, you may be able to enroll yourself and your dependents. However, you must request enrollment within [*insert "30 days" or any longer period that applies under the plan*] after the marriage, birth, adoption, or placement for adoption.

To request special enrollment or obtain more information, contact [*insert the name, title, telephone number, and any additional contact information of the appropriate plan representative*].[27]

---

[27]    DOL Reg. § 2590.701-6(c).

A plan using the alternative method of administering creditable coverage must:

- prominently state in any disclosure statements that it has elected to use the alternative method; and
- inform each enrollment in enrollment statements that it has elected to use the alternative method.[28]

The statements must include a description of the effect of electing the alternative method.

**Health coverage certification**

Group health plans and health plan insurers are required to provide health coverage certification when an individual:[29]

- loses plan coverage,
- becomes covered under COBRA,
- loses COBRA coverage; or
- requests certification within 24 months after coverage ends.

A sample certificate of coverage jointly issued by the DOL, IRS, and CMS is shown in Figure 10-3. The sample includes information on the Family and Medical Leave Act of 1993, which is contained in the DOL's proposed regulations.

(See Section C in Chapter 3 for a description of the electronic safe harbor rules.)

**Special rules for multi-employer plans or multiple employer plans**

A multiemployer plan or multiple employer plan cannot deny coverage to employees unless one of the following conditions applies:[30]

- The employer fails to contribute to the plan.
- The plan learns that the employer committed fraud or intentionally misrepresented material facts.
- The employer did not comply with material plan provisions.
- The plan is ceasing coverage in a geographic coverage area.
- In the case of a plan that offers benefits through a network, none of the employer's employees work or reside within the service area.
- The employer fails to meet the terms of a collectively bargained agreement, fails to renew the terms of an agreement requiring or authorizing contributions to the plan, or fails to employ individuals covered by the agreement.

---

[28] ERISA § 701(c)(3)(C).
[29] ERISA § 701(e)(1).
[30] ERISA § 703; I.R.C. § 9803.

## Figure 10-3

## Sample Certificate of Coverage

*Note:* If a plan uses the model certificate or the proposed model certificate prepared by the DOL, IRS, and CMS, it will be deemed to have complied with the content requirements for the certificate of coverage as required under HIPAA.

---

### CERTIFICATE OF GROUP HEALTH PLAN COVERAGE

1. Date of this certificate: _____

2. Name of group health plan: _____

3. Name of participant: _____

4. Identification number of participant: _____

5. Name of individual(s) to whom this certificate applies: _____

6. Name, address, and telephone number of plan administrator or issuer responsible for providing this certificate:

   _____

   _____

   _____

7. For further information, call: _____

8. If the individual(s) identified in line 5 has (have) at least 18 months of creditable coverage (disregarding periods of coverage before a 63-day break), check here ☐ and skip lines 9 and 10:

9. Date waiting period or affiliation period (if any) began: _____

10. Date coverage began: _____

11. Date coverage ended (or if coverage has not ended, enter "continuing"): _____

[*Note: Separate certificates will be furnished if information is not identical for the participant and each beneficiary.*]

---

**Figure 10-3 (*cont'd*)**

**Sample Certificate of Coverage**

---

### Statement of HIPAA Portability Rights

**IMPORTANT—KEEP THIS CERTIFICATE.** This certificate is evidence of your coverage under this plan. Under a federal law known as HIPAA, you may need evidence of your coverage to reduce a preexisting condition exclusion period under another plan, to help you get special enrollment in another plan, or to get certain types of individual health coverage even if you have health problems.

<u>Preexisting condition exclusions.</u> Some group health plans restrict coverage for medical conditions present before an individual's enrollment. These restrictions are known as "preexisting condition exclusions." A preexisting condition exclusion can apply only to conditions for which medical advice, diagnosis, care, or treatment was recommended or received within the 6 months before your "enrollment date." Your enrollment date is your first day of coverage under the plan, or, if there is a waiting period, the first day of your waiting period (typically, your first day of work). In addition, a preexisting condition exclusion cannot last for more than 12 months after your enrollment date (18 months if you are a late enrollee). Finally, a preexisting condition exclusion cannot apply to pregnancy and cannot apply to a child who is enrolled in health coverage within 30 days after birth, adoption, or placement for adoption.

If a plan imposes a preexisting condition exclusion, the length of the exclusion must be reduced by the amount of your prior creditable coverage. Most health coverage is creditable coverage, including group health plan coverage, COBRA continuation coverage, coverage under an individual health policy, Medicare, Medicaid, State Children's Health Insurance Program (SCHIP), and coverage through high-risk pools and the Peace Corps. Not all forms of creditable coverage are required to provide certificates like this one. If you do not receive a certificate for past coverage, talk to your new plan administrator.

You can add up any creditable coverage you have, including the coverage shown on this certificate. However, if at any time you went for 63 days or more without any coverage (called a break in coverage), a plan may not have to count the coverage you had before the break.

- Therefore, once your coverage ends, you should try to obtain alternative coverage as soon as possible to avoid a 63-day break. You may use this certificate as evidence of your creditable coverage to reduce the length of any preexisting condition exclusion if you enroll in another plan.

<u>Right to get special enrollment in another plan.</u> Under HIPAA, if you lose your group health plan coverage, you may be able to get into another group health plan for which you are eligible (such as a spouse's plan), even if the plan generally does not accept late enrollees, if you request enrollment within 30 days. (Additional special enrollment rights are triggered by marriage, birth, adoption, and placement for adoption.)

- Therefore, once your coverage ends, if you are eligible for coverage in another plan (such as a spouse's plan), you should request special enrollment as soon as possible.

## Figure 10-3 (*cont'd*)

## Sample Certificate of Coverage

**Prohibition against discrimination based on a health factor.** Under HIPAA, a group health plan may not keep you (or your dependents) out of the plan based on anything related to your health. Also, a group health plan may not charge you (or your dependents) more for coverage, based on health, than the amount charged a similarly situated individual.

**Right to individual health coverage.** Under HIPAA, if you are an "eligible individual," you have a right to buy certain individual health policies (or in some states, to buy coverage through a high-risk pool) without a preexisting condition exclusion. To be an eligible individual, you must meet the following requirements:

• You have had coverage for at least 18 months without a break in coverage of 63 days or more;

• Your most recent coverage was under a group health plan (which can be shown by this certificate);

• Your group coverage was not terminated because of fraud or nonpayment of premiums;

• You are not eligible for COBRA continuation coverage or you have exhausted your COBRA benefits (or continuation coverage under a similar state provision); and

• You are not eligible for another group health plan, Medicare, or Medicaid, and do not have any other health insurance coverage.

The right to buy individual coverage is the same whether you are laid off, fired, or quit your job.

• Therefore, if you are interested in obtaining individual coverage and you meet the other criteria to be an eligible individual, you should apply for this coverage as soon as possible to avoid losing your eligible individual status due to a 63-day break.

[*Note: The proposed rules modify the required elements for the certificate of creditable coverage to require a disclosure about the FMLA.*[31] *The following FMLA paragraph is suggested model language and, until the proposed rule is finalized, may be included or omitted.*]

**Special information for people on FMLA leave.** If you are taking leave under the Family and Medical Leave Act (FMLA) and you drop coverage during your leave, any days without health coverage while on FMLA leave will not count towards a 63-day break in coverage. In addition, if you do not return from leave, the 30-day period to request special enrollment in another plan will not start before your FMLA leave ends.

• Therefore, when you apply for other health coverage, you should tell your plan administrator or health insurer about any prior FMLA leave.

**State flexibility.** This certificate describes minimum HIPAA protections under federal law. States may require insurers and HMOs to provide additional protections to individuals in that state.

**For more information.** If you have questions about your HIPAA rights, you may contact your state insurance department or the U.S. Department of Labor, Employee Benefits Security Administration (EBSA) toll-free at 1-866-444-3272 (for free HIPAA publications ask for publications concerning changes in health care laws). You may also contact the CMS publication hotline at 1-800-633-4227 (ask for "Protecting Your Health Insurance Coverage"). These publications and other useful information are also available on the Internet at http://www.dol.gov/ebsa, the DOL's interactive web pages—Health Elaws or http://www.cms.hhs.gov/hipaa1.

---

[31]    69 Fed. Reg. 78,802 (Dec. 30, 2004).

# B. Health Plan Nondiscrimination Rules

The Health Insurance Portability and Accountability Act of 1996 (HIPAA) prohibits group health plans from discriminating against individuals based on health factors when determining eligibility, benefits, or required contributions.[32] The Genetic Information Nondiscrimination Act of 2008 modifies the HIPAA rules with specific constraints imposed on the use of genetic information by health plans.[33]

**Eligibility to enroll**

Group health plans may not establish an enrollment rule that discriminates against any individual based on any health status-related factor. The eight health factors are health status, medical condition (including both physical and mental illness), claims experience, receipt of health care, medical history, genetic information, evidence of insurability, and disability.

Plan eligibility may not discriminate based on evidence of insurability. This includes conditions arising out of domestic violence or participation in activities such as motorcycling, snowmobiling, skiing, or other similar activities.[34] Plans may treat late enrollees differently from individuals who enroll when first eligible but may not require an individual to provide evidence of good health to obtain coverage.[35]

**Benefits**

A group health plan is not required to provide coverage for any particular benefit. Plans may limit or exclude coverage for specific diseases or for specific treatments or drugs. However, any restriction must apply uniformly to all similarly situated individuals and must not be directed at individuals based on a health factor. When a health plan design is changed, the plan amendment will not be considered aimed at any particular individual if it is applicable to all similarly situated individuals in the plan and effective no earlier than the first day of the first plan year after the amendment is adopted.[36]

For example, a plan may apply a separate $2,000 lifetime maximum for treatment of TMJ (temporomandibular joint syndrome) or limit prescription drug benefits to drugs listed on a formulary and not discriminate based on health factors if the benefit limits are applied uniformly to

---

[32]  ERISA § 702.
[33]  P.L. 110-233, enacted May 21, 2008.
[34]  DOL Reg. § 2590.702(a)(2).
[35]  DOL Reg. § 2590.702(b)(1).
[36]  DOL Reg. § 2590.702(b)(2).

all similarly situated individuals and not directed at an individual participant.[37]

Although health plans cannot exclude individuals for engaging in specified high-risk activities, they can exclude coverage for an injury based on the source of the injury (e.g., a head injury caused by bungee jumping). However, plans may not exclude coverage for an injury if the injury results from an act of domestic violence or a medical condition (physical or mental) otherwise covered by the plan. Also, a plan may not exclude coverage for self-inflicted injuries if the claimant suffers from depression and, as a result, attempts suicide.[38]

**Preexisting condition limitations**

A preexisting-condition limitation that satisfies HIPAA requirements does not violate the nondiscrimination provisions if it is applied uniformly to all similarly situated individuals and is not directed at individuals based on their adverse health factors. However, a plan may not shorten the length of an individual's preexisting-condition exclusion period for not incurring claims during the first part of the exclusion period.[39]

**Required contributions**

HIPAA does not restrict the aggregate amount that an employer may be charged for coverage under a group health plan. However, individuals may not be required to pay a higher contribution based on a health factor.[40]

**Similarly situated individuals**

HIPAA's nondiscrimination requirements apply within each group of "similarly situated individuals." Plan participants may be treated as different groups of similarly situated individuals if the distinction between the groups is based on a bona fide employment-based classification consistent with the employer's usual business practice. These classifications include full-time versus part-time employment status, different geographic locations, collective bargaining units, current employment versus former employment status, and different occupations.

Beneficiaries may be classified based on their relationship to the participant, such as spouse or child, or marital status. Children may be classified based on age or student status. However, employers may not

---

[37]   DOL Reg. § 2590.702(b)(2)(D), Example 4.
[38]   DOL Reg. § 2590.702(b)(2)(iii).
[39]   DOL Reg. § 2590.702(b)(3).
[40]   DOL Reg. § 2590.702(c)(1).

modify an employment-based classification to single out an individual and deny coverage based on a health factor.[41]

**Nonconfinement and "actively at work" provisions**

Health plan eligibility may not be denied or delayed based on the hospital confinement of an employee or dependent. Plans are also prohibited from denying or delaying eligibility based on whether the employee is actively at work at the time coverage would normally become effective. However, plans may establish an initial eligibility rule that requires individuals to report for their first day of work before coverage becomes effective as long as the rule applies regardless of the reason for absence.[42]

For example, if employees become eligible to enroll for coverage after 30 days of employment, the plan may not delay the effective date of coverage for an employee who is not actively at work due to health reasons at the end of the 30-day period. Health plans may, however, base continued eligibility on whether employees are currently performing services or are on leave.[43]

**Favorable treatment based on adverse health factors**

HIPAA does not prohibit plans from treating individuals with adverse health factors more favorably under plan eligibility rules. For instance, plans may allow dependent children who are handicapped to continue to be eligible for plan coverage beyond the plan's limiting age even though coverage would terminate at that age for able-bodied dependent children.[44]

Plans may charge individuals lower premiums or contributions if the lower charge is based on an adverse health factor. For example, a plan may waive premiums for disabled employees.

**Wellness programs**

HIPAA's nondiscrimination rules do not prevent a health plan from providing discounts or rebates, or modifying copayments or deductibles, in return for participating in a wellness program to promote good health. However, to prevent wellness programs from being used to circumvent HIPAA's nondiscrimination rules, four requirements are imposed on wellness programs that reward (or penalize) plan participants based on the ability of an individual to meet a health standard.[45] The requirements are (1) reasonable design, (2) uniform availability, (3) reward limitation, and (4) disclosure.

---

41  DOL Reg. § 2590.702(d).
42  DOL Reg. § 2590.702(e).
43  DOL Reg. § 2590.702(e)(3).
44  DOL Reg. § 2590.702(g).
45  DOL Reg. § 2590.702(f)(2).

Note that complying with HIPAA rules for wellness programs does not necessarily ensure compliance with other laws such as the Americans with Disabilities Act.

**Reasonable design**

To satisfy the reasonable design requirement, there must be a reasonable connection between a wellness program's health standard and the promotion of good health. At a minimum, wellness programs must give individuals an opportunity to qualify for the reward at least once a year. Thus, a wellness program that permanently excludes unhealthy individuals is not reasonably related to improving health if an individual cannot qualify for the reward by adopting healthier behavior after initial enrollment.[46]

**Uniform availability**

A wellness program reward must be available to all similarly situated individuals. An alternative health standard must also be available to individuals for whom it is unreasonably difficult, or medically inadvisable due to a medical condition, to satisfy the wellness program's health standard.[47] For example:

| Health Standard | Reasonable Alternative |
| --- | --- |
| • Achieve cholesterol count less than 200 | • Comply with low-cholesterol diet |
| • Have body mass index between 19 and 26 | • Walk for 20 minutes 3 days a week |
| • Not use tobacco products for 12 months | • Participate in smoking cessation program |

**Reward limitation**

The total reward for meeting a health standard must not exceed 20 percent of the cost of employee-only coverage, taking into account both employee and employer contributions.[48]

**Disclosure**

All materials describing wellness programs must disclose the availability of the reasonable alternative if those materials describe the health standard. The DOL offers the following model language:

> If it is unreasonably difficult due to a medical condition for you to achieve the standards for reward under this program, or if it is medically inadvisable for you to attempt to achieve the standards for the

---

[46]   DOL Reg. § 2590.702(f)(2)(ii).
[47]   DOL Reg. § 2590.702(f)(2)(iv).
[48]   DOL Reg. § 2590.702(f)(2)(i).

reward under this program, call us at [*insert telephone number*] and we will work with you to develop another way to qualify for the reward.

If the materials for the wellness program merely mention that a program is available and do not describe the health standard, disclosure of the availability of the reasonable alternative is not required.[49]

**Programs without rewards**

The four requirements (i.e., reward limit, reasonable design, uniform availability, and disclosure) apply only to wellness programs that provide rewards based on health factors.[50] For example, without complying with the four requirements, a wellness program could:

- Reimburse all or part of the cost for membership in a fitness center
- Provide a reward for participation in a diagnostic testing program without basing any part of the reward on outcomes
- Encourage preventive care such as well-baby visits through the waiver of the plan's copayments or deductibles
- Reimburse employees for the costs of smoking cessation programs even if the employee does not quit smoking
- Provide a reward to employees for attending a monthly health education seminar

**DOL checklist for wellness programs**

A checklist offering examples and tips on applying the wellness program rules is available on the DOL's Web site in Field Assistance Bulletin 2008-02.

**Genetic information**

The Genetic Information Nondiscrimination Act of 2008 (GINA) amends ERISA, the Internal Revenue Code, and the Public Health Service Act to prevent group health plans and health insurance companies in both the group and individual markets from basing enrollment decisions, premium costs, or participant contributions on genetic information.[51] These groups will also be prohibited from requiring individuals to undergo genetic testing. Similarly, employers may not condition hiring or firing decisions on the basis of genetic information. In addition, the new law extends medical privacy and confidentiality rules to the disclosure of genetic information.

GINA does not limit the authority of a health care professional to ask an individual to undergo a genetic test,[52] or preclude a group health plan

---

49  DOL Reg. § 2590.702(f)(2)(v).
50  DOL Reg. § 2590.702(f)(2).
51  ERISA § 702(b)(3).
52  ERISA § 702(c)(2).

from obtaining or using the results of a genetic test in making a determination about payment.[53] However, the plan may only ask for the minimum amount of information needed for the intended purpose.[54]

GINA allows a group health plan to request, but not require, a participant or beneficiary to undergo a genetic test for research purposes if:

- the plan clearly indicates that compliance is voluntary and that noncompliance will have no effect on enrollment status or premium or contribution amounts;
- no genetic information collected or acquired is used for underwriting purposes; and
- the plan notifies the Secretary of Health and Human Services that it is conducting activities under this exception and describes the activities.[55]

The Secretary of Health and Human Services is directed to revise the HIPAA privacy regulations to:

- treat genetic information as health information; and
- prohibit the use or disclosure of genetic information about an individual for underwriting purposes by a group health plan, health insurance coverage, or Medicare supplemental policy.[56]

GINA's ERISA health plan rules will apply to plan years beginning after May 21, 2009.[57]

---

[53] ERISA § 702(c)(3)(A).
[54] ERISA § 702(c)(3)(B).
[55] ERISA § 702(c)(4).
[56] P.L. 110-233, § 106.
[57] P.L. 110-233, § 101(f).

# C. Minimum Maternity Benefits

The Newborns' and Mothers' Health Protection Act of 1996 established minimum periods of hospitalization for mothers and their newborn children. These minimum maternity benefit requirements apply to insured and self-insured group health plans with two or more participants who are current employees on the first day of the plan year.[58]

**Minimum length of hospital stay**

Group health plans must cover at least 48 hours of hospitalization for mothers and newborns after conventional deliveries and at least 96 hours of hospitalization after cesarean deliveries. The attending health care provider does not need authorization from a group health plan to provide the mother and newborn with the minimum required length of hospital stay.[59]

**Plan design flexibility**

Shorter hospital stays are permitted if the attending health care provider, in consultation with the mother, determines that this is the best course of action. However, group health plans may not offer incentives to the mother or health care provider to shorten the hospital stay.[60]

**Summary plan descriptions**

Group health plans must inform participants of their minimum maternity benefit rights in the summary plan description. The DOL has issued model language that may be used for this purpose.[61] (See Figure 7-5, Section C in Chapter 7, for the DOL's model minimum maternity benefits statement.)

**State laws**

The NMHPA does not override any state law requiring health insurance to cover maternity or pediatric care in accordance with professional medical association guidelines. Similarly, it does not preempt state laws that allow the attending provider, in consultation with the mother, to decide the appropriate length of hospital stay.[62]

---

[58] ERISA § 711.
[59] ERISA § 711(a).
[60] ERISA §§ 711(a)(2), 711(b)(2).
[61] DOL Reg. § 2520.102-3(u).
[62] ERISA § 711(f).

# D. Women's Health and Cancer Rights Act

Under the Women's Health and Cancer Rights Act of 1998 (WHCRA) group health plans covering a mastectomy must also provide coverage for breast reconstruction performed in connection with the mastectomy.[63]

**Affected plans** By amending ERISA and the Public Health Service Act, the breast reconstruction mandate applies to all ERISA health plans, state and local government plans, and health insurers. However, self-insured state and local government plans can elect out.

Coverage must be provided for reconstruction of the breast, surgery and reconstruction of the other breast for symmetrical appearance, and prostheses and physical complications in all stages of a mastectomy.[64]

The group health plan must determine the manner of coverage in consultation with the attending physician and patient. Coverage may be subject to the same deductibles and coinsurance provisions as other benefits under the plan.

**Notice requirement** Group health plans must provide plan participants with two separate notices of WHCRA benefits. The first notice of the WHCRA's mandated benefits must be provided to new plan enrollees at enrollment time. A second, similar notice must be furnished annually thereafter.[65]

The law requires the written notices to be "prominently positioned in any literature or correspondence" transmitted to plan participants or beneficiaries. The first notice may be delivered in the plan's SPD if it is given at the time of enrollment.

The notices may be distributed electronically pursuant to the DOL's electronic distribution safe harbor rules (see Section C in Chapter 3).

---

[63]  ERISA §713.
[64]  ERISA §713(a).
[65]  ERISA §713(a).

**Enrollment notice**

The enrollment notice must describe the WHCRA's benefit requirements. It must say that for persons receiving benefits in connection with a mastectomy, coverage will be provided in a manner determined in consultation with the attending physician and the patient for reconstructive surgery, and coverage includes surgery for the other breast to produce a symmetrical appearance as well as for a prosthesis and for treatment of physical complications. Deductibles or coinsurance limits also must be described.

The following model notice is provided by DOL:[66]

---

## Sample Language for WHCRA Enrollment Notice

---

If you have had or are going to have a mastectomy, you may be entitled to certain benefits under the Women's Health and Cancer Rights Act of 1998 (WHCRA). For individuals receiving mastectomy-related benefits, coverage will be provided in a manner determined in consultation with the attending physician and the patient, for:

- all stages of reconstruction of the breast on which the mastectomy was performed;
- surgery and reconstruction of the other breast to produce a symmetrical appearance;
- prostheses; and
- treatment of physical complications of the mastectomy, including lymphedemas.

These benefits will be provided subject to the same deductibles and coinsurance applicable to other medical and surgical benefits provided under this plan. Therefore, the following deductibles and coinsurance apply: [insert deductibles and coinsurance applicable to these benefits].

If you would like more information on WHCRA benefits, call your Plan Administrator [insert telephone number].

**Model annual notice**

The DOL has issued the following model annual notice:[67]

Did you know that your plan, as required by the Women's Health and Cancer Rights Act of 1998, provides benefits for mastectomy-related

---

[66] See www.dol.gov/ebsa.

[67] *Id.*

services including reconstruction and surgery to achieve symmetry between the breasts, prostheses, and complications resulting from a mastectomy (including lymphedema)? Call your Plan Administrator [*insert phone number*] for more information.

# E. Mental Health Parity Act

**Caution.** The rules described below are stated to expire at the end of 2008. However, in the past Congress has typically acted to extend the expiration date. In addition, congressional efforts to expand the parity rules beyond the rules described here were under serious consideration as this edition went to print.

The Mental Health Parity Act of 1996 (MHPA), requires most group health plans that have coverage for physical and mental conditions to maintain the same annual and lifetime dollar limits for both types of coverage.[68]

In general, the MHPA applies to all group health plans with two or more participants who are current employees on the first day of the plan year. There are, however, two exceptions:

- The Act does not apply to small employers who employed 50 or fewer employees on average during the preceding calendar year. If the employer did not exist in the preceding year, the exception will be based on the average number of employees expected to work in the current calendar year. For purposes of determining if the exemption applies, all businesses treated as a single employer under the controlled group rules are considered a single employer.[69]
- The Act does not apply if its application would increase plan costs by 1 percent or more. To make this 1 percent determination, a plan must have at least six months of claims and administrative expense experience.[70] The exception cannot be effective until at least 30 days after the plan provides notice to plan participants and beneficiaries.[71] In addition, the plan must file the notice with the DOL, the IRS, or the Health Care Financing Administration, depending on the type of employer organization. Group health plans subject to ERISA file with DOL.[72]

---

[68] ERISA § 712.
[69] ERISA § 712(c)(1); DOL Reg. § 2590.712(e).
[70] DOL Reg. § 2590.712(f)(1), (2)(iv).
[71] DOL Reg. § 2590.712(f)(3)(i).
[72] DOL Reg. § 2590.712(f)(3)(ii).

**Plan design, benefits, and coverage**

Under the MHPA, if a plan provides physical and mental health benefits, it must apply the same annual and lifetime dollar limits to both types of coverage. For example, if the plan has no annual or lifetime limits on medical and surgical benefits, it cannot impose limits on mental health benefits.[73] If a plan has two or more benefit options (e.g., indemnity coverage and an HMO), the parity requirements apply separately to each option.[74]

The MHPA does not affect plan design for mental health coverage other than the annual and lifetime dollar limits. It also does not require plans to provide mental health benefits (although other federal laws, such as the Americans with Disabilities Act, may do so).[75]

In addition, the MHPA does not affect the amount, duration, or scope of mental health benefits under the plan. Mental health coverage can vary from coverage for physical conditions on deductibles and copayments, limitations on number of service provider visits, and requirements of proof of medical necessity.[76]

---

[73] DOL Reg. § 2590.712(a), (b).
[74] DOL Reg. § 2590.712(c).
[75] DOL Reg. § 2590.712(d)(3).
[76] *Id.*

# F. COBRA Requirements

The Consolidated Omnibus Budget Reconciliation Act of 1985 (COBRA) requires most health plans to offer continuation coverage to "qualified beneficiaries" who would otherwise lose coverage because of certain "qualifying events."[77]

**Exceptions**

The COBRA continuation coverage requirements apply to all group health plans except:[78]

- church plans; and
- plans maintained by employers that employed fewer than 20 employees on a typical business day during the preceding calendar year.

While governmental plans are not subject to the COBRA requirements of ERISA or the Code, group health plans maintained by state and local governments are generally subject to parallel rules under the Public Health Service Act. Federal employees are covered by generally similar rules under the Federal Employees Health Benefits Amendments Act of 1988.[79]

**Qualified beneficiary**

A *qualified beneficiary* is an employee or an employee's spouse or dependent child who, on the day before a qualifying event, is covered by the employer's group health plan.[80] A qualified beneficiary also includes a covered employee's newborn child or children placed for adoption with the covered employee during the continuation period.[81]

**Qualifying events**

*Qualifying events* are certain types of events that would, except for COBRA continuation coverage, cause an individual to lose health coverage. The qualifying events are:[82]

- The employee's termination of employment for any reason except gross misconduct

---

[77]  I.R.C. § 4980B; ERISA §§ 601–608; PHSA §§ 2201–2208.
[78]  I.R.C. § 4980B(d).
[79]  IRS Reg. § 54.4980B-2, Q&A 4(d).
[80]  I.R.C. § 4980B(g)(1)(A).
[81]  *Id.*
[82]  I.R.C. § 4980B(f)(3).

- A reduction in hours to fewer than the number of hours required for plan participation
- The employee's divorce or legal separation from his or her spouse
- The employee's death
- The employee's entitlement to Medicare
- The employee's child's loss of dependent status as defined under the plan
- The retired employee's (or retired spouse's or child's) substantial loss of coverage within one year before or after the employer becomes subject to a Title XI bankruptcy proceeding

**Maximum coverage period**

Generally, coverage must continue for up to 18 months if the qualifying event is the employee's termination or reduction in hours, and for up to 36 months for other qualifying events. Certain disabled qualified beneficiaries and their family members can receive up to 29 months coverage. Retirees who would have lost coverage due to the employer's bankruptcy may have lifetime continuation rights.[83]

**Canceling coverage**

An employer may cancel a qualified beneficiary's continuation coverage, before the maximum coverage period ends, on the following date(s):[84]

- The date the beneficiary first becomes, after his or her election, covered by another employer's group health plan, if that plan does not limit or exclude coverage for any of the beneficiary's preexisting conditions
- The date the beneficiary first becomes, after election, covered by Medicare[85]
- The date the employer fails to receive a timely payment for the beneficiary's continuation coverage
- The date the employer stops providing health coverage for any active employee

**Premiums**

An employer may require qualified beneficiaries to pay for their continuation coverage.[86]

In general, an employer cannot require qualified beneficiaries to pay more than 102 percent of the total cost of coverage for their period of

---

83  I.R.C. § 4980B(f)(2)(B)(i).
84  I.R.C. § 4980B(f)(2)(B).
85  IRS Reg. § 4980B-7, Q&A 3(b).
86  I.R.C. § 4980B(f)(2)(C).

continuation coverage. However, for disabled beneficiaries and their family members entitled to 29 months of continuation coverage, the plan can increase the amount of the premium after 18 months to 150 percent of the total coverage cost.

**General notice**   The plan administrator must notify employees and their spouses, generally within the first 90 days of receiving group health plan coverage, of their right to COBRA continuation coverage under the plan.[87] Among other distribution methods, this notice may be included in the SPD, or it may be provided electronically, pursuant to the DOL's electronic distribution safe harbor rules.[88] (See Section C in Chapter 3.)

The general notice requirement to provide notice to the spouse can be satisfied by the notice to the employee if, based on the most recent information available to the plan:

- the employee & spouse reside at the same location;
- the notice is addressed to both parties; and
- the spouse's coverage starts contemporaneously with the employee or up to the notice deadline, if late.

DOL's Model General Notice is reproduced in Figure 10-4.

---

[87]  DOL Reg. § 2590.606-1(b).
[88]  DOL Reg. § 2590.606-1(e) and (f).

## Figure 10-4

## Model General Notice Of COBRA Continuation Coverage Rights
### (For use by single-employer group health plans)

---

### **Continuation Coverage Rights Under COBRA**

#### Introduction

You are receiving this notice because you have recently become covered under a group health plan (the Plan). This notice contains important information about your right to COBRA continuation coverage, which is a temporary extension of coverage under the Plan. **This notice generally explains COBRA continuation coverage, when it may become available to you and your family, and what you need to do to protect the right to receive it.**

The right to COBRA continuation coverage was created by a federal law, the Consolidated Omnibus Budget Reconciliation Act of 1985 (COBRA). COBRA continuation coverage can become available to you when you would otherwise lose your group health coverage. It can also become available to other members of your family who are covered under the Plan when they would otherwise lose their group health coverage. For additional information about your rights and obligations under the Plan and under federal law, you should review the Plan's Summary Plan Description or contact the Plan Administrator.

#### What is COBRA Continuation Coverage?

COBRA continuation coverage is a continuation of Plan coverage when coverage would otherwise end because of a life event known as a "qualifying event." Specific qualifying events are listed later in this notice. After a qualifying event, COBRA continuation coverage must be offered to each person who is a "qualified beneficiary." You, your spouse, and your dependent children could become qualified beneficiaries if coverage under the Plan is lost because of the qualifying event. Under the Plan, qualified beneficiaries who elect COBRA continuation coverage [*choose and enter appropriate information:* must pay *or* are not required to pay] for COBRA continuation coverage.

If you are an employee, you will become a qualified beneficiary if you lose your coverage under the Plan because either one of the following qualifying events happens:

- your hours of employment are reduced; or

- your employment ends for any reason other than your gross misconduct.

If you are the spouse of an employee, you will become a qualified beneficiary if you lose your coverage under the Plan because any of the following qualifying events happens:

- your spouse dies;

- your spouse's hours of employment are reduced;

- your spouse's employment ends for any reason other than his or her gross misconduct;

- your spouse becomes entitled to Medicare benefits (under Part A, Part B, or both); or

- you become divorced or legally separated from your spouse.

**Figure 10-4 (*cont'd*)**

**Model General Notice Of COBRA Continuation
Coverage Rights**

Your dependent children will become qualified beneficiaries if they lose coverage under the Plan because any of the following qualifying events happens:

- The parent-employee dies;

- the parent-employee's hours of employment are reduced;

- the parent-employee's employment ends for any reason other than his or her gross misconduct;

- the parent-employee becomes entitled to Medicare benefits (Part A, Part B, or both);

- the parents become divorced or legally separated; or

- the child stops being eligible for coverage under the plan as a "dependent child."

[*If the Plan provides retiree health coverage, add the following paragraph:*]

Sometimes, filing a proceeding in bankruptcy under title 11 of the United States Code can be a qualifying event. If a proceeding in bankruptcy is filed with respect to [*enter name of employer sponsoring the plan*], and that bankruptcy results in the loss of coverage of any retired employee covered under the Plan, the retired employee will become a qualified beneficiary with respect to the bankruptcy. The retired employee's spouse, surviving spouse, and dependent children will also become qualified beneficiaries if bankruptcy results in the loss of their coverage under the Plan.

### When is COBRA Coverage Available?

The Plan will offer COBRA continuation coverage to qualified beneficiaries only after the Plan Administrator has been notified that a qualifying event has occurred. When the qualifying event is the end of employment or reduction of hours of employment, death of the employee, [*add if Plan provides retiree health coverage:* commencement of a proceeding in bankruptcy with respect to the employer,] or the employee's becoming entitled to Medicare benefits (under Part A, Part B, or both), the employer must notify the Plan Administrator of the qualifying event.

### You Must Give Notice of Some Qualifying Events

**For the other qualifying events (divorce or legal separation of the employee and spouse or a dependent child's losing eligibility for coverage as a dependent child), you must notify the Plan Administrator within 60 days [*or enter longer period permitted under the terms of the Plan*] after the qualifying event occurs. You must provide this notice to: [*Enter name of appropriate party*]. [*Add description of any additional Plan procedures for this notice, including a description of any required information or documentation.*]**

### How is COBRA Coverage Provided?

Once the Plan Administrator receives notice that a qualifying event has occurred, COBRA continuation coverage will be offered to each of the qualified beneficiaries. Each qualified beneficiary will have an independent right to elect COBRA continuation coverage. Covered employees may elect COBRA continuation coverage on behalf of their spouses, and parents may elect COBRA continuation coverage on behalf of their children.

## Figure 10-4 (*cont'd*)
## Model General Notice Of COBRA Continuation Coverage Rights

COBRA continuation coverage is a temporary continuation of coverage. When the qualifying event is the death of the employee, the employee's becoming entitled to Medicare benefits (under Part A, Part B, or both), your divorce or legal separation, or a dependent child's losing eligibility as a dependent child, COBRA continuation coverage lasts for up to a total of 36 months. When the qualifying event is the end of employment or reduction of the employee's hours of employment, and the employee became entitled to Medicare benefits less than 18 months before the qualifying event, COBRA continuation coverage for qualified beneficiaries other than the employee lasts until 36 months after the date of Medicare entitlement. For example, if a covered employee becomes entitled to Medicare 8 months before the date on which his employment terminates, COBRA continuation coverage for his spouse and children can last up to 36 months after the date of Medicare entitlement, which is equal to 28 months after the date of the qualifying event (36 months minus 8 months). Otherwise, when the qualifying event is the end of employment or reduction of the employee's hours of employment, COBRA continuation coverage generally lasts for only up to a total of 18 months. There are two ways in which this 18-month period of COBRA continuation coverage can be extended.

### Disability extension of 18-month period of continuation coverage

If you or anyone in your family covered under the Plan is determined by the Social Security Administration to be disabled and you notify the Plan Administrator in a timely fashion, you and your entire family may be entitled to receive up to an additional 11 months of COBRA continuation coverage, for a total maximum of 29 months. The disability would have to have started at some time before the 60th day of COBRA continuation coverage and must last at least until the end of the 18-month period of continuation coverage. [*Add description of any additional Plan procedures for this notice, including a description of any required information or documentation, the name of the appropriate party to whom notice must be sent, and the time period for giving notice.*]

### Second qualifying event extension of 18-month period of continuation coverage

If your family experiences another qualifying event while receiving 18 months of COBRA continuation coverage, the spouse and dependent children in your family can get up to 18 additional months of COBRA continuation coverage, for a maximum of 36 months, if notice of the second qualifying event is properly given to the Plan. This extension may be available to the spouse and any dependent children receiving continuation coverage if the employee or former employee dies, becomes entitled to Medicare benefits (under Part A, Part B, or both), or gets divorced or legally separated, or if the dependent child stops being eligible under the Plan as a dependent child, but only if the event would have caused the spouse or dependent child to lose coverage under the Plan had the first qualifying event not occurred.

### If You Have Questions

Questions concerning your Plan or your COBRA continuation coverage rights should be addressed to the contact or contacts identified below. For more information about your rights under ERISA, including COBRA, the Health Insurance Portability and Accountability Act (HIPAA), and other laws affecting group health plans, contact the nearest Regional or District Office of the U.S. Department of Labor's Employee Benefits Security Administration (EBSA) in your area or visit the EBSA website at www.dol.gov/ebsa. (Addresses and phone numbers of Regional and District EBSA Offices are available through EBSA's website.)

**Figure 10-4 (*cont'd*)**

**Model General Notice Of COBRA Continuation
Coverage Rights**

---

**Keep Your Plan Informed of Address Changes**

In order to protect your family's rights, you should keep the Plan Administrator informed of any changes in the addresses of family members. You should also keep a copy, for your records, of any notices you send to the Plan Administrator.

**Plan Contact Information**

*[Enter name of group health plan and name (or position), address and phone number of party or parties from whom information about the plan and COBRA continuation coverage can be obtained on request.]*

---

**Notice of qualifying events**

The employer must notify the plan administrator within 30 days of a qualifying event that is:

- A termination of employment or reduction in hours
- The employee's entitlement to Medicare
- The death of the employee
- A proceeding in the employer's bankruptcy case[89]

The plan administrator then has 14 days from the date it is notified of the qualifying event to notify the qualified beneficiaries of their right to elect continuation coverage. If the employer is also the plan administrator, it has 44 days in which to notify the qualified beneficiary.[90]

DOL's Model Continuing Coverage Election Notice is reproduced in Figure 10-5.

---

[89] DOL Reg. § 2590.606-12.
[90] DOL Reg. § 2590.606-4.

**Figure 10-5**

**Model COBRA Continuation Coverage Election Notice
(For use by single-employer group health plans)**

---

[*Enter date of notice*]

Dear: [*Identify the qualified beneficiary(ies), by name or status*]

**This notice contains important information about your right to continue your health care coverage in the [*enter name of group health plan*] (the Plan).** Please read the information contained in this notice very carefully.

To elect COBRA continuation coverage, follow the instructions on the next page to complete the enclosed Election Form and submit it to us.

If you do not elect COBRA continuation coverage, your coverage under the Plan will end on [*enter date*] due to [*check appropriate box*]:

| | |
|---|---|
| ☐ End of employment | ☐ Reduction in hours of employment |
| ☐ Death of employee | ☐ Divorce or legal separation |
| ☐ Entitlement to Medicare | ☐ Loss of dependent child status |

Each person ("qualified beneficiary") in the category(ies) checked below is entitled to elect COBRA continuation coverage, which will continue group health care coverage under the Plan for up to ___ months [*enter 18 or 36, as appropriate and check appropriate box or boxes; names may be added*]:

☐ *Employee or former employee*

☐ *Spouse or former spouse*

☐ *Dependent child(ren) covered under the Plan on the day before the event that caused the loss of coverage*

☐ *Child who is losing coverage under the Plan because he or she is no longer a dependent under the Plan*

If elected, COBRA continuation coverage will begin on [*enter date*] and can last until [*enter date*].

[*Add, if appropriate:* You may elect any of the following options for COBRA continuation coverage: [*list available coverage options*].

COBRA continuation coverage will cost: [*enter amount each qualified beneficiary will be required to pay for each option per month of coverage and any other permitted coverage periods.*] You do not have to send any payment with the Election Form. Important additional information about payment for COBRA continuation coverage is included in the pages following the Election Form.

If you have any questions about this notice or your rights to COBRA continuation coverage, you should contact [*enter name of party responsible for COBRA administration for the Plan, with telephone number and address*].

**Figure 10-5 (*cont'd*)**

## Model COBRA Continuation Coverage Election Notice
## (For use by single-employer group health plans)

**COBRA Continuation Coverage Election Form**

**Instructions:** To elect COBRA continuation coverage, complete this Election Form and return it to us. Under federal law, you must have 60 days after the date of this notice to decide whether you want to elect COBRA continuation coverage under the Plan.

Send completed Election Form to: [*Enter Name and Address*]

This Election Form must be completed and returned by mail [*or describe other means of submission and due date*]. If mailed, it must be post-marked no later than [*enter date*].

If you do not submit a completed Election Form by the due date shown above, you will lose your right to elect COBRA continuation coverage. If you reject COBRA continuation coverage before the due date, you may change your mind as long as you furnish a completed Election Form before the due date. However, if you change your mind after first rejecting COBRA continuation coverage, your COBRA continuation coverage will begin on the date you furnish the completed Election Form.

Read the important information about your rights included in the pages after the Election Form.

I (We) elect COBRA continuation coverage in the [*enter name of plan*] (the Plan) as indicated below:

Name    Date of Birth    Relationship to Employee    SSN (or other identifier)
a. _____

        [*Add if appropriate:* Coverage option elected: _____]

b. _____

        [*Add if appropriate:* Coverage option elected: _____]

c. _____

        [*Add if appropriate:* Coverage option elected: _____]


_____      _____
Signature                                Date

_____      _____
Print Name                           Relationship to individual(s) listed above

_____
_____

_____      _____
Print Address                         Telephone number

**Figure 10-5 (*cont'd*)**

## Model COBRA Continuation Coverage Election Notice
## (For use by single-employer group health plans)

---

**Important Information About Your COBRA Continuation Coverage Rights**

**What is continuation coverage?**

Federal law requires that most group health plans (including this Plan) give employees and their families the opportunity to continue their health care coverage when there is a "qualifying event" that would result in a loss of coverage under an employer's plan. Depending on the type of qualifying event, "qualified beneficiaries" can include the employee (or retired employee) covered under the group health plan, the covered employee's spouse, and the dependent children of the covered employee.

Continuation coverage is the same coverage that the Plan gives to other participants or beneficiaries under the Plan who are not receiving continuation coverage. Each qualified beneficiary who elects continuation coverage will have the same rights under the Plan as other participants or beneficiaries covered under the Plan, including [*add if applicable:* open enrollment and] special enrollment rights.

**How long will continuation coverage last?**

In the case of a loss of coverage due to end of employment or reduction in hours of employment, coverage generally may be continued only for up to a total of 18 months. In the case of losses of coverage due to an employee's death, divorce or legal separation, the employee's becoming entitled to Medicare benefits or a dependent child ceasing to be a dependent under the terms of the plan, coverage may be continued for up to a total of 36 months. When the qualifying event is the end of employment or reduction of the employee's hours of employment, and the employee became entitled to Medicare benefits less than 18 months before the qualifying event, COBRA continuation coverage for qualified beneficiaries other than the employee lasts until 36 months after the date of Medicare entitlement. This notice shows the maximum period of continuation coverage available to the qualified beneficiaries.

Continuation coverage will be terminated before the end of the maximum period if:

- any required premium is not paid in full on time;
- a qualified beneficiary becomes covered, after electing continuation coverage, under another group health plan that does not impose any pre-existing condition exclusion for a pre-existing condition of the qualified beneficiary;
- a qualified beneficiary becomes entitled to Medicare benefits (under Part A, Part B, or both) after electing continuation coverage; or
- the employer ceases to provide any group health plan for its employees.

Continuation coverage may also be terminated for any reason the Plan would terminate coverage of a participant or beneficiary not receiving continuation coverage (such as fraud).

[*If the maximum period shown on page 1 of this notice is less than 36 months, add the following three paragraphs:*]

**Figure 10-5 (*cont'd*)**

## Model COBRA Continuation Coverage Election Notice
## (For use by single-employer group health plans)

### How can you extend the length of COBRA continuation coverage?

If you elect continuation coverage, an extension of the maximum period of coverage may be available if a qualified beneficiary is disabled or a second qualifying event occurs. You must notify [*enter name of party responsible for COBRA administration*] of a disability or a second qualifying event in order to extend the period of continuation coverage. Failure to provide notice of a disability or second qualifying event may affect the right to extend the period of continuation coverage.

### Disability

An 11-month extension of coverage may be available if any of the qualified beneficiaries is determined by the Social Security Administration (SSA) to be disabled. The disability has to have started at some time before the 60th day of COBRA continuation coverage and must last at least until the end of the 18-month period of continuation coverage. [*Describe Plan provisions for requiring notice of disability determination, including time frames and procedures.*] Each qualified beneficiary who has elected continuation coverage will be entitled to the 11-month disability extension if one of them qualifies. If the qualified beneficiary is determined by SSA to no longer be disabled, you must notify the Plan of that fact within 30 days after SSA's determination.

### Second Qualifying Event

An 18-month extension of coverage will be available to spouses and dependent children who elect continuation coverage if a second qualifying event occurs during the first 18 months of continuation coverage. The maximum amount of continuation coverage available when a second qualifying event occurs is 36 months. Such second qualifying events may include the death of a covered employee, divorce or separation from the covered employee, the covered employee's becoming entitled to Medicare benefits (under Part A, Part B, or both), or a dependent child's ceasing to be eligible for coverage as a dependent under the Plan. These events can be a second qualifying event only if they would have caused the qualified beneficiary to lose coverage under the Plan if the first qualifying event had not occurred. You must notify the Plan within 60 days after a second qualifying event occurs if you want to extend your continuation coverage.

### How can you elect COBRA continuation coverage?

To elect continuation coverage, you must complete the Election Form and furnish it according to the directions on the form. Each qualified beneficiary has a separate right to elect continuation coverage. For example, the employee's spouse may elect continuation coverage even if the employee does not. Continuation coverage may be elected for only one, several, or for all dependent children who are qualified beneficiaries. A parent may elect to continue coverage on behalf of any dependent children. The employee or the employee's spouse can elect continuation coverage on behalf of all of the qualified beneficiaries.

In considering whether to elect continuation coverage, you should take into account that a failure to continue your group health coverage will affect your future rights under federal law. First, you can lose the right to avoid having pre-existing condition exclusions applied to you by other group health plans if you have more than a 63-day gap in health coverage, and election of continuation coverage may help you not have such a gap. Second, you will lose the guaranteed right to purchase

**Figure 10-5 (*cont'd*)**

**Model COBRA Continuation Coverage Election Notice
(For use by single-employer group health plans)**

individual health insurance policies that do not impose such pre-existing condition exclusions if you do not get continuation coverage for the maximum time available to you. Finally, you should take into account that you have special enrollment rights under federal law. You have the right to request special enrollment in another group health plan for which you are otherwise eligible (such as a plan sponsored by your spouse's employer) within 30 days after your group health coverage ends because of the qualifying event listed above. You will also have the same special enrollment right at the end of continuation coverage if you get continuation coverage for the maximum time available to you.

### How much does COBRA continuation coverage cost?

Generally, each qualified beneficiary may be required to pay the entire cost of continuation coverage. The amount a qualified beneficiary may be required to pay may not exceed 102 percent (or, in the case of an extension of continuation coverage due to a disability, 150 percent) of the cost to the group health plan (including both employer and employee contributions) for coverage of a similarly situated plan participant or beneficiary who is not receiving continuation coverage. The required payment for each continuation coverage period for each option is described in this notice.

[*If employees might be eligible for trade adjustment assistance, the following information may be added*: The Trade Act of 2002 created a new tax credit for certain individuals who become eligible for trade adjustment assistance and for certain retired employees who are receiving pension payments from the Pension Benefit Guaranty Corporation (PBGC) (eligible individuals). Under the new tax provisions, eligible individuals can either take a tax credit or get advance payment of 65 percent of premiums paid for qualified health insurance, including continuation coverage. If you have questions about these new tax provisions, you may call the Health Coverage Tax Credit Customer Contact Center toll-free at 1-866-628-4282. TTD/TTY callers may call toll-free at 1-866-626-4282. More information about the Trade Act is also available at www.doleta.gov/tradeact/2002act_index.cfm.

### When and how must payment for COBRA continuation coverage be made?

*First payment for continuation coverage*

If you elect continuation coverage, you do not have to send any payment with the Election Form. However, you must make your first payment for continuation coverage not later than 45 days after the date of your election. (This is the date the Election Notice is post-marked, if mailed.) If you do not make your first payment for continuation coverage in full not later than 45 days after the date of your election, you will lose all continuation coverage rights under the Plan. You are responsible for making sure that the amount of your first payment is correct. You may contact [*enter appropriate contact information, e.g., the Plan Administrator or other party responsible for COBRA administration under the Plan*] to confirm the correct amount of your first payment.

*Periodic payments for continuation coverage*

After you make your first payment for continuation coverage, you will be required to make periodic payments for each subsequent coverage period. The amount due for each coverage period for each qualified beneficiary is shown in this notice. The periodic payments can be made on a monthly basis. Under the Plan, each of these periodic payments for continuation

## Figure 10-5 (*cont'd*)

## Model COBRA Continuation Coverage Election Notice
## (For use by single-employer group health plans)

coverage is due on the [*enter due day for each monthly payment*] for that coverage period. [*If Plan offers other payment schedules, enter with appropriate dates:* You may instead make payments for continuation coverage for the following coverage periods, due on the following dates:]. If you make a periodic payment on or before the first day of the coverage period to which it applies, your coverage under the Plan will continue for that coverage period without any break. The Plan [*select one:* will *or* will not] send periodic notices of payments due for these coverage periods.

*Grace periods for periodic payments*

Although periodic payments are due on the dates shown above, you will be given a grace period of 30 days after the first day of the coverage period [*or enter longer period permitted by Plan*] to make each periodic payment. Your continuation coverage will be provided for each coverage period as long as payment for that coverage period is made before the end of the grace period for that payment. [*If Plan suspends coverage during grace period for nonpayment, enter and modify as necessary:* However, if you pay a periodic payment later than the first day of the coverage period to which it applies, but before the end of the grace period for the coverage period, your coverage under the Plan will be suspended as of the first day of the coverage period and then retro-actively reinstated (going back to the first day of the coverage period) when the periodic payment is received. This means that any claim you submit for benefits while your coverage is suspended may be denied and may have to be resubmitted once your coverage is reinstated.]

If you fail to make a periodic payment before the end of the grace period for that coverage period, you will lose all rights to continuation coverage under the Plan.

Your first payment and all periodic payments for continuation coverage should be sent to:

[*enter appropriate payment address*]

### For more Information

This notice does not fully describe continuation coverage or other rights under the Plan. More information about continuation coverage and your rights under the Plan is available in your summary plan description or from the Plan Administrator.

If you have any questions concerning the information in this notice, your rights to coverage, or if you want a copy of your summary plan description, you should contact [*enter name of party responsible for COBRA administration for the Plan, with telephone number and address*].

For more information about your rights under ERISA, including COBRA, the Health Insurance Portability and Accountability Act (HIPAA), and other laws affecting group health plans, contact the U.S. Department of Labor's Employee Benefits Security Administration (EBSA) in your area or visit the EBSA website at www.dol.gov/ebsa. (Addresses and phone numbers of Regional and District EBSA Offices are available through EBSA's website.)

### Keep Your Plan Informed of Address Changes

In order to protect your and your family's rights, you should keep the Plan Administrator informed of any changes in your address and the addresses of family members. You should also keep a copy, for your records, of any notices you send to the Plan Administrator.

A qualified beneficiary, or employee, has 60 days in which to notify the plan administrator if the qualifying event is:

- The divorce or legal separation of the beneficiary or employee
- The loss of dependent status of a child under the terms of the plan

A qualified beneficiary must also notify the plan administrator if a second qualifying event occurs while the qualified beneficiary is on COBRA continuation coverage due to the termination of employment or a reduction in hours and when determined to be disabled by the Social Security Administration.[91]

**Other notices** The plan administrator must notify individuals who erroneously file a qualifying event notice or who have not experienced a second qualifying event of the reason they are not entitled to elect or extend COBRA continuation coverage. The plan administrator is also required to notify qualified beneficiaries when their coverage will be canceled before the end of the maximum continuation coverage period.[92]

**Penalties for non-compliance** The IRS can impose on an employer or plan administrator an excise tax equal to $100 per day for each qualified beneficiary affected by a failure to comply with COBRA.[93] In addition, the IRS can impose an excise tax, up to a specified maximum, if the failure is discovered after notice of an audit.[94]

The DOL may also impose on a plan administrator a penalty of $110 per day for each employee the plan administrator fails to notify.[95]

---

[91] DOL Reg. § 2590.606-3.
[92] DOL Reg. § 2590.606-4(c) and (d).
[93] I.R.C. § 4980B(b).
[94] I.R.C. § 4980B(b)(3)(A).
[95] ERISA § 502(c)(1)(A).

# G. Qualified Medical Child Support Orders

ERISA requires group health plans to honor qualified medical child support orders (QMCSOs) issued by state courts or through an administrative process established under state law that has the force and effect of state law. These orders require health coverage for a participant's child even if the child would not normally be covered under the plan's provisions.[96]

**Affected health plans**

All ERISA-covered group health plans, regardless of size, are subject to the QMCSO rules. For QMCSO purposes, a *group health plan* is defined as an employee benefit welfare plan providing medical care to participants or beneficiaries through insurance, reimbursement, or otherwise.[97]

**Qualification requirements**

A medical child support order is an order from the appropriate state court requiring a group health plan to provide coverage for a participant's child. It is qualified only if it:[98]

- creates or recognizes an alternate recipient's right to receive benefits under the plan;
- provides the name and last-known mailing address, if any, of the participant and each alternate recipient covered by the order;
- provides a reasonable description of the coverage or the manner in which coverage will be determined;
- specifies the period covered by the order; and
- does not require the plan to provide any type or form of benefit (or optional benefit) that is not normally available under the plan.

**Alternate recipient**

An *alternate recipient* is a participant's child who has been given a right to enroll in the plan under a medical child support order.[99] The QMCSO provisions do not define the term *child* or provide a maximum age limit for children.

---

[96] ERISA § 609(a).
[97] ERISA § 607(l).
[98] ERISA § 609(a)(2)(A), 609(a)(3), 609(a)(4).
[99] ERISA § 609(a)(2)(C).

**Alternate recipient's rights**

Generally, alternate recipients are entitled to receive the same coverage as other beneficiaries normally covered under the plan.[100] However, if the alternate recipient (or the alternate recipient's custodial parent or guardian) pays medical expenses that should have been paid by the plan under the QMCSO, the plan must directly reimburse the alternate recipient (or the alternate recipient's custodial parent or guardian).[101]

**Benefits**

A QMCSO generally cannot require the plan to provide any form or type of benefit coverage not normally provided to active participants. However, the plan must comply with state medical child support laws on eligibility and enrollment, even if the plan has more restrictive rules.[102]

**State medical child support laws**

To receive federal Medicaid funding, states are required to enact laws that:[103]

- Prohibit a health plan that provides family coverage from denying enrollment of a child who is
  — born out of wedlock
  — not claimed by the employee as a dependent on his or her federal income tax form
  — not residing with the employee
  — not living within the plan service area.
- Require health plans that provide family coverage to follow QMCSOs and enroll children who are otherwise eligible for coverage in the plan regardless of the plan's open enrollment period. (If the employee does not enroll the child, the plan must allow the child's custodial parent or certain state agencies to do so. Required employee contributions may be withheld from the employee's paycheck.)
- Require that a child's coverage pursuant to a QMCSO cannot be terminated unless the plan receives written evidence that the order is no longer in effect or proof that the child is enrolled, as of the date of coverage termination, in a comparable health plan.
- Require the plan to give the custodial parent information needed to obtain benefits for the child and permit the custodial parent to make claims and collect benefits.

---

[100] ERISA § 609(a)(7)(A).
[101] ERISA § 609(a)(8).
[102] ERISA § 609(a)(4).
[103] 42 U.S.C. § 1908.

**National medical support notice**

The DOL has issued final regulations outlining the use of a National Medical Support Notice by state agencies when they issue QMCSOs to group health plans.[104] A portion of the notice is designed to meet the QMCSO requirements for individual court orders.

The National Medical Support Notice has two parts. Part A identifies the employee as well as the child or children to whom the order applies, and it instructs the employer to forward Part B of the Notice to the plan administrator within 20 business days. The employer is told to withhold any required plan contributions from the employee's income. The Notice also has an employer response section that the employer may use to inform the issuing agency if (1) it does not have a group health plan, (2) the employee is not eligible for plan coverage, or (3) the individual is no longer an employee.

Part B of the Notice contains the QMCSO-required items and informs the plan administrator that the employee is obligated to provide coverage and enroll his or her child. The plan administrator must respond to the issuing agency within 40 business days to notify it that the child has been enrolled. If the employee is not enrolled in a plan, and there is more than one option for coverage, the plan administrator must inform the issuing agency of the options available for the child's coverage.

**DOL guidance**

The DOL has released a publication titled "Compliance Guide for Qualified Medical Child Support Orders" to answer questions about QMCSOs and the National Medical Support Notice.[105] The publication includes a list of additional resources providing information about ERISA and how to obtain health coverage and medical care for children.

The Guide states that:

- If an employee is not enrolled in the plan when a QMCSO is issued for the employee's child, the plan must enroll both the employee and the child.
- A plan administrator need not determine whether a court or agency order is legally valid (e.g., ascertain the proper interpretation of facts, jurisdiction, or law); it need only determine whether the order meets the ERISA requirements for a QMCSO.
- If an order submitted to a plan is lacking certain identifying information that is easily obtained by the plan administrator, the plan administrator should supplement the order with the appropriate information.

---

[104] DOL Reg. § 2590.609-2.
[105] The Guide is posted on the DOL's Web site (*see www.dol.gov/ebsa/publications/qmcso.html*).

- If federal or state withholding limitations prevent the withholding of necessary employee contributions, the plan is not required to extend coverage to the child.

**Reporting and disclosure**

For reporting and disclosure purposes, the plan must treat each alternate recipient as a participant.[106] Thus, each alternate recipient must receive a summary annual report and a summary plan description if otherwise required. Each alternate recipient is also counted as a participant for Form 5500 annual report purposes.

**Written procedures**

The plan administrator must establish written procedures to determine an order's qualified status and administer benefits under a qualified order.[107] The procedures:

- should be in writing;
- should provide for prompt notification of the procedures to each person named in the order (at the address included in the order); and
- allow for the naming of a representative to receive copies of any notices.

**Administrative procedures**

When a plan receives a medical child support order, the plan administrator must:[108]

- promptly provide a notice to the participant and each alternate recipient stating that the plan has received a medical child support order and outlining the procedure(s) to determine if the order is qualified;
- determine if the order is qualified within a reasonable time; and
- notify the participant and alternate recipients of the results within a reasonable time.

ERISA does not define *promptly* or *a reasonable time* for providing notices or determining an order's qualified status. The notices may be provided electronically pursuant to the DOL's electronic distribution safe harbor rules (see Section C in Chapter 3).

---

[106]   ERISA § 609(a)(7)(B).
[107]   ERISA § 609(a)(5)(B).
[108]   ERISA § 609(a)(5)(A).

# H. HIPAA Privacy Requirements

**Overview**

Under HIPAA's privacy rules, a health plan generally cannot use or disclose individually identifiable health information, that is, ***protected health information*** (PHI), except as authorized by the individual or by regulations issued by the U.S. Department of Health and Human Services (HHS). However, de-identified health information (e.g., health information from which the patient's name, Social Security number, and all other identifying information have been removed) is not protected. In addition, the privacy rules broadly authorize claims administrators and other health plan vendors to use and disclose protected health information for three "routine" purposes: treatment, payment, and health care operations.

**Covered entities**

The privacy rules apply to health plans, health care providers, and health care clearinghouses. These are known as ***covered entities***. The term ***health plan*** means a group health plan, whether insured or self-funded, that has 50 or more participants or is administered by a third party. The term encompasses governmental plans, church plans, health maintenance organizations, health care flexible spending accounts, and insurers, including Medicare supplement issuers.[109]

**Protected information**

The privacy standards protect medical records and other confidential health information that identifies (or could reasonably be used to identify) an individual, and relates to a past, present, or future physical or mental condition of the individual or the payment of health care for that individual. PHI can be in any form (i.e., electronic, written, or oral) that is created or received by a health plan (or other covered entity) or employer.[110]

**Notice of privacy practices**

Most covered health plans must issue a Notice of Privacy Practices to plan participants. This notice should describe the health plan's uses and disclosures of PHI.[111] A notice to a covered participant is also effective for the participant's dependents.[112]

---

[109]   HHS Reg. § 160.103.
[110]   *Id.*
[111]   HHS Reg. § 164.520(a).
[112]   HHS Reg. § 164.520(c)(1)(iii).

However, if a fully insured plan has no access to PHI except for enrollment information, the insurer, not the plan, has the obligation to provide the notice.[113]

**Contents of privacy notice**

The privacy notice must include the following text either as a header or otherwise prominently displayed:[114]

THIS NOTICE DESCRIBES HOW MEDICAL INFORMATION ABOUT YOU MAY BE USED AND DISCLOSED AND HOW YOU CAN GET ACCESS TO THIS INFORMATION. PLEASE REVIEW IT CAREFULLY.

The notice must describe the following in sufficient detail:

- The types of disclosures that the plan is permitted to make for treatment, payment, and health care operations and how the information is used
- Any other uses of the information that can be made without the individual's authorization
- Other limitations on disclosure due to other applicable laws (e.g., state privacy laws)[115]

The notice must also contain a statement that other uses and disclosures will only be made with the individual's written authorization, and that the individual may revoke such authorization.

**Separate statements for certain uses**

The privacy notice must also describe whether the plan or another covered entity may do any of the following:[116]

- Contact the individual to provide information about treatment alternatives or other health-related benefits and services
- Contact the individual to raise funds for the plan
- Disclose PHI to the plan sponsor

**Individual rights**

The privacy notice must contain a statement of the individual's rights with respect to PHI, including:[117]

- The right to request restrictions on certain uses and disclosures of PHI (e.g., disclosure made for payment, treatment, or plan operations)
- The right to receive confidential communications of PHI from the plan

---

113   HHS Reg. § 164.520(a)(2).
114   HHS Reg. § 164.520(b)(1)(i).
115   HHS Reg. § 164.520(b)(1)(ii).
116   HHS Reg. § 164.520(b)(1)(iii).
117   HHS Reg. § 164.520(b)(1)(iv).

- The right to inspect PHI and correct inaccurate information
- The right to receive an accounting of certain PHI disclosures made by the plan
- The right to receive a paper copy of the notice upon request

**Duties of covered entities**

The privacy notice must contain statements indicating that:[118]

- The covered entity is required by law to maintain the privacy of PHI and to provide this notice
- The covered entity is required by law to abide by the terms of the notice currently in effect
- If applicable, the covered entity reserves the right to change the terms of the notice and provide individuals with a revised notice

**Delivery of notice**

The Notice of Privacy Practices must be provided to all plan participants no later than the privacy rule's effective date, and then to all new participants at enrollment. A new notice must be given to all participants within 60 days after the notice has been materially changed. The notice must also be available upon request. In addition, the plan must notify participants of the availability of the privacy notice at least once every three years.[119] The privacy notice can be delivered using a paper copy or, if certain conditions are satisfied, electronically.[120] Privacy notices may be included with other materials provided to participants such as annual open enrollment materials.[121]

**Plan document provisions**

A health plan (or insurer) may disclose summary health information (e.g., claims information from which most individually identifiable information has been deleted) to allow the plan sponsor to obtain premium bids or to modify, amend, or terminate a plan. However, a health plan (or insurer) can only disclose PHI to a plan sponsor if the health plan document includes privacy provisions.[122]

Among other things, the plan document's privacy provisions must establish the permitted uses and disclosures of PHI by the plan sponsor and must state that:[123]

- The plan sponsor will not use or further disclose PHI, except as permitted by the plan documents or as required by law, and, if applicable, report to the plan any improper disclosures.

---

[118] HHS Reg. § 164.520(b)(1)(v).
[119] HHS Reg. § 164.520(c)(1).
[120] HHS Reg. § 164.520(c)(3)(ii).
[121] HHS FAQ at http://www.hhs.gov/hipaafaq/notice/1065.html.
[122] HHS Reg. § 164.504(f)(1)(i).
[123] HHS Reg. § 164.504(f)(2)(ii).

- The plan sponsor will not use the information for any employment-related action or in connection with any other benefit plan.
- The plan sponsor will allow individuals access to their own PHI, consider their amendments, and, upon request, provide an accounting of the disclosures made.
- The plan sponsor will ensure that its agents and subcontractors agree to similar restrictions.
- The plan sponsor will make its internal practices and records available to the Department of Health and Human Services.
- If feasible, the plan sponsor will return or destroy all PHI received from the plan when such information is no longer needed.

The plan document must also:

- Describe which employees of the plan sponsor may access PHI
- Restrict their use of PHI to the plan's administrative functions
- Provide a mechanism for resolving those employees' noncompliance with the plan sponsor's privacy policy[124]

Finally, the plan documents must provide that the group health plan will disclose PHI to the plan sponsor only upon receipt of the sponsor's certification that the plan documents have been amended as indicated above.[125]

**Penalties**

Covered entities that violate the privacy standards will be subject to penalties of $100 per incident, up to $25,000 per person, per year, per standard.

In addition, criminal penalties of up to $50,000 and one year in prison may be imposed for obtaining or disclosing PHI; $100,000 and five years in prison for obtaining PHI under "false pretenses"; and $250,000 and 10 years in prison for obtaining or disclosing PHI with the intent to transfer or use it for commercial or personal advantage or malicious harm.[126]

---

[124] HHS Reg. § 164.504(f)(2)(iii).
[125] HHS Reg. § 164.504(f)(2)(ii).
[126] Social Security Act, Title XI, §§ 1176, 1177.

# I. EDI and Security Requirements

HIPAA's administrative simplication provisions require the Department of Health and Human Services (HHS) to adopt standards to enable health information to be exchanged electronically. HIPAA also requires all health plans, providers, and clearinghouses that maintain or transmit health information electronically to maintain security standards to ensure the integrity and confidentiality of health-related information.

**Definition** *Electronic data interchange* (EDI) is the electronic transfer of health information, such as claims data, in a standard format between trading partners (e.g., claims processors and health care providers). EDI allows health system entities to exchange billing, enrollment, medical, and other information and to process transactions in a quicker and more cost-effective manner than conducting such exchanges and transactions on paper.[127]

**EDI standards** The final standards adopted by HHS address transactions and code sets to be used in electronic health information exchanges in eight areas:[128]

- Health care claims
- Health care payment and remittance advice
- Health care claim status requests
- Participant enrollment and disenrollment
- Health plan premium payments
- Participant eligibility
- Referral certification and authorization
- Coordination of benefits

Generally, the EDI standards mandate both the format of the transaction and the type of data the typical transaction must include. In addition to these eight standards, HIPAA requires HHS to issue standards for "health claims attachments" and "first report of injury," which will affect workers' compensation programs.

**Security standards** The security standards apply to health plans, health care providers, and health care clearinghouses that transmit or store individually identifiable health information electronically. These are known as "covered entities."[129] *Health plans* are defined to mean group health

---

[127] HHS Final Rule Pts. 160 and 162, Preamble 8-17-2000, p. 50312.
[128] HHS Reg. §§ 162.1102, 162.1202, 162.1302, 162.1402, 162.1502, 162.1602, 162.1702, 162.1802.
[129] HHS Reg. § 164.104.

plans (whether insured or self-funded) that have 50 or more participants or are administered by a third party, governmental plans, church plans, HMOs, and health insurers, including Medicare supplement issuers.[130]

HIPAA's privacy standards essentially say that a health plan cannot use or disclose PHI except as authorized by the individual or by HHS regulations. The security standards go a step further to say that a health plan must adopt safeguards to prevent unauthorized electronic access or unauthorized destruction of such information (e.g., by hackers breaking into a health plan's claims records).

**Safeguard categories**

There are three broad categories of security standards:[131]

1. Administrative safeguards are defined as the administrative actions, policies, and procedures used to manage the security process.
2. Physical safeguards are those physical methods, procedures, and policies intended to protect the electronically protected health information from unauthorized access and natural and environmental hazards.
3. Technical safeguards include the technology used to protect electronic PHI.

These categories are further subdivided into 18 "standards" composed of 42 "implementation specifications."

**Security official and plan documentation**

A health plan must designate a security official responsible for developing and implementing its security privacy policy and procedures. A health plan's responsibility to safeguard electronic PHI extends to its entire workforce regardless of location.[132]

A health plan document must contain the appropriate and reasonable security standards for the plan, and the employer, as plan sponsor, must agree to abide by the standards before the plan may disclose PHI to the plan sponsor. A limited exception to the plan documentation requirement allows a health plan to disclose enrollment/disenrollment data and summary health information (e.g., claims history data from which most individually identifiable information has been deleted).[133]

---

130   HHS Reg. § 160.103.
131   HHS Reg. § 164.304.
132   HHS Reg. § 164.308.
133   HHS Reg. § 164.314.

## J. Multiple Employer Welfare Arrangement

Under the Multiemployer Pension Plan Amendments Act of 1980, Congress amended ERISA to allow states to regulate multiple employer welfare arrangements (MEWAs).

A *MEWA* is defined as an employee welfare benefits plan, or any other arrangement that is established or maintained for the purpose of offering or providing welfare benefits to the employees of two or more employers. The definition does not include any plan or arrangement that is established or maintained by a controlled group of employers or a group of employers under "common control" or pursuant to one or more collective bargaining agreements, or by a rural electric cooperative, or by a rural telephone cooperative.[134]

**Collectively bargained MEWA**

For a collectively bargained MEWA to be exempt from state regulation, it must be an employee welfare benefit plan within the meaning of ERISA Section 3(1). In addition, at least 85 percent of the participants covered by the arrangement must have a nexus, or connection, to the bargaining relationships under which the plan is established. DOL regulations specified the factors that must be considered in determining whether a plan is maintained under a bona fide collective bargaining agreement.[135]

**State regulation**

As shown in Table 10-1, the extent of permitted state regulation depends on whether the MEWA is an ERISA-qualified plan and whether the benefits are insured.[136]

**Table 10-1**
**Permitted State Regulation of MEWAs**

| If the MEWA is: | And if it is: | Then it is subject to: |
|---|---|---|
| *not* an ERISA plan | | all state laws |
| an ERISA plan | Fully insured | only state rating and reserve laws |
| | *not* fully insured | all state insurance laws "to the extent not inconsistent with" ERISA |

---

[134] ERISA § 3(40).
[135] DOL Reg. § 2510.3-40.
[136] DOL Adv. Op. 90-18A.

# K. Additional Standards for Group Health Plans

The Omnibus Budget Reconciliation Act of 1993 (OBRA '93) amended ERISA by adding three provisions that affect group health plans. Group health plans were required to:

- Treat children placed for adoption in a participant's home the same as the participant's natural children[137]
- Pay benefits in accordance with any assignment of rights under Medicaid as secondary payer rules and not discriminate against individuals eligible for Medicaid[138]
- Maintain coverage for pediatric vaccines at least at the level provided on May 1, 1993[139]

**Adoption requirements**

Children placed for adoption with a participant (or beneficiary) must receive group health coverage under the same terms and conditions as a participant's (or beneficiary's) natural children. A child becomes eligible for coverage when placed for adoption, not when the adoption becomes final.[140]

The health plan cannot restrict coverage based on a child's preexisting conditions at the time the child is adopted or placed for adoption with a participant or beneficiary.[141]

A *child*, for the purposes of these regulations, is an individual who has not attained age 18 at the time he or she is adopted or placed for adoption.[142]

A child is *placed for adoption* when the plan participant or beneficiary becomes legally responsible for the child's support, either totally or partially, in anticipation of adoption. Placement for adoption ceases when the participant's or beneficiary's legal obligation terminates.[143]

---

[137] ERISA § 609(c).
[138] ERISA § 609(b).
[139] ERISA § 609(d).
[140] ERISA § 609(c).
[141] ERISA § 609(c)(2).
[142] ERISA § 609(c)(3)(A).
[143] ERISA § 609(c)(3)(B).

**Medicaid requirements**

A group health plan is required to reimburse Medicaid payments made to participants and beneficiaries as provided under state Medicaid laws.[144] Such a plan is required to ignore Medicaid eligibility when enrolling a participant or beneficiary or making any benefit payment determination.[145] Finally, the plan must comply with any subrogation rights required under state Medicaid laws.[146]

**Pediatric vaccines**

A group health plan may not reduce its coverage of the costs of pediatric vaccines below the coverage it provided on May 1, 1993.[147]

---

[144]   ERISA § 609(b)(1).
[145]   ERISA § 609(b)(2).
[146]   ERISA § 609(b)(3).
[147]   ERISA § 609(d).

# L. Medicare Part D "Creditable Coverage" Notices

Employers providing prescription drug coverage to employees or retirees covered by Medicare Part A or B must provide them with "creditable coverage" notices. The notices inform Medicare beneficiaries whether or not the employer's drug coverage is "as good as" Medicare Part D prescription drug coverage.[148] Individuals who do not enroll for Part D coverage when they initially become eligible will pay a late enrollment penalty in the form of higher premiums when they enroll later, unless they were covered by creditable coverage under their employer's plan.

**Who receives notice**

The creditable coverage notices must be provided to active employees or their spouses if they are covered by an employer's group health plan (including COBRA coverage) and if they are also covered by Medicare because of their age, disability, or end-stage renal disease. The creditable coverage notice requirements apply to most employers, *including those without retiree health plans*. Employers with retiree health plans also will be required to provide notices to retirees or their spouses over age 65.

*Note.* Separate notices are sent to employees/retirees and spouses if they reside at different addresses.

In addition, employers notify CMS about whether their prescription drug coverage is creditable or non-creditable using an online form at *https://www.cms.hhs.gov/CreditableCoverage/45_CCDisclosureForm.asp.*

**Content**

The employee/retiree disclosure statement of creditable coverage must contain all of the following elements:

- Individual's first and last name
- Individual's date of birth or unique member identification number
- Entity name and contact information
- Statement that the entity's plan was determined by the entity to be creditable or non-creditable coverage
- The date ranges of creditable coverage

---

[148]   42 CFR § 423.56(e)

CMS' Model Personalized Disclosure Notice on Creditable Coverage also includes the individual's social security number, or health insurance claim number. See Figure 10-6 for this model notice.[149]

**Due date**    At a minimum, the appropriate notice must be provided at the following times:[150]

- Within the past 12 months of an individual's initial enrollment period for Medicare Part D
- Within the past 12 months of the annual Medicare Part D enrollment period running November 15 through December 31 of each year
- Within the past 12 months of the effective date of a Medicare beneficiary's coverage under the employer's health plan
- Whenever prescription drug coverage ends or changes so that it is no longer creditable or becomes creditable
- Upon a Medicare beneficiary's request

---

[149] This and other notices, including Spanish versions, are available at http://www.cms.hhs.gov/CreditableCoverage/10_CCafterFeb15.asp#TopOfPage.
[150] 42 CFR § 423.56(f)

**Figure 10-6**

## Important Notice from [Insert Name of Entity] About Your Prescription Drug Coverage and Medicare

Please read this notice carefully and keep it where you can find it. This notice has information about your current prescription drug coverage with [Insert Name of Entity] and about your options under Medicare's prescription drug coverage. This information can help you decide whether or not you want to join a Medicare drug plan. If you are considering joining, you should compare your current coverage, including which drugs are covered at what cost, with the coverage and costs of the plans offering Medicare prescription drug coverage in your area. Information about where you can get help to make decisions about your prescription drug coverage is at the end of this notice.

There are two Important things you need to know about your current coverage and Medicare's prescription drug coverage:

1. Medicare prescription drug coverage became available in 2006 to everyone with Medicare. You can get this coverage if you join a Medicare Prescription Drug Plan or join a Medicare Advantage Plan (like an HMO or PPO) that offers prescription drug coverage. All Medicare drug plans provide at least a standard level of coverage set by Medicare. Some plans may also offer more coverage for a higher monthly premium.
2. [Insert Name of Entity] has determined that the prescription drug coverage offered by the [Insert Name of Plan] is, on average for all plan participants, expected to pay out as much as standard Medicare prescription drug coverage pays and is therefore considered Creditable Coverage. Because your existing coverage is Creditable Coverage, you can keep this coverage and not pay a higher premium (a penalty) if you later decide to join a Medicare drug plan.

---

**When Can You Join A Medicare Drug Plan?**

You can join a Medicare drug plan when you first become eligible for Medicare and each year from November 15th through December 31st

However, if you lose your current creditable prescription drug coverage, through no fault of your own, you will also be eligible for a two (2) month Special Enrollment Period (SEP) to join a Medicare drug plan.

**What Happens To Your Current Coverage If You Decide to Join A Medicare Drug Plan?**

If you decide to join a Medicare drug plan, your current [Insert Name of Entity] coverage will [or will not] be affected. [The entity providing the Disclosure Notice should insert an explanation of the prescription drug coverage plan provisions/options under the particular entity's plan that Medicare eligible individuals have available to them when they become eligible for Medicare Part D (e.g., they can keep this coverage if they elect part D and this plan will coordinate with Part D coverage; for those individuals who elect Part D coverage, coverage under the entity's plan will end for the individual and all covered dependents, etc.). *See* pages 7-9 of the CMS Disclosure of Creditable Coverage To Medicare Part D Eligible Individuals Guidance (available at http://www.cms.hhs.gov/CreditableCoverage/), which outlines the prescription drug plan provisions/options that Medicare eligible individuals may have available to them when they become eligible for Medicare Part D.]

**Figure 10-6 (*cont'd*)**

## Important Notice from [Insert Name of Entity] About Your Prescription Drug Coverage and Medicare

If you do decide to join a Medicare drug plan and drop your current [Insert Name of Entity] coverage, be aware that you and your dependents will [or will not] [Medigap issuers must insert *"will not"*] be able to get this coverage back.

**When Will You Pay A Higher Premium (Penalty) To Join A Medicare Drug Plan?**

You should also know that if you drop or lose your current coverage with [Insert Name of Entity] and don't join a Medicare drug plan within 63 continuous days after your current coverage ends, you may pay a higher premium (a penalty) to join a Medicare drug plan later.

If you go 63 continuous days or longer without creditable prescription drug coverage, your monthly premium may go up by at least 1% of the Medicare base beneficiary premium per month for every month that you did not have that coverage. For example, if you go nineteen months without creditable coverage, your premium may consistently be at least 19% higher than the Medicare base beneficiary premium. You may have to pay this higher premium (a penalty) as long as you have Medicare prescription drug coverage. In addition, you may have to wait until the following November to join.

**For More Information About This Notice Or Your Current Prescription Drug Coverage . . .**

Contact the person listed below for further information [or call [Insert Alternative Contact] at [(XXX) XXX-XXXX]. **NOTE:** You'll get this notice each year. You will also get it before the next period you can join a Medicare drug plan, and if this coverage through [Insert Name of Entity] changes. You also may request a copy of this notice at any time.

**For More Information About Your Options Under Medicare Prescription Drug Coverage . . .**

More detailed information about Medicare plans that offer prescription drug coverage is in the "Medicare & You" handbook. You'll get a copy of the handbook in the mail every year from Medicare. You may also be contacted directly by Medicare drug plans.

For more information about Medicare prescription drug coverage:

- Visit www.medicare.gov
- Call your State Health Insurance Assistance Program (see the inside back cover of your copy of the "Medicare & You" handbook for their telephone number) for personalized help
- Call 1-800-MEDICARE (1-800-633-4227). TTY users should call 1-877-486-2048.

If you have limited income and resources, extra help paying for Medicare prescription drug coverage is available. For information about this extra help, visit Social Security on the web at www.socialsecurity.gov. or call them at 1-800-772-1213 (TTY 1-800-325-0778).

**Remember: Keep this Creditable Coverage notice. If you decide to join one of the Medicare drug plans, you may be required to provide a copy of this notice when you join to show whether or not you have maintained creditable coverage and, therefore, whether or not you are required to pay a higher premium (a penalty).**

**Figure 10-6 (*cont'd*)**

## Important Notice from [Insert Name of Entity] About Your Prescription Drug Coverage and Medicare

| | |
|---:|:---|
| Date: | [Insert MM/DD/YY] |
| Name of Entity/Sender: | [Insert Name of Entity] |
| Contact—Position/Office: | [Insert Position/Office] |
| Address: | [Insert Street Address, City, State & Zip Code of Entity] |
| Phone Number: | [Insert Entity Phone Number] |

# Chapter 11

# Other ERISA Requirements

**Introduction**  In addition to reporting and disclosure requirements, ERISA-covered pension and welfare benefit plans must comply with certain other ERISA requirements. This chapter discusses these other ERISA requirements.

**Contents**  This chapter has nine sections:

# A. Plan Documentation Requirements

In general, ERISA-covered pension and welfare benefit plans must be established and maintained in writing.[1]

**Exempted plans**

The plan document requirements apply to all ERISA-covered pension and welfare plans, except for:[2]

- unfunded plans maintained solely to provide deferred compensation for a select group of management or highly compensated employees; and
- partnership agreements that provide payments to retired or deceased partners or the successors of deceased partners.

**Content requirements**

For affected plans, the plan document must:[3]

- provide for one or more named fiduciaries who have authority to control and manage the plan's operation and administration;
- provide a procedure for establishing and carrying out a funding policy (not applicable to unfunded welfare plans);[4]
- describe any procedure for allocating responsibility for the plan's operation and administration;
- provide a procedure for amending the plan and identify those who have authority to amend the plan; and
- specify the basis for making payments to and from the plan.

**Named fiduciary**

The *named fiduciary* is named in the plan document or identified by the employer and/or the employee organization as a fiduciary by a procedure specified in the plan document.[5]

**Additional fiduciaries**

The plan document may also provide that:[6]

---

[1] ERISA § 402(a)(1).
[2] ERISA § 401(a).
[3] ERISA § 402(b).
[4] DOL Reg. § 2509.75-5.
[5] ERISA § 402(a)(2).
[6] ERISA § 402(c).

- Any person or persons may serve in more than one fiduciary capacity for the plan, including serving as both trustee and plan administrator.
- A named fiduciary or a fiduciary designated by the named fiduciary may employ one or more persons to provide advice on the fiduciary's responsibility.
- A named fiduciary responsible for asset management may appoint an investment manager with authority to buy and sell plan assets.

**Group health plans**   Additional provisions are mandated for group health plans under the privacy requirements of the Health Insurance Portability and Accountability Act of 1966 (HIPAA).

(For details concerning HIPAA, see Chapter 10.)

# B. Claims Procedure Requirements

Every ERISA-covered pension or welfare benefit plan must establish a claims procedure for participants to follow when they file claims for benefits and request reviews of denied claims.[7]

**Affected plans** The claims procedure requirements apply to *all* ERISA-covered pension and welfare benefit plans with the exception of apprenticeship training programs.[8]

**Documenting and communicating claims procedure** In general, a plan must establish and maintain "reasonable" claims procedures, which:[9]

- must be described (or if provided in another document, be referenced) in the plan's summary plan description (SPD);
- must *not* be administered in any way that would interfere with making or processing a claim;
- must permit a participant's authorized representative to pursue a claim;
- must inform participants, in writing and in a timely fashion, of the time limits for filing benefit claims and requesting reviews of denied claims; and
- must contain administrative safeguards to ensure consistency.

Slightly different procedures may apply to collectively bargained plans.[10]

**Claims denial notice deadline** If a claim is partially or wholly denied, the claimant must be notified of the decision within 90 days from the date the claim was filed.[11]

If more time is required for a special circumstance, the plan administrator may take an additional 90 days, provided the claimant receives a written notice before the end of the first 90-day period.[12]

(For health and disability deadlines see Table 11-1.)

---

7   ERISA § 503.
8   DOL Reg. § 2560.503-1(n).
9   DOL Reg. § 2560.503-1(b).
10   DOL Reg. § 2560.503-1(b)(6)(i).
11   DOL Reg. § 2560.503-1(f)(1).
12   *Id.*

**Claims denial notice content requirements**

The notice of claims denial must:[13]

- state the specific reasons for denial;
- refer to the plan provision on which the denial is based;
- describe any additional information needed and why; and
- describe the plan's review procedures and time limits, including the claimant's right to sue.

In addition to the above requirements, the notice of claims denials for disability or health plans must disclose any internal rule, guidelines, protocol, or similar criterion relied on in making the adverse determination (or state that such information will be provided free of charge upon request).[14]

If the denial is based on medical necessity or experimental treatment, the notice must provide an explanation of the scientific or clinical judgment for the determination, applying plan terms to the participant's medical condition (or state that such information will be provided free of charge upon request).

For urgent health plan care claims, the notice of claims denial must include a description of the expedited review process applicable to such claims. (This denial may be given orally, provided that a written or electronic notification is furnished to the participant no later than three days after the oral notification.)

**Review request procedure**

Every plan must establish and maintain procedures a claimant can follow to request a full and fair review of a denied claim by an appropriate, identified fiduciary.[15]

This procedure must permit the claimant to:[16]

- have at least 60 days after receiving the denial to request a review (180 days for disability or health plans);
- have reasonable access to pertinent documents relevant to the claim;
- submit issues, records, and comments in writing; and
- have a review that takes into account all comments and documents submitted by the claimant during the review process and, for health and disability plans, have a review that is not influenced by the initial claim decision and is conducted by a different person than the one

---

13  DOL Reg. § 2560.503-1(g).
14  DOL Reg. § 2560.503-1(g)(1)(iv).
15  DOL Reg. § 2560.503-1(h).
16  *Id.*

who made the initial determination and who is not under the first person's authority.

For health and disability plans, if a claim is denied on the grounds of medical judgment, the plan administrator must consult a health care professional with appropriate experience. In addition, the claims procedure must identify medical or vocational experts whose advice was obtained in connection with the adverse determination, regardless of whether the advice was relied on.

If a health plan claim involves urgent care, a request for an expedited appeal may be submitted orally or in writing, and claims procedures must allow all necessary information to be transmitted between the plan and claimant by phone, fax, or other available similarly expeditious method.

**Review decision deadline**

The plan must notify a claimant of a named fiduciary's decision, in an easily understandable manner, no later than 60 days after receiving the request for review. If special circumstances exist, the period may be extended an additional 60 days, provided the claimant is notified in writing.[17]

However, if a plan committee reviews claims and meets at least quarterly, the review may be held at the next scheduled meeting or, if the request is filed within 30 days of the meeting, at the second scheduled meeting.[18]

(For health and disability deadlines see Table 11-1.)

**Review decision content requirements**

The decision on review must:[19]

- Be in writing or in electronic form
- State the specific reasons for the decision
- Refer to the plan provisions on which the decision is based
- State that the claimant is entitled to receive, free of charge, reasonable access to, and copies of, all relevant documents
- Describe any voluntary appeals procedures and the claimant's right to sue

---

[17]  DOL Reg. § 2560.503-1(i).
[18]  *Id.*
[19]  DOL Reg. § 2560.503-1(j).

- In the case of a group health plan or a plan providing disability benefits:
  — provide any internal rule, guideline, protocol, or similar criterion relied upon in making the adverse determination (or state that this material will be provided free of charge to the claimant upon request)
  — provide either an explanation of the scientific or clinical judgment for the determination, or a statement that such explanation will be provided free of charge upon request, if the adverse benefit determination is based on a medical necessity or experimental treatment or similar exclusion or limit
  — include the following statement: "You and your plan may have other voluntary alternative dispute resolution options, such as mediation. One way to find out what may be available is to contact your local U.S. Department of Labor Office and your State insurance regulatory agency."

**Claims time limits for health and disability plans (including retirement plans providing disability benefits)**

Table 11-1 summarizes the claims processing deadlines for health and disability benefits. As noted in the table, a plan can extend the time needed to make a claim decision, or to review a claim denial on appeal, if the plan needs more information from the claimant. In addition, time is "tolled" (i.e., not counted) from the point that the plan notifies the claimant about the need for the additional information until the claimant responds with the information. For purposes of the deadlines, urgent health claims generally involve medical care needed quickly to avoid seriously jeopardizing the life or health of the claimant. Pre-service health claims require obtaining plan approval in advance of obtaining medical care. Most other health claims are considered post-service health claims.

*Note.* Table 11-1 does not include special rules for multiemployer plans.

**Table 11-1**
**Health and Disability Claims Deadlines**

| New Rules | Urgent Health Claims | Pre-Service Health Claims | Post-Service Health Claims | Disability Claims |
|---|---|---|---|---|
| Plan Notice of Improper Pre-Service Claim | 24 hours after receiving improper claim.[1] | 5 days after receiving improper claim.[1] | N/A | N/A |
| Plan Notice of Incomplete Claim | 24 hours after receiving incomplete claim.[2] | N/A | N/A | N/A |
| Claimant Deadline to Complete Urgent Claim | At least 48 hours after receiving notice.[3] | N/A | N/A | N/A |
| Plan Notice of Initial Claim Denial Decision | 48 hours[4,5] (i) after receiving completed claim or (ii) after the 48-hour claimant deadline, whichever is earlier. 72 hours[4,5] after receiving the initial claim, if it was proper and complete. | 15 days[5] after receiving the initial claim. 30 days[5] after receiving the claim if plan needs more claimant information and if plan provides an extension notice during initial 15-day period. | 30 days after receiving the initial claim. 45 days after receiving the claim if plan needs more claimant information and if plan provides an extension notice during initial 30-day period. | 45 days after receiving the initial claim. 75 days after receiving the claim if plan needs more claimant information and if plan provides an extension notice during initial 45-day period. 105 days if plan needs another extension. |
| Claimant Deadline to Complete Non-Urgent Claim | N/A | At least 45 days after receiving extension notice. | At least 45 days after receiving extension notice. | At least 45 days after receiving extension notice. |
| Claimant Deadline to Appeal Decision | At least 180 days[6] after receiving claim denial. | At least 180 days after receiving claim denial. | At least 180 days after receiving claim denial. | At least 180 days after receiving claim denial. |

| Plan Notice of Appeal Decision | 72 hours after receiving appeal. | 30 days after receiving the appeal. | 60 days after receiving the appeal. | 45 days after receiving the appeal. |
| --- | --- | --- | --- | --- |
| | | 15 days after receiving an appeal if plan allows two levels of appeal.[7] | 30 days after receiving an appeal if plan allows two levels of appeal.[7] | 90 days after receiving the appeal if plan needs an extension. |

1. Plan may provide notice orally unless the claimant requests written notification.
2. Plan should be able to provide notice orally, but the regulation is silent.
3. Claimant should be able to provide information by telephone, fax, or similar method, but the regulation is silent.
4. Plan may provide notice orally if written or electronic notice is provided within three days after oral notification.
5. Plan notice requirement applies to claim approvals as well as claim denials.
6. Plan must allow claimant to provide information on appeal by telephone, fax, or similar method.
7. Both levels of appeal must be completed within the deadline that would apply if there were only one level of appeal.

# C. Record Retention Requirements

ERISA requires plan administrators to retain certain records for inspection by the DOL. The agency can inspect these records to verify or clarify the accuracy and completeness of the plan's reports and documents.[20] In addition, ERISA requires the retention of records necessary to determine plan benefits.

**Required records for reports**

Plans administrators are required to retain record of any description, report, or certification of information they have filed with the IRS or the DOL or would have filed had it not been for an exemption or simplified reporting requirement.[21]

These records include:

- Documents and reports of matters subject to the ERISA reporting and disclosure requirements (e.g., annual reports, summary annual reports, summary plan descriptions, summaries of material modifications)
- Supporting documents with sufficient detail to allow for verification or clarification (e.g., vouchers, worksheets, receipts)

(For further discussion of filing exemptions, see Section B in Chapter 3.)

**Electronic recordkeeping**

The DOL allows the use of electronic media to satisfy ERISA's recordkeeping requirements if:[22]

- the system has reasonable controls to ensure the integrity, accuracy, authenticity, and reliability of the electronic records;
- the electronic records are maintained in reasonable order and in a safe and accessible place so they may be readily inspected or examined (e.g., the system should be capable of indexing, retaining, preserving, retrieving, and reproducing the electronic records);
- the electronic records can be readily converted into legible and readable paper copy;
- the system is not subject to any agreement that would compromise compliance with ERISA's reporting and disclosure requirements; and
- adequate records of management practices are established and implemented.

---

[20] ERISA §§ 107 and 209.
[21] ERISA § 107.
[22] DOL Reg. § 2520.107-1(b).

All electronic record must exhibit a high degree of legibility and readability[23] when displayed on a video display or some other method of electronic transmission and when reproduced in paper form. Original paper records may be disposed of after they are transferred to an electronic recordkeeping system, except if the record would not constitute a duplicate or substitute record under the terms of the plan and applicable federal or state law.[24]

**Retention period**

Plans must maintain required records for at least: six years after filing the reports or documents (based on the information they contain) or six years after the reports or documents would have been filed if not for an exemption or simplified reporting requirement.[25]

**Required records for benefit determinations**

Employers are required to maintain records necessary to determine the benefits due or which may become due to each employee. The plan administrator is required to make a report to each plan participant who requests a report, terminates service, or has a one-year break in service. The report must inform the participant of his or her accrued benefit under the plan and the extent of his or her vesting. The employer has to provide the plan administrator with the information necessary to make these reports.[26] The recordkeeping requirements of ERISA Section 209 are not limited to the six-year period described above for ERISA Section 107, thus, these records must be retained indefinitely.

Failure to comply with this recordkeeping requirement can result in a civil penalty of $11 for each employee for whom records are missing, unless the failure is due to reasonable cause.[27]

---

[23]  DOL Reg. § 2520.107-1(c).
[24]  DOL Reg. § 2520.107-1(d).
[25]  *Id.*
[26]  ERISA § 209(a)(1).
[27]  ERISA § 209(b); DOL Reg. § 2575.209b-1.

# D. Document Disclosure Requirements

**Affected plans** Most ERISA-covered pension and welfare benefit plans must furnish certain information to participants and beneficiaries on request and make certain information available to participants and beneficiaries for inspection. Affected plans must comply with these document disclosure requirements unless ERISA specifically exempts them from the requirements.[28]

**Exempt plans** ERISA-covered plans and programs exempt from the document disclosure requirements are:

- Apprenticeship and training programs[29]
- Executive pension and welfare plans[30]
- Employer-provided day care centers[31]
- Simplified employee pension (SEP) plans[32]
- Savings incentive match plans for employees (SIMPLEs)[33]

These plans are exempt only if they meet certain conditions. (For further discussion about the conditions of exemption, see Section B in Chapter 3.)

**Furnishing information upon request** Upon written request, plans must furnish copies of the following documents to participants and beneficiaries receiving benefits under the plan:[34]

- The most recent SPDs and SMMs
- The most recent annual report
- Terminal reports, plan documents, collective bargaining agreements, and other instruments under which the plan is established or maintained

---

[28] ERISA § 104(a)(1).
[29] DOL Reg. § 2520.104-22.
[30] DOL Reg. §§ 2520.104-23, 2520.104-24.
[31] DOL Reg. § 2520.104-25.
[32] DOL Reg. § 2520.104-49.
[33] ERISA § 101(h).
[34] ERISA § 104(b)(4).

Plans may charge recipients a reasonable fee (not to exceed $0.25 per page) to cover the cost of copying these documents, but they may not charge for postage.[35]

**Copies available for inspection**

A plan must make available for inspection by participants and beneficiaries its most recent annual report, as well as plan documents, collective bargaining agreements, and other instruments under which the plan is established or maintained.[36]

**Availability**

The documents available for inspection must be current and clearly identified and enough copies of them must be kept on hand to meet the expected volume of requests. These documents must be made available in the principal office of the plan administrator at all times and within ten days following a request at the following locations:[37]

- In the case of a union plan, at the union's principal offices and at any employer location where at least 50 participants work[38]
- In the case of a non-union plan sponsored by an employer, including a plan with more than one location, a multiple employer plan, or a plan a controlled group of corporations maintains, the principal office of the employer, and any location where at least 50 participants work[39]
- In the case of a plan sponsored solely by an employee organization, at any office of any local representing 50 or more participants[40]

**Penalty for non-compliance**

If a plan refuses or otherwise fails to provide documents within 30 days after receiving a written request, the requesting party may file a civil action. At the court's discretion, the plan administrator may be held personally liable to the participant or beneficiary for a penalty of up to $110 a day from the date of the failure or refusal to provide requested materials.[41]

---

35  *Id.*
36  ERISA § 104(b)(2).
37  DOL Reg. § 2520.104-1(b)(3).
38  DOL Reg. § 2520.104-1(b)(3)(iii).
39  DOL Reg. § 2520.104(b)-1(b)(3)(i).
40  DOL Reg. § 2520.104(b)-1(b)(3)(ii).
41  ERISA § 502(a), 502(c)(1).

# E. Fiduciary Responsibility

**Affected and exempt plans**   Most ERISA-covered pension and welfare plans are subject to the fiduciary responsibility rules. The plans exempt from these rules are unfunded plans maintained solely to provide deferred compensation for a select group of management or highly compensated employees, and partnership agreements that provide payments to retired or deceased partners or successors of deceased partners.[42]

**Fiduciary**   A *fiduciary* is any person who[43]:

- exercises discretionary authority or control over plan management or plan asset management or disposition;
- provides investment advice relating to any money or other property of the plan, or has any authority or responsibility to do so, for a fee or other direct or indirect compensation; or
- has any discretionary authority or discretionary responsibility in plan administration.

**Fiduciary duties**   Fiduciaries must perform their duties solely in the interest of participants and beneficiaries:[44]

- for the exclusive purpose of providing benefits and defraying the plan's reasonable administrative costs;
- with the care, skill, prudence, and diligence that a prudent man acting in a like capacity would use;
- by diversifying investments to minimize risk, unless it is clearly prudent not to do so; and
- according to the plan documents to the extent they are consistent with ERISA.

DOL offers a Web-based module designed to help ERISA fiduciaries understand their responsibilities. The module can be found at http://www.dol.gov/elaws/ERISAfiduciary.htm.

---

[42]   ERISA § 401(a).
[43]   ERISA § 3(21)(A).
[44]   ERISA § 404(a)(1).

**Investment duties**

A fiduciary must invest assets prudently. This requirement is satisfied if the fiduciary has appropriately considered the facts and circumstances relevant to each investment, including the role the investment plays in the plan's investment portfolio, and acted accordingly.[45]

Also, a fiduciary must diversify investments unless it is clearly prudent not to do so.[46]

Plan participants who direct the investment of their own accounts in certain defined contribution plans (i.e., profit-sharing plans, stock bonus plans, thrift plans, employee stock ownership plans) are not subject to these investment rules.[47] However, these plans must comply with certain rules the DOL imposes to take advantage of this exception.[48]

**Breach of fiduciary duties**

Fiduciaries are liable for their own breach of fiduciary duties as well as a co-fiduciary's breach of fiduciary duties. Thus, Fiduciary A is liable for Fiduciary B's breach if Fiduciary A:

- participates in or conceals an action or omission by Fiduciary B, knowing it is a breach;
- enables Fiduciary B to commit a breach by failing to comply with ERISA; or
- knows about Fiduciary B's breach and makes no reasonable effort to remedy the breach.[49]

**Penalties**

The fiduciary is liable to the plan for the actual amount lost and any profits made through the use of the assets resulting from a breach of fiduciary duty.[50] If the fiduciary is a plan participant, a court or government agency may order or agree to offset retirement plan benefits by amounts owed resulting from a breach of fiduciary duty.[51]

In addition, the DOL may penalize the fiduciary 20 percent of the amount recovered from the fiduciary.[52]

---

[45]   DOL Reg. § 2550.404a-1(b).
[46]   ERISA § 404(a)(1)(C).
[47]   ERISA § 404(c).
[48]   DOL Reg. § 2550.404c-1.
[49]   ERISA § 405(a).
[50]   ERISA § 409(a).
[51]   I.R.C. § 401(a)(13); ERISA § 206(d).
[52]   ERISA § 502(*l*)(1).

# F. Voluntary Fiduciary Correction Program

**Eligibility for VFCP**

DOL's Voluntary Fiduciary Correction (VFC) Program allows plan fiduciaries to avoid certain penalties if they voluntarily correct specified violations.[53] Eligibility for the VFC Program is conditioned on the following:[54]

- Neither the plan nor the applicant is under investigation.
- The application contains no evidence of potential criminal violations as determined by the DOL.
- DOL has not conducted an investigation that resulted in written notice to a plan fiduciary that the transaction, for which the potential applicant could otherwise have sought relief under the VFC Program, has been referred to the IRS.[55]

**Scope of VFCP**

The VFC Program outlines examples of specific transactions that would constitute breaches of ERISA and provides acceptable means of correction under the program. Transactions covered by this program are limited to those that would, in the absence of the fiduciary violation, have been appropriate for the plan. For example, if a plan fiduciary purchases real estate from the plan sponsor (a prohibited transaction) and the purchase also causes the plan's investments to stop being diversified, the VFC Program would apply to the prohibited transaction, but not to the failure to diversify.

The breaches that may be corrected under VFC are:[56]

- Delinquent participant contributions and participant loan repayments to pension and welfare plans
- Delinquent participant contributions to insured welfare plans and welfare plan trusts
- Loans to a party-in-interest at fair market rates or less
- Loans to a person who is not a party-in-interest at less than market rates
- Loans at below market interest rates solely due to a delay in perfecting the plan's security interest

---

[53] EBSA Notice RIN 1210-AB03 (April 19, 2006).

[54] EBSA Notice RIN 1210-AB03 (April 19, 2006), Section 4.

[55] This condition applies only to those transactions specifically identified in DOL's written notice of referral to the IRS.

[56] EBSA Notice RIN 1210-AB03 (April 19, 2006), Section 7.

- Participant loans failing to comply with plan provisions for amount, duration, or level amortization
- Defaulted participant loans
- Purchase from or sale of an asset, including real property, to a party-in-interest
- Sale and leaseback of real property to the employer
- Purchase of assets from a person who is not a party-in-interest at more than fair market value
- Sale of assets to a person who is not a party-in-interest at less than fair market value
- Holding of an illiquid asset previously purchased by plan
- Payment of benefits without properly valuing plan assets on which payment is based
- Duplicative, excessive, or unnecessary compensation paid by a plan
- Improper payment of expenses by plan
- Payment of dual compensation to a plan fiduciary

Under the VFC Program, upon discovery of one of the specified violations, the plan fiduciaries must:[57]

- follow the prescribed process for correcting the breach;
- calculate and restore any losses and profits with interest and distribute any supplemental benefits; and
- file an application with the regional DOL office that includes documentation showing corrective actions taken.

**Scope of relief**   If the DOL approves the correction, it will issue a "no action" letter, and the fiduciaries listed in the application "will be relieved of the possibility" of civil investigation and the imposition of the 20 percent penalty under ERISA and the penalty on prohibited transactions.[58]

If an application fails to satisfy the terms of the VFC Program, DOL reserves the right to investigate and take any other action with respect to the transaction and/or plan that is the subject of the application, including refusing to issue a no action letter.[59] In addition, the relief granted by the DOL will not preclude the DOL from:[60]

- conducting a criminal investigation of the transaction identified or any other governmental agency from conducting an investigation;
- providing assistance to such other agency;

---

57   EBSA Notice RIN 1210-AB03 (April 19, 2006), Sections 1–7.
58   EBSA Notice RIN 1210-AB03 (April 19, 2006), Section 2(a).
59   EBSA Notice RIN 1210-AB03 (April 19, 2006), Section 2(c)(4).
60   EBSA Notice RIN 1210-AB03 (April 19, 2006), Sections 2(c)(5), (6).

- making the appropriate referrals of criminal violations as required by ERISA § 506(b);
- seeking removal from positions of responsibility with respect to a plan or other non-monetary injunctive relief against any person responsible for the transaction at issue;
- referring information regarding the transaction to the IRS; or
- imposing penalties for failure to file accurate annual reports.

The DOL notes that "full correction" under the VFC Program does not prevent any other governmental agency, including the IRS, from exercising any rights it may have with respect to the transactions.[61] However, to encourage use of the VFC Program and to address concerns raised about the imposition of the IRS excise tax, the DOL has issued a class exemption to provide limited relief from the excise tax on prohibited transactions.[62] The IRS has also advised the DOL that it will not impose excise taxes on transactions covered by the program.[63]

---

[61]   EBSA Notice RIN 1210-AB03 (April 19, 2006), Section 2(c)(7).
[62]   DOL PTE 2002-51.
[63]   I.R.S. Ann. 2002-31, 2002-15 I.R.B. 747.

# G. Prohibited Transactions

A fiduciary or other party-in-interest of an ERISA-covered pension or welfare benefit plan may not engage in certain prohibited transactions under ERISA.

**Prohibited transaction defined**

A *prohibited transaction* is the direct or indirect[64]

- sale, exchange, or lease of property between the plan and a party-in-interest;
- loan or extension of credit between the plan and a party-in-interest;
- furnishing of goods, services, or facilities between the plan and a party-in-interest;
- transfer of plan assets to a party-in-interest or a transfer for the use or benefit of a party-in-interest; or
- acquisition or holding of employer securities or real estate leased to the employer, unless specific conditions are met.

In addition, a fiduciary is prohibited from[65]

- dealing with the plan assets in his or her own interest or for his or her own account;
- acting as an individual, or in any other capacity, in any transaction involving the plan, on behalf of a party whose interests are adverse to the interests of the plan, its participants, or beneficiaries; and
- receiving any consideration for his or her own account from any party dealing with the plan, in connection with a transaction involving plan assets.

**Party-in-interest defined**

A *party-in-interest* includes, among others:[66]

- any plan fiduciary;
- any person rendering a service to the plan;
- the employer and any director, officer, employee, owner, or subsidiary of that employer; and
- an employee organization whose members are plan participants.

---

[64] ERISA § 406(a).
[65] ERISA § 406(b).
[66] ERISA § 3(14).

*Note.* The Internal Revenue Code uses the term *disqualified person,* which is similar to *party-in-interest.*[67]

**Prohibited transaction exemptions**

Certain transactions are exempt from the prohibited transaction rules by law.[68] For a detailed list of the transactions exempt by law, see Table 11-2.

**Requesting exemptions**

Plan fiduciaries and parties-in-interest may request additional exemptions from the prohibited transaction rules. The DOL is authorized to exempt individual transactions and classes of transactions if such exemption (1) is administratively feasible, (2) is in the interest of the plan and the participants and beneficiaries, and (3) protects the rights of the plan's participants and beneficiaries.[69]

**Penalties**

The DOL imposes a civil penalty of 5 percent and the IRS imposes an excise tax on plan fiduciaries and certain parties-in-interest for prohibited transactions.

The IRS excise tax is equal to 10 percent of the dollar amount involved for the tax year in which the transaction occurred and for each additional year in which it is not corrected.[70] The excise tax increased to 15 percent for prohibited transactions involving retirement plans occurring after August 5, 1997.

In addition, the transaction must be corrected within a certain period after receiving notice from the IRS or the DOL; otherwise, the agency will impose a further tax equal to 100 percent of the dollar amount involved.[71]

"Correction" means to undo the transaction to the extent possible—or at least undo it to the point where the plan's financial position would be no

---

[67]  I.R.C. § 4975(e)(2).
[68]  ERISA § 408(b).
[69]  ERISA § 408(a).
[70]  I.R.C. § 4975(a).
[71]  I.R.C. § 4975(b).

worse than what it would have been had the prohibited transaction not occurred.[72]

The tax must be paid by the party-in-interest engaging in the prohibited transaction.[73]

---

[72]   I.R.C. § 4975(f)(5).
[73]   I.R.C. § 4975(a), 4975(b).

## Table 11-2
### Prohibited Transactions Exemptions

*Note:* This list of prohibited transactions exempt by law is based on ERISA Section 408.

| Item | Description |
|------|-------------|
| 1 | Receipt of benefits from the plan as a participant or beneficiary so long as the benefits are consistent with the terms of the plan as applied to all other participants and beneficiaries |
| 2 | Receipt of reasonable compensation for services as a plan fiduciary unless fiduciary receives full-time pay from the employer or employee organization |
| 3 | Receipt of reimbursement for expenses incurred |
| 4 | Service as a fiduciary in addition to service as an officer, employee, agent, etc., of a party-in-interest |
| 5 | Loans by the plan to plan participants or beneficiaries if the loans: <br>• are expressly allowed by the plan; <br>• are available to all participants and beneficiaries on an equal basis; <br>• are not available to officers, shareholders, and highly compensated employees on a disproportionate basis; <br>• bear a reasonable interest rate; and <br>• are adequately secured. |
| 6 | Payment of reasonable compensation to parties-in-interest for office space and legal, accounting, and other services necessary to operate plan |
| 7 | Deposit of all or part of the plan's assets in a bank or similar financial institution bearing reasonable interest rates, even when the bank or similar financial institution is a plan fiduciary or other party-in-interest, if: <br>• the investment is expressly authorized by the plan, or by a fiduciary other than the bank or financial institution responsible for investing plan assets that is authorized by the plan; or <br>• the financial institution's employees are the only participants in the plan. |
| 8 | Use of life, health, or annuity contracts by an insurance company to fund a plan for its employees or, with certain restrictions, for employees of a company that owns or is owned by the insurance company |
| 9 | Payment of reasonable compensation for "ancillary services" a bank or similar financial institution performs for a plan, if: <br>• the bank or similar financial institution has adopted adequate safeguards assuring the ancillary service is consistent with sound banking and financial practice; or <br>• the ancillary service is subject to guidelines in the best interests of the participants and beneficiaries and is not excessive or unreasonable. |
| 10 | Exercise of a privilege to convert securities for adequate consideration |

**Table 11-2** (*cont'd*)
**Prohibited Transactions Exemptions**

| Item | Description |
|------|-------------|
| 11 | Transactions between a plan and a common or collective trust fund or a pooled investment fund, under specified circumstances, if:<br>• the transaction is a sale or purchase of an interest in the fund and expressly allowed by the plan; and<br>• the bank, trust company, or insurance company receives only reasonable compensation. |
| 12 | Loans to an employee stock ownership plan (ESOP) if:<br>• the loans benefit plan participants and beneficiaries; and<br>• the loans bear a reasonable interest rate. |
| 13 | Distribution of assets upon plan termination according to the rules relating to asset allocation |
| 14 | Any transaction permitted or required for multiemployer plans under the rules for employer withdrawals |
| 15 | The merger or transfer of assets or liabilities between multiemployer plans permitted under other rules |
| 16 | Any qualified transfer of excess pension assets to a retiree health account under Internal Revenue Code Section 420 before January 1, 2014 |
| 17 | Purchase or sale of employer securities and leasing of real property to the employer by the plan if certain conditions are met |
| 18 | Providing investment advice to participants and beneficiaries with the right to self-direct investments in their account even if the adviser receives fees for providing the advice, as long as provided under an "eligible investment advice arrangement." |
| 19 | Transactions involving block trades where aggregate plan interests of the employer are no more than 10% of the size of the block trade, and terms and fees meet arm's length transaction criteria. |
| 20 | Electronic and other alternative trading systems designed to effect best price available trades, subject to conditions. |
| 21 | Sales exchanges, loans between plans and service providers who are not investment fiduciaries for adequate consideration. |
| 22 | Arm's length foreign exchange transactions for the plan by the plan's trustee, custodian, fiduciary, or other party-in-interest. |
| 23 | Limited cross-trading among accounts of an investment manager. |
| 24 | Certain transactions involving commodities and other securities that are corrected within 14 days of discovery. |

# H. Bonding Requirements

Fiduciaries and persons handling funds or property of most ERISA-covered pension or welfare benefit plans must be bonded. Bonding protects a plan against loss caused by fraud or dishonesty on the part of fiduciaries or other persons handling funds.[74]

**Exempted plans**

The bonding requirements apply to all ERISA-covered pension and welfare plans except totally unfunded plans[75] and insured plans where premiums are paid out of the employer's general assets, except to the extent funds (such as dividends) returned by the insurer belong to the plan and are subject to handling.[76]

All fiduciaries must be bonded except those that meet *all* the following conditions:[77]

- The fiduciary is a U.S. corporation.
- The fiduciary is authorized to exercise trust powers or to conduct insurance business.
- The fiduciary is subject to federal and state supervision.
- The fiduciary has combined capital and surplus in excess of $1 million at all times.

Effective for plan years beginning after August 17, 2006, no bond is required of any entity that is registered as a broker or dealer under Section 15(b) of the Securities Exchange Act of 1934, if the broker or dealer is subject to the fidelity bond requirements of a self-regulatory organization.

**Handling funds**

*Handling* refers to any occasion on which there is a risk that plan funds could be lost because of fraud or dishonesty on the part of a particular person or group. The criteria for handling are:[78]

- Physical contact, unless under these conditions and circumstances it would prevent loss

---

[74] ERISA § 412(a).
[75] ERISA § 412(a)(1).
[76] DOL Reg. § 2580.412-6(b)(7).
[77] ERISA § 412(a)(2).
[78] DOL Reg. § 2580.412-6.

- The power to exercise physical contact or control, such as access to a safe deposit box
- The power to transfer funds to oneself or a third party, or to negotiate for value
- Disbursement of funds, including signing or endorsing checks
- Supervisory or decision-making responsibility over any of the above actions

**Amount of bond**

The amount of a bond must equal 10 percent of the funds handled, but no less than $1,000 and no more than $500,000, unless required by the DOL.[79] For plan years beginning after 2007, the maximum bond amount is $1 million in the case of a plan that holds employer securities.

To compute the value of the bond, use the amount of plan assets handled for the previous year or, in the case of a new plan, estimate the plan funds handled in the current year.[80]

**Fiduciary liability insurance**

Fiduciary liability insurance, which protects only the fiduciary and not the plan, is different from ERISA-required bonding.

Fiduciary liability insurance is purchased with fiduciary or employer assets to protect the fiduciary against liability to the plan for a breach of fiduciary duty.[81] A plan may also purchase fiduciary liability insurance for its fiduciaries if such insurance permits recourse by the issuer against the fiduciary for a fiduciary breach.[82] ERISA does not require fiduciary liability insurance.

---

[79] ERISA § 412(a).
[80] *Id.*
[81] ERISA § 410(b)(2), 410(b)(3).
[82] ERISA § 410(b)(1).

# I. Trust Requirements

The assets of most ERISA-covered pension and welfare plans must be held in trust.[83]

**Affected plans and assets**

The trust requirements apply to all ERISA-covered pension and welfare plans and assets except:[84]

- Insurance contracts or policies
- Assets of an insurance company or plan assets held by an insurance company
- A plan in which some or all of the participants are self-employed or that consists of one or more individual retirement accounts (IRAs) to the extent the plan's assets are held in qualified custodial accounts
- A contract established for a tax-sheltered annuity to the extent the plan's assets are held in qualified custodial accounts
- Certain plans of employee-owned companies used to restore pension benefits forfeited before the plan became subject to ERISA

**Exceptions**

The DOL currently does not require salary reduction contributions to cafeteria plans to be held in trust. In addition, employee contributions to other insured contributory welfare plans are not subject to the trust requirements if they meet the small-employer exemption or the exemption from including an accountant's opinion in the annual report.[85]

(For further discussion of various types of exemption, see Section B in Chapter 3; for discussion of annual reports, see Chapter 5.)

**Employee contribution deposit requirement**

Plan assets must be deposited in a trust or functional equivalent when they become plan assets.

Employee contributions to welfare plans become plan assets as soon as they can reasonably be segregated from the employer's assets, but not later than 90 days after the employer withholds the contributions from the employee's pay or receives the contributions from the employee.[86]

---

[83]  ERISA § 403(a).
[84]  ERISA § 403(b).
[85]  ERISA Tech. Release 92-1; DOL News Release, 58 Fed. Reg. 45,359 (Aug. 27, 1993).
[86]  DOL Reg. § 2510.3-102(a), (c).

Retirement plan contributions become assets as soon as they can reasonably be segregated from the employer's assets, but no later than 15 business days after the month in which the employer receives or withholds the employee contributions.[87] Saturdays, Sundays, and federal holidays are not counted.[88]

An employer can extend the 15-day, but not the 90-day, deposit period for an additional 10 business days if certain conditions are met—for example, sending a written notice to plan participants and obtaining a performance bond.[89]

The 90-day and 15-day periods are not safe harbors; they are simply the maximum period during which an employer may hold employee contributions before depositing them. For example, where a 3-day deposit schedule is in keeping with the employer's practice, DOL may challenge a delay beyond three days. DOL has proposed adding a 7-day safe harbor for small plans.[90]

**Look-through rule**

Certain investments made by employee benefit plans in an entity can cause the entity's underlying assets to be considered plan assets.[91]

When this occurs, the entity's managers are considered plan fiduciaries.[92]

**Exceptions to look-through rule**

The primary exceptions to the look-through rule are investments in:

- debt instruments;[93]
- publicly offered securities, if widely held and freely transferable;[94]
- companies that primarily produce or sell products or services other than capital investment;[95] and
- companies where employee benefit plans and "similar investors" (e.g., IRAs and tax-sheltered annuities) do not hold more than 25% of the value of any class of equity interests in the entity.[96]

---

87  DOL Reg. § 2510.3-102(a), (b).
88  DOL Reg. § 2510.3-102(e).
89  DOL Reg. § 2510.3-102(d).
90  DOL Prop. Reg. § 2510.3-102(a).
91  DOL Reg. § 2510.3-101(a)(2).
92  Id.
93  DOL Reg. § 2510.3-101(b)(1).
94  DOL Reg. § 2510.3-101(b)(2).
95  DOL Reg. § 2510.3-101(c).
96  DOL Reg. § 2510.3-101(f).

PPA narrowed the determination of the 25% similar investors rule to ERISA plans, plans subject to prohibited transaction rules under the Code, and other look-through assets.[97]

---

[97] ERISA § 3(42).

# Appendix A

**Employee Benefit Plan Limits**

Many of the dollar thresholds used in limiting the level of benefits available through tax-advantaged programs are adjusted annually to reflect changes in the consumer price index (CPI) relative to the base period used for each limit. The limit for a particular year is adjusted based on the cumulative increase through the third quarter of the preceding calendar year. The adjusted limits are then rounded down to the nearest multiplier specified for the particular limit. The limits for 2009, for example, are based on the CPI factors through the third quarter of 2008. The Economic Growth and Tax Relief Reconciliation Act of 2001 (EGTRRA) overrides many of the pre-EGTRRA CPI adjustments with specific increases over a five-year period before CPI increases restart for items with fixed increments. The following table reflects these fixed limits. Estimates calculated by the author for 2009 reflect CPI though July 2008. Barring cost of living retrenchment, the actual figures for 2009 will not be less.

### Indexing of Employee Benefit Limits

| Purpose | Calendar Year | | |
| --- | --- | --- | --- |
| | *2007* | *2008* | *Estimated 2009* |
| Base 402(g) deferral limit | $15,500 | $15,500 | $16,500 |
| 457 limit | $15,500 | $15,500 | $16,500 |
| 401(k)/403(b)/457/SAR-SEP,[1] catch-up deferrals | $5,000 | $5,000 | $5,500 |
| SIMPLE limit | $10,500 | $10,500 | $11,500 |
| SIMPLE catch-up deferrals | $2,500 | $2,500 | $2,500 |
| IRA/Roth-IRA limit | $4,000 | $5,000 | $5,000 |
| IRA/Roth-IRA catch-up contributions | $1,000 | $1,000 | $1,000 |
| DB[2] maximum benefit | $180,000 | $185,000 | $195,000 |
| DC[3] maximum addition | $45,000 | $46,000 | $49,000 |
| HCE compensation[4] | $100,000 | $105,000 | $110,000 |
| Key Employee: | | | |

### Indexing of Employee Benefit Limits (*cont'd*)

| Purpose | Calendar Year | | |
|---|---|---|---|
| | *2007* | *2008* | *Estimated 2009* |
| Officer[5] | $145,000 | $150,000 | $160,000 |
| 1% Owners | $150,000 | $150,000 | $150,000 |
| Compensation[6] | $225,000 | $230,000 | $245,000 |
| SEP threshold | $500 | $500 | $550 |
| ESOP (5-year distribution factor) | $180,000 | $185,000 | $195,000 |
| ESOP (account balance) | $915,000 | $935,000 | $995,000 |
| Taxable wage base[7] | $97,500 | $102,000 | $106,500 |
| SECA tax for self-employed individuals, combined rate | 15.3% | 15.3% | 15.3% |
| Old-age, survivors, and disability insurance tax rate | 12.4% | 12.4% | 12.4% |
| Hospital insurance (Medicare) | 2.9% | 2.9% | 2.9% |
| Social Security tax for employees and employers, | 7.65% | 7.65% | 7.65% |
| Combined rate Old-age, survivors, and disability insurance tax rate | 6.20% | 6.20% | 6.20% |
| Hospital insurance (Medicare) | 1.45% | 1.45% | 1.45% |

[1] This number represents the catch-up limit available under Code Section 414(v). Code Sections 457(b)(3) and 402(g)(7) provide separate catch-up rules that must also be considered in an appropriate situation.

[2] Defined Benefit limit applies to limitation years ending in indicated year.

[3] Defined Contribution limit applies to limitation years ending in indicated year.

[4] Compensation during the plan year beginning in the indicated year identifies Highly Compensated Employees for the following plan year.

[5] Generally, compensation during the determination year ending in the indicated year identifies Key Employees for the following plan year.

[6] Compensation limit applies to plan years beginning in indicated year. Annual compensation limits for certain eligible participants in governmental plans that followed Code Section 401(a)(17) limits (with indexing) on July 1, 1993 are: $365,000 for 2009 (estimated), $345,000 for 2008, and $335,000 for 2007.

[7] Calculation differs from CPI description provided above.

# Glossary

---

**Alternate payee.** A participant's spouse, former spouse, child, or other dependent that a domestic relations order recognizes as having a right to receive all, or a portion of, the benefits payable under a pension plan to the participant.

**Alternate recipient.** A participant's child that a medical child support order recognizes as having a right to enroll under the participant's group health plan.

**Annual report.** A report about a specific pension or welfare plan filed each year with the DOL that includes information, for a specified plan year, about the plan's type, administration, participation, funding, and other financial information. Annual reporting is done by filing 5500 series forms.

**Apprenticeship training program.** An employee welfare benefit plan that exclusively provides apprenticeship training and/or other training benefits.

**Beneficiary.** Any person designated by a participant, or by the terms of a plan, who is or may become entitled to benefits.

**Cafeteria plan.** A plan that allows participants to choose among various taxable and nontaxable benefits. The plan must offer at least one taxable benefit and one nontaxable benefit.

**Church plan.** In general, a plan established and maintained by a church or by a convention or association of churches that includes many plans established for employees of tax-exempt organizations controlled or associated with a church.

**COBRA.** The Consolidated Omnibus Budget Reconciliation Act of 1985, the law that, among other things, requires most employers to offer continuation coverage to employees and dependents who would otherwise lose group health plan coverage because of certain events such as termination of employment.

**Code.** The Internal Revenue Code of 1986, as amended.

**Code Section 6039D.** Added in 1984 to impose independent annual reporting requirements on certain welfare benefit plans, regardless of whether those plans report under ERISA. In some cases, a Code Section 6039D plan may also be a welfare plan.

**Commerce.** Trade, traffic, commerce, transportation, or communication between any state and any place outside the state.

**Common control.** Corporations, trades, or businesses—including sole proprietorships and partnerships—where one entity owns at least 80 percent of the stock, profit, or capital interest in the other organization or the same five or fewer people own a specified controlling interest in each entity.

**Controlled group.** A corporate group with common ownership. A parent-subsidiary controlled group exists if one corporation owns at least 80 percent of the stock of another. A brother-sister controlled group exists if five or fewer persons own at least 80 percent of the stock of two or more corporations and a 50 percent test, based on stock ownership of each person in each corporation, is met.

**Defined benefit plan.** Any pension plan not meeting the definition of an individual account plan.

**Defined contribution plan.** See **individual account plan.**

**Dependent care reimbursement program.** An arrangement under which an employee selects a day care or other dependent care facility and is reimbursed for expenses by the employer, often through a cafeteria plan.

**Disability benefits.** Payments to an employee who is unable to work for a period of time due to illness or injury. Short-term disability plans generally cover the first six months of disability, paying no more than an employee's normal compensation from the employer's general assets. Long-term disability plans generally provide benefits during an extended period beginning after six months of disability.

**Disclosure.** Mandatory distribution of materials to plan participants and/or beneficiaries by plan administrators. Disclosure requirements include supplying plan participants with copies of summary plan descriptions, summary of material modifications, summary annual reports, and special notices for pension plans, and making certain documents available for inspection by participants and providing copies on request.

**DOL.** U.S. Department of Labor, the agency responsible for enforcing most of ERISA's reporting and disclosure requirements as well as ERISA's fiduciary responsibility and prohibited transaction provisions.

**DRO.** A domestic relations order, a judgment, decree, or order made under a state's domestic relations law related to child support, alimony payments, or marital property rights for a spouse, former spouse, child, or other dependent of a participant.

**Dues-financed pension or welfare plan.** An unfunded plan maintained by an employee organization for its members and their beneficiaries. Benefits are paid solely from the organization's assets, derived in whole or in part from membership dues.

**Educational assistance programs.** Programs that permit tax-free payments by an employer of certain educational expenses of its employees. The program must meet the requirements of Code Section 127.

**Employee.** Any individual employed by an employer.

**EAP.** Employee assistance program, which provides employees with advice on or actual treatment of a variety of problems, including medical or psychological conditions, stress reduction, and personal (e.g., financial) problems.

**Employee benefit plan.** A welfare or pension plan, or a plan that is both.

**Employee organization.** A labor union or organization that exists (in whole or in part) to negotiate with employers about an employee benefit plan or other matters incidental to employment relationship. Also, an employees' beneficiary association organized (in whole or in part) to establish an employee benefit plan.

**Employer.** Any person acting directly as an employer, or indirectly in an employer's interest, in relation to an employee benefit plan. This includes a group or association of employers.

**Employer-provided day care center.** A center established and maintained by the employer for dependents of employees.

**ERISA.** The Employee Retirement Income Security Act of 1974—the legal basis for most employee benefit plan compliance—mandates, among other things, comprehensive employee benefit plan reporting and disclosure.

**ERISA rights statement.** An explanation of participant (and beneficiary) rights under ERISA.

**Excess aggregate contributions.** After-tax contributions made by participants or matching contributions made by the employer that do not satisfy the discrimination test under Code Section 401(m).

**Excess benefit plan.** A plan maintained by an employer to provide benefits that exceed the limits on contributions and benefits imposed by Code Section 415.

**Excess contributions.** Pretax contributions made by participants that do not satisfy the discrimination test under Code Section 401(k).

**Excess deferrals.** Pretax amounts contributed by participants that exceed the maximum limit under Code Section 402(g) for the taxable year.

**Executive medical reimbursement program.** A program that provides executives with medical benefits not provided by the employer's standard plan for rank-and-file employees.

**Fiduciary.** Any person who exercises discretionary authority or control over managing the plan or managing or disposing of the plan's assets, renders investment advice for a fee or other direct or indirect compensation concerning any money or other property of a plan, or has any authority or responsibility to do so, or who has any discretionary authority or responsibility for administering the plan.

**FSA.** Flexible spending account, an account through which a participant is reimbursed, on a tax-exempt basis, for health care or dependent care expenses.

**Fringe benefits.** Benefits defined by Code Section 132 and not subject to tax. Such benefits include: employer-operated facilities offering meals to employees at limited discounts; programs providing employees limited discounts on property or services offered to customers in the employer's ordinary course of business; no-additional-cost services; and working condition fringes.

**Fully subsidized benefit.** A benefit for which no increase in cost or decrease in benefits to the participant may result from the failure to waive the benefit.

**Funded plan.** A plan paying benefits in any manner other than through an employer's or employee organization's general assets, including an insured plan and a plan paying benefits or premiums from a trust.

**General assets.** Assets owned by an employer or employee organization; they do not include employee contributions or other plan assets.

**Government plan.** In general, a plan established or maintained by a federal, state, or local government or by any of their agencies and instrumentalities for their employees. Such a plan also includes any plan financed though contributions required by the Railroad Retirement Acts of 1935 and 1937 or a plan or an international organization exempt from taxation by the International Organization Immunities Act.

**Group health plan.** Any plan providing health benefits given favorable tax treatment under Code Section 105; a plan described in ERISA Section 607(1) that is subject to COBRA continuation obligations; and for purposes of HIPAA portability, access, and renewability requirements (as defined in ERISA Section 733), a welfare plan that provides amounts paid through insurance reimbursement or otherwise for such things as diagnosis, cure, mitigation, treatment, or prevention of disease or for the purpose of affecting any structure or function of the body, transportation primarily for medical care, and insurance covering medical care.

**Group term life insurance.** Insurance provided to a group of employees through a single contract. Code Section 79 limits the amount and type of group term life insurance that can be provided on a tax-free basis.

**HIPAA.** The Health Insurance Portability and Accountability Act of 1996, which amended ERISA and Internal Revenue Code provisions for group health plans to implement rules that govern preexisting condition limitations, establish special enrollment periods, and prohibit plans from excluding individuals because of health-related factors.

**Individual account plan.** A pension plan that provides individual accounts for participants with benefits based solely on contributions, income, expenses, gains and losses, and forfeitures. Aellso referred to as a defined contribution plan.

**IRA.** Individual retirement account, a personal retirement program that meets the requirements of Code Section 408.

**Industry or activity affecting commerce.** Any activity, business, or industry in commerce or in which a labor dispute would hinder or obstruct commerce or the free flow of commerce.

**IRC.** The Internal Revenue Code of 1986, as amended.

**IRS.** The Internal Revenue Service, the agency responsible for administering the requirements for qualified pension plans as well as tax rules for other retirement and welfare plans. It shares responsibility with the DOL and the PBGC for developing the Form 5500 series and monitoring the information submitted on these annual reports. The IRS is also responsible for taxes related to employee benefit plans, including excise taxes for prohibited transactions.

**Material modification.** A change in information required to be in an SPD or the terms of the plan considered important to plan participants.

**Medical child support order.** A judgment, decree, or order (including approval or a settlement agreement) that provides support for a participant's child under a group health plan or provides health benefit coverage, and is made under a state's domestic relations law, and relates to benefits under the plan or that enforces a law relating to medical child support under a group health plan.

**MEWA.** A multiple employer welfare arrangement that offers health or welfare coverage to the employees of two or more employers. Arrangements established or maintained under collective bargaining agreements and established or maintained by rural electric cooperatives or rural telephone cooperative associations are not MEWAs.

**MSA.** A medical savings account, an account used to pay health care expenses for employees of small businesses or self-employed individuals who are covered under health plans with high deductibles.

**Minimum funding standards.** Standards imposed to ensure plans are sufficiently funded to meet their accrued benefit liabilities.

**Multiemployer plan.** A plan to which more than one employer contributes and that is maintained according to one or more collective bargaining agreements. For purposes of this definition, employers under common control are considered a single employer.

**Named fiduciary.** An individual with authority to control and manage the operational and administration of a plan. A named fiduciary is named in the plan documents and identified by the employer and/or an employee organization as a fiduciary by a procedure specified in the plan document.

**No-additional-cost service.** A service offered to employees that is also offered to the public in the employer's normal course of business and that results in no substantial additional cost to the employer.

**Participant.** An employee, former employee, employer, or any member or former member of an employee organization who is or who may become eligible for benefits from an employee benefit plan or whose beneficiaries may become eligible for benefits.

**Party-in-interest.** A party to a plan, such as a plan fiduciary, any person rendering a service to the plan, the employer of plan participants, any director, officer, employee, owner, or subsidiary of that employer, or any employee organization whose members are participants in the plan.

**PBGC.** The Pension Benefit Guaranty Corporation, the federal agency that insures defined benefit pension plans and that steps in and pays guaranteed benefits up to a specified maximum if a plan terminates and is unable to pay all required benefits.

**Pension plan.** In general, any plan, fund, or program established or maintained by an employer, employee organization, or both that provides retirement income to employees or results in a deferral of income by employees for periods extending to the termination of covered employment or beyond.

**Plan administrator.** An individual, group of individuals, or corporation identified in plan documents who is responsible for plan duties. If a plan administrator is not named in the document, the plan sponsor generally is the plan administrator.

**Plan sponsor.** The employer, employee organization, joint board of trustees, or other entity representing parties establishing or maintaining the plan.

**Plan year.** The fiscal year on which a plan's records are kept. The plan year should be stated in the plan document and does not have to coincide with any insurance policies or other contracts relating to the plan.

**Prohibited transaction.** A direct or indirect sale, exchange, or lease of property between the plan and a party-in-interest; loan or extension of credit between the plan and a party-in-interest; furnishing of goods, services, or facilities between the plan and a party-in-interest; transfer of plan assets to a party-in-interest or a transfer for the use or benefit of a party-in-interest; or acquisition or holding of employer securities, or real estate that is leased to the employer, unless specific conditions are met. A fiduciary is prohibited from dealing with the assets or the plan in his or her own interest or for his or her own account; acting as an individual, or in any other capacity, in any transaction involving the plan, on behalf of a party whose interests are adverse to the interests of the plan, its participants, or its beneficiaries; or receiving any consideration or his or her own account from any party dealing with the plan, in connection with a transaction involving plan assets.

**Qualified beneficiary.** For COBRA purposes, an employee or an employee's spouse of dependent child who, on the day before a qualifying event, is covered by the employer's group health plan. Effective January 1, 1997, a qualified beneficiary includes a child born or placed for adoption with a covered employee during the continuation coverage period.

**QDRO.** Qualified domestic relations order, a domestic relations order that creates and recognizes the existence of an alternate payee's right to receive all or a portion of a participant's benefit, does not alter the amount and form of plan benefits, and includes certain required information.

**QMSCO.** Qualified medical child support order, a court order that creates or recognizes the rights of an alternate recipient to receive benefits for which a participant or beneficiary is eligible under a group health plan; states the name and last known mailing address (if any) of the participant and each alternate recipient under the order, a reasonable description of the coverage to be provided or the manner in which coverage will be determined, the period covered by the order, and each plan to which the order applies; and that does not require the plan to provide any type or form of benefit (or optional benefit) that is not normally available under the plan.

**QJSA.** Qualified joint and survivor annuity, an annuity payable for the life of the participant with a survivor annuity, equal to at least 50 percent (but not more than 100 percent) of the participant's benefit, payable to the spouse upon the participant's death.

**Qualified pre-retirement survivor annuity.** An annuity benefit payable, beginning at the time the participant would have attained the earliest retirement age under the plan, for the life of the deceased participant's surviving spouse.

**Qualifying events.** Certain types of events that would cause, except for COBRA continuation coverage, an individual to lose group health coverage, such as an employee's termination of employment for any reason except gross misconduct; an employee's reduction in hours to fewer than the number required for plan participation; an employee's divorce or legal separation from spouse; an employee's death; an employee's entitlement to Medicare; a child's loss of dependent status as defined under the plan; or a retiree's (or a retiree's spouse's or child's) substantial loss of coverage within one year before or after the employer is subject to a Title XI bankruptcy proceeding.

**Remembrance fund.** A fund, generally organized by unions, that provides a small gift (e.g., flowers or cash) on occasions such as sickness, death, or termination of employment.

**Reportable event.** Any designated event generally requiring notice to the PBGC.

**Reporting.** Refers to government filing requirements. Reporting requirements include filing annual reports with the IRS, filing annual premium reports with the PBGC, and making certain documents available for inspection by the DOL. In most cases, plan administrators must use a designated form for reporting purposes.

**SIMPLE.** Savings incentive match plan for employees, an arrangement sponsored by a small employer that (1) employs no more than 100 employees who received at least $5,000 in compensation in the preceding year; (2) is maintained by an employer that does not maintain another qualified plan; (3) allows employees to contribute up to $10,500 (see Appendix A for current limit); and (4) is maintained by an employer required to make either matching or nonelective contributions. The contributions to a SIMPLE are fully vested at all times.

**Scholarship programs.** Generally, programs that provide scholarships for employees' dependents. If a program meets the requirements of Code Section 117, the benefits are tax free; otherwise, they are taxable income to the employee.

**Service provider.** Any person—accountant, enrolled actuary, insurance carrier, administrator, investment manager, trustee, other plan fiduciary—or entity providing any service to a plan.

**Severance pay programs.** Payments made after involuntary termination of employment. They are welfare benefits if payments do not exceed twice the terminated employee's annual pay at the time of termination and the payments are completed within two years; otherwise, these are pension plans under ERISA.

**SEP.** Simplified employee pension plan, an arrangement under which an employer makes direct contributions to an IRA established by an employee.

**Small welfare plan.** An employee welfare benefit plan that covers fewer than 100 participants at the beginning of the plan year. Such plans meeting certain conditions are exempt from some of ERISA's reporting and disclosure requirements.

**Split dollar life insurance.** Arrangements that generally split insurance premium payments between the employer and the employee.

**SAR.** Summary annual report, an abstract of the information in the plan's annual report provided to plan participants. Its primary purpose is to inform participants and beneficiaries of the plan's financial condition.

**SMM.** Summary of material modifications, a written summary describing a material modification to a plan.

**SPD.** Summary plan description, a summary of the benefits provided by one or more plans that must include all information required by ERISA, such as a description of benefits, eligibility requirements, funding arrangements, claims procedures, and participant rights under ERISA.

**Supplement payment plan.** An arrangement under which an employer makes payments to supplement an employee's retirement income.

**TSA.** Tax-sheltered annuity (or 403(b) plan), a program under which employees of certain tax-exempt employers (e.g., public schools) can defer taxes on contributions to certain annuity contracts or custodial accounts. Such programs must meet the requirements of Code Section 403(b).

**Tuition reduction plans.** Programs of one or more educational institutions under which their employees and/or dependents may enroll in classes at reduced costs, or at no cost. If the plan meets the requirements of Code Section 117(d), the benefits are tax free.

**Unfunded.** A plan that is not insured or trusteed. Benefits are paid solely from the employer's general assets.

**Vacation benefit.** A benefit provided through an employer's current assets that is exempt from ERISA as a payroll practice providing compensation to employees absent from work for vacation.

**Vacation pay plan.** A plan, usually established through collective bargaining, in which the employer generally makes a contribution to a trust that pays the benefits. These plans are covered by ERISA.

**Welfare plan.** Any plan, fund, or program established or maintained by an employer, employee organization, or both for providing certain benefits to participants and their beneficiaries, through the purchase of insurance or other means. Benefits provided include medical, surgical, or hospital benefits; sickness, accident, or disability benefits; death benefits; unemployment benefits; vacation benefits; severance benefits; apprenticeship or other training programs; scholarship funds; day care centers; and prepaid legal services.

# Index

## A

## B

## C

## D

### E

# F

## G

## H

# I

# L

# M

## N

# O

## P

## Q

## S

## T